# BREAKING
# BOUNDS

# BREAKING BOUNDS

### ≋

## Whitman and American Cultural Studies

*Edited by*

Betsy Erkkila

and Jay Grossman

*New York    Oxford*

OXFORD UNIVERSITY PRESS

1996

Oxford University Press

Oxford   New York
Athens   Auckland   Bangkok   Bombay
Calcutta   Capetown   Dar es Salaam   Delhi
Florence   Hong Kong   Istanbul   Karachi
Kuala Lumpur   Madras   Madrid   Melbourne
Mexico City   Nairobi   Paris   Singapore
Taipei   Tokyo   Toronto

and associated companies in
Berlin   Ibadan

Published by Oxford University Press, Inc.,
198 Madison Avenue, New York, New York 10016

Oxford is a registered trademark of Oxford University Press

Library of Congress Cataloging-in-Publication Data
Breaking bounds: Whitman and American cultural studies / edited by
Betsy Erkkila and Jay Grossman.
p. cm.   Includes bibliographical references and index.
ISBN 0-19-509349-6;—ISBN 0-19-509350-X (pbk.)
1. Whitman, Walt, 1819–1892—Criticism and interpretation.
2. Homosexuality and literature—United States—History—19th
century.   3. Politics and literature—United States—History—19th
century.   4. Literature and society—United States—History—19th
century.   5. National characteristics, American, in literature.
I. Erkkila, Betsy, 1944–   . II. Grossman, Jay.
PS3238.B74   1996
811'.3—dc20          95-6861

1 3 5 7 9 8 6 4 2

Printed in the United States of America
on acid-free paper

*To the memory of*
*Tom Yingling*
*1951–1992*

# Acknowledgments

Among the bounds this volume breaks are those that routinely police the perimeters between individual and collective work and commitments. *Breaking Bounds* has been at every stage a collaborative achievement, drawing upon the assistance and generosity of a wide range of organizations and individuals. It is therefore with a great deal of pleasure that we call attention to those whose support and labors have made this volume possible.

The essays in this book were originally presented at a three-day public symposium on Whitman's life and work that was held at the University of Pennsylvania in October 1992. This symposium was part of a yearlong program of events called "Breaking Bounds: A Whitman Centennial Celebration," which included poetry readings throughout the Philadelphia and Camden communities, an improvisatory keynote address by Allen Ginsberg at the Pennsylvania Academy of the Fine Arts, and a library exhibit of rare Whitman materials and publications held in the Kamin Exhibition Gallery of the Van Pelt Library at the University of Pennsylvania. This public program of events, which was sponsored by the Department of English and the Van Pelt Library of the University of Pennsylvania in collaboration with the Walt Whitman Association, was funded in part by grants from the New Jersey Committee for the Humanities, the New Jersey Council on the Arts, the Pennsylvania Council on the Arts, the Pennsylvania Humanities Council, and the University of Pennsylvania. We would like to express our gratitude to all these funding sources, as well as to Margo Burnette, the former director of the Walt Whitman Association, Joan Wilmarth, the president of the Whitman Association, Doug Winterich, the curator of the Walt Whitman House in Camden, New Jersey, Chris Bethmann of the New Jersey State Park Service, Michael Ryan, the director of special collections, and Dan Traister, the curator for research services of the Van Pelt Library, for their financial assistance and their special help in arranging events on both sides of the Whitman Bridge and the Delaware River. We would also like to thank David Boyd, Stuart Curran, and Calvin Thomas for their memorial presentations on Tom Yingling at the Whitman symposium.

Paula Geyh coordinated every aspect of the Philadelphia symposium with admirable grace, efficiency, and commitment. It is not too much to say that this public event could not have succeeded without her organizing skills, her energies, and her attention to the manifold details such a project creates. We owe her our warmest gratitude and our sincerest thanks.

We acknowledge with appreciation the following institutions and individuals for formal permissions that have enabled the movement of these pages from manuscript to print: Duke University Library, for permission to reprint excerpts from the letters of Louisa Van Velsor Whitman; the Estate of Thomas Yingling (David E. Kartalia, Esq., agent, and Robyn Wiegman, literary executor), for permission to publish "Homosexuality and Utopian Discourse in American Poetry"; Fabian Baber Communications Inc., for permission to reprint a still photo from a public service announcement produced by the Philadelphia Lesbian and Gay Task Force.

The photograph of the International Display of the Entire NAMES Project AIDS Memorial Quilt, October 9–11, 1992, is reproduced with the generous permission of Mark Thiessen and the NAMES Project Foundation, San Francisco. Composed of over twenty-seven thousand individual memorial panels, the quilt (or portions of it) is displayed over two hundred times each year to help promote awareness, inspire compassion, and raise funds for people living with HIV. For more information about the NAMES Project AIDS Memorial Quilt, call (415) 882-5500.

Our hearty thanks to Liz Maguire, Paul Schlotthauer, Nancy Hoagland, and the staff at Oxford University Press for shepherding the project through its various stages, and to the anonymous reader for the Press, whose careful and insightful attention to the manuscript helped us to clarify the volume's overall goals as well as the breadth and scope of many of the individual essays.

Many other individuals have contributed their time, their patience, their support, and their good humor toward this volume's success. We would like especially to thank Rick Beeman, Eric Cheyfitz, Miriam Mann, John Richetti, and Valerie Savage.

When we say that our families have been indulgent with regard to our completion of this project, we are leaving a great deal unspoken. But Larry, Suli, and Jeffrey know where our hearts and thanks are.

This volume is dedicated to the memory of Tom Yingling, committed scholar, committed activist, and gentle man, who died of complications associated with AIDS on July 27, 1992. The worlds he inhabited and to which he brought so much are sorely lacking now that he is gone, and he is missed by many whose lives, hearts, and minds he deeply touched.

# Contents

# Abbreviations

| | |
|---|---|
| *Corr* | Walt Whitman, *Correspondence*. Ed. Edwin Haviland Miller. New York: New York UP, 1961–67. |
| *EPF* | Walt Whitman, *Early Poetry and Fiction*. Ed. Thomas L. Brasher. New York: New York UP, 1963. |
| *I Sit* | Walt Whitman, *I Sit and Look Out: Editorials from the* Brooklyn Daily Times. New York: AMS Press, 1966. |
| *LG* | Walt Whitman, *Leaves of Grass*. Ed. Sculley Bradley and Harold W. Blodgett. New York: Norton, 1973. |
| *LG* 1855 | Walt Whitman, *Leaves of Grass: The First (1855) Edition*. Ed. Malcolm Cowley. New York: Penguin, 1959. |
| *LG* 1860 | Walt Whitman, *Leaves of Grass, 1860 Facsimile Text*. Ed. Roy Harvey Pearce. Ithaca: Cornell UP, 1961. |
| *NUP* | Walt Whitman, *Notebooks and Unpublished Prose Manuscripts*. Ed. Edward F. Grier. 6 vols. New York: New York UP, 1984. |
| *PW* | Walt Whitman, *Prose Works 1892*. Ed. Floyd Stovall. 2 vols. New York: New York UP, 1963–64. |
| *TV* | Walt Whitman, *Leaves of Grass: A Textual Variorum of the Printed Poems*. Ed. Sculley Bradley et al. New York: New York UP, 1980. |
| *UPP* | Walt Whitman, *Uncollected Poetry and Prose*. Ed. Emory Holloway. 2 vols. New York: Doubleday, 1921; rpt., Gloucester, Mass: Peter Smith, 1972. |
| *WWC* | Horace Traubel. *With Walt Whitman in Camden*. Vols. 1–3: 1905–14; rpt., New York: Rowman and Littlefield, 1961. Vol. 4: Philadelphia: U of Pennsylvania P, 1953. Vols. 5–7: Carbondale: Southern Illinois UP, 1964, 1982, 1992. |

# BREAKING
# BOUNDS

# Introduction: Breaking Bounds

## BETSY ERKKILA

Unscrew the locks from the doors!
Unscrew the doors themselves from their jambs!
Walt Whitman, *LG* 1855

One of the most controversial dimensions of this volume is certain to be
the picture on the cover, a nude photograph of an old man taken by
Thomas Eakins that bears a striking resemblance to Walt Whitman. Discovered by Ed Folsom in an exhibition catalog of previously unpublished photographs by Eakins (*Photographer Thomas Eakins* 33), the picture is part of a
sequence of seven nude photographs, taken sometime in the 1880s, showing frontal, side, and posterior shots (Fig. I.1). Although we are unaccus-
tomed to seeing our major American writers in the flesh, given Whitman's
words at the outset of the long opening poem of the 1855 edition of *Leaves
of Grass*—"I will go to the bank by the wood and become undisguised and
naked" (*LG* 1855: 25)—and the interest that Whitman and Eakins shared
over many years in the glories of the undraped body, the existence of a
nude photograph of Whitman taken by Eakins should come as no surprise.
Indeed, rumors of the existence of such a photograph or painting have
circulated for many years.

Taken sometime after Herbert Gilchrist made sketches of Whitman sun-
bathing in the nude at Timber Creek in 1878 (Fig. I.2) and sometime before Eakins began painting his well-known "Rabelaisian" portrait of Whitman in 1887 (Fig. 10.8), the "old man" appears to be part of "the naked
series," a series of photographic studies of male and female nude bodies
that Eakins made at the Pennsylvania Academy of Fine Arts between 1882
and 1886. But among the eighty pictures we have of Eakins's young students and models, this particular picture is anomalous: it is the only picture
we have of an older man taken by Eakins. Moreover, as Folsom observes
in his essay on Whitman's male-male photographs in this volume, sometime
between 1886 and 1892 Bill Duckett, Whitman's housemate in 1886 and
companion in the late 1880s, also posed as one of Eakins's nude models in
a remarkably explicit and traditionally "feminine" pose (Fig. 13.10).

If the sequence of nude photographs now simply entitled "old man" is

3

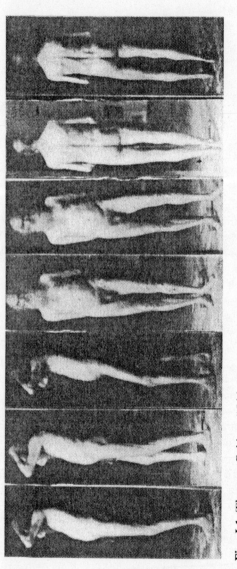

**Fig. I.1** Thomas Eakins, "Old Man, seven photographs," 1880s. Albumen, 8.1 x 19.4 cm. The Collection of the J. Paul Getty Museum, Malibu, California.

**Fig. I.2** Herbert Gilchrist, pen and ink drawing of Whitman at Timber Creek, 1878. New York Public Library.

not Whitman, it is at least worth speculating on why Eakins would choose a model who was, in Folsom's words, "a ringer for Whitman, a stand-in who could serve Eakins as Whitman's body-double for his form studies" (213). In fact, the very ambiguity of this nude photograph (is it really Walt Whitman or somebody else?), with its erasure of individual identity and its blurred but nevertheless culturally charged conjuncture between the democratic poet Walt Whitman and the democratic painter Thomas Eakins around the site of the body, nakedness, homoeroticism, and American nationality, raises questions about identity, queerness, the body politic, and the making and breaking of boundaries at once national and transnational, cultural and social that the essays in this volume centrally address.

These essays were originally presented at a public conference entitled "Breaking Bounds: A Whitman Centennial Celebration," held at the University of Pennsylvania in 1992. While this program of events was supported by grants from numerous public and private agencies, it was denied funding by the National Endowment for the Humanities because, in the words of the program officer, it was "too esoteric." I want to draw attention to this denial because I believe it is relevant to the "bound-breaking" theme of these essays. In a year when thousands of dollars were spent to commemorate the quincentennial of Columbus's arrival in America, it cannot be entirely insignificant that Washington, D.C., where Whitman served as a volunteer nurse in the hospitals during the Civil War, and the Library of Congress, which holds the largest and most substantial collection of Whitman materials in the world, chose not to hold any public event in commemoration of Walt Whitman's death. Although the reasons for this silence are not entirely clear to me, I understand from officials in Washington, D.C. with whom I have spoken that in the Reagan/Bush political climate, Whitman was regarded as much too volatile a figure for national exhibition.

As a means of reflecting on this volatility, the "esoteric," and the uses to which Whitman may and may not be put in contemporary American culture, I would like to begin by describing a brief public service announcement produced by the Philadelphia Lesbian and Gay Task force in 1990. A young man stands at the Delaware River's edge, with the Walt Whitman Bridge in the background, and says:

"Hey, I just found out Walt Whitman was gay . . . you know, the guy they named the bridge after.

"I wish I had known that when I was in high school. Back then, I got hassled all the time by the other kids, 'cause I'm gay—and the teachers— they didn't say anything.

"Why didn't they tell me Walt Whitman was gay?" (Fig. I.3)

All six television stations in the Philadelphia market refused to air this public service announcement, arguing that it was too "controversial" and that it "advocated a particular lifestyle." When two of the stations called the Walt Whitman Cultural Arts Center in Camden, New Jersey, the director said that to tell the world that Whitman was gay "would really be detrimental to the Center. A lot of our programming is geared to teens. Kids don't need a lot to scare them off" (qtd. in David Warner 4). At issue in this controversy was not the question of whether or not Whitman was gay: there seemed to be widespread or at least covert agreement that he was. At issue, instead, was the idea that Whitman's gayness must not be aired publicly and that such public airing would be detrimental to the American people and "scare" young kids. What the controversy suggests, finally, is the extent to which Whitman's image has become an American public property whose image is bound up with the maintenance of American public health and American national policy. It is not only the academic and critical establishment but those in positions of social and cultural power, and I would add, the national government itself, that are heavily invested in keeping Whitman's sexuality, and specifically his sexual love for men, out of any discussion of his role as the poet of democracy, and *the* American poet. The fantasy seems to be, at least in part, that if we can control Whitman's sexuality we can somehow control the sexuality of the nation.

I wanted to begin with this public service announcement, and the controversy surrounding its public display, because I believe it suggests the extent to which Whitman is still, a century after his death, a sexually and politically charged figure who works on the boundaries of traditional sexual, social, and cultural taboos. "Unscrew the locks from the doors! / Unscrew the doors themselves from their jambs!" (*LG* 1855: 48), Whitman exclaimed in the long opening poem of the first edition of *Leaves of Grass*, which was published on or about July 4, 1855. In this and subsequent edi-

**Fig. I.3** Young man with the Walt Whitman Bridge in the background. Public Service Announcement produced by the Philadelphia Lesbian and Gay Task Force, 1990.

tions of *Leaves of Grass* that Whitman continued to revise and publish over the course of his life, he broke away from the form and content of traditional verse. His rhythmic and fluid free verse lines not only broke the pentameter but in the words of Ezra Pound, he also broke the "new wood" that would be "carved" and explored by the poets, writers, and social thinkers who followed him (Pound, *Personae* 89). Presenting himself as a model democrat who speaks as and for rather than apart from the people, Whitman's poet is a breaker of bounds: he is female and male, farmer and factory worker, prostitute and slave, citizen of America and citizen of the world. Shuttling between past, present, and future, he is "an acme of things accomplished" and "an encloser of things to be" (*LG* 1855: 77). His songs are songs not only of workers and occupations but of sex and the body. Celebrating the body as the luxuriant growth of nature and sexual energy as the regenerative law of the universe, Whitman sang of masturbation, the sexual organs, and the sexual act; he was one of the first poets to write openly of the "body electric," female eroticism, homosexual love, and the anguish of repressed desire. By equating democracy with sexual liberation, Whitman was also the first poet to provoke among his unsympathetic readers what was (and perhaps still is) the deepest underlying fear of democracy in America: that in its purest form democracy would lead to a blurring of sexual bounds and thus the breakdown of a social and bourgeois economy based on the management of the body and the polarization of male and female spheres.

*Breaking Bounds: Whitman and American Cultural Studies* seeks to engage, to query, to wrestle with, and to extend into the present the bound-breaking dimensions of Whitman's life and work. This volume assembles a distinguished group of poets, writers, and critics who are, in one way or another, reconstituting the boundaries of American cultural studies. Like Whitman, and like what Tony Bennett calls the "fairly dispersed array of theoretical and political positions" that might be described by the term "cultural studies" (23), this collection breaks disciplinary, generic, and national bounds. Bringing together contributors from the fields of literature, the history of art, gay studies, Latin American studies, American studies, and European studies, *Breaking Bounds* considers Whitman's multiple and often contradictory legacies in South as well as North America, in Europe as well as the United States. Moreover, by linking traditional perspectives with new theoretical paradigms for the study of American literature and culture, these essays cross generational bounds by placing more established critics of American culture in dialogue with a new generation of gay and straight, feminist and cultural critics who are challenging and rethinking the very meanings we bring to such terms as American, literature, history, culture, and Walt Whitman himself.

In structuring this collection, Jay Grossman and I deliberately tried to work against what have become fairly standard divisions in Whitman stud-ies—the aesthetic Whitman, the sexual Whitman, the historic Whitman, the political Whitman—because we believe these divisions tend to mask the complexly interactive social, sexual, and historical engagements of Whit-man's work. The essays in the first section, "Genealogies," consider the multiple points of departure of Whitman's work, focusing in particular on the popular, familial, working-class, vernacular, journalistic, homoerotic, and political sources of Whitman's writing. Beginning with the *genea,* or specifically familial origins of Whitman's work in the queer working-class voice of Whitman's mother (Moon and Sedgwick), the essays in this section trace not only the sexual, social, and cultural lines of descent out of which Whitman's writing emerged, but also the multiple and sometimes repres-sive critical and political genealogies to which the figure of "Walt Whitman" has given rise, from the tradition of "selfing" in American criticism (War-ner), to the nationalist figure of Whitman that emerged side by side with the American Studies movement in the Cold War period (Arac), to contem-porary philosophical reflections on the ideology of the liberal political self that Whitman helped to create (Dimock).

The essays brought together in the next section, "America's Whitmans," examine Whitman's writings from a variety of critical, disciplinary, and geographical perspectives. Representing a range of approaches and indeed "styles" of addressing Whitman—gay, feminist, and straight, reader-response, psychobiographical, and orphic, Latino and Anglo-American, essayistic and prose-poetic—this section marks this volume's underlying assumption that the reading and production of Whitman is a constantly fluctuating and undeniably plural process. Thus the section's rubric seeks to resist any static or iconic approach to "America's Poet of Democracy" and the commonsensical identification of "America" or "the American" with the United States, installing in its place an already present, but traditionally neglected, geographical ambiguity that insists—like the continental imprint of North and South America that appears throughout the 1860 *Leaves of Grass*—on the poet's full hemispheric influence: from José Martí in Cuba (Molloy) to Emily Dickinson in Amherst (Pollak); from Allen Grossman's American poet as novitiate in the service of Whitman as esoteric master to Pablo Neruda in Chile and Jorge Luis Borges in Argentina (Salessi and Quiroga).

Appropriately signaled by its chiamus, the third section, "Whitman's Americas," shifts our focus from "inside" the Whitmanian text to the "outside." In this section, four distinguished scholars turn their attention toward the relationships that can be established between Whitman and a range of worlds with which he interacted: the interlinked discourses of utopia, homosexuality, and America (Yingling); the democratic masses and their representation in the visual arts (Johns); the modern American city (Trachtenberg); the massive carnage of the Civil War (Kinney). Like the leveling dynamics of Whitman's catalogs, the interdisciplinary comparisons of this section highlight the comparative and interrelational dialectics of the volume as a whole, which attempts to work its own kind of contemporaneous leveling: to witness Whitman's literary productions in relation to an entire web of social, sexual, cultural, artistic, scientific, technological, and political practices that his writing simultaneously inhabited, contested, and worked to constitute.

The last section of this volume, "Legacies," addresses the question of Whitman's multiple and often contradictory bequests to the future, the range of interpretations, cultural exchanges, and histories—sexual, political, and artistic—in which Whitman has been made to play a role. Focusing on the performative and staged dimensions of the figure "Walt Whitman" and the constructedness of his reputation among writers, artists, critics, and social activists in the United States and throughout the world, the essays in this section explore Whitman's many poses—as Broadway dandy, American rough, tenderest lover, wound-dresser, good gray poet, motherman, new husband, nationalist bard, and prophet of internationalism—and the ways these poses (including those he staged for the camera) have been deployed by his early disciples and later critics (Folsom), by contemporary gay male poets (Davidson), and by an internationalist network of followers and advocates (Grünzweig).

The section divisions that structure this volume are intended not as prescriptions for some future state of Whitman studies but as invitations to an alternative critical practice. While the essays in each section are in valuable dialogue with each other, they are also in dialogue with other essays across these divides in a manner that we hope will suggest alternative modes of reading this volume and the territory of Whitman studies as well. We want to mark this fluidity of structure and division at the outset because, as the title suggests, the essays in *Breaking Bounds* centrally contest the critical taxonomies, interpretive strategies, and regimes of knowledge that have governed past and recent approaches not only to Whitman, but to American literature and culture more generally.

In one of his conversations with Horace Traubel, Whitman attributed the feminine sensibility of *Leaves of Grass* to the influence of his mother, Louisa Van Velsor Whitman. "*Leaves of Grass* is the flower of her temperament active in me," he said (*WWC* 2: 113). In past approaches to Whitman's work, critics have conveniently passed over this comment, either not mentioning Louisa Whitman at all, or, when they do, treating her as an emotional nuisance and financial drag on Whitman's creative genius. Drawing on two hundred pages of extant letters of Louisa Whitman to her son in the Duke University library, Michael Moon and Eve Sedgwick, in their essay "Confusion of Tongues," interweave critical commentary with a performative enactment of the relationship between Louisa and Walt Whitman in which the voices of mother and son, queer female and queer male desire interchange. Against the critical neglect of Louisa Whitman in past approaches to Whitman and "pop-culture (mis)understandings of the family dynamics of queerness" (25), Sedgwick and Moon reopen for serious consideration the question of the relationship between Louisa and Walt Whitman at the same time that they explore Louisa Whitman's writing as an instance of the relation between Whitman's innovations in *Leaves of Grass* and his social and specifically epistolary exchanges with working-class and "semiliterate" correspondents.

Like Whitman, whose radical experiments in poetic form were directly connected with his bound-breaking thematics, several of the essays in *Breaking Bounds* experiment with alternative modes of critical writing. Just as in their splendidly dialogic essay, Moon and Sedgwick enact the blurring of bounds, or "confusion of tongues," that is the subject of their writing, so in their provocative essay, "Errata sobre la erótica, or the Elision of Whitman's Body," Jorge Salessi and José Quiroga make use of a simultaneously autobiographical and double-voiced narration that enacts the complicated relationship between the erotic body of Whitman's poems and the homoerotic scenes of reading and translation that have informed Whitman's reception in Latin America. Similarly, in Allen Grossman's prose-poetic essay, "Whitman's 'Whoever You Are Holding Me Now in Hand': Remarks on the Endlessly Repeated Rediscovery of the Incommensurability of the Person," the bounds that are broken pertain to the category of criticism itself and its demands for directed (rather than evolving) logic and evidentiary subordination (rather than simultaneity). Adapting Whitman's oracular voice to contemporary criticism, Grossman the poet-critic becomes for his own readers the "esoteric master" that he discovers in the schoolroom of Whitman's poetry.

Although past critics have recognized the blurring of the bounds between poetry and prose that grounds Whitman's experimental poetics, they have continued to scan his verse in the hope of finding a regular poetic meter, to canonize those poems that seem most formally coherent ("Crossing Brooklyn Ferry," "Out of the Cradle Endlessly Rocking," and "When Lilacs Last in the Dooryard Bloom'd"), and to insist on the essential distinction between the early prose writer and political journalist, Walter Whitman, and the later poet and transcendent artist figure who, in Malcolm Cowley's terms, "miraculously" emerged as "Walt Whitman, an American, one of the roughs, a kosmos" in the 1855 edition of *Leaves of Grass* (*LG* 1855: 48). In "Whitman Drunk," Michael Warner complicates these distinctions between prose writer and poet, temperance journalist and democratic bard, mass culture and high culture, by reading Whitman's 1842 temperance novel, *Franklin Evans; or the Inebriate,* in the context of the temperance movement, the discourse of addiction, the emergence of nonstate, voluntarist forms of public association, and the dialectics of self-mastery and self-abandonment in Whitman's early and later work. Against a long tradition of "selfing" in Whitman criticism, Warner's examination of the relation between temperance rhetoric and the temperance movement and the "later Whitman's perverse self-characterization" in *Leaves of Grass* subtly rethinks and in effect "queers" traditional representations of Whitman as the prophet of "the liberal self." Although "Whitman Drunk" does not address the publication history of *Leaves of Grass* directly, Warner's essay also provides a convincing explanation for why the phrenological firm, Fowler and Wells, well-known authors and publishers of a number of sexual purity tracts (including Orson Fowler's *Amativeness: Or Evils and Remedies of Excessive and Perverted Sexuality* [1844]), also served as agents for *Leaves of Grass* (1855) and secret publishers of *Leaves of Grass* (1856), notwithstanding Whitman's own poetic self-characterization as sexual liberator and masturbator.

Nowhere are the contestations over Whitman more heated than in discussions of his sexuality and its relation to his poetry and his politics. Like Sedgwick and Moon reading Whitman in the context of the "queerness and queer desire" of his mother, Warner reading Whitman in the context of "the emergent same-sex subculture of New York," and Salessi and Quiroga reading Whitman in the context of the "erratic and erotic encounters" that "lie over and under Whitman's Latin American literary body" (25, 38,127), several other contributors seek to restore to visibility and legibility the sexual love for men that has been by turns erased, silenced, and marginalized in traditional accounts of Whitman's life, work, and influence.

In "Homosexuality and Utopian Discourse in American Poetry," Tom Yingling addresses the relationship between homosexuality and the uto-

pian idea of America that has gone largely unremarked in past approaches
to American literature and culture. Focusing on a range of theoretical issues and cultural texts associated with the discourses of utopia, homosexuality, and America in the work of Whitman, Crane, and Ginsberg, Yingling's essay, which is powerfully introduced by his literary executor,
Robyn Wiegman, contends that it is precisely because "homosexuality" and
"America" remain undefined, fluid, and unfixed terms of unlimited possibility in Whitman's work that his text continues to be a source of radical
seduction and pleasure. Like the incompletion of Whitman's own homosexual utopia, Yingling's essay, which was left unfinished at the time of his
death from complications associated with AIDS, sets the terms for future
work on the relation between homosexuality and America by rearticulating
that relation not as a question of either/or but rather as one of both/and.

In "His America, Our America: José Martí Reads Whitman," Sylvia Molloy also foregrounds the relation between Whitman, homoeroticism, and
the revolutionary idea of America in the Latin American cultural imaginary. Revising the conventional reading of Martí's famous 1887 essay, "El
Poeta Walt Whitman," which emphasizes Martí's sympathetic evocation of
Whitman as "good gray poet" and democratic model for the Latin American political project, Molloy explores the family centered and intensely
male centered homoerotic dynamics that inform Martí's simultaneously
sexual and political reading of Whitman as revolutionary model for "Our
America." "To his credit," Molloy writes, "Martí will have been the only
Latin American to consider, in Whitman, the erotic together with the political, and to register his anxiety, even his panic, before that explosive alliance" (90). To her credit, too, Molloy refuses to observe the culturally man-
dated bound between the family, father/son desire, and homosexuality, on
the one hand, and politics, revolution, and America, on the other hand, as
discrete realms of activity and inquiry. For Whitman as for Martí, Molloy
suggests, the articulation of new models of the family and new modes of
social organization, grounded in the "polymorphous, unhierarchical exchange of all-male feeling," is at the very center of their shared utopian
vision of the revolutionary political potential of America.

In addition to leaving a written legacy of images of male-male desire
that has functioned centrally in the constitution of modern homosexual
identities and communities, Whitman also left a visual legacy of portraits,
a small cache of "marital" photographs taken with his boyfriends Peter
Doyle (in the 1860s), Harry Stafford (in the 1870s), Bill Duckett (in the
1880s), and Warren (Warry) Fritzinger (in the 1890s). Although these photographs were not "published" until after Whitman's death in 1892 (and
they are still little known or remarked upon by Whitman scholars), they
were circulated among Whitman's friends and critics during his lifetime
and used in the decade after his death both to canonize Whitman as a
good, gray (unhomosexual) poet, as in Richard Maurice Bucke's edition of
Whitman's letters to Doyle in *Calamus* (1897); and, as in John Addington

Symonds's *Walt Whitman: A Study* (1893) and Eduard Bertz's "Walt Whitman: Ein Charakterbild" (1905), to circulate Whitman's visual image as part of the cultural and constitutive capital of a newly emerging international homosexual community.

In "Whitman's Calamus Photographs," Folsom brings together this legacy of male-male photographs from the post-Civil War period. These revisionary portraits, Folsom argues, stage new identities and new versions of the family, marriage, and social relationships that blur the traditional roles of mother, father, husband, wife, brother, lover, friend. Through their stunning visual enactments of the ways Whitman might be said to speak not so much *for* woman, bride, wife, and mother, but *as* woman, bride, wife, and mother, these "family" and "marital" photographs suggest some of the more radically transgressive dimensions of Whitman's gender politics. In fact, the photographs are all the more striking because they were taken during the last twenty-five years of Whitman's life, the very years when, in traditional accounts of his life and work, he is said to have sublimated his sexual passion for men in the more conventional roles of the "wound-dresser," the "good gray poet," and the patriotic nationalist.

Whitman's fluid and multiply productive performances of gender and their relation to the national imaginary are also the subject of Michael Davidson's essay, " 'When the World Strips Down and Rouges Up': Redressing Whitman." Engaging the figure of dress—addressing, cross-dressing, re-dressing—Davidson brings into new visibility the radically staged character of identity and sexuality in Whitman's poetry as he retheorizes the specifically gendered lineage of Whitman's performances among contemporary American gay male poets. "What seems considerably more important than defining the ways Whitman's figuration 'hides' a given sexual act," Davidson writes, "is the way that it 'reveals' the multiplicity of erotic possibilities made possible through the shifting of roles" (225). Whereas modernist poets, such as Eliot and Pound, redressed Whitman in the sense of correcting or neutralizing his "excesses," contemporary poets, Davidson argues, embraced these very excesses, redressing Whitman in "contemporary garb" as a measure of the social and political failings of America. In addition to the more prophetic and insistently masculine response to Whitman among the "new American poets," especially Robert Duncan and Allen Ginsberg, Davidson finds another less obvious mode of redressing Whitman in the campy, cosmopolitan voice of Frank O'Hara, who "signals the limits to Whitman's expansive self," at the same time that he reinvests and extends Whitman's cross-dressed and gender-bending performance of identity as "a series of theatrical roles" (228).

One sign of the extent to which Whitman's democratic vision of America has entered into the national imaginary is our tendency to forget that his poetic representations of what he called the "simple separate person" and the democratic "en masse" performed the cultural work of inventing, rather than merely reflecting an already existing American nationality.

Through an interdisciplinary comparison between visual representations of democracy in nineteenth-century American painting and those Whitman offered in the poetry and prose annexes of *Leaves of Grass,* art historian Elizabeth Johns, in her essay "America on Canvas, America in Manuscript: Imaging the Democracy," denaturalizes any simple or transparent notion of democratic representation or American nationality. By contrasting the negative representations of "yankee farmers, westerners, blacks, women, and the urban poor" in paintings of the 1850s with Whitman's more sympathetic representations in the 1855 edition of *Leaves of Grass,* Johns suggests how extraordinary and exceptional Whitman's democratic images were in the context of widespread antidemocratic and antinational feeling in the antebellum period, especially in the visual arts. Rather than relating these differences between Whitman and early nineteenth-century American painters to differences in personal temperament or taste among individual artists, however, Johns attributes them to disparities in the relations of production among painters and writers. Whereas the print and journalistic culture out of which Whitman arose sought to appeal to a broad mass public, Johns argues that painters and their patrons still belonged to an elite tradition in which the focus of pictorial representation was more exclusive, regional, and even hostile to the democratic masses. It was not until after the Civil War that the painters Winslow Homer and Thomas Eakins assumed what Johns calls the "mantle" of Whitman, creating "visual counterparts to Whitman's community of the American body" (156).

Whitman's poetry presents some of the most palpable images we have not only of democracy and the common people, but of the modern city. More so than any nineteenth-century poet, with the possible exception of Charles Baudelaire, Whitman was the inventor of the city for the modern world. The city crowd, the promenade, the spectacle of people and goods on display, anonymity, the furtive exchange of gazes, the phenomenology of cruising—these were the very texture of the new urban space that Whitman's poet inhabits and represents. In "Whitman's Lesson of the City," Alan Trachtenberg provides a kind of companion piece to Wai Chee Dimock's essay "Whitman, Syntax, and Political Theory" in the opening section. If Dimock explores Whitman's constitution of the self within the democratic context of the antebellum American republic, Trachtenberg contextualizes these same processes by resituating Whitman within the urban settings through which he wandered and found the materials for his metropolitan poetics. The Whitmanian poet "comes to himself through the intermediary of the crowd," Trachtenberg argues, finding in Whitman's "rapturous city poet" a pragmatic analogue for William James's accounts of the multiple and multiply shifting perspectives, and rapturous modes of seeing and being, accessible to inhabitants of the city in the nineteenth-century United States (170,166).

And yet, Whitman's city is a site not only of rapture, but also of agitation, discord, and siege. What sets Trachtenberg's account of Whitman's city poetry apart is his insistence on "a violence immanent in Whitman's version of the city, in his crowds, in his apparent surrender as passive panoramist to their inducements and promises" (168). Noting that the first appearance of the urban place in the 1855 edition of *Leaves of Grass* is discordant and hallucinatory—closer to Baudelaire and Eliot than to the Whitman of William James—Trachtenberg traces the ways the form of the procession, what he calls "seeing processionally," functions in Whitman's poetry as his "most radically urban way of seeking the soul, a way of freeing people from the hold of money and ownership to seek possession of themselves" (173).

Katherine Kinney also explores a particularly resonant aspect of Whitman's relation to the city in her essay "Making Capital: War, Labor, and Whitman in Washington, D.C." Moving from a consideration of Whitman's sensuously human acts of memorialization in his wartime prose to other acts of memorialization, such as the Army Medical Museum, the Washington Monument, the Vietnam Veteran's War Memorial, and the NAMES Project AIDS Memorial Quilt, Kinney presents one of the most broad-ranging and culturally nuanced accounts of Whitman's Civil War writings yet to appear. Always attentive to the material conditions and implications of Whitman's wartime prose and what she calls its "bodily abundance," Kinney is the first to notice the eerie and prophetic effect of juxtaposing wounded bodies and machines in Whitman's description of the "Patent-Office Hospital." In this physical space, she writes, "the historical connections underwriting the power and terror of the metaphor of 'the war machine'—a metaphor which gains increasing currency from the Civil War to Vietnam—become visible" (178).

Kinney's comparison of the Washington Monument, which she describes as "one of the most perfectly phallic representations of power ever conceived" (185), with Whitman's tactile and decentered acts of memorialization, complements Yingling's discussion of the anti-institutional and antipatriarchal dimensions of Whitman's work. Whereas Yingling focuses on Whitman's homosexual utopia as a "political strategy of displacement" and Kinney focuses on the "bodily excess" of Whitman's Civil War writing as a form of sensuous, anti-institutional activity, both emphasize Whitman's displacement of what Yingling calls "the cultural authority of existing centers," a cultural authority powerfully signified by the conjunction between patriarchal "edifices" and "America" that Kinney makes legible in her reading of the Washington Monument.

As Molloy wittily elucidates in her rereading of Martí's "El Poeta Walt Whitman," acts of interpretation and cultural translation can reveal as much about the interpreter as they do about Whitman. Although several essays in this volume address the question of Whitman's national and transnational reception and influence, their goal is not to get back to what Quiroga and Salessi call "a pristine original" but rather to explore the ways

Whitman's reception, like the critical processes of interpretation and translation in general, is always mediated by "acts of imaginative, erotic, and
necessarily cultural, intervention" (124,128). Thus, Davidson's examination
of Whitman's reception among contemporary American gay male poets is
not an influence study in any traditional sense of the term, but rather a
dazzling and revisionary meditation on questions of influence, poetic tradition, and literary history seen through the lens of postmodernist aesthetics
and contemporary performance theory. Reading against both the Bloo-
mian notion of American poetic history as an oedipal struggle against
strong precursors—especially Emerson—and the "identitarian logic" that
informs past and recent approaches to Whitman, Davidson argues that
"the perennial topic of Whitman's influence must take into consideration
not only the 'outsetting bards' he produced but the multiple identities from
which he was productive" (221).

Whereas Davidson, Molloy, Quiroga and Salessi, and Yingling consider
the homoerotic and specifically male-male sites from which Whitman's
work has been productive, Vivian Pollak's essay, "'In Loftiest Spheres':
Whitman's Visionary Feminism," examines a few representative strands of
the multifarious responses Whitman has engendered among women readers and contemporary feminist critics, linking these compellingly to questions raised by the "cult of true womanhood" and other structures of female oppression in the nineteenth century. Seeking to demystify
Whitman's maternal poetics from a feminist point of view, Pollak notes that
unlike Whitman, Emily Dickinson "had very little to say about the erotics
of maternity or about mothers as morally and biologically superior beings"
(99). Although the uncanny relation—or disrelation—between these two
major writers of the nineteenth century has frequently been alluded to by
critics, Pollak goes further than others in presenting a detailed account
of Dickinson's possible knowledge of Whitman: what she may have read
(including excerpts from "As I Ebb'd With the Ocean of Life" and "Song
of Myself"); who may have cautioned her against Whitman; and what she
might have meant when she told Thomas Higginson in 1862, "I never read
his Book—but was told that he was disgraceful" (*Letters* 2:404).

Unlike Pollak, Davidson, and others in this volume who focus on the
gendered dimensions of reading and interpretation, in "Whitman and
Problems of the Vernacular," Jonathan Arac intervenes in the putatively
neutral and transparent process of critical reception and canonization by
examining the crucial relation of Whitman and the idea of an authentic
American vernacular to the formation of American national identity, the
institutionalization of American Studies, and the shaping of "an American
past that would serve postwar liberalism" in the Cold War period. Challenging the critical tradition set in place by Henry Nash Smith and Leo
Marx, who focus on Whitman and Mark Twain as key figures in the emergence of an authentically American language, Arac, like Warner, argues
that Whitman's idiom has its origins in the printed prose of mass journal-

ism. Against the notion of a native or pure American expression, Arac's discussion of Whitman in the "creolized" context of newspapers and global capitalism breaks the bound between America and Europe, between authentic and inauthentic American by connecting Whitman "back to Europe, not as an argument for influence, but in order to redefine the grounds for transatlantic comparative study of Whitman" (51-52).

In the study of Whitman in a transatlantic context, no one has been more important than Walter Grünzweig, whose own work over the last decade reflects the internationalist spirit he attributes to Whitman and his followers worldwide. Creating a global map of Whitman contacts, Grünzweig's essay, " 'For America—For All the Earth': Walt Whitman as an International(ist) Poet," traces the multiple political, cultural, and literary uses to which Whitman's work has been put by an international and especially intercultural and collaborative Whitman network. What distinguishes Grünzweig's work is his insistence on treating influence not as a one-way or static relationship but as a dynamic and highly politicized moment of cultural encounter and exchange. Locating the origins of Whitman's internationalist perspective in the revolutions of 1848, Grünzweig, like Arac, emphasizes the creolized or "composite" quality of Whitman's vision of America. Although Whitman has been critically constructed as a nationalist and distinctively American poet, Grünzweig argues, "even Whitman's American nationalism can be interpreted *internationally*" (239).

As I have attempted to demonstrate, the essays in *Breaking Bounds* are not only in productive dialogue with each other; they also reveal some of the critical faultlines, or major areas of contestation, in Whitman studies and in the broader arena of cultural studies. These faultlines cluster around questions of identity, subjectivity, and authorship; gender, sexuality, and the role of "woman"; the relations between homosexuality, writing, reading, and politics; the relation between literature and history; and the culturally and politically charged question of "breaking bounds" itself.

Some of these contests emerge around differential readings of the same passages or poems from *Leaves of Grass*. Whereas Warner reads Whitman's "Calamus" poem "To a Stranger" as a representative instance of "the imperfect success of *selfing*" in Whitman's work, Arac—reading Whitman "under the rubric" of Walter Benjamin's study of Charles Baudelaire, as a poet "in the age of high capitalism"—compares "To a Stranger" with Baudelaire's "A Une Passante" ("To a Passing Woman"), interpreting the work of both poets in the context of the global rise of commodity capitalism, the city, the crowd, the newspaper, and mass culture. If Warner focuses on Whitman's exploitation of the anonymity and mutual nonknowledge of the print medium as a means of representing the self-other relation and as "a provocation against the ideology of self-characterization," Trachtenberg reads the self-other relation as an enactment of "Whitman's lesson of the city," "its instruction in the mutuality and interdependence of I and You" that "constitutes Whitman's poesis" (40,164). Whereas for Trachtenberg, as for William James, Whitman's city poet represents a mode of "seeing processionally," for Davidson, the cross-dressed, city poetry of Whitman and O'Hara represents a mode of *being* processionally—"as a series of costumes, attitudes and positions"—in a world that, in O'Hara's terms, "strips down and rouges up" (234).

Unlike Davidson, Arac, Warner, and Jay Grossman, whose essays address in different registers the workings and consequences of liberal ideology in American culture and criticism, Dimock gives an exceptionally eloquent account of the more compelling and potentially contradictory dimensions of noncontingent rationality and liberal personhood not simply in writings by Whitman, but in the larger social texts of liberal democracy that Whitman's writings have helped to constitute. If Moon and Sedgwick, Folsom, Davidson, and others emphasize the fluid, performative, and queer dimensions of Whitman's self-representations, Dimock, like Allen Grossman, focuses on Whitman's attempt to give sacred legitimacy to the person and to love in a universe defined and moved only by material practices.

Whereas Allen Grossman reads Whitman's "Calamus" poem, "Whoever You Are Holding Me Now in Hand," in relation to its specifically literary "prehistory in the poetry of the West" as the expression of a universal person, or body—the "gender is indifferent," he writes—several of the essays in this volume contest this potentially universalizing interpretive strategy. In their examination of the ways Latin American writers "read, misread, desired, repressed, and had to come to terms with Whitman" (124), for example, Quiroga and Salessi foreground the scenes of homoerotic instruction that get elided in Grossman's more vatic account of Whitman as culturally productive poet and teacher. Beginning with an autobiographical account of an erotic encounter between two young men mediated by the body of Whitman's *Leaves of Grass,* Salessi and Quiroga present a vividly physical homosexual enactment of what Grossman calls, more abstractly, "Whitman's reinstauration of love by poetic means" (116).

In his discussion of the "homocentric vision of unity and transcendent possibility" that grounds the poetry of Whitman, Crane, and Ginsberg, Yingling wonders "whether the male homocentric vision of utopia is based on an elimination of the female, and whether the gay male vision of the good life is merely an orgy of male bodies" (139). Whereas Yingling decides, with some qualification, that for Whitman, as for Crane and Ginsberg, "the desire for utopia" "involves a rethinking of social organization on a scale that includes a rethinking of the question of woman (although it seems not often to include a rethinking of the question of the lesbian)" (139), Pollak argues that Whitman's "claim to speak *for* women and to understand their experience better than they understand it themselves emerges as the most consistently problematized element of his social, psychological, and political feminist vision" (93). Unlike Moon and Sedgwick, who emphasize the sympathetic identification of Louisa and Walt Whitman, Pollak represents Whitman's mother as a more repressive figure in the text of the poet's life and work. "Whitman experienced himself as having been subjected to the 'empire of the mother,' " she contends, "though at the same time he was also painfully conscious of his mother's thwarted aspirations for a more self-determining life" (108).

Against the tendency of past critics to subscribe to Whitman's own self-representation—"I have no mockings or arguments . . . . I witness and wait" (*LG* 1855: 28)—either removing Whitman's work from history into a transcendent realm called "literature" or treating Whitman as a sublimely affirming singer of American democracy, several of the essays in this volume consider Whitman's life, work, and influence in relation to the vexed political histories not only of his time but of ours. While past critics have granted Whitman's status as the poet of democracy, few have been willing to make any grand claims for him as a political theorist or philosopher. Dimock in effect reverses this critical consensus and the rigid boundary it inscribes between poetry and political theory, when, at a key moment in her essay, she turns to Whitman "to work out in greater detail" and possibly to resolve the "fatal contradiction" she perceives in contemporary political theory "between the language of democratic equality on the one hand and the language of affective preferences on the other, between our political need for formal universals and our emotional attachment to substantive particulars" (70).

What Grünzweig calls "the international Whitman movement" also suggests the ways Whitman has been taken seriously as a social and political writer whose vision must be translated into action worldwide. Thus, Horace Traubel's *Walt Whitman Fellowship International* was founded at the turn of the century not just to sip tea and talk poetry, but, as Grünzweig notes, "to transport a leftist and internationalist ideology" (243). In addition to breaking the traditional bound between literature and politics, this internationalist Whitman also suggests a difference in critical perspective. Whereas United States critics have tended to emphasize Whitman's individualism, his transcendentalism, and his aesthetic revolution, the writers and critics in the internationalist network that Grünzweig maps tend to emphasize Whitman's collectivism, his democratic politics, and the revolutionary implications of his verse. If to some Whitman appears to be the mythologizer of bourgeois capitalism, liberal ideology, and the imperial self, from an internationalist perspective Whitman also played a constitutive role in the emergence and formation of the international left. (In fact, one wonders if the later use of the term "comrade" among leftists to signal an international brotherhood may have originated with Whitman.) Bringing Whitman's internationalist vision seriously into history, Grünzweig's essay is itself a political meditation, written from the point of view of an Austrian leftist who has lived and taught in the former East Germany, on the situation in Europe—especially Eastern Europe—and the current internationalist stakes, both positive and negative, of living in a world without bounds.

In the epilogue to this volume, "Whitman's Centennial and the State of Whitman Studies," Jay Grossman also takes Whitman seriously into history as he reflects on the crucial relation between our approaches to Whitman in the classroom and in our critical writing and what he calls "the sequence of consequences that result in macro genocide or micro despair" as evidenced by the tragic prevalence of gay teenage suicide and the mounting deaths from AIDS. There is, Grossman argues, an "interconnectedness"— a homology—among "the methodologies and institutional structures that render homosexuality invisible or inapplicable across" a range of "cultural scenes," including past and present approaches to Whitman, the International AIDS Conference in San Francisco in 1990, the centennial conferences on Walt Whitman in 1992, and those agencies in Washington, D.C. "that continue to make invisible the suffering and the bravery of a pandemic of colossal proportions" (260,261).

By seeking to intervene in the critical and cultural practices that would keep Whitman's homosexuality neatly separated from his poetry and his politics, literature safely isolated from history, and the state of Whitman studies unrelated to the state of the world—or as Jay Grossman puts it, "from *Breaking Bounds*, by breaking bounds"—we hope that the essays in this centennial volume will help to propagate new states of Whitman studies, alternative social and cultural practices, and other possible worlds.

# Genealogies

# 1

## Confusion of Tongues

### MICHAEL MOON and
### EVE KOSOFSKY SEDGWICK

*MM:* My mother was a Van Velsor: I favor her: "favor" they call it up on Long Island—a curious word so used, yet a word of great suggestiveness.

*EKS:* Often people would say—men, women, children, would say—

*MM:* "You are a Whitman: I know you."

*EKS:* When I asked how they knew they would up with a finger at me:

*MM:* "By your features, your gait, your voice: they are your mother's."

*EKS:* I think all that was, is, true: I could see it in myself (*WWC* 2: 280).

*MM:* In this exchange we want to re-examine the matter of Walt Whitman's relationship with his mother, Louisa Van Velsor Whitman—his intense identifications and disidentifications with her and hers with him, as well as some possible connections between her writing and style (in the broadest sense of the term) and his.

*EKS:* My mother was illiterate in the formal sense but strangely knowing: she excelled in narrative—had great mimetic power: she could tell stories, impersonate: . . . was very original in her manner, her style (*WWC* 2: 113–14).

*MM:* *Leaves of Grass* is the flower of her temperament active in me (*WWC* 2: 113).

*EKS:* We've undertaken this project not only out of our dissatisfaction with the prevailing ideas of Louisa Whitman in Whitman criticism and biography, but from our even stronger dissatisfaction with prevailing ideas of the significance of relations between queer men and the women who are our mothers. Louisa Whitman, Lady Wilde, Julia Warhola: adult women, mothers, collaborators and coconspirators in the generativity of adult queer men who knew them, and were known to them, as few adults of any sexuality learn to know one another across the divide of gender. We want

23

to represent Louisa Whitman and her desires as fully as we can, especially those that aren't a part of conventional notions of maternal characteristics or of maternal desire.

*MM:* i pity Andrew very much but i think sometimes how much more those poor wounded and sick soldiers suffer with so much patience   poor souls I think much about them and always glad to hear you speak of them   i don't think walt after you being amongst them so long you could content yourself from them   it becomes a kind of fasination and you get attached to so many of the young men [1]

*EKS:* George came home last saturday very unexpected   he came to see about getting the inspecting of some pipe for the gas compa-ny . . .   he is well   looks most too fat and pussy but seems to be well)

*MM:* My dear darling walt i have just got your letter   i am glad my dear walt you are as well as you are   i know its bad enoughf to be confined in your room and unable to walk but i am glad to hear your friends is so kind   i thought of peter i knew if it was in his power to be with you he would and cherefully doo everything that he could for you )

*EKS:* well Walt here we are yet in the same old place but i doo want to get out of it very much indeed   there is so many children and not the best i ever see but a continual traveling up and down from morning till night   one good thing their dog is dead

*MM:* lou has had quite a run of company this week mostly girls from the place where she used to work   all have to be taken up in my room   i stayed down in the kitchen part of the time   their discourse was not inter-esting to me

*EKS:* Now what my mother told me one day as we sat at dinner together.
  Of when she was a nearly grown girl living home with her parents
   on the old homestead.

  A red squaw came one breakfast-time to the old homestead,
  On her back she carried a bundle of rushes for rush-bottoming
   chairs,
  Her hair, straight, shiny, coarse, black, profuse, half-envelop'd
   her face,
  Her step was free and elastic, and her voice sounded exquisitely
   as she spoke.
  My mother look'd in delight and amazement at the stranger,
  She look'd at the freshness of her tall-borne face and full and
   pliant limbs,
  The more she look'd upon her she loved her,
  Never before had she seen such wonderful beauty and purity,
  She made her sit on a bench by the jamb of the fireplace, she
   cook'd food for her,

She had no work to give her, but she gave her remembrance and fondness. (*LG* 429–30)

*MM:* I keep going back to that crucial passage in "The Sleepers." It's the most extended treatment of desire between women and also between races in all of *Leaves of Grass*. And the fact that this central scene of cross-racial *and* female-female attraction is represented by Whitman as being his mother's desire, long and fondly remembered by both of them, raises questions about queerness and queer desire: aren't they among the capacities that the poet imagined he acquired from his mother, or shared profoundly with her?

*EKS:* Whitman's critics and biographers since the 1950s have frequently patronized the poet and his parents, typecasting Whitman as the pathetic fag son of a mean and withholding father and a possessive and demanding mother. Whitman and his parents have too frequently been conscripted to illustrate the thesis, long popular among psychoanalysts and still ubiquitous in pop-culture (mis)understandings of the family dynamics of queerness, that—as one analyst puts it—a "predilection for a same-sex love object is caused by a close-binding, hostile mother who undermines her son's masculinity by blocking the development of his independence, interfering with the father-son relationship, and inducing a fear of women. Other [theorists] emphasize the role of an absent, weak, detached, or hostile father who makes it impossible for the child to separate from his dominating mother" (Isay 14). In the context of this tradition of thought, which so powerfully welds homophobia with misogyny—homophobia because of the assumption that something has to go *wrong* to produce homosexuality; misogyny because of the assertion that what goes wrong is excess of female—it's easy to see how the whole landscape of thinking about gay men and their mothers has become so poisoned that most gay-affirmative theorists now feel they must avoid the terrain entirely. Current antihomophobic developmental work, such as that of psychoanalysts Richard Friedman and Richard Isay, focuses instead on the enabling potential of the young gay man's relationship with his father. To do that is still, however, for these writers also to equate any man's sense of personhood and power with the strength of (in Friedman's phrase) his "masculine self-regard" (245); it is still to privilege the idea that in gay men's—in any men's—development as adult individuals, father-son relations must be qualitatively different from and, indeed, innately superior to the ties between mother and son.

*MM:* Anyone who knows anything about Whitman's family knows that relations among them were often tense and strained by the usual kinds of difficulties that poverty exacerbates—poor health, lack of money and adequate housing. We have been reading through Louisa Van Velsor Whitman's extant letters to Walt: a couple of hundred pages of them, most of them still unpublished. The letters have the look on the page of *archy and mehitabel:* Louisa Whitman writes entirely in lower case letters and never uses any marks of punctuation, except for a rare close parenthesis. The letters span the years from 1860 to the terrible months in 1873 marked by the news of Walt's having had a paralytic stroke in Washington, by the loss of her beloved daughter-in-law Mattie, and finally by her own death. Among the stories these letters can be used to tell there certainly is a very sad one about one nineteenth-century working-class Brooklyn woman's extremely difficult life, as she strives hopelessly to take care of herself and her children in the face of overwhelming experiences of disease and early death, intense emotional disturbance, unremitting physical labor, and want of material essentials for living—decent and ample food and living space.

*EKS:* Dear Walt  . . .  i received your letter yesterday after looking all day for one   i was glad to have the letter and glad to have the 2 dollars   at noon i hadent one cent and i asked georgee to give me 50 cents and after looking for a considerable time he laid me down 50 cents   well Walt i felt so bad and child like i cried because he dident give me more   if i had got the 2 dollars a little sooner i should not have asked   i have got along very well up to about 2 weeks ago and since that time george has been moody and would hardly speak only when i spoke to him   well of course you will say mother put the worst construction on it   well walt i did not the first few days  . . .  i thought of every thing   sometimes i would think maybee he is tired of having me and edd and then i would think george is too noble a fellow for that to be the cause and i know that . . . he had not been to more expence than if he paid his board   Jeffy told me to have a talk with george and ask him what made him so but i dident like to i would ask him if he wasent well and so on   but i doo hope it will go over   i acted just the same as if i did not notice any change but i felt awful bad and what has made him act so god only knows but i beleive it runs in the Whitman family to have such spells

*MM:* But there is another story one can use her letters to tell and that is about her extraordinary gifts and her legacy to her extraordinary son— of her sheer love of articulation and narration, especially outspoken and sardonic narration; her relish of grotesque incident; her strong sense of pity and her zest, at the same time, for the pithy framing of pitiless truths; her graphic interest in the dissolution and wearing away of self, and equally in the perseveration of need, of desire, of individual voice.

*EKS:* O walt it is terrible here in the winter   matt is getting as tired of it as i am   it will not look like any thing again even in the summer   its all dug and redug between this and the avenue   great trenches   it looks like destruction

*MM:* well walter dear we are getting along quite smart   matty is improving but far from well   the doctor is doctoring her throat with great success i think   . . .   but O dear if you could hear her talk   it would make me hoarse to talk a steady stream as she does when any one comes in to see her   i dread to see any one come in   i talk and talk to her but it does no manner of good   she gets almost offended at me   Perbasco was here the other evening and staid quite late and the way mats toung went it certainly would have made me have had the headach to have talked such a length of time steady but so it is  . . .   when we doo every thing to have her comfortable it makes me real out of patience

*EKS:* My dear Walter i did feel so anxious to hear from you and i cant help but feel quite down hearted to hear your thumb is so bad yet   i am so sorry for you to have such a tedious long time but i hope you will have it all come right in time   but it seems a long time   it seemes sometimes as if a sore never will get well and then at other times it will heal very quick   it is too bad)   how doo you do to write at the office or dont you   i wish you could write what the doctor thinks of it and what you put on it but i dont want to have you write any extras beause i know by the writing it must be difficult for you   i long for a letter so bad thinking you will be better the next one but i hope you will not get discouraged my dear walter for it certainly will get well)

*MM:* Our essay takes its title, "Confusion of Tongues," from a 1932 essay of Sandor Ferenczi's in which the psychoanalytic theorist argues that children have an uncanny faculty for miming the erotic desire that adults feel for them (Ferenczi). And this mimetic relation may not be one-directional. Ferenczi argues that children are capable—often to their own detriment—of turning themselves into what he calls "love-automatons" as they enact seductions that arise not so much from their own sexualities *per se* as from their desire to please adults. According to Ferenczi, the adult who is convinced he or she has been seduced by a child is missing the uncanny and compulsive mimeticism—itself a form of resistance—that comprises the child's behavior. But in that case, when Whitman points to his *mother's* "great mimetic power" and facility at "impersonation" as among her dearest gifts to him—among the things he acquired, that is, in *imitation* of this beloved and resisted model—then how many voices, and the voices of what kinds of passion and resistance, and toward whom, are we to imagine being transmitted in this relation? Here's a letter from Louisa to Walt that reflects her fascination (her enforced fascination) with the son-in-law, Charlie Heyde, who is abusing her daughter Hanna:

*EKS:* Walter dear i write a few lines to say i received a letter from heyde yesterday  . . .   he first began with saying hanna was so she came out to the kitchen and eat her meals but she is very far from complete recovery   she is very frail constitutionally yet her hand or rather her thumb by what he says is quite bad and the flesh scrinks from the bone )

*MM:* this may all be true probably is )

*EKS:* then he goes on to say that she is better off with him   that any change would not benefit her or to that affect with his highfullatin phrases )   well now for the second act )   he says he received a very stupid letter from Walt addressed to han which he humanely concluded not to deliver to her and then he goes on to quote the first part of the letter   he says it ran thus )

*MM:* i suppose my dear sister you are by this time perfectly recovered

*EKS:* and the next )

*MM:* what a stupid man

*EKS:* and the balance

*MM:* *he says*

*EKS:* is about nothing   hours of stuff   i am out of patience   let him stay in washington   he has but small credit here   i dont want to see him )

*MM:* all this i have copied from his letter except where i marked above now walter what doo you think such a man is capable of doing[2]

*EKS:* This not uncharacteristic letter of Louisa Whitman's is truly "a confusion of tongues," but without this confusion she could not have made the complex transaction we see her making here: enlisting Walt on her side in her longstanding quarrel with her truculent son-in-law, while insulting Walt at the same time with her copious interlineations of Heyde's trenchant abuse of him, while concurrently soliciting Walt's identification with *her* relishing identification with Heyde's relish in the production and (as I'm sure he anticipated) circulation of aggressive language and quotation.

*MM:* Whitman's representations of his family and their home belie the stereotypes of Victorian domesticity and the sanctity of maternity and of filial and fraternal love; the alleged undersides of all these official ideals don't get erased from Whitman's and his family's discourse about themselves and their relationships. I've been writing recently about incestuous desire between brothers as a crucially important focus of energy in Whitman's poetry, looking at poems and passages in *Leaves of Grass* that seem to structure and destructure themselves around an older and a younger brother's desire for each other. Looking beyond the kinds of representations of fraternal desire that supposedly produce some of the most exalted satisfactions depicted in Whitman's poetry—as in "Passage to India":

*EKS:* As fill'd with friendship, love complete, the Elder Brother found,
The Younger melts in fondness in his arms.

　　　　　　　　　*LG* 420)

*MM:* This work has been looking instead at what one might call the career of the term and the practice of "eddying" in Whitman's poetry as a set of traces of the poet's desire for his youngest brother, Eddy, who was born physically disabled and "feebleminded" and with whom Whitman was sharing a bed during the years when he was writing the first two editions of *Leaves of Grass* (Walt was thirty-six in 1855, Eddy twenty).

*EKS:* It's hard to say which is more disruptive: making visible what seem to be the traces of the poet's incestuous practice, or—and I think this *is* the harder one—coming to see this figure of poetic autonomy in the

matrix of everyday intimacies that, like all family relations, are both diz-
zyingly contingent and undiscretionary, and at the same time dense with
creative adult overdetermination. The Whitman whose most constant physical intimacy is with a mentally retarded youth, his brother, defies the
needs of readers in something like the same way as the Whitman whose
verbal culture emerged from decades of risky mimetic negotiations with a
highly talented, near-illiterate, passionate, and often exhausted older
woman.

*MM:* The queerness of each of these figures takes on new aspects when
we see them in each other's context. The word "queer" itself, of course,
means *across*—it comes from the Indo-European root *-twerkw,* which also
yields the German *quer* (transverse), Latin *torquere* (to twist), English
*athwart.* The correspondence of this nonheterosexual man and this woman-
loving woman is scored across and across with their passions for and debts
to one another; neither of them had a home of their own during Louisa's
lifetime, yet each succeeded in offering something like a home to the
other's openness to further transverse desires. But these engagements
don't occur between what is most archetypally "the mother" in Louisa
Whitman and most archetypally "the son" in Walt. "One is not born a
woman," Simone de Beauvoir famously wrote in *The Second Sex.* Certainly
one is not born a mother; perhaps one is not born even a son. Among the
voices we hear in Walt Whitman's poetry is the tongue of Louisa Whitman's
inspired resistance to these fates.

## Notes

1. Quotations from Louisa Whitman's letters are from an unpaginated typescript of letters housed in Special Collections at Duke University.
2. We have italicized in place of Louisa Whitman's markings above the
words.

# 2

# Whitman Drunk

## MICHAEL WARNER

I am as independent as the United States of America.
Anonymous drunk of the 1840s, being escorted from a bar

In November 1842, New Yorkers would have been able to buy, for twelve and a half cents each, or for eight dollars per hundred, an object that would be hard to classify today. It was called *Franklin Evans; or, the Inebriate*. Now it is encountered as a book, and is usually described as a novel. In 1842 it was a newspaper supplement—a special issue of the *New World*, unbound, printed on cheap paper, in newspaper columns. Any reader would have recognized it as a tract as well. The *New World*'s advertisements for it had begun, "Friends of Temperance, Ahoy!" (*EPF* 124). The first sentence makes no bones about these extranovelistic features: "The story I am going to tell you, reader, will be somewhat aside from the ordinary track of the novelist" (*EPF* 126).

Those who read *Franklin Evans* today, as a novel, often find it unsatisfactory; one reason for this is that the work addressed publics that were not simply novelistic publics. Newspaper subscribers and "Friends of Temperance" would have brought to the object the mass-mediated self-understanding of the temperance movement. And that was a public in a new way. Temperance publications like *Franklin Evans* brought together two tendencies of the early national period: an ever more aggressive press, which had become strongly entrepreneurial; and a tradition of association that by the time of Tocqueville's American tour could seem to be the defining feature of American culture. Temperance activism had been a prominent part of this early national pattern of association. In the ten or fifteen years before *Franklin Evans*, however, the press and voluntary association had transformed each other in the context of temperance. The early national entrepreneurial press became a mass medium, and the temperance reform societies that had been popping up in every American locale became a full-scale, mass-mediated social movement—that is, one that understood itself as such.

Temperance and the mass press planted each other on the national scene. The American Temperance Society from its beginnings in 1826 drew on a tradition of tract-distributing reform groups, especially the American Tract Society, and pushed the publishing trade to an unprecedented outreach. Temperance tracts—five million copies by 1851—dominated the American Tract Society's output. And papers such as the *Albany Temperance Recorder* achieved mass circulation in exactly the same years that saw the first penny daily newspapers. Even before the arrival of the new steam presses—the first penny daily, the *New York Sun*, was printed on a flatbed hand press—tractarians and newspapermen were developing the basis of a mass public. Not only were temperance societies and newspapers expanding; they incorporated an awareness of nonstate "society" in the culture of their membership and readership. As Charles Sellers tellingly notes:

> Americans were first habituated to statistics by the Benevolent Empire's bourgeois passion for enumerating souls saved, money raised, Bibles circulated, tracts printed, missionary years expended. Endlessly temperance reformers calculated the dollar costs of alcohol, including crime, pauperism, and lost labor. The $94,425,000 total of one tally would "buy up all the houses, lands, and slaves in the United States every five years." (265)

This statistical consciousness, combined with a vast network of nonstate associations and an equally vast body of print, brought a mass public into awareness of itself and its distinctness from the national state. The Washington Temperance Society, founded in 1840, was especially emphatic about the social scale of the voluntary movement; and the Washingtonians quickly outstripped the more elite-based ATS.

In this essay I will argue that the thematic language of temperance rhetoric had much to do with the emergence of the cultural form of the social movement, which from the 1830s to the present has been one of the givens of the political world. Temperance ideology shifted so radically in this process as to become virtually the opposite of temperance, as will become clear. I will also argue that both temperance rhetoric and the temperance movement were the context in which the tract's author, the newspaperman Walter Whitman, first articulated what would later become the major issues of his career. I will be especially interested in two residues from his temperance publishing: a dialectic or tension that would eventually become sexual expressivism; and the strange conception of a public that distinguishes his poetic writing and his publishing practice.

For all his trumpeting about the friends of temperance, when he is talking about alcohol in *Franklin Evans* Whitman often seems to be thinking about something else. Franklin Evans has his first encounter with musical drinking-shops shortly after he arrives in New York from the country, when his new city-boy friend says to him, "Let us go out and cruise a little, and see what there is going on" (*EPF* 152). "How delicious everything seemed!" Franklin exclaims.

Those beautiful women—warbling melodies sweeter than ever I had
heard before, and the effect of the liquor upon my brain, seemed to
lave¹ me in happiness, as it were, from head to foot!

Oh, fatal pleasure! There and then was my first false step after coming
in the borders of the city—and *so soon* after, too! . . .

Colby saw at length that he had been too heedless with me. Used as
he was to the dissipation of city life, he forgot that I was from the country, and never in my life before engaged in such a scene of *pleasure*. (*EPF*
153–54, italics in original)

This passage tries simultaneously to articulate pleasure and to manage it.
Self-mastery and self-abandonment struggle for supremacy in a way that is
visibly absent from earlier writing on alcohol, such as Benjamin Franklin's
or Washington Irving's. Fatal pleasure, but also *Oh,* fatal pleasure.² The-
matically, the focus is on drink. But Whitman does not write, "Oh, fatal alcohol."

If alcohol does not quite seem to be the subject here, still it is no accident that Whitman's first extended treatment of a dialectic between self-
mastery and self-abandonment should occur in the form of temperance
fiction. The temperance movement *invented* addiction. DeQuincey never
uses the term (though current editions supply it in prefaces and notes),
and only some decades after the concept was developed in temperance was
it extended to drugs other than alcohol. Addiction had been a legal term
describing the performative act of bondage before it became a metaphor to
describe a person's self-relation. Someone who is addicted to, say, Sabbath-
breaking could be understood as having developed a habit, bound himself
to a custom. In temperance rhetoric the concept loses the sense of an active
self-abnegation on the part of the will. Desire and will became distinct in a
way that Jonathan Edwards had rejected as a Lockean confusion: "A man
never, in any instance, wills any thing contrary to his desires, or desires
any thing contrary to his Will" (199). Edwards concedes that "a drunkard,
under such and such circumstances, may be unable to forbear taking
strong drink" (216); but this is a habitual inability, and thus an expression
of the will rather than its limitation. "It cannot truly be said . . . that a
drunkard, let his appetite be never so strong, cannot keep the cup from
his mouth" (218).³

Temperance reformers began imagining the reverse—that the drunkard *cannot* keep the cup from his mouth even if he wants to do so. At this
point they gave up on the traditional concept of temperance itself, in favor
of abstinence and the treatment of addiction as disease. In the culture of
modernity, where people are held responsible for the disposition of their
lives as an act of will, it became possible to imagine desire no longer as self
but rather as the paradigm case of heteronomy. Controlling your body *had*
made you temperate. Now it made you free. Where desire and will had
been one for Edwards, temperance reformers—like liberal evangelicals—

began radicalizing the concept of volition. The corollary was an expanded concept of desire as the limit on the will.

In *Franklin Evans* Whitman is on the cutting edge of addiction theory when he writes,

> Reader! perhaps you despise me. Perhaps, if I were by you at this moment, I should behold the curled lip of scorn, and the look of deep contempt. Oh, pause stern reverencer of duty, and have pity for a fellow-creature's weakness! . . . Thou sayest, perhaps—Begin a reformation, and custom will make it easy. But what if the beginning be dreadful? The first steps, not like climbing a mountain, but going through fire? What if the whole system must undergo a change, violent as that which we conceive of the mutation of form in some insects? What if a process comparable to flaying alive, have to be endured? Is the weakness which sinks under such struggles, to be compared with the pertinacity which clings to vice, for itself and its gross appetites? (*EPF* 179)

What if it isn't vice at all, this, or at least not vice *for itself*? What if it's, well, what could it be called? Flaying, infrapersonal trouble, the shudders of a mutating bug. "[I]mpotent attempts to make issue with what appears to be our destiny" (*EPF* 180). Whitman or Evans pleads by this logic for humanity. "The drunkard, low as he is, is a *man*" (*EPF* 180). He articulates an antinomy between will and desire, the moral solution to which is in fact a much more radical valuing of will: "the GLORIOUS TEMPERANCE PLEDGE" (*EPF* 180).

How does a picture of the body's own heteronomy (so to speak) produce the alien solution of the voluntary pledge? Eve Kosofsky Sedgwick has astutely observed this pattern in our own day, witnessed in a wild proliferation of addiction theories to the point that she speaks of epidemics of the will:

> So long as an entity known as "free will" has been hypostatized and charged with ethical value, . . . for just so long has an equally hypostatized "compulsion" had to be available as a counterstructure always internal to it, always requiring to be ejected from it. The scouring descriptive work of addiction attribution is propelled by the same imperative: its exacerbated perceptual acuteness in detecting the compulsion behind everyday voluntarity is driven, ever more blindly, by its own compulsion to isolate some new, receding but absolutized space of *pure* voluntarity. (*Tendencies* 133–34)

The glorious temperance pledge marks the receding horizon of that relatively absolute voluntarity. Whitman, pursuing the voluntarist utopia of pledging to an extreme, interpolates a dream-vision; a jacobin fantasy about a stateless festival republic, in which every last peasant will have

signed the temperance pledge, bringing all born persons into the Washingtonian associational network. In Franklin's dream, he appears in the crowd
during this big event:

> A venerable old man came forward upon the scaffold, and presented a
> document to the speaker. He received it with evident delight; and
> snatching a pen from a table, he wrote his name under it, and held it up
> to the view of the people.
>
> It were impossible to describe the thunder-peal of hurrahs that arose
> in the air, and sounded to the skies, as the Full Work was consummated
> thus. They cried aloud—
>
> "Victory! Victory! The Last Slave of Appetite is free, and the people
> are regenerated!" (*EPF* 222–23)

If it weren't so queer, this passage would be a true nightmare of democratic totalitarianism. It *is* rather queer, partly because the ideal of political
union, this delirious consummation, takes place in the public witnessing of
a man's relation to his own appetitive body; partly because of the campy
feudalism involved in calling John Doe the Last Vassal; partly because of
the odd mixture of humiliation and heroization involved in parading him
about; partly because of Franklin Evans's phantom self on the margin of
the whole scene.

What interests me most here is the fantasy of stateless public association,
because I think this points to the institutional context for addiction culture.
Temperance was not just another discourse, but a rather special kind of
social movement. The assumptions of addiction discourse silently explicate
the associational style of temperance, which was of course a civil society
phenomenon, arguably the largest and most sustained social movement in
modernity. In the year of the novel's publication, 1842, hundreds of American cities had held temperance festivals on Washington's birthday; but, as
one temperance lecturer announced, "the festival at New York surpassed
all others in its extent, beauty, and appropriateness" (Stovall 36). There
were even more festivals on July 4 of that year. There were also new temperance publications, including the *New York Washingtonian,* in which Whitman published a temperance story in March 1842, and where he would
publish the beginning of a second novel, *The Madman,* in 1843. Festivals
and publications alike helped to mediate for temperance participants a
sense of the social movement as part of a repertoire of action. Their sense
of membership and the very nature of their action were mediated by an
understanding that temperance organizing was an action on the part of
nonstate society. *Franklin Evans* also helped to mediate that constitutive
self-understanding.

Whitman in later life told Traubel that *Franklin Evans* was essentially
commissioned by two temperance activists, "Parke Godwin and another
somebody"—probably, in fact, Park Benjamin and James Burns (*WWC* 2:

124n). The idea of commissioning fiction as propaganda had been part of the public strategy of the temperance movement since 1836, when the second convention of the American Temperance Union, in Saratoga, formally voted to endorse fiction and other "products of the fancy" as public sphere instruments (Brown 201). Whitman echoed this notion of the instrumental role of fiction in the preface and conclusion of his novel:

> Issued in the cheap and popular form you see, and wafted by every mail to all parts of this vast republic; the facilities which its publisher possesses, giving him the power of diffusing it more widely than any other establishment in the United States; the mighty and deep public opinion, . . . its being written *for the mass* . . . all these will give "THE INEBRIATE," I feel confident, a more than ordinary share of patronage. (*EPF* 126–27)

Both the temperance movement in general and *Franklin Evans* in particular are therefore embedded in a context of nonstate political association.

Just seven years before the publication of the novel, Tocqueville had given this social form the ideologization by which it has been known ever since: voluntary association.

> In no country in the world has the principle of association been more successfully used or applied to a greater multitude of objects than in America. . . . The citizen of the United States is taught from infancy to rely upon his own exertions in order to resist the evils and the difficulties of life; he looks upon the social authority with an eye of mistrust and anxiety, and he claims its assistance only when he is unable to do without it. . . . If some public pleasure is concerned, an association is formed to give more splendor and regularity to the entertainment. Societies are formed to resist evils that are exclusively of a moral nature, as to diminish the vice of intemperance. (*Democracy in America* 1: 198–99)

In Tocqueville's account, as in *Franklin Evans,* the imperative of will for the individual ("to resist the evils and the difficulties of life") translates directly into a form of association. Americans fill up their social space with a vast network of associations all formed occasionally, entered and left at will, existing only to make the exercise of will more powerful. Temperance was shaped organizationally by this ideologization, not only in being open member associations like so many other moral reform groups, but also in calling attention to voluntarism by the ritual of pledge-signing. The thematic content of self-management and addiction, in this context, was able to provide an implicit metalanguage by which association might be perceived as valuable *because* voluntary. (Compare Thoreau's statement of only a few years later: "Know all men by these presents, that I, Henry Thoreau, do not wish to be regarded as a member of any incorporated society which I have not joined." [79])

Perhaps another way of showing how important these metasocial themes are in Whitman's treatment of alcohol is to show how unimportant alcohol itself is. Certain moralizing passages claim that all bad things in the story came from drink. But actually very little follows directly from alcohol in the plot. The "Oh, fatal pleasure" scene is perfectly typical: Franklin's dissipation comes as much from sopranos as from gin. Alcohol never plays more than an ancillary role in such gothic disasters as his marriage, on impulse, to a creole slave who later turns into a homicidal madwoman. (It's a very male text.)

Indeed, so unimportant is alcohol to the plot that Whitman was able to republish the novel with a new title that made no reference to it—twice: first as *Franklin Evans; or the Merchant's Clerk: A Tale of the Times* (advertised through the same *New World* in 1843); then again in 1846 in Whitman's own paper, the *Brooklyn Daily Eagle*, as *Fortunes of a Country Boy.* The latter version especially is no longer a temperance novel. The interpolated tales have been removed, but most of these had little to do with alcohol itself, as for example in the tale of Wind-Foot (an exquisite Indian boy who does what Indians do best in white American literature: die in erotically thrilling ways). By means of such cuts and some discreet alterations—"dissipation" replaces "drunkenness"—*Fortunes of a Country Boy* becomes a novel about self-development and urban associational space. Addiction is replaced by a character flaw: "weakness of resolution, and liability to be led by others" (*EPF* 212). Franklin's final conversion to the total abstinence pledge is dropped, which means that his return from the dark night of his Southern sojourn is marked only by the sudden reappearance of Stephen Lee, who leaves him a large inheritance. "So, at an age which was hardly upon the middle verge of life, I found myself possessed of a comfortable property; and, as the term is 'unincumbered' person" (*EPF* 232). (When Evans asks the reason for this largesse Lee says, "My own fancy" [*EPF* 230]. At the beginning of the novel he had said, "I do not wish to conceal that I am somewhat interested in your case" [*EPF* 151].)

What both versions share is an interest in the dilemmas of self-coherence. In the following passage from *Franklin Evans,* Whitman sounds almost DeQuincian:

> How refreshing it is to pause in the whirl and tempest of life, and cast back our minds over past years! I think there is even a kind of satisfaction in deliberately and calmly reviewing actions that we feel were foolish or evil. It pleases us to know that we have the learning of experience. The very contrast, perhaps, between what we are, and what we were, is gratifying. . . .
>
> From no other view can I understand how it is, that I sometimes catch myself turning back in my reflection, to the very dreariest and most degraded incidents which I have related in the preceding pages, and thinking upon them without any of the bitterness and mortification which they

might be supposed to arouse in my bosom. The formal narration of them, to be sure, is far from agreeable to me—but in my own self-communion upon the subject, I find a species of entertainment. I was always fond of day-dreams—an innocent pleasure, perhaps, if not allowed too much latitude. (*EPF* 219)

As a pretext for introducing the daydream about the Last Slave of Appetite this transitional passage assumes a fair amount of latitude, and stands out all the more for that reason as an index to the novel's characteristic obsessions. Franklin indicates the autobiographical act as a version of liberal individual morality, an act of taking responsibility for one's entire disposition. But he quickly begins instead to describe the perverse pleasures of self-discontinuity, even self-repudiation and -abjection. The scenes he contemplates are dreary, even degrading; though he says he contemplates them without bitterness or mortification he also tells us that the contemplation is pleasurable because he knows it *should* be bitter and mortifying.

The dialectic between these two moments—liberal self-integration and perverse self-contemplation—governs the entire narrative. *Franklin Evans* seems designed more than anything else to narrate its title character into as many disparate social spaces as possible, and to compound his integration problems with the endless resurgence of appetite. From his first appearance *en route* from rural Long Island to Manhattan, Franklin is the subject of his elective associations, especially male (he will marry twice and take one mistress, with fatal consequences for all three women). He falls in with some fast boys who introduce him to male circles of urban appetitive decadence. He also meets Lee, the mysterious older widower who takes a special interest in him. His path between these affinitive influences leads him in and out of various states of self-coherence, where integration tends to be associated with capital and temperance, disintegrative tendencies with alcohol, sexuality, time, death, the city, sickness, poverty, market dependency, crime, prison, shame, singing, and pleasure. "How delicious everything seemed!"

At the end of *Franklin Evans*, Whitman summarizes the moral of the story: "I would warn that youth whose eye may scan over these lines, with a voice which speaks to him, not from idle fear, but the sad knowledge of experience, how bitter are the consequences attending these musical drinking-shops . . . pestilent places, where the mind and the body are both rendered effeminate together" (*EPF* 239). It's not difficult to hear attraction here. Something that cannot be openly avowed is nevertheless coming to expression. Modern bourgeois culture gets a lot of things done this way, but nowhere more visibly than in the literature of addiction, to which *Franklin Evans* belongs. Addiction literature is marked by a dialectic: no sooner do scenes of self-abandonment conjure up the necessity of self-mastery than this instrumental self-relation in turn gives way to the possibility of self-contemplation, of an abandonment newly regarded as expressive. Though the theme is addiction, it's hard not to hear some reference to the emergent same-sex subculture of New York in the following passage, which describes a lower Manhattan theater of exactly the sort where that subculture flourished:

> The Demon of Intemperance had taken possession of all our faculties, and we were his alone.
>
> A wretched scene! Half-a-dozen men, just entering the busy scenes of life, not one of us over twenty-five years, and there we were, benumbing our faculties, and confirming ourselves in practices which ever too surely bring the scorn of the world, and deserved disgrace to their miserable victims! It is a terrible sight, I have often thought since, to see *young men* beginning their walk upon this fatal journey! . . . To know that the blood is poisoned, and that the strength is to be broken down, and the bloom banished from the cheek, and the lustre of the eye dimmed, and all for a few hours' sensual gratification, now and then—is it not terrible! . . . [It] saps the foundations, not only of the body's health, but places a stigma for the future on their worldly course, which can never be wiped out, or concealed from the knowledge of those about them. (*EPF* 167–68)

Alcohol discriminates finely; it assaults young blood, manly strength, blooming cheeks, and bright eyes. Its symptoms, scarcely distinguishable from those associated with onanism in the mass reform literature of the time, appear in whole numbers of men at once. Seeing such men in public, you recognize them by an epistemology of stigma. This is where they hang out. I have often thought about it.

Alcohol becomes a figure for self-incoherence in general; any "Demon" that has "taken possession of all our faculties" will do. "I sicken as I narrate this part of my story," he says at another point. "The recollection comes of the sufferings of my poor wife, and of my unkindness to her. I paid no attention to her comforts, and took no thought for her subsistence. I *think* I never proceeded to any act of violence—but God only knows what words I spoke in my paroxysms of drunken irritation . . ." (*EPF* 175). Franklin has problems of self-characterization; God only knows what words I spoke. Whitman heightens his difficulty of autonarration by a number of odd voicing devices: the first scene, for example, is told in omniscient third-person until the narrator says of the main character, "Reader, I was that youth"—a device later repeated in the interpolated tales. Drunkenness, however, allows or requires Franklin to treat his problems of self-characterization as part of his self-characterization. He is a person subject to "paroxysms," self-sickenings, involuntary amnesias, alien thrills of retrospection. These forms of internal heteronomy take on special significance because they contrast with the confessional performance of the narration itself, which is organized by a metalanguage of choice, responsibility, and association through affinity and self-characterization rather than through kinship and status.

At the end of the novel, when Whitman strives for closure within the voluntarist rhetoric, Franklin's internal recognition problems suddenly find an equivalent in his double. He sees in the street a "tipsy loafer" begging, "going through his disgusting capers."

> Pausing a moment, and looking in the man's face, I thought I recollected the features. A second and a third glance convinced me. It was Colby, my early intimate, the tempter who had led me aside from the paths of soberness.
>
> Wretched creature! . . . His apparel looked as though it had been picked up in some mud hole; it was torn in strips and all over soiled. His face was bloated, and his eyes red and swollen. I thought of the morning when I awoke upon the dock, after my long fit of intemperance: the person before me, was even more an object of pity than myself on that occasion. (*EPF* 234)

Since Franklin's association with Colby had been the paradigmatic instance of affinitive, voluntary association in the novel, Franklin can only repudiate him with some cost, leading him rather inconsistently to say, in the penultimate paragraph, "I would advise every young man to marry as soon as possible, and have a home of his own" (*EPF* 236).

The later Whitman's perverse self-characterization is not so far removed from the bourgeois propriety of the temperance novel as one might expect. Nor is his insistence on bringing sexuality into public view, given the peculiar nature of *Franklin Evans*'s public. Whitman's commitment to voluntarist culture never completely relaxed. Like *Franklin Evans, Leaves of Grass* imagines a stateless society, constituted in the public sphere through performative discourse. The significant difference is that the poetry imagines this associational style as yoked to—and explicated by—the contemplative or self-abandoning moment in the dialectic of individualism rather than its instrumental or self-mastering moment. Where *Franklin Evans* had imagined civil society association as organized by voluntariness and self-mastery, condensed in the image of a pledging association, Whitman in the 1850s and 1860s imagined nonstate association as called into being by desire, by contemplative recognition, by the imperfect success of selfing.

Unfortunately, this difference has been obscured by the central tradition of Whitman criticism. With its obsessive discourse about Whitman's so-called "self," Whitman criticism has provided the most extreme instance I know of the ideology of self analyzed by Vincent Crapanzano. Crapanzano has argued that in middle-class American culture pragmatic features of discourse tend to be perceived in a referential language of character.[4] These texts are no exception, since their pragmatics are uniformly taken as indices of Whitman's "self," and their peculiarities are taken to be peculiarities of that self. (Sometimes with a great deal of unintended comedy, as when Malcom Cowley explains that Whitman had "an abnormally developed sense of touch" [Introduction xv]). "Self" seems to be a concept without which it is impossible to do Whitman criticism. In a long tradition of Whitman criticism, from Anderson's *Imperial Self* to recent essays by Doris Sommer and Philip Fisher, Whitman has been regarded as a prophet of "the liberal self," a self that regards itself as universal, that does not "recognize difference." In my view, this reading of Whitman gets almost everything wrong, though it's a misreading partly developed by the late Whitman, as it were, himself.

Whitman's writing thematizes a modern phenomenology of self everywhere: "I celebrate myself, and sing myself." But it almost always does so in order to make the pragmatics of selfing a mess: "And what I assume you shall assume" (*LG* 28). The second line can be taken as elaborating the indicatively modern and liberal problem of the other, the problem of mutuality—a problem frequently enough taken up by Whitman, as for example in "Crossing Brooklyn Ferry." But it can also be taken as thematizing the pragmatics of self-attribution. It announces that "I" and "you" bear no relation to content, action, choice, self-knowledge or mutual knowledge, the attribution of traits, the reciprocal confirmation of identity through action, or any other condition of selfing: "what I assume you shall assume."

Moreover, the impossibility of selfing is driven home in the way the line parrots interpersonal drama while deploying the special discursive conventions of print-mediated publicity. Whitman's poetry, more than any other body of writing I know, continually exploits public sphere discourse conventions as its condition of utterance. In this case it relies on a discourse context defined by the necessary anonymity and mutual nonknowledge of writer and reader, and therefore on the definitional impossibility of intimacy. Assuming what I assume, you and I have neither an identity together, mediated as we are by print, nor apart, since neither pronoun attributions nor acts of assuming manage to distinguish us.

From the first word of "Song of Myself" ("I") to the last ("you"), in every major poem he wrote, Whitman tries out an enormous range of strategies for frustrating the attempt to "self" his language, both by thematic assertion—"I resist anything better than my own diversity"—and by attribution problems: "My voice is the wife's voice, the screech by the rail of the stairs." I interpret the metadiscursive queerness of the poems as a provocation against the ideology of self-characterization. "To a Stranger," for example, invokes the communicative medium of intimacy—the medium to which character attribution is most indispensable—in a way that toys with the nonintimate, depersonalizing conventions of print publication.

> Passing stranger! you do not know how longingly I look upon you,
> You must be he I was seeking, or she I was seeking, (it comes to me as of a dream,)
> I have somewhere surely lived a life of joy with you,

All is recall'd as we flit by each other, fluid, affectionate, chaste, matured,
You grew up with me, were a boy with me or a girl with me,
I ate with you and slept with you, your body has become not yours only
    nor left my body mine only,
You give me the pleasure of your eyes, face, flesh, as we pass, you take of
    my beard, breast, hands, in return,
I am not to speak to you, I am to think of you when I sit alone or wake at
    night alone,
I am to wait, I do not doubt I am to meet you again,
I am to see to it that I do not lose you. (*LG* 127)

When the speaker says, "you do not know how longingly I look upon you," we know that Whitman is not looking longingly upon us, that we cannot possibly *be* the self addressed in second-person attributions. But we also cannot simply fictionalize either the speaker or the scene of address, in the manner of "My Last Duchess," because the speaker himself indicates the genericizing conventions of publication. It is addressed "to a stranger," and that we certainly are. He is not to speak to us, he says, and that he certainly is not. When the speaker says in the last line, "I am to see to it that I do not lose you," we are able to recognize his sense of difficulty simultaneously as (a) his personal commitment to me, whom he loves; and (b) his attempt to acknowledge our anonymity, our mutual nonknowledge, our mediation by print.

The same tension marks all the lines that grope for particularity: "You grew up with me, were a boy with me or a girl with me." You can imagine that one of these recognizes you in particular, but the effort of imagination involved in being recognized both ways serves to remind you that this "you" is, after all, not you but a pronomial shifter, addressing the in principle anonymous and indefinite audience of the print public sphere. At the same time, you know that you are not being addressed by a complacently generic you, of the kind that I am using to address you in this sentence. In "To a Stranger," while we remain on notice about our place in nonintimate public discourse, we are nevertheless solicited into an intimate recognition exchange. Like so much of Whitman's poetry, "To a Stranger" mimes the phenomenology of cruising.

Now the first thing I want to say about this is that it connects with the contemplative, expressive side of individualism, which Whitman in the 1850s radicalized out of the dialectic visible in the 1842 novel. The language of *Leaves of Grass* presents challenges for the pragmatics of selfing, in a way that bears out the speaker's talk of inner divisions, shifting personal boundaries, cross-identifications, and so forth. And this erratically selfed language frequently announces an erotics or even ethics of contemplative self-abandonment. Whitman's poetry may in fact be the earliest instance of a theme that has come to be taken for granted in Euro-American culture: the idea of sexuality as an expressive capacity of the individual.

The second thing I would want to say about the poem is that it links its erotics of self-abandonment to its own perverse publicity, to its use of a print public sphere mode of address. A more famous example would be these lines, with which Whitman began the second poem of his 1855 *Leaves of Grass*, a poem later given the title "Song for Occupations":

> Come closer to me,
> Push close my lovers and take the best I possess,
> Yield closer and closer and give me the best you possess.
>
> This is unfinished business with me . . . . how is it with you?
> I was chilled with the cold types and cylinder and wet paper between us.
>
> I pass so poorly with paper and types . . . . I must pass with the contact
>     of bodies and souls. (*LG* 1855: 87)

If I were to read these lines to you, you would know that I was quoting rather than soliciting; that would have been clear, if you hadn't already recognized the passage, when I got to the reference to paper and types. If you were to read the lines on the page, however, you would recognize a certain fictionality in the scenario from the first line, "Come closer to me," since the deictics of that line indicates exactly the kind of embodied sociality that modern public print discourse negates. Reading the passage, you might be drawn into its erotic fantasy—pubic hairs on the ink rollers and so on—but you would still realize that the speaker references the speech situation itself in a way that is manifestly wrong, that there is no question of coming closer to this speaker *or not*, that part of what makes the passage kinky is not just that Ballard-like image of cold lead on skin, pre-come on the platen, but rather the parasitic relation of one discourse context to another, a cultivated perversity at the metadiscursive level. In this as in so many other passages, Whitman wants to make sex public, and doing so involves jarring conventions of representation.

There are of course other poems that fictionalize their own discursive status. In a work like Browning's "My Last Duchess," the reader is expected to suspend recognition of the publication context of the poem in order to construct the fictional scenario of the Duke's embodied speech, which includes several deictic phrases that, like "Come closer to me," are impossible references in the print context: "That's my last Duchess painted on the wall"; "Will't please you rise?"; "We'll go / Together down, sir," and so on. Whitman's method is different because he does not suspend awareness of the publication context, which therefore becomes the ground of his perversity.[5]

In sections 27 and 28 of "Song of Myself" the dialectic of sexual expressivism becomes explicit, as it does also in section 5, where Whitman turns a fictive internal I/you scenario—the soul's speech to the body—into an erotic relation: "the other I am must not abase itself to you." As in Thoreau, the self-relation of expressive individualism takes the form of a self-other relation, which is also to say that selfing becomes problematic even as the phenomenology of self is radically broadened. As in Thoreau, the internal problematics of the expressive self become difficult to distinguish from the paradigmatically liberal erotic dilemmas of recognition and mutuality. And, as in Thoreau, Whitman's interest in those dilemmas is strongest when they are not stabilized by heterosexuality, which is to say by the modern ideology that interprets gender difference as the form of self-other difference.[6]

The distinctive pragmatics of Whitman's poetry refigure the conventions of temperance fiction in a number of ways that are equally relevant to the valuation of sexuality. Whitman takes voluntarist culture as a context in which internal dissonances of appetite, the involuntary, or amnesia can be read simultaneously as expressive of a self *and* as selfing problems. What had been internal heteronomy in the addiction rhetoric of the novel becomes both the other of self-contemplation and a limit to the responsibilizing language of self. This dialectic is at the core of the Whitmanian sublime.

## Notes

1. Brasher's edition reads "have."
2. The rhetorical weight accorded to mere italicization in that last phrase, "such a scene of *pleasure*"—like the conclusion's emphasis on the voice which speaks to the reader in these lines, or like the women's ability through "warbling" to lave Evans in happiness—indicates Whitman's characteristic (and characteristically faggy) attachment to voice as a limit-case both of embodied self-mastery and of boundary problems.
3. The history of addiction theory and temperance is best analyzed in Levine, who discusses Edwards at 149ff.
4. See especially chapter 4, "Self-Characterization."
5. In "To a Stranger," by the way, the effect of metadiscursive perverseness was heightened in revision. Where the published version ends with "I am to see to it that I do not lose you," the manuscript had continued with two more lines:

> I listen to the different voices winding in and out, striving, contending with fiery vehemence to excel each other in emotion,
> I do not think the performers know themselves—But now I think I begin to know them. (*Whitman's Manuscripts* 105)

By eliminating this reference to the speech-mediated scene of the street, Whitman focused the reader's own impossible insertion in the poem.

6. I have elaborated this reading of Thoreau in "Thoreau's Bottom" and "Walden's Erotic Economy."

# 3

# Whitman and Problems of
# the Vernacular

## JONATHAN ARAC

Let me start well within bounds, with a commonplace. Someone eager to learn about the author of *Leaves of Grass* could turn to recent works of good repute and find that Whitman is notable for his use of "the American vernacular" (Loving 453), that he was "the first genuine master of the American vernacular" (Zweig 182). But what is meant by this laudatory description? How did this term *vernacular* come to occupy a key place in discussions of Whitman? What is the value of maintaining it? The term was not part of nineteenth-century discussions of what Cmiel (1991) calls "popular language" in the United States, nor does it figure in the path-breaking discussion of Whitman's language in F. O. Matthiessen's *American Renaissance* (1941). So far as I can tell, the term begins to play its current role in the early postwar period, functioning among the founding premises for the institutionalization of literary American Studies. The specific premise is that Whitman, together with Mark Twain, inaugurated what Henry Nash Smith in the 1948 *Literary History of the United States* called, in praise, "the intrusion of the vernacular into consciously literary usage" (650). A decade later, Leo Marx developed this claim in "The Vernacular Tradition in American Literature," which as late as 1988 Marx placed first in the warmly-reviewed volume of his collected essays.

Departing from this well-established view, I explore conceptual problems in the notion of *vernacular*, especially its frequent linkage to nationalist myths of purity. I argue instead for a comparatist perspective that emphasizes *mixture:* a "creole" mixture associated with the "Black Atlantic" (Gilroy) or "Circum-Atlantic Performance" (Roach); the heterogeneity of life and language associated with the big city, whether Whitman's New York or Baudelaire's Paris; and finally even the impurity that joins this self-consciously American writer to the literary practices of British romanticism.

## From Vernacular to Creole

The years after the end of World War II were imagined to inaugurate the "American Century" that would follow from the rise of the United States to the position of morally best and economically and militarily most powerful state in the world. The establishment and proliferation of scholarly research in American Studies renewed nationalist themes familiar from more than a century earlier, when the United States had first tried to define itself as an independent culture. Leo Marx—through his experience just before the war as a Harvard undergraduate student of F. O. Matthiessen and Perry Miller and then as a graduate student after the war, next as a junior colleague of Henry Nash Smith at Minnesota in the early 1950s—stands as one of the few still active figures who reaches back to the beginnings of organized American Studies. His work remains in print, and despite problems that I will raise with it, its quality makes it worth attention even now, for he combines history, close reading, and political concerns in a blend that remains a compelling model.

Marx's essay on "The Vernacular Tradition" begins from the question of national cultural identity. He claims that before 1850 "the boundary between British and American literature remains uncertain" (3). So it is apt in this volume to note that the topic of vernacular may involve establishing bounds more than breaking bounds. Walt Whitman and Twain are "the two great seminal figures of modern American writing" because in "Song of Myself" and *Huckleberry Finn*, "the line" between British and American becomes "much more distinct" (4). These works "establish once and for all the literary usefulness of the native idiom" (4). Because they "fashioned a vernacular mode," they made possible a "national style" (4). Vernacular, Marx explains (xv, 265) stands in contrast to what George Santayana had called the "genteel tradition," the traditional mentality from which a younger generation had diverged. For Marx, then, the vernacular tradition is not only a matter of characteristic language; it also carries with it social, specifically political, values: "the core of the American vernacular . . . is not simply a style, but a style with a politics in view" (8); its "political ideal is freedom" (16).

To make his point, Marx compares a poem by Longfellow ("The Slave in the Dismal Swamp") with these lines from section 10 of "Song of Myself":

The runaway slave came to my house and stopt outside,
I heard his motions crackling the twigs of the woodpile,
Through the swung half-door of the kitchen I saw him limpsy and weak,
And went where he sat on a log and led him in and assured him,
And brought water and fill'd a tub for his sweated body and bruis'd feet,
And gave him a room that enter'd from my own, and gave him some
    coarse clean clothes,

And remember perfectly well his revolving eyes and his awkwardness,
And remember putting plasters on the galls of his neck and ankles;
He staid with me a week before he was recuperated and pass'd north.
I had him sit next me at table, my fire-lock lean'd in the corner. (*LG* 37–
   38)

Marx claims that Whitman "imagines a completely different kind of relation to the black man" from that in Longfellow's poem, achieved through
the "extraordinary sense of immediacy that the vernacular mode conveys"
(7). Marx praises the "indirection" by which Whitman's speaker "at the end
. . . casually mentions the gun in the corner" (8). For Marx here, "the
image *is* the meaning; it is a perfect example of the democratic hero's relaxed but militant egalitarianism" (8). Stylistically, Whitman "anticipates the
kind of ironic understatement" (8) that would flourish in the twentieth
century.

However, I find it painfully evident that the aesthetic principles of
American new-critical modernism—an emphasis on irony and imagery, on
"showing" rather than "telling"—have saturated Marx's socially, culturally,
and politically concerned argument, and further, that those principles un-
derwrite a Cold War, American Century stance even in this leftist critic.
Whitman's speaker's soft talk and big stick form a recognizable style of
boasting, later brought by Teddy Roosevelt from his macho western experiences to the stage of world diplomacy and reinforced in the days of massive deterrence when Marx wrote. Now that Eliot and Hemingway no
longer reign, it may be acknowledged that image and irony alone are
merely formal criteria, not tests of moral substance. A national style it has
been, perhaps, but can all find freedom in its bounds? In essays published
well before Marx's, Ralph Ellison had already criticized the twentieth-
century American literary convention of "understatement" for relying on
shared understandings not necessarily available to minorities, and had argued that Hemingway took from Twain only stylistic techniques, but not
moral vision (*Shadow and Act* 35, 103).

Marx continues by arguing that Whitman "does not need to proclaim
the solidarity between the two men . . . because he can describe it so vividly" (8). Yet as I read this scene, the slave remains an object by means of
which the narrator is morally empowered. Every single transitive verb in
the passage has the narrator's "I" as its subject and the slave (or some part
or feature of him—body, sweat, feet, eyes, awkwardness) as its object. The
"model society," the "ideal . . . egalitarian community" (8) Marx sees im-
aged here lacks the pronoun *we*. I say this not to hold Whitman to some
after-the-fact standard of correctness. Rather, I regret the degree of cosmetic remodeling scholars and critics were driven to by their wish to shape
an American past that would serve postwar liberalism after the earnest
style of the prewar Popular Front had been stigmatized as Stalinist.[1]
Despite Leo Marx's own concern to distance himself from any "chauvin-

ism" (8) and his acknowledgment that the turn to vernacular was "international" (9), as witnessed by William Wordsworth's earlier *Lyrical Ballads* (1800) in England, his argument enforces an American nationalism. The same difficulty marked *Made in America* (1948), a work on American vernacular across the arts by the cultural historian John Kouwenhoven, which was highly influential in giving the term the privilege it accrued in the postwar period.[2] In the paperback reissue, Kouwenhoven protested against the isolationist, anti-European reading given to his work by many reviewers (ix–x). Yet I think anyone encountering the book's sympathetic exposition of "Fordism" and "Taylorism" (181–87) might be forgiven this interpretation. Kouwenhoven, like Marx, insists that democracy is an essential value within American vernacular (186), but the form of experience that Kouwenhoven emphasizes is above all "technical and industrial" (128): tool design is the paradigm case from which he develops his larger definition (13–26). In his long chapter, "What Is Vernacular?" Kouwenhoven names it as "the folk arts of the first people in history who, disinherited of a great cultural tradition, found themselves living under democratic institutions in an expanding machine economy" (12, italicized in the original). Thus near the end Kouwenhoven can summarize, "If there ever was an unabashed product of the vernacular tradition as this book has defined it, the Model-T Ford was it" (179). Kouwenhoven does not refer to Santayana, but his argument bears out Santayana's sense that the only existing alternative to genteel tradition was "aggressive enterprise" (188), not exactly the value Marx wished to find in vernacular.

To return to Marx's argument, we must recognize that in Whitman's own time the lines between politics and aesthetics were as complex as in the postwar period and now. Whittier's abolitionist verse was not formally distinguishable from Longfellow's; it was genteel, not vernacular. Yet in his 1845 *Narrative*, Frederick Douglass quoted Whittier as "the slave's poet" (48), and Douglass's own style is closer to the genteel Daniel Webster than to the vernacular Mark Twain.[3] So, too, it is not the vernacular Davy Crockett but the sentimental *Uncle Tom's Cabin*, in the Quaker settlement of Rachel Halliday, which provides a textual model of deeply felt interracial proximity from which Whitman's beautiful impersonation may arise.[4] Yet Stowe's imagination also allows George Harris to bear and use firearms himself. The drive to freedom may cross the bounds of styles.

As I consider Marx's argument further, I am struck by the instability of the key term *vernacular*. Marx does not remark upon its etymological history, which, however, seems to predict his examples. *Vernacular* comes from Latin *verna*, a slave born in the master's house,[5] and it thus carries from its beginnings the problematic of domination and domestication. (The Latin word is apparently of Etruscan derivation and so itself a domesticated, subjugated alien.)

The current senses in the *American Heritage Dictionary* for the noun *vernacular* suggest the problems I find. Sense one is "the standard native language of a country or locality"; sense two is the "nonstandard or substandard everyday speech of a country or locality." In considering these senses, we might think of the model of Latin vis-à-vis the emerging Romance languages (the "vernaculars"). From the point of view of the Roman empire, the second sense (substandard, everyday) predominated, but from the point of view of nations in formation the first sense (standard, native) prevailed. The distinction between standard native language and non- or substandard everyday speech throws back into crisis the bounds of American literary nationality: is there a standard "American" national language of the "country" or are there only innumerable everyday variations differing by "locality"?[6] What does it mean to imply that, as masterpieces of "the vernacular," *Leaves of Grass* and *Huckleberry Finn* have the relation to past British and future American languages that the *Divine Comedy* and the *Decameron* do to past Latin and future Italian? At least it makes us ask whether Marx's praise of vernacular does not in fact work to fix a vernacular *standard*, as the great Renaissance writers did for their European cultures through the prestige they were accorded in critical and educational practices. That is, having been used to define one set of bounds (America versus the Old World), vernacular becomes a means for drawing further bounds within the United States, as to what will count as authentically "American." The third sense of *vernacular* in the *American Heritage Dictionary* further emphasizes this problem of representativeness: "the idiom of a particular trade or profession." In other words, here *vernacular* means much the same as *jargon*, not what is common, but what is peculiar or particular to a closed group, although that group may claim for itself, or have claimed for it, the right to stand for the whole.

Marx's usages display the complications that the dictionaries make explicit. He wrote of the vernacular as an American "native idiom" and thus the basis for a "national style." But what is the relation of native and national here? To begin, we may note that the dictionaries mention vernacular as not only *native* but also *indigenous*. The difference between these terms lies precisely in the historical depth of settlement. While the U.S.-born children of immigrants might be native, and proudly called themselves so, they were not indigenous. Only those known now as "native Americans" would count as indigenous. In the earlier nineteenth-century discussions of the possibilities of an American literary nationality for the United States, this problem was directly addressed, namely, that the Indians, the historically rooted inhabitants of what had become the United States, spoke as their mother tongues languages that were not the English language of the politically dominant culture. The opposite problem, certainly by the time Whitman was writing, was felt even more immediately, that is, the problem of nonanglophone immigrants. Marx's discussion of vernacular seems to leave no room for either of these features of the language and life of the United States.

Whitman, with whatever success, did deliberately incorporate non-

English words into his poetry, and many twentieth-century students of American English have found much of its distinctive difference from British English to spring precisely from idioms (words, inflections, syntactic patterns) drawn from other languages. The example of Whitman moves me to claim that the "creolization" of American English is what produces its difference from the English that served as the standard of literary language.[7] The emphasis on "native," however useful in polemics against transatlantic domination from England, ignores fundamental features of the society, culture, and politics of the United States, and it thereby, however inadvertently, gives comfort to some of the most distressing tendencies of American nativism. It may be more useful to take American English as a "new type of colonial language," which will always have the character of a "second language."[8]

Although the term *creole* is known to most who live in the United States as relevant only to Louisiana, the basic sense of *creole* refers to peoples in all the North and South American and Asian areas colonized by Europeans, specifically to individuals born in the colonized area whose parents came from Europe or Africa. The term in itself carries no specification of color or race, except insofar as it distinguishes the creoles both from immigrants or transients of the colonizing area and from the aboriginal or indigenous population. Part of its conceptual force as a term is that its model is not binary, but involves three or more terms. Moreover, in the actual politics of creolization that have emerged, the term implies a hyphen: for instance Hirsch and Logsdon discuss "Franco-Africans and African-Americans" (189–319). "Creole" as a term for thinking about Whitman's language, then, links his experience in New Orleans to his major work done in New York.

The *Oxford English Dictionary* further glosses *vernacular* by adding, "usually applied to the native speech of a populace, in contrast to another or others acquired for commercial, social, or educative purposes; now frequently employed with reference to that of the working classes or peasantry." This emphasizes that the standard of proper vernacularity depends on a system of social stratification and its attendant structures of value. Marx understands vernacular as insurgent, representing popular values that oppose those of an elite. But the people, it seems, must not rise by raising themselves linguistically: no feature of Whitman's language has been more universally put down, by purists of the genteel and purists of the vernacular alike, than his *camerados* and *Mannahatta* and *promulges*, that is, the linguistic signs of the autodidact, the self-making man, the creole.[9]

## City Languages: New York and Paris

I have suggested that the line of vernacular theory represented by Leo Marx and John Kouwenhoven may be understood as part of the Cold War remaking of American culture, and I noted that the major authoritative work of American Popular Front literary scholarship, Matthiessen's *American Renaissance*, did not use the notion of vernacularity, even though its title implied such a concern (based on the European model it evoked). I want now to turn to some of the resources the 1930s offer for thinking about Whitman's American language, in the hope of linking them to current concerns and thus perhaps establishing an alternative tradition of thought, outside the main lines of Cold War American Studies.

A neglected Soviet essay of the Popular Front era, by the notable critic D. S. Mirsky, who died in the Gulag,[10] forthrightly asserts of Whitman what the authoritative line of postwar literary American Studies cannot acknowledge: "The prose idiom that Whitman employed in bringing new life to poetry was not the colloquial tongue of the street, the factory or the barracks; it was, rather, the language of printed prose, of newspapers and of popular science" (251). Matthiessen does not make the claim with the same equanimity of tone, but he clearly agrees with Mirsky. The fifteen pages of *American Renaissance* on "Words! book-words! What are you?" keep finding that Whitman's language is closer to mass print than Matthiessen wishes. Matthiessen values Whitman for his contrast to the "neurotic strain oppressing present-day man," who is filled more with "read lives" than with "concrete actuality" (518), yet he finds in Whitman a constant liability to go "beyond slang into the rawest jargon, the journalese of the day" (526). Whitman will often use a "bastard word"; his "curious amalgamation of homely and simple usage with half-remembered terms he read once somewhere" makes him seem to be using "a language not quite his own" (531). Matthiessen must conclude that Whitman's language does not come primarily "from contact with the soil" of America (532). That language is a "natural product" only insofar as it is exactly what could arise from "a Brooklyn journalist of the 1840s" (532).

Whitman's "American Primer" notes and similar documents provide an especially rich resource for working through his own positions on these issues, for he was himself a theorist and polemicist about American language.[11] However, I do not wish to "get right" the question of Whitman and the vernacular; I would rather accept the invitation to break bounds, by reconsidering the question. Matthiessen shows a professor's common squeamishness about mass culture, but Whitman's friend William O'Connor did not hesitate to proclaim *Leaves of Grass* "purely and entirely American, autochthonic," precisely because "in no literary form, except our newspapers, has there been anything distinctively American" (23). And in this view, O'Connor prefigures Kouwenhoven. Unlike many literary critics, the cultural historian who helped establish the prestige of the term *vernacular* was not committed to linking that value with a residual orality. For Kouwenhoven the rifle and the newspaper were alike products of democratic, mechanical, vernacular arts.

I have already suggested that *creole* might be a more useful term than *vernacular* for thinking about American language. This terminological shift would start to place less weight on distinguishing the culture of the United States from the cultures of Britain and Europe and more on relating, both as similar and as different, the cultures of the United States to those of other areas once held as colonies of Britain and Europe. Moreover, in recognizing that questions of empire were not terminated by the Revolutionary War, a "creole" perspective would foster the understanding of the United States not only as itself a postcolonial nation but also as itself an imperial nation.[12] (And so this essay will carry its analysis of Whitman from New World creolism back across to France and Britain.) Although the notion of creole has indeed at times been used as part of an ideology of racial purity (see Hirsch and Logsdon), its wider connotations, as seen in its usage as a term of linguistics, suggest "mixture" rather than "purity." Thus I find the term especially apt for the figure of Whitman I am delineating, since the journalistic practice and language of Whitman have also been understood as impure (recall Matthiessen's "bastard" and "amalgamation"), in contrast to what I have tried to demonstrate are the national-racial identitarian purisms of "vernacular."

Thus a "creole" perspective encourages thinking about Whitman and the emergence of American literary nationality not as something in the first place unique and exceptional, but instead as one among many occasions—around the globe and over centuries—where colonialism precipitated resistances that became nationalism. Yet the process of nationalism has not been uniquely (post)colonial; it has also, of course, transformed the colonizing powers. Benedict Anderson locates the emergence of nationalism in the creole elites of the new world, first in northern and then in southern America, and sketches its transfer from the Americas back to Europe of the Napoleonic wars, and from Europe to Asia and Africa through later colonial-imperial encounters. Anderson recognizes that "colonizers' languages may be the basis for the identity of new nations" (122), exactly the embarrassing case with English in the United States. In evoking the powers of imagination required to feel "community in anonymity" (40), Anderson describes, in terms that resonate with Whitman, the "complete confidence" an American may feel in the "steady . . . simultaneous activity" of millions of fellow-Americans never met, never known by name (31). For Anderson the basic "literary convention" of the newspaper as a form, the "arbitrariness of . . . inclusion and juxtaposition" for persons and events (37), shows the same mode of imagination as that on which nationhood depends. He argues that the two bases for this kind of imaginative connection are the "homogeneous, empty time" (31) of historical chronology, the secular calendar that replaces the religious shaping of time, and the relations of monetary exchange in the market (37–38).

I am about to discuss Whitman further as a poet in the culture of newspapers and the economy of capitalism, and I will connect him back to Europe, not as an argument for influence, but in order to redefine the grounds for transatlantic comparative study of Whitman. In pursuing this argument, I will make use of the work of Walter Benjamin, a great critic of the thirties, whose writing is crucial to the arguments of Anderson laid out in the previous paragraph. If we define for Whitman the historical ground he shares with his French contemporary Charles Baudelaire, what interesting differences will then emerge? I approach this task circumspectly, because the press referee's response to the typescript of my "Breaking Bounds" conference paper, which first sketched this topic, was defensively dismissive. This response shows how strongly the bounds for Whitman study are presupposed. The referee complains:

"Rather than follow current Whitman scholarship by exploring the vernacular in terms of popular writing and its influence on Whitman, Arac swerves into a discussion of Benjamin. . . . More pertinent would be an extended analysis of Whitman's briefly noted debt to Fanny Fern, whose *Fern Leaves from Fanny's Portfolio* gave Whitman not only the cover of the 1855 edition, but the inspiration for his polyvocal imitation of voices. . . . Ignoring her in favor of Benjamin is a symptom of Arac's seduction by high theory."

Let me pass by the question of why Benjamin, a powerful writer of urban memoir and prose-collage, a journalistic book reviewer and *feuilletoniste*, should be scored as high theory rather than as a practitioner in the tradition of city-writing that he critically investigates. Let me not even begin to explore the distressing sexual and gender politics of the referee, who criticizes me for my "swerve" away from the proper goal of a Protestant American woman, "ignoring" her because misled—indeed, a victim of "seduction"—by a German-Jewish man. Nor will I ask why anyone need honor the bounds of a scholarly subspeciality and "follow" its leaders. What most distresses me in this response, and what I feel to be symptomatic of a long-standing, deep-rooted problem in postwar literary American Studies, even now, is the failure even to note my attention to Baudelaire. If I am not exploring the influence of a fellow American, then I must be making an application of foreign theory; it is not legible to this scholar-critic that I might be trying to find a way to think together about great poets from different national traditions, a small first step toward a nonhomogeneous *Weltliteratur*.

I do not wish to join David Reynolds in condescending to Fanny Fern's writings as "at their best" possessing, "on occasion, preliterary complexity" (*Beneath* 403); in my own arguments in the *Cambridge History of American Literature* concerning the emergence of the "literary" in the United States around Whitman's time, I treat urban-sketch writing as an alternative practice rather than as pre- or subliterary. But there are features that join Whitman and Baudelaire and distinguish them from much other city-writing of their time. Above all, I think of what Erich Auerbach in *Mimesis* defined as stylistic techniques of mixture which dignify everyday reality as problematic and deeply serious, rather than simply comic or base, as was traditional.[13]

In order to maintain this claim, I must at least briefly indicate why I think Whitman's poetry is more deeply democratic in spirit than the writing I know by other characteristically urban writers of his time and place, whether Fanny Fern or George Foster, whom Reynolds characterizes as "lovingly recording the kinds of quotidian images that would fascinate Whitman" (317). I choose for comparison Foster's *New York by Gas-Light* (1850), since Reynolds claims the "New-York-by-gaslight" genre was especially intimately linked to the emergent urban culture of the Bowery known by the figure of the "b'hoy" (*Beneath*, 510), a culture with which Whitman may associate himself in his self-proclamation as "an American, one of the roughs." Yet in a bravura set-piece that Foster proclaims as a "catalogue of the audience" (155) at the Bowery Theater, I find his description very much that of a superior observer, not an example of writing "by and for" (Reynolds, *Beneath* 510) the social group being portrayed. It is spirited city sketching, but the ever more extended compound adjectives build to hilarity as Foster renders the "laughing, children-nursing, baby-quieting, orange-sucking, peanut-eating, lemonade-with-a-stick-in-it-drinking unconventionality of the 'dress circle' " (155). And he concludes that "Hogarth, Hood, Doyle, Leach, Gavarni" would all be required to render the scene. These were estimable figures in the culture of the time, but in Auerbach's terms their work was not serious, for they were understood as comic caricaturists not great artists, producing laughter, not feeling and especially not the sense that the reader or viewer might be implicated.

In another of Foster's catalogs, he expatiates on an identity among Americans that has made his list a favorite for quotation (Spann 344; Reynolds *Beneath*, 464; Stott 253; Thomas 651): "The b'hoy of the Bowery, the rowdy of Philadelphia, the Hoosier of the Mississippi, the trapper of the Rocky Mountains, and the gold-hunter of California are so much alike that an unpracticed hand could not distinguish one from the other" (170). In a language he shares with French and British "physiognomy" writers of the time, including Balzac, Foster offers "the secret and key" of this "entire class of characters," as "represented by Mose and Sykesey in New York and by Davy Crockett and the 'Yaller-Flower' of the forest on our whole western and south-western frontier, (extending and including any where from the Mississippi to the Pacific)" (170). The secret is not one that the modern enthusiasts for Foster quote, for it makes the ugliness of Foster's nationalism too evident and thus might chill the warm American feeling of current readers. Writing shortly after the U.S. conquest of Mexico, Foster finds that the secret is *"free development to Anglo-Saxon nature"* (170). Vernacularism as a theory of American literary language has often, intentionally in some cases and unintentionally in others, come down to some form of Anglo-Saxonism.[14]

Instead of constructing in "vernacular" an intellectual and political tool by which to link *Leaves of Grass* to America, as part of what I have called nationalist "hypercanonization," what if we sought instead to link Whitman, through a global process of capitalist modernity, to great French poetry quite contemporary with his own activity? Charles Baudelaire's *Les Fleurs du Mal* appeared in 1857, and then with substantial changes a second edition in 1861. However "heterogeneous" their leaves and flowers, as T. S. Eliot observed (206), both Whitman and Baudelaire are profound innovators in the poetry of the big city. Moreover, the language of each has been widely recognized as strikingly mixed, despite the American Studies vernacularist line. Charles Eliot Norton in *Putnam's Monthly* reviewed the 1855 *Leaves of Grass*, which he found a "mixture of Yankee transcendentalism and New York Rowdyism" (321), as Emerson later found Whitman's language "a remarkable mixture of the *Bhagvat-Gheeta* and the *New York Herald*" (Matthiessen 526). Theodor Adorno put to use the similar judgment of Paul Claudel that Baudelaire's style mixed Racine with Paris journalism (50).

It requires fresh thought to consider why Whitman and Baudelaire alike make seriously moving poetry out of the materials of life which had long been thought least propitious for great art. Baudelaire did not believe in democracy or progress; indeed he polemicized against such ideals and the view of human nature that supported them. Precisely this difference between Whitman and Baudelaire arises once as a disturbing question in a notebook of the interpreter of Baudelaire whose work has meant the most to me, Walter Benjamin: "That Baudelaire was hostile to progress was an indispensable condition of his being able to cope with Paris in his poetry. Compared to his, later city poetry must be accounted feeble, and not least where it sees the city as the seat of progress. But Walt Whitman?" ("Central Park" 50).

It has been usual to compare the social significance of mid-nineteenth-century American literature with that of transatlantic writings by contrasting the American concern with freedom to Old World concerns with poverty: Victor Hugo's Jean Valjean in *Les Misérables* first goes to prison for stealing a loaf of bread; the death of Dickens's Jo in *Bleak House* speaks to the national urgency of assisting those who lack food, housing, and health care; but Stowe's Eva dies in *Uncle Tom's Cabin* because the national sin of slavery is too great to bear, and the fates of George Harris and Uncle Tom no less testify that freedom far outweighs economic issues. The force of Benjamin's work is to help make understandable a fundamental structure by which the same economic system that produced European (and of course American) poverty also established the basis for fierce concern with human equality in freedom. The replacement of what had been considered "organic" bonds of hierarchical interdependency left every individual in principle free, and the poor free to starve; the transformation of patterns of work on the model of mass production, of the analytical separation of tasks, made it increasingly likely that a worker performed the same repetitive action rather than being responsible for producing a whole; the growth of commercial-industrial urban centers on a new scale brought people together who showed themselves to each other in anonymous, heterogeneous, fascinating masses; and newspapers became the newly dominant medium for the linguistic exchange of information.[15] Benjamin understood the condition of possibility of Baudelaire's poetry as the Paris of crowds and of newspapers that cut up the doings of the world into atomized bits, each equal and isolated, like members of a city crowd.[16] Benjamin helps us imagine that the journalistic, along with its appeal to self-remaking, rather than some "native" vernacular, may join Whitman to his age, and not necessarily specifically to his nation.

What, then, if we question Whitman under the rubric of Benjamin's study of Baudelaire, as a poet "in the age of high capitalism," a system that a later student of the mid-nineteenth century has characterized as "unification through monetarization" (Harvey 202)? The measure of Whitman's verse is a syntax which poses an equation between elements that would conventionally be understood as different from each other in as many ways as possible.[17] To Leo Marx and American Studies this is radical democracy. To Roman Jakobson, it lays bare the poetic principle of projecting equivalence from the axis of combination to the axis of selection (358). But to Karl Marx, it is the logic of the commodity: "Just as every qualitative difference between commodities is extinguished in money, so money, on its side, like the radical leveller that it is, does away with all distinctions" (1: 132).[18] This principle of uniformity, which makes possible modern industry as well as politics, in Benjamin's analysis also encompasses the crowd and the newspaper and sets the challenge to old models of experience that Baudelaire brings into his poetry.

## Past Refinements and Present Improvisations

This line of speculation brings me to a text. Benjamin offers a strong reading of Baudelaire's sonnet "A une Passante" ("To a Passing Woman," in my very literal translation).

The deafening street howled around me.
Tall, slim, in deep mourning, majestic sorrow,
A woman passed, with a stately hand
Lifting, balancing the scallop of her hem;

Quick and noble, with her leg like a statue's.
Me, I drank, twisted like a madman,
Deep in her eye, ashen sky where hurricanes grow,
The sweetness that binds and the pleasure that kills.

A flash . . . then night!—Transient beauty
Whose look has brought me suddenly to rebirth,
Will I not see you again except in eternity?

Somewhere else, far from here! Too late! *Never* perhaps!
For I don't know where you're fleeing, you don't know where I'm going,
O you I would have loved, O you who knew it!

Number 22 of the 1860 "Calamus" is the sonnet-sized poem that begins, "Passing stranger!" (from 1867 entitled "To a Stranger"). Benjamin emphasizes that in Baudelaire's poem the crowd is not represented; it emerges only through an allusion to the noise of the street in the opening line (*Charles Baudelaire* 44–45; 124–25). In Whitman there is not even the allusion; it is as though the speaker were alone with the stranger, although I read the poem under the sign of the "populous city":

Passing stranger! you do not know how longingly I look upon you,
You must be he I was seeking, or she I was seeking, (it comes to me as of a
    dream,)
I have somewhere surely lived a life of joy with you,
All is recall'd as we flit by each other, fluid, affectionate, chaste, matured,
You grew up with me, were a boy with me or a girl with me,
I ate with you and slept with you, your body has become not yours only
    nor left my body mine only,
You give me the pleasure of your eyes, face, flesh, as we pass, you take of
    my beard, breast, hands, in return,
I am not to speak to you, I am to think of you when I sit alone or wake at
    night alone,
I am to wait, I do not doubt I am to meet you again,
I am to see to it that I do not lose you. (*LG* 127)

Whitman imagines an intimacy so great that the speaker and stranger are figured as "we." The public space of the street produces the solidarity and exchange that were impossible for the private unrepresentability of the runaway slave. The temporality of Baudelaire's poem differs strongly from Whitman's. Baudelaire's strong "never" closes a moment of melodramatically rich loss; in contrast Whitman's "again" prolongs into a shared future the shared past already produced by this encounter. Whitman brings together the acts of reading and city-strolling, the chaos and anonymity of the crowd with the multiplication of copies of one book among all the others. (I will return shortly to Whitman's renewal of the figure of the stranger as reader.) Neither Whitman nor Baudelaire represents the crowd,[19] but each is implicated in it: they are not protected by the distance of observation; even in passing, an encounter may count.

Through this essay, I have argued against the purism lurking in the critical discourse on *vernacular* and have argued instead for a "creole" perspective. A creole perspective not only registers more clearly the complex mixtures forming American language and culture; it also links America to a globally transformative history of colonialism and capitalism, in which the newspaper—emerging in cities as a medium of commercial information and advertisement—became a means of formation for national consciousness and new language practices. In partial dialogue with the American Studies movement, Ralph Ellison defined a distinctive sense of "vernacular" by which he tried to evade the suggestions of purist nativism, in a way that I find in keeping with my argument for "creolization." He defined vernacular as "far more than popular or indigenous language" (*Going to the Territory* 139). In Ellison's expanded sense, *vernacular* names a "dynamic process" in which "the most refined styles from the past are continually merged" with American everyday life, "the improvisations which we invent in our efforts to control our environment and entertain ourselves" (139). Ellison's abstraction provides a beautifully and craftily dignified phrasing for technology and mass culture.[20] In this sense of Ellison's we may further reconsider Whitman's poetry. His grand poetry of catalogs and visions has been polemically, powerfully redefined by Josephine Miles. Drawing on her analysis of the eighteenth-century British "sublime poem" (49–57), she reconceptualizes the stylistic history of American poetry by arguing that the American "Protestant-democratic style," such as Whitman's, is not the "plain English style" (that is, what one might assume to be a "vernacular" mode) but rather the "high Greek and Biblical" sublime style (239). In other words, "when the two nations separated politically," it was "America, not England" that "carried on the eighteenth-century poetic tradition" (240), while England instead went through the stylistic revolution of romanticism. Yet despite her standing as an American poet, Miles's formulation has had little impact.

Certainly "To a Stranger" does not seem to fit Miles's model; it has none of the gestures of the sublime style. Yet the mode of thought that Miles and Ellison together open leads me to a powerful essay by Geoffrey Hartman, which charts the encounter between a refined and elevated tradition of poetry and the vagaries of everyday life in England around 1800. Hartman notes that the address to a passing stranger is the traditional form of the poetic epitaph, that is, the inscription on a gravestone or memorial (211). Indeed, the earliest epitaph I know is the one Herodotus records for the Lacedemonians fallen at Thermopylae, those soldiers who before the battle were seen by Persian spies engaged in the Whitmanesque camaraderie of athletic games and combing each others' hair: "Stranger, tell the Spartans that we lie here, obedient to their commands."

The work of romantic poetry, Hartman suggests (extending the model of stylistic mixture developed by his teacher Erich Auerbach), is to regenerate "archaic formulae" (226) so that they are felt to come from the speaker's own situation, not from convention or tradition. In "Calamus," then, we may say that Whitman reinvents the situation of the epitaphic speaker, the posthumous voice, in "Scented Herbage of My Breast," in which the speaker writes "tomb-leaves, body-leaves." The impossible goal of the modern (romantic) postepitaphic poem will then be a "monument to spontaneity" (Hartman 228), bringing the chastity and gravity of language developed through the long traditions of epitaphs and epigrams, while conveying a sense of the speaker's continuing vitality, which means evading the closure of wit no less than that of death. We may think here of Whitman's "City of . . . walks and joys," with its "shifting tableaus" and "frequent and swift flash of eyes offering me love" (*LG* 125–26). The necessary condition for the romantic lyric, then, will be that "fugitive feelings are taken seriously" (Hartman 221), that is, that even a passing stranger not be forever lost.

Hartman finds a starting point for this poetic movement in English: Mark Akenside, one of the British writers Miles considered especially relevant to American verse (56). His 1758 "Inscriptions" first used unrhymed verse so as to make possible the "liberated epigram" (Hartman 219) that is the generic skeleton of many romantic lyrics. In William Wordsworth's recategorization of his poetry for his edition of 1815 (a self-shaping in a volume of verse that must have been significant for Whitman), there is a section entitled "Inscriptions," as there is after 1871 at the beginning of Whitman's *Leaves*.

Connecting Whitman to Baudelaire brought together their two poems of passing strangers, which then led to a distinction between them, based on English-language traditions of poetic history. Yet this combination of perspectives on Whitman's poetic mode helps make clear the "creole"-hyphenated character of even his highly nationally defined work. The global, imperial-colonial process of creolization was part of the economic transformation that brought into existence the daily life of a world metropolis, which Wordsworth in London, Baudelaire in Paris, and Whitman in New York all lived through, and which marked all of their poetry in different ways. Wordsworth turned to the country to counter the city;[21] Baudelaire and Whitman made the city the center of much of their greatest work. Yet their relations to the city still greatly differed. Benjamin's Baudelaire wrote against his age; in Benjamin's terms, his "experience" challenged the "information" of the news. Whitman wrote with his age. Whitman lacked the purity of folk-vernacular or of cultivated art-speech, and he made journalism into his experience. Whitman's nation-building culture was not folk but mass, that is to say capitalist, and from that, as we now say hopefully of the world stretching—as Whitman would see it—westward from China to Poland, real democracy may follow.

## Acknowledgment

My concern with problems of vernacular grows from my book in progress on "*Huckleberry Finn* and the Functions of Criticism." I am grateful to Michael Riffaterre for inviting me to the School of Criticism and Theory in July 1990, where I first developed my main lines of thought on vernacular in lectures on "Writing Literary History Now," and to Betsy Erkkila and Jay Grossman for inviting me to join them and Whitman in "Breaking Bounds." Thanks also to Paul A. Bove, Nancy Glazener, and Kathryne V. Lindberg for closely attentive readings.

## Notes

1. I discuss the Popular Front and Stalinism in chapters on Matthiessen and on New York intellectuals in *Critical Genealogies;* see esp. 164–67, 309–14. For a recent polemical reconsideration, see the first chapter of Foley. And for a reading of the Whitman passage quite different from mine or Marx's, see Sánchez-Eppler 76–77.

2. As Kouwenhoven acknowledges, the germ of this book was his prize essay "Arts in America." The essay devotes half its space to literature, a much higher proportion than in the final book. Only halfway through does he introduce the term *vernacular* as his preferred name for the peculiarly American version of folk art, which in its literary form he associates with "mass-produced . . . journalism" (178). In a contributor's note (unpaginated), Kouwenhoven explains that the essay grew from his previous two years' teaching at Bennington College. Stanley Edgar Hyman, Ralph Ellison's longtime friend and "intellectual sparring partner" (*Shadow and Act* 45), was also a member of the Bennington community at this time.

3. For a challenging critique of Douglass precisely for his use of language approximating that of public political discourse of the 1840s, see Baker, *The Journey Back* 39–43.

4. Do I contradict myself in calling "beautiful" what I have also criticized for its shortcomings? I think not. As a human product poetry is limited, not perfect. Beauty need not be flawless nor rise absolutely beyond its historical occasion; indeed, I think it cannot do these things. Yet it exists and may be praised even though it does not achieve what salvationist theories of aesthetics have claimed for it, at great cost to the honesty of critics, teachers, and students.

5. Baker in *Blues, Ideology, and African-American Literature* cites this etymology as first epigraph to the book, which tries to develop what its subtitle calls a "vernacular theory," and which cites as its second epigraph Whitman from the 1855 preface. As I do in this essay, Baker sees "vernacular" as inseparable from problems of cultural nationalism, which in his book take the form of redefining what he calls "AMERICA" (the capitals to indicate that the term is an ideological construct).

6. In my contribution on mid-nineteenth century American prose narra-

tives to the *Cambridge History of American Literature*, the relations between "local" narratives and "national" narratives form one of my major topics.

7. I adapt the notion of *creolized language* from the *OED* definition (in the *Supplement* and second edition): "a language which has developed from that of a dominant group, first being used as a second language, then becoming the usual language of a subject group, its sounds, grammar, and vocabulary being modified in the process." Obviously the most difficult issue in this adaptation for the purposes of American English is the question of "subject [in the sense of subordinated] group" (after the Revolution, the formerly subject free white Americans were no longer subject). A 1932 citation, although it introduces another problem, offers a useful alternative: "a language of a civilized people, especially European, mixed with that of one or more savage tribes." What these awkwardnesses make clear is that the term, however much a part of "scientific" linguistics, is inseparable from political relations of inequality, which are therefore open to struggle.

The term *creole* has much the same etymological meaning as *vernacular: creole* comes to English from French *créole*, from Spanish *criollo*, from Portuguese *crioulo*, "animal or person born at home, then . . . a black African slave in Brazil who was born in his or her master's house" (McArthur 270). But the long and complex overtly political deployment of the term (for excellent insights on which, see Hirsch and Logsdon) makes it more salutary and stimulating than vernacular for current critical use. I am grateful to Mary Louise Pratt for insights and provocations on this topic when she visited Pittsburgh in February 1993.

8. This useful phrasing comes from Fisher (71), who does not, however, engage the issue of creolization.

9. Erkkila is unusual in offering a sympathetic and politically nuanced understanding of this issue, particularly with regard to Whitman's use of French ("Walt Whitman: The Politics of Language"). See also Lindberg on the response to Whitman's non-English vocabulary by José Martí.

10. On Mirsky's life and work, see Stacy; and Wilson.

11. The richest recent discussion of these materials is in Nathanson, who uses as his key term not *vernacular* but "demotic." See, for instance, 191–96, where the phrase "demotic energies" appears on each page of this discussion of Whitman's "linguistic populism" (192). Yet even under the Bakhtinian umbrella of "heteroglossia" (also adapted by Marx in conjunction with *vernacular*, x–xi), the same hypercanonic story is told: "The mode is quintessentially American, and the discursive melange of 'Song of Myself' already anticipates the more ambitiously orchestrated cacophony of *Huckleberry Finn*" (389).

12. On U.S. literature as postcolonial, see Buell; and on America and empire, see the massive, pathbreaking collection edited by Kaplan and Pease.

13. As his essay shows, Auerbach himself was quite equivocal about Baudelaire, whom he does not discuss in *Mimesis*.

14. Foster's "key" produces instead a mystery about the term *b'hoy*. In the culture of the time, the extra aitch marked the term as styling itself after a common Irish way of pronouncing English (see Mathews in the first entry under "boy"), and the Bowery political leader and journalist Mike Walsh (the "prototypical b'hoy politician" according to Reynolds *Beneath*, 464) was born in Ireland. Yet neither Reynolds nor Wilentz in any way illuminates this connec-

tion, which, however, needs explanation. In the United States people from Ireland were still subjected to many forms of nativist prejudice, including ethnically derogatory humor (see Harris, who wrote two different versions of the same brutal story twenty years apart), and were by no means automatically included as "American." It is not enough to say that Walsh "always considered himself a 'true American' " (Wilentz 327); the question is why everyone else accepted his self-definition, even while the group for which he was "chief spokesperson" (Reynolds *Beneath*, 509) bore an Irish stigmatized title. No answers, but further materials for thought, may be found in important work by Stott; Roediger; and Lott.

15. This sentence necessarily condenses far too much, yet I also wish to enter in evidence a formulation of Karl Marx's which would require yet more space to develop. Marx's explanation of why Aristotle had reached an impasse, rather than achieving a successful answer to the question of value, has real potential as a line of thought for understanding the relations of the north and south in antebellum America:

> Greek society was founded upon slavery, and had, therefore, for its natural basis, the inequality of men and of their labour-powers. The secret of the expression of value, namely, that all kinds of labour are equal and equivalent, because, and so far as they are human labour in general, cannot be deciphered until the notion of human equality has already acquired the fixity of a popular prejudice. This, however, is possible only in a society in which the great mass of the produce of labour takes the form of commodities, in which, consequently, the dominant relation between man and man is that of owners of commodities (1: 60).

16. In a discussion of Emily Dickinson together with Baudelaire, I analyze, use, and challenge these formulations of Benjamin's in *Critical Genealogies* 194–214. See also Brand, who makes good use of Benjamin, but to remarkably unsympathetic effect, in assessing Whitman as a city-writer.

17. I draw here from Allen Grossman's classic essay, especially his characterization of Whitman's "translator," which rewrites every hierarchy as equality, every duality as identity (194).

18. Although not directly citing Karl Marx, Sommer's interpretation is in line with this principle (77), as well as offering suggestive remarks on the reception of Whitman in relation to the Popular Front and to Latin American populist political ideologies (71–72).

19. I have already mentioned Benjamin's argument to this effect concerning Baudelaire. The most powerful argument on the implications of Whitman's work as not performing representation but rather constructing interhuman potentiality may be found in Pease (for example, 153).

20. Ellison here seems to adapt Kouwenhoven, who discusses the music of George Gershwin as exemplifying an "evolutionary process whereby the vernacular . . . . interacts creatively with the cultural tradition, losing none of the former's vitality and immediate relevance but greatly augmenting its expressive range" (223). For Kouwenhoven, however, jazz is the vernacular, while in Ellison's model of the vernacular process, jazz is itself understood as having a long tradition and so may be included among "the most refined styles from the past."

21. I discuss this in greater detail in *Critical Genealogies* 180–83.

# 4

# Whitman, Syntax, and Political Theory

## WAI CHEE DIMOCK

I want to begin at what might appear a surprising distance from Whitman, although I hope that, in good time, this unorthodox starting point will seem not altogether unwarranted. I want to begin, in any case, with John Rawls's *A Theory of Justice* (1971), perhaps the most celebrated text in twentieth-century political philosophy. The work of a self-acknowledged Kantian, this is not only a theory of justice, but very much a theory of *noncontingent* justice, aspiring, that is, to a principle of "absolute necessity," absolute enough to be the "ground of obligation," and "cleansed of everything that can only be empirical and appropriate to anthropology," as Kant recommends in the *Groundwork of the Metaphysics of Morals* (57). Justice, for Kant as well as for Rawls, is incompatible with circumstantial vagaries, but it is also imaginable outside of those vagaries. It is imaginable, that is, as the logical outcome of noncontingent reason, the logical endpoint of a deliberative process carried out under a hypothetical condition of freedom.

To his great credit, however, enamored as he is of noncontingent reason, Rawls never tries to naturalize it, never imagines it as effortlessly at home in the world, in the state of nature. Indeed, the "state of nature" for him—the starting point for his political theory—is notable for being arbitrary, and harshly arbitrary. For it is here, at this initial stage, that we are faced with the most glaring instance of distributive *in*justice: the random inequality of natural endowments. At the heart of Rawls's theory of justice, then, is something like a constitutive theory of luck. It is the sense that luck has always been there, from the very beginning—the sense that we are its creature, its handiwork—that pushes him to some of his most radical conclusions, especially his argument about desert, and about its relation to distributive entitlement. Desert is, of course, seen by most sensible laymen (and mainstream political philosophers) as the basis of our entitlement, and therefore as the moral foundation of distributive justice.[1] Rawls disagrees. He rejects the idea that "distributive shares should be in accordance with moral worth," that merit should be rewarded by a corresponding benefit (314, 310–15). For him, such an idea is not only undemocratic in practice, but untenable in theory. He argues, instead, that what counts as our "merit" is actually something that accrues to us through the accident of birth, through "luck in the natural lottery" (75). We cannot be said to deserve it any more than we can be said to deserve those material advantages that accrue to us through the same accident. In short, to allow "the distribution of wealth and income to be determined by the natural distribution of abilities and talents" is to do no more than to submit to "the outcome of the natural lottery, and this outcome is arbitrary from a moral perspective" (74).

Rawls's vigorous rejection of desert is therefore the starting point for an alternative theory of justice. It is also the starting point for an alternative theory of the person. Since we do not actually deserve those attributes that happen to be lodged in us, we also cannot be said to own them. For Rawls, this thought gives rise to an exhilarating (and some would say phantasmagoric) vision of the world: here, natural talents are imagined to be showered upon the earth, like manna from heaven (the phrase is Robert Nozick's [219]), unowned, unmarked, undeserved by any particular person, and free to be used for the good of all. This notion of common usability— applied to attributes long considered private and personal—makes for a distributive domain larger than anything previously imagined. Out of this radically enlarged pool of resources, Rawls is thus able to argue for an equally radical mode of distribution, based not on the moral reflexity within particular persons, not on the supposed correspondence between merit and desert, but on the political will of the community, on its concerted policy decision. In other words, the benefit each person receives would not be self-evident or self-executing, would not reflect the sort of person he or she happens to be or the sort of work he or she happens to have done. It would reflect, instead, the principles of fairness of the entire society, the choices that it makes regarding the individual and collective well-being of its members. Such principles would speak not only to those lucky enough to be naturally talented, but also to those so unlucky as to be without rewardable talents.

Critics of Rawls have, of course, objected to his theory of justice as an elegant but thinly disguised scheme for the redistribution of wealth, a scheme that, in refusing to reward excellence in particular persons, must end up destroying the ethical (not to say the economic) primacy of the person. This objection, forceful as it is, also seems to me somewhat beside the point. Rawls himself, indeed, is reassuringly emphatic here. "Each person," he announces on the first page of his book, "possesses an inviolability founded on justice that even the welfare of society as a whole cannot override" (3). What is especially fascinating here, then, both in the context of thinking about Whitman, but also in the more general context of thinking about the political consequences of personhood, is the way Rawls has managed to jettison the notion of personal desert without jettisoning, at the same time, either the category of the "person," or its political centrality within a theory of democratic justice. The challenge for him is thus to defend a distributive justice based on policy decision rather than on private endeavor, and to demonstrate (appearances to the contrary) that this rejection of individual entitlement is nonetheless not a violation of individual rights, nor incompatible with a respect for persons.

His strategy is an ingeniously Kantian one. The political subject is conceived, that is, in strictly *categorical* terms, lifted from the vagaries of circumstances, and "cleansed" in the process of many features ordinarily held to be his. Indeed, any tangible or rewardable attributes, any marks of excellence or lack thereof, all these particularizing features of the self are now relegated to a domain defined as being not quite the self. For Rawls, such ontological cleansings are crucial if the "person" is to remain democratically defensible, for a democratic subject must be, first and foremost, a universal subject, one whose political dignity is absolute, about whom one can make a categoric claim. To secure such a subject, actual selves would have to be stripped bare, would have to be removed from all those accidental features, all those inequities of chance, which make them unfit for such a categoric description.

The upshot of this exercise is ultimately to bring about a refinement in what we might call the syntax of the self: a small but crucial distinction between what a person *is* and what a person *has*, between what is *me* and what is *mine*. It is a matter of luck that I am some particular person, that I have attributes I can call my own. But, because those attributes that are "mine" are assigned to me by luck, because they just happen to have attached themselves to me, they cannot properly be said to be "me." Indeed, to give the paradox an even sharper edge, what is "mine" is, for that very reason, not "me." Rawls's theory of justice therefore operates on something like a postulate of detachability. It both assumes and requires a categoric subject apprehensible apart from all its substantive descriptions. Only such a "me," conceived in contradistinction to what is "mine," can make justice more than an apology for the accident of birth. Only such a "me" can make democratic equality not just a policy but also an epistemology.

This rigorous distinction between "me" and "mine" thus commits Rawls to what he himself acknowledges to be a "thin" theory of the person, one that bears, if not exactly an inverse relation, then at least a suspended one, to people as they ordinarily appear and as they are ordinarily perceived, people thick with particular traits, which they innocently call his or hers, yours or mine. Such usages are unacceptable to Rawls, because to be democratically defensible, the "person" must be defensible as a categoric idea, rather than as people with actual features and attributes. This is, in a sense, the logical consequence of yet another (and perhaps analytically prior) paradox in Rawls: his simultaneous acknowledgment of and revulsion against luck, his sense not only of its abiding centrality in human life, but also of its unconscionable tyranny. For if his rejection of desert is based on the insight that desert is merely luck in disguise, the ubiquity of luck is, at the same time, a grievous wrong for him, one that carries with it a silent directive, a demand for rectification. And so, as Rawls himself admits, his theory of justice is very much a theory to combat luck, a theory to "nullify the accidents of natural endowment and the contingencies of social circumstances" (15). His cleansing of the political subject is an effort in that direction, an effort to free the self of the incrustations of luck, to save the essential "me" from the accidental "mine," so that the category of the person can finally be categoric, and justice can finally be noncontingent.

## Syntax and Democracy

Central, then, to Rawls's political theory is a syntactic proposition about the self—a distinction between "me" and "mine"—a syntactic distinction which is then transposed into an ontological distinction. I use the word "syntax" advisedly, knowing that it is not a neutral word, but heavily accented by its association with Noam Chomsky, an association which, as it happens, Rawls himself has likewise remarked upon. Indeed, he calls attention to a parallel between his theory of justice and Chomsky's theory of linguistics. Both, he says, operate at some remove from "familiar common sense precepts," and both involve "principles and theoretical constructs which go much beyond the norms and standards cited in everyday life" (47).[2] And both aspire, we might add, to a level of noncontingency which can only be found in what Chomsky calls a "formalized general theory" (Chomsky, *Syntactic Structures* 5). I want to explore further this point of contact between Chomsky and Rawls, both to study Rawls's language of justice as *language*, and to anticipate any possible connections in Whitman himself between syntactic theory and democratic theory. Chomsky is uniquely helpful here, for not only is he a formidable practitioner of both linguistics and politics, but his syntactic theory, in its ambitions and limits, also brings into focus some of the ambitions and limits of a syntax of political personhood.

Chomsky begins his challenge to traditional linguistics by taking issue with its self-conception as a taxonomic system, and urges, instead, that a proper study of language focus not on its classifications but on its "generative" character. And for him syntax, above all, is what makes a natural language "generative"—both in the sense that it is syntax that assigns structural properties to the semantic and phonological components of a sentence, and in the sense that it is syntax that enables us to substitute words within the same structural category, thus creating an infinite number of new sentences, all equally rule-observing, and all syntactically equivalent. Substitutability and interchangeability, in short, are the central generative features of syntax. They make syntax the wellspring of language, its source of perpetual renewal and perpetual regularity. Indeed, for Chomsky, syntax represents not only the deep structure of sentences in one particular language, but also (in its "transformational" capacity) the deep structure of *all* natural languages. It is the foundation of a "universal grammar," common to all human beings, at work in all mental processes, and indistinguishable from human cognition itself.

Chomsky's virtual equation of syntax and cognition, of course, comes at the expense of semantics, a time-honored area of linguistic (and philosophical) inquiry.[3] Chomsky, however, is openly impatient of semantic analysis, an impatience having to do, I suspect, with the way he defines the objectives of linguistics and the way he delimits its domain. While it is "of course, impossible to prove that semantic notions are of no use in grammar," Chomsky says, he cannot help pointing out that the "correspondences . . . between formal and semantic features in language" are so "imperfect" and "inexact" that "meaning will be relatively useless as a basis for grammatical description." For that reason, "grammar is best formulated as a self-contained study independent of semantics" (*Syntactic Structures* 100, 101, 106). In short, semantics is not a fruitful object of study for Chomsky because, being always at the mercy of context, it is highly erratic, cannot sustain a grammar, does not lend itself to formalizable rules, and does not exhibit the properties of substitutability and interchangeability, whereas syntax does.[4]

Chomsky's privileging of syntax over semantics, in turn, opens outward into a set of definitional demarcations that map out the domain of linguistics as he understands it, demarcations that assign primacy in every instance to terms that are universal and noncontingent. Chomsky thus distinguishes between *competence* and *performance*, arguing that linguistics can adequately study only the former, only the grammatical knowledge internalized in all speakers of a natural language, rather than the specific verbal behavior of some particular user. He also argues that language is primarily a vehicle of thought, an activity self-sufficient unto itself, rather than a vehicle of communication, an activity dependent on an audience.[5] And, since he equates syntactic knowledge with cognitive capability, he also argues, most controversially of all, that linguistic competence is innate, that it resides in a congenital faculty of language, unindebted to educational input and environmental influence. Putting himself squarely in the camp of the rationalist tradition associated with Descartes,[6] Chomsky thus turns language acquisition itself into a noncontingent phenomenon, "free from the control of detectable stimuli, either external or internal" (*Language and Mind* 12), not varying with particular environments, and not even varying with particular individuals . It is, instead, a guaranteed feature of human cognition, uniformly and categorically present to all, "independen[t] of intelligence, motivation, and emotional state" (*Aspects of the Theory of Syntax* 58).

Chomsky's peculiar insistencies might be better gauged, I think, if we contrast him briefly with the later Wittgenstein, whose position on natural language, on grammar, and on grammatical rules is close enough to Chomsky's for the divergences to be instructive. Like Chomsky, Wittgenstein believes that grammatical description is constitutive of thought, that "grammar tells us what kind of object anything is" (Wittgenstein, *Philosophical Investigations* 373). Also like Chomsky, he believes that the "various transformations and consequences of the sentence" are possible only "in so far as they are embodied in a grammar," a grammar which "has the same relation to the language as the description of a game, the rules of a game, have to the game" (Wittgenstein, *Philosophical Grammar* 104, 23). Unlike Chomsky, however, Wittgenstein has no desire to produce a *foundational* theory of grammar, no desire to locate a necessary basis for syntactic knowledge in human cognition. To the contrary, he argues that "grammar is not accountable to any reality," and that the "only correlate in language to an intrinsic necessity is an arbitrary rule" (Wittgenstein, *Philosophical Grammar* 133). Language cannot be foundational for Wittgenstein because it is contingent at its core, because it can only render back to us our customs, our communities, our shared agreements about how things are. It has its being not in the innateness of cognition but in the socialness of convention, or, as Wittgenstein puts it in his famous dictum, "to imagine a language means to imagine a form of life" (Wittgenstein, *Philosophical Investigations* 19).

Against Wittgenstein's emphatic rejection of the innateness of language, Chomsky's equally emphatic assertion of that innateness becomes all the more striking. He has been savagely attacked, in fact, on just this point.[7] Questioned about this in an interview with the *New Left Review,* Chomsky replies:

> I would like to assume on the basis of fact and hope on the basis of confidence in the human species that there are innate structures of mind. If there are not, if humans are just plastic and random organisms, then they are fit subjects for the shaping of behaviour. If humans only become as they are by random changes, then why not control that randomness by the state authority or the behaviourist technologist or anything else? (Chomsky, "Linguistics and Politics" 31–32)

For Chomsky, then, "innate structures of mind" are, above all, a defense against the threats of "randomness," which, for him, mean especially political threats, threats from the state against its citizens. It is in this context, against the historical gravity of that threat, that we can best understand his foundationalist impulse, his desire to locate and to affirm linguistic "principles that are universal by biological necessity and not mere historical accident" ("On Cognitive Capacity," *Reflections on Language* 4). An unlearned competence, a universal grammar, a knowledge of syntax embedded in human cognition—these issues, brilliantly technical as they are, are none-

theless not strictly technical issues for Chomsky. They are so many bul-
warks against the political vulnerabilities of human life, against the intolerable odds in favor of injustice and oppression. And so, even though
Chomsky's acknowledged intellectual debt is Cartesian rather than Kantian,[8] we might nonetheless speak of a categorical imperative in his linguistic theory as well, a desire to imagine an ethical domain free from contingency, free from the less than benign presence of the arbitrary, and free,
for that reason, to pass judgment on the arbitrary. For him as for Rawls,
the postulate of an ontological given—a guaranteed linguistic knowledge,
a guaranteed deliberative rationality—is also the founding moment of political faith. And it is from this point of faith, this point of ethical inviolability, that the contingencies of politics might be adjudged, amended if necessary, resisted if necessary.[9] Chomsky's linguistic theory, then, like Rawls's
political theory, is a tribute to, a protest against, and a self-conscious battle
with that all-too-elusive, all-too-ubiquitous, demon of luck, whether it inheres in the "lottery" of life, or whether it inheres in the "randomness" of
unjust regimes. And, ultimately, the triumph of democracy is measured by
the elimination of luck: by replacing its inequities and irregularities with
something like a syntactic theory of justice, so that the political subject can
finally resemble the grammatical subject, its basic rights as uniform and as
categoric as the structural properties of the latter.

## Grammatical Subjects

Within such a grammar, human attachment thus becomes something of an
enigma, something of a conceptual puzzle. For, given the "thinness" of the
subject, it is not at all clear how that attachment is to be anchored, let alone
what it is anchored to, or what inferences one might draw for its being
anchored to one particular object and not to another. Rawls, oddly, remains untroubled by this problem, and, in a passage memorable for its
equanimity, he writes:

> The active sentiments of love and friendship, and even the sense of jus-
> tice, arise from the manifest intention of other persons to act for our
> good. Because we recognize that they wish us well, we care for their well-
> being in return. Thus we acquire attachments to persons and institutions
> according to how we perceive our good to be affected by them. The basic
> idea is one of reciprocity, a tendency to answer in kind. . . . For surely
> a rational person is not indifferent to things that significantly affect his
> good; and supposing that he develops some attitude toward them, he
> acquires either a new attachment or a new aversion. (494–95)

The keyword here is clearly "a rational person," liberally defined, for it is
only under the most liberal definition that love and friendship can proceed

with such commendable regularity, as an exchange of goodwill beneficial to both: routine, unvarying, matter-of-fact. There is nothing arbitrary about the loves of the rational person; they are strictly proportionate, strictly accountable, always "answering in kind" to the love he receives. His outgoing affection will always match the incoming goodwill. And, since it is a category of *sentiment*—rather than some particular *individual*—that he is responding to, we can assume that substitutability and interchangeability will be vital features of his affective life. Without much exaggeration, then, we might call Rawls's "rational person" a grammatical subject, for his affections are happily rule-observing, governed by a generative syntax that not only maintains a structural form, but also endlessly renews that form by replacing any given term with an infinite number of syntactic equivalents.

If this sounds jarring, no doubt it is because we are not always so grammatical in love and friendship. A theory of formal universals, in this case, is virtually a parody of itself. Rawls, of course, is not the only philosopher to have trouble making ethical sense of affective preferences. As Gregory Vlastos has pointed out, personal affection also fares badly in Plato, for whom the highest form of love turns out to be "one furthest removed from affection for concrete human beings" (32). Even so, there is something particularly comical, particularly threadbare, about Rawls's account of love and friendship. Michael Sandel, one of Rawls's ablest commentators, has seized upon just this point not only to highlight the unpersuasive thinness of the Rawlsian self, but also to put forward a sustained critique of the language of justice, focusing especially on its inability to account for the phenomenon of friendship except as a secondary, indeed a derivative, virtue. The thinness of the Rawlsian self means that it will have no responsive chord, that its capacity for friendship will always be limited by its "restricted access to the good of others," and so "every act of friendship thus becomes parasitic on a good identifiable in advance" (Sandel, *Liberalism* 181).

My own critique of the language of justice, while indebted to Sandel's, will focus less on its trivialization of love and friendship than on its tendency to locate these phenomena in a relation of externality to itself, as that which philosophy is not and cannot be concerned with. I have in mind not only Rawls's respectful dismissal of love and friendship as "higher-order sentiments" (191), elevated above the supposedly humdrum domain of political philosophy, but also the obsessively repetitive pages in *Groundwork of the Metaphysics of Morals*, where Kant insists, over and over again, that "the highest and unconditioned good can alone be found" in those instances when one "does good, not from inclination, but from duty" (69, 66). The language of justice, in the end, renders a good part of our lives analytically unintelligible. And, to the extent that this unintelligibility is necessary for its coherence, the return of the repressed can appear only as a fatal contradiction, a fatal incompatibility of opposing claims: between

the language of democratic equality on the one hand and the language of
affective preferences on the other, between our political need for formal
universals and our emotional attachment to substantive particulars. Since
Rawls is unhelpful on this point, I want to turn now to Whitman, both to
work out in greater detail the terms of this contradiction, and possibly to
gesture toward a philosophy that more closely approximates our experiential sense of the world, one in which "inclination" will have a place.

Whitman would have been pleased with the company of Chomsky and
Rawls, I think, not only because his commitment to democracy is itself a
formal commitment, but also because his poetry, with its endless catalogs,
its endless collections of attachable, detachable parts, one as good as the
other, one substitutable for the other, is perhaps as close as any poetry can
get to being a generative grammar. Within the terms of our discussion, we
would expect this poetry to be governed by syntax, and that is indeed the
case in "Song of Myself." Perhaps also not surprisingly, then, at the heart
of the poem is a grammatical entity, the "myself" who is both the author
and subject of his song. And, since this "myself" is democratically defensible only as a formal universal, it too has to be purified, abstracted, turned
into a categoric idea, so that it can remain structurally inviolate even as it
undergoes many substantive variations, even as it entertains an infinite
number of contingent terms. By means, then, of a series of grammatical
distinctions—a series of complexly articulated and scrupulously nonequiva-
lent uses of "me," "mine," and "myself"—Whitman (even more so than
Rawls) works his way through the various syntactic modes of the subject in
order to recover a truly foundational subject, one whose democratic dignity
is absolute, transcendent, and unconditional.

Given this categoric conception, the problematics of the self that we
have seen in Rawls—its much-discussed "thinness," its tendency to propagate a corresponding thinness in human affections, its rational practice of
substitutability and interchangeability—would perhaps plague Whitman as
well. In any case, as much as it is a poetry of accumulation, "Song of Myself" is also a poetry of divestment, a poetry that spins out an endless catalog of the self's many attachments only to distinguish the self from all those
attachments. We see this in familiar lines such as the following, in which,
beginning with things that are obviously external, Whitman moves on to
things that are less obviously so, things that might even have been thought
of as intrinsic to him, which he nonetheless disavows, nonetheless imagines
as being somehow distinct from him, distinct from the "Me myself" which
is anterior to and curiously untouched by what he happens to be possessing
or even experiencing at any given moment:

My dinner, dress, associates, looks, business, compliments, dues,
The real or fancied indifference of some man or woman I love,
The sickness of one of my folks—or of myself . . . . or ill-doing . . . . or
    loss or lack of money . . . . . or depressions or exaltations,

They come to me days and nights and go from me again,
But they are not the Me myself. (*LG* 1855: 28)

By the time Whitman is through, quite a few things that might have been considered a part of him—things like physical well-being, emotional affliction, or satisfaction—are all consigned to the realm of the contingent, which is also to say, the realm of the nonessential. To arrive at a democratic subject, Whitman, like Rawls, is quite willing to do some ontological cleansing, rearranging the very contents of the person. This means, in practice, removing the self from all its contingencies, and defining these contingencies as the "not Me myself," so that, finally detached from them, the self can also be defined against them, as a principle of absolute necessity. As Whitman spins out his catalogs, then, the domain of the "*Not* Me myself" thus becomes broader and broader, more and more crowded, even as the "Me myself" is increasingly stripped bare, put through an increasingly rigorous set of refinements, until it is purified into no more than an idea, an empty form, but for that very reason, a form of transcendent dignity. Like Rawls, Whitman is quite willing to give up what is "mine," to write it over to the world as part of its bounty as well as its caprice, in order to rescue "me" as an absolute concept, free from all circumstantial encumbrances, free from the vagaries of the accidental.

In the 1855 Preface to *Leaves of Grass,* Whitman writes that the poet "judges not as the judge judges but as the sun falling around a helpless thing" (9). This statement stands not only as a democratic manifesto, but also, I think, as a noncontingent poetics, which, in its unfastidious, unconditional generosity, in effect eliminates luck by eliminating the invidious distinctions it fosters, so that the whole world is now taken in, wrapped in a kind of cosmic tenderness, without exception and without fail, leaving nothing to chance. The objects of Whitman's attention are admitted as strict equals, guaranteed equals, by virtue of both the mininal universal "Me" they all have in common, and of a poetic syntax which greets each of them in exactly the same way, as a grammatical unit, equivalently functioning and structurally interchangeable. To say this is perhaps to say the obvious: that there is an intimate connection between Whitman's poetic language and political philosophy, a shared commitment to syntax, which, I argue, not only underwrites the universality of the self in "Song of Myself," but also inscribes in it a democratic hospitality to the world, a refusal to tolerate exclusions, a refusal, indeed, to register distinctions, an openness as impartial as it is impersonal.

The problem in Whitman (to the extent that it is one) can be restated, then, as one version of the conflict we have been discussing: a conflict between the opposing claims of universality and particularity in the definition of personhood, and between the opposing domains of human experience to which each corresponds. How can we reconcile the categoric conception of the self in democratic theory with our experiential sense of the self in human attachments, attachments that are, after all, not universal, but highly particular, anchored to the self not in its commonality, but in its distinctive features and substantive attributes—anchored, in short, not to what is "me," but to what is "mine"? How can we reconcile the democratic need for substitutability and interchangeability with the phenomenon of memory, with our selective attachment to our past and to figures from our past, and with the sense that people never matter to us uniformly, not at any given moment, and certainly not in time? How can we, in short, imagine a "me" adequate both to the requisite impartiality of political life and to the requisite partiality of personal affections?

These questions have been raised by Whitman himself—or at least raised by him in the form of a statement—when he writes in what would become section 3 of "Song of Myself": "Out of the dimness opposite equals advance . . . . Always substance and increase, / Always a knit of identity . . . . always distinction . . . . always a breed of life" (1855 *LG:* 26–27). Identity and distinction, the contrary claims of personhood, and the contrary claims, I have tried to suggest, of democratic politics and affective preferences, are here conjoined by Whitman, made to appear as syntactic equivalents, in a parallel construction, with neither one subordinated to the other. But if this raises one's hope, there is also a sense in which the hope is rigged, since the very form of the syntax, the logical primacy it assigns to equivalence, would seem to have foreclosed the very question it is meant to address. This sense of foreclosure—of a conclusion syntactically settled ahead of time—is especially noticeable in the lines we examined earlier, Whitman's catalog of all those things that comprise the "not Me myself."

In that fateful passage, a succession of objects and events are adduced, paratactically, as analogous terms: equally contingent, equally peripheral to the self, and equally detachable from the self. Since the syntax here focuses only on the phenomenon of equivalence—only on the fact that all the items enumerated here are equally "not Me myself"—what cannot be recognized is not only the appositional difference among these items, but also the sequential difference that each might conceivably bring, the difference that each might make to what comes after it. In "Song of Myself" that difference hardly exists, since the fact of prior occurrence is in no way a determining condition for what follows. To mention just one example, "the real or fancied indifference of some man or woman I love" is offered here as a sequel, a syntactic equivalent, to "My dinner, dress, associates, looks, business, compliments, dues," and is in turn followed by yet another syntactic equivalent, "The sickness of one of my folks—or of myself . . . . or ill-doing . . . . or loss or lack of money . . . . or depressions or exaltations"—as if all three were comparable, separated by no emotional distance, and as if the significance of each were exhausted by its appearance, so that each departs as it arrives, leaving behind no residue, no constraints on the syntax, nothing to make it less fresh or less open for each succeeding term.[10]

## Syntax, Semantics, and Memory

"Song of Myself" is thus a poetry of sequence without sedimentation, a poetry that sallies forth, its syntactic possibilities unmarked and undiminished by what it has been through.[11] It is a poetry that dwells ever in the present, not because it refuses to look back, but because past events are so strangely foreshortened, so devoid of any weight of time, that they have the effect of being contemporaneous with all events subsequent to them. The operative process here is something like the transposition of seriality into simultaneity—the constitution of memory as a field of spatial latitude rather than temporal extension—a process that, I argue, makes for the perpetual openness of the poem, its boundless horizons of experience. Since I see this as a rather crucial feature of Whitman's democratic poetics, I want to discuss in some detail one particular stanza in "Song of Myself"— the famous encounter with the runaway slave in what would become section 10—in which the word "remember" actually figures, and figures curiously:

The runaway slave came to my house and stopped outside,
I heard his motions crackling the twigs of the woodpile,
Through the swung half-door of the kitchen I saw him limpsey and weak,
And went where he sat on a log, and led him in and assured him,
And brought water and filled a tub for his sweated body and bruised feet,
And gave him a room that entered from my own, and gave him some
   coarse clean clothes,
And remember perfectly well his revolving eyes and his awkwardness,
And remember putting plasters on the galls of his neck and ankles;
He staid with me a week before he was recuperated and passed north,
I had him sit next me at table . . . . my firelock leaned in the corner.
(*LG* 1855: 33–34)

In its scrupulousness and restraint, restraint especially from undue effusiveness or familiarity, this passage must stand as one of the most compelling moments of democratic affections in "Song of Myself." The runaway slave is not a *particular* slave, he is *any* slave, for the poet would have done as much for anyone bearing that generic identity, his goodwill also being offered generically, occasioned not by any qualities peculiar to the slave but by his membership in a collective category and transferable, one would imagine, to any other member of that category. The poet is behaving "grammatically," then, as I have disparagingly used that term. But if so, what this passage reminds us is the tremendous need for grammar in this world, the tremendous need for structural provisions unattached to particular persons, and responsive to all analogous persons. Substitutability and interchangeability, from this perspective, hardly detract from human dignity. They guarantee it.

Still, it must be said as well that this dignity, while guaranteed, is also carefully shielded from any hint of that very substitutability and interchangeability that make it possible. And so the object of the poet's attention is introduced not as *a* runaway slave, but as *the* runaway slave, as if he were some previously mentioned figure, specially known to the poet, rather than the categoric person which he is. What Whitman encourages us to forget, then, is the very condition under which the slave is admitted into "Song of Myself," as one of its representative figures, one of its formal equivalents, succeeding the trapper and his Indian bride in the previous stanza, and to be succeeded, in turn, by the twenty-eight young men bathing by the shore in section 11. Indeed, these other figures—the trapper and his bride, and the bathing young men—must be forgotten as well, their lack of sequential connection to the slave being in no way a lapse, but a necessity, a desired effect. This tender forgetfulness—this ceaseless transformation of "a" into "the"—thus generates a peculiar shape of time in "Song of Myself," turning it into an arena of simultaneity, an arena in which antecedence carries no particular weight because it is simply not registered as antecedence.

The transposition of seriality into simultaneity thus makes memory in "Song of Myself" democratic in a rather troubling sense, in that no particular event can claim to have a special place in it, to be more cherished or more enduring.[12] The extension of time, or rather, the emotional weight inhering in that extension, is something of an incomprehensible (or inadmissible) phenomenon, and it is this, I think, that accounts for that strange confusion of tenses here surrounding the word "remember." That fateful word is used not once but twice, in two consecutive sentences: "And remember perfectly well his revolving eyes and his awkwardness, / And remember putting plasters on the galls of his neck and ankles." Indeed, not just these two lines, but the entire stanza—from the "swung half-door of the kitchen" to the famous "firelock leaned in the corner"[13]—might be read as a tribute to memory, to its minuteness and tenacity. And yet, this tribute notwithstanding, the exact status of memory—its location and extension in time—remains more than a little dubious. After all, the most striking feature of the stanza is surely the odd, incongruous placement of the act of remembering—something supposedly being done in the present—among the recorded deeds of the past. Presided over by the conjunctive "and," "remember" becomes syntactically equivalent to all the verbs that precede it: "went," "led," "brought water," "filled a tub," "gave him a room." It is made analogous to, and put into the company of, verbs depicting concrete acts, of definite duration and tangible result, acts begun in the past and ended in the past.

And yet, what makes memory special is surely that it resembles none of the above: it is not concrete, has no definite duration, no tangible result, and knows neither beginnings nor endings. It can be put in the midst of the others, can be pronounced the equivalent of the others, only through a syntactic dictate that amounts to a kind of epistemological violence. Being harnessed in this manner by the syntax, memory becomes coterminous and coextensive with the event that occasions it. It is woven into the incident that it recalls, sealed and sewn within it. This is what gives memory in Whitman its tapestry-like quality, its strange sense of being without compulsion, without mobility in time. Relieved from the weight of antecedence, past events can now become cheerful additions to the present, swelling its ranks and multiplying its opportunities. The transposition of temporal extension into spatial amplitude thus makes for a self so resilient, so able to accommodate all contingencies as to be beyond contingency. This is, of course, the fantasized ideal of "Song of Myself": a self endlessly renewed by its procedures, a self whose perennial innocence translates into an imaginative largesse, a self always open to new experience, but always unencumbered by that experience.

An "unencumbered self," Michael Sandel has argued, is the ideal citizen for a "procedural republic" ("The Procedural Republic"), a Kantian political utopia, aspiring always to the exercise of noncontingent reason, and founded always on the possibility of a universal subject, one who might "be made the ground for all maxims of action" (Kant 105). If so, "Song of Myself" must count as one of the most compelling portraits of that utopia, an experiment to devise for the unencumbered self a credible embodiment and a credible home. From the poem, though, we might glimpse not only the political necessities for such an ideal, but also some of its experiential difficulties. For, more dramatically here than elsewhere, we see the extent to which the language of democratic justice is a language of syntax, a language signally porous both in relation to the varieties of human experience and in relation to the textures of affective lives. It captures for us the expansiveness of space but not the endurance of time, the rhythms of fresh beginnings but not the music of familiar affections, the renewability of syntax but not the sedimentation of meanings.

In this context, it is worth returning briefly to Noam Chomsky to recall some of *his* problems in elevating syntax into the principal (or perhaps even sole) object of study. From the first, Chomsky's critics have argued that the phenomenon of language is richer, more contingent, and less formalizable than a syntactic theory would allow, and have called for a supplement in the form of a *semantic* theory.[14] John Searle, one such critic, has objected (not surprisingly) to the inability of syntax to account for actual speech behavior, actual linguistic performances. Language, Searle argues, is not primarily an instrument of thought and only secondarily an instrument of communication (as Chomsky would have it), but irreducibly, constitutively shaped by its communicative needs, and thus centrally organized by semantics, the production and reception of meaning (2–33). Of course, Searle himself is speaking from a partisan position—that of speech-act theory, of which he and J. L. Austin are the leading exponents. That tradition, in giving pride of place to the contexts of utterance, has built its case, understandably, not on the formal universals of syntax, but on the substantive contingencies of semantics. The meanings of words—their situational variations occasioned by different rules and intentions, and their etymological variations occasioned by historical change—these make up the life of language as Austin and Searle understand it. Words come to us accompanied by "trailing clouds of etymology," Austin writes, for "[a] word never—well, hardly ever—shakes off its etymology and its formation. In spite of all changes in and extensions of and additions to its meanings, and indeed rather pervading and governing these, there will still persist the old idea" (201).

Semantics, then, is that domain in which the historical life of language is honored and preserved, and in which human history itself is also silently but indelibly recorded. Words have memories here, and the passing away of a usage, a manner of speaking, or a mode of association is never without residue, never without a shower of deposits, clouding up the orthographic clarity of words, giving them their particular thickness and opacity. Unlike syntax, then, which begins as a clean slate each time it is used, empty of any traces of the words that previously comprised it, semantics is a slate that can never be wiped clean, being written upon over and over again, accumulating meanings that settle and thicken in time. This is what Mikhail Bakhtin has in mind when he refers to semantics as a domain in which language becomes "saturated," each word pervaded by the "tastes of the context and contexts in which it has lived its socially charged life" (293). Bakhtin is speaking of the saturation of words within the historical life of an entire society, but on a more modest scale we might also imagine the same process of saturation within the biographical life of a single individual, or within the textual life of a long poem such as "Song of Myself." Here, too, prior usages might have left behind memories of their passing, accumulated nuances and inflections that make it impossible for words to be quite innocent, quite neutral, quite pristine, impossible for them to begin unencumbered.

This historical memory of words is what the poetic form of "Song of Myself" is out to combat. It is syntax, then, rather than semantics, that gives "Song of Myself" its peculiar resilience and regularity, its promise of renewal and guarantee of permanence.[15] This is its great source of strength, a strength that, in Whitman as in Chomsky, comes from a necessary abstraction, an insistence on formal universals, an insistence that transforms the randomness of the world, its accidents and its vulnerabilities, into the orderly form of its syntax. "All goes onward and outward . . . . and nothing collapses, / And to die is different from what any one supposed, and luckier," Whitman writes at the end of his famous paean to the grass which, like language, and most particularly like syntax ("so many uttering tongues!"), is ever substitutable, and ever renewable. And he immediately goes on to repeat that crucial concluding word all over again: "Has any one supposed it lucky to be born? / I hasten to inform him or her it is just as lucky to die, and I know it" (*LG* 1855: 30).

Luck, that bane of democracy, is here mentioned by name, three times in the space of three lines, and even in face of death, its most terrible ally. It can be mentioned because, like the self which it overshadows, it too has been formalized, neutralized, made amenable to reason through the agency of syntax. In a complex play of crescendo that might be called the rationalization of luck, the syntax here focuses on the different degrees and gradations of it—"lucky," "luckier," "just as lucky"—using these degrees and gradations to ask some rather abstruse questions (is it luckier to live or to die, or are both just as lucky?). What is happily missing here, among the available options, is one item which, ordinarily, would perhaps be of the greatest concern to most people, namely, the category of the "unlucky." That, however, belongs to a different syntactic order, a different progression of logical possibilities, and its absence here is virtually a given. The Whitmanian self is thus always lucky, he can only be lucky, whether he lives or dies. And he is just as lucky as everybody else. In being so assured of that fact, in having so little room for surprise, let alone for complaint, he might also be said, paradoxically, to be beyond luck, beyond its caprice and, above all, beyond its inequities.

What does it mean for a self to be beyond luck? Martha Nussbaum has argued that an ethical life that aspires to be noncontingent is also one that is necessarily impoverished. There can be no goodness without vulnerability, she suggests. "Song of Myself" affirms her insight, qualifies it, and offers perhaps an alternative political context for its interpretation. Taking the noncontingent self, then, both as a necessary foundation of democratic justice as Whitman urges, but possibly also as a case of experiential impoverishment as Nussbaum warns, I want to think further about the epistemology underwritten by such a figure, and about the shape of the world radiating outward from its particular form. Whitman, as always, has indirectly supplied an answer here. In "Song of Myself," immediately following his declaration that "it is just as lucky to die," he goes on to invoke a world of "manifold objects, no two alike, and every one good, / The earth good, and the stars good, and their adjuncts all good" (*LG* 1855: 30–31).

These particular lines here, celebratory in a way that borders on the syrupy, might perhaps lend themselves to the charge of facile optimism, but it would be unfair to read them in that light. Rather, they have to do, I think, with a democratic impulse (driven perhaps as much by anxiety as by hope) to so construe the world as to render the faculty of discrimination unnecessary. After all, judgment can cease, can truly cease, only in a world where there is no call for it. Luck—of the Whitmanian sort, predicated on the syntactic elimination of the unlucky—makes such a world thinkable, credible, habitable. And so, under its dispensation, one can live one's life "judg[ing] not as the judge judges but as the sun falling around a helpless thing," secure in the belief that the "helpless thing" will not turn out to be a snake, a porcupine, a snapping turtle. It is that belief, tenuous as it is and utopian as it is, that enables Whitman to imagine a world that is epistemologically democratic, and that allows him to dispense with preference altogether, so that, even among objects "no two alike," he is still able to consecrate a syntax that is nothing if not a chant of equivalence: "and every one good, / The earth good, and the stars good, and their adjuncts all good" (*LG* 1855: 31).

Good, good, good, good. That chant of equivalence brings to a head the hope as well as the frailty of a democratic poetics, as of a democratic polity. The equivalence is secured, of course, by the regularity of the syntax, which neutralizes luck by making all eventualities equally *indifferent*, both in the sense that none is distinguishable from the others, and in the sense that none is preferred to the others. For preference is indeed hard to justify, hard even to imagine, given the blanket attribution of goodness. In a world filled with objects all generated by the same syntax, and all described by the word good, how can we make sense of the fact that some particular object, some particular person, will appeal to us in a manner altogether disproportionate to their grammatical description? And how can we make sense of the fact that some other object, some other person, will not appeal to us, certifiably (because categorically) good as they are?

A self that is beyond luck is not simply *beyond* the contingent, it is also *barred* from the contingent. It is barred, that is, from that circumstantial domain, inhabited by densely-featured people, some of whom are miracles and some of whom are just unhappy freaks of accident, but all of whom, in any case, whether as objects of affection or as objects of aversion, can materialize for us only through a particularizing language. Whitman's democratic poetics, in short, can have no access to that chaotic world of special loves and hates. It is silent about those objects that, for us, are not categoric, not interchangeable or substitutable, not adequately described by grammar or fully accounted for by syntax. In that silence, "Song of Myself" is at one with the entire Western philosophical tradition from Immanuel Kant to Noam Chomsky and John Rawls. It is not at one with that tradition, however, in making that silence so eerie, so restless and untranquil in its willed uniformity. If nothing else, Whitman makes us long for what he does not and cannot offer: an ethics of preference, one that, in giving voice to what is not exhausted by a language of formal universals, what remains its conceptual or emotional residue, might suggest some way of reconciling the democratic and the affective, some way of rescuing "love" from being the lost soul of political theory.

### Notes

1. For a classic statement, see Ross. For a vigorous defense of desert and a response to Rawls, see Sher. Robert Nozick, in face of Rawls's argument against desert, has retreated, on the other hand, to the weaker claim of "entitlement" as the ground of distributive justice. See Nozick 185–231.

2. See also 491, where Rawls once again compares ethical understanding to grammatical knowledge.

3. A cursory list of theorists here would include Rudolf Carnap, Donald Davidson, Michael Dummett, Hilary Putnam, W. V. Quine, Alfred Tarski, the later Wittgenstein, Paul Ziff. Some of these, needless to say, themselves have complicated arguments about the analyzability of semantics. (Quine, for example, argues against the factuality of semantics in favor of its indeterminacy.)

4. Chomsky's own impatience with semantics, of course, has not prevented other Chomskian linguists from trying to work out a generative semantic theory. See, for example, Fodor and Katz.

5. This point emerges most clearly in Chomsky's critique of Paul Grice, Peter Strawson, and especially John Searle. See Chomsky, "The Object of Inquiry," in *Reflections on Language*, esp. 53–77. For a useful (and complicating) account of this debate, see Dummett.

6. Chomsky, *Cartesian Linguistics;* and *Language and Mind*, 1–23.

7. See Thompson.

8. On the whole, Chomsky is much more impressed by Descartes than he is by Kant, whom he tends to assimilate into the Cartesian tradition, noting that Kant's ideas are "rather similar" to the "rich and varied work of seventeenth-century rationalists." See *Reflections on Language* 7, also 131.

9. Chomsky's commitment to civil disobedience is well known. For Rawls's detailed discussion of this subject, see 363–91.

10. Allen Grossman has written that Whitman's is "a world composed of a limitless series of brilliant finite events each of which imposed closure at the grammatical end of its account" (189).

11. I want to emphasize that this is a particular feature of "Song of Myself," a feature that I associate with its democratic poetics. It is certainly not true of all of Whitman's poetry. In the poem later entitled "There Was a Child Went Forth," for example, Whitman writes, "There was a child went forth every day, / And the first object he looked upon and received with wonder or pity or love or dread, that object he became, / And that object became part of him for the day or a certain part of the day . . . . or for many years or stretching cycles of years" (*LG* 1855: 138).

12. Allen Grossman is exactly right, I think, when he writes that "the fullness of articulation of Whitman's poem" depends "on the failed predecessor system of which all that survives is love without an object" (199).

13. Whether the firelock is meant to protect the runaway slave or to protect the poet *against* the slave is, of course, a much debated question. For a fine reading of this detail, see Sánchez-Eppler 77.

14. The body of literature on this subject is formidable. See, for example, Ziff; Fodor and Katz, "The Structure of a Semantic Theory." For more recent discussions, see Hornstein; and Dummett.

15. In this sense, syntax might be said to be the primary linguistic vehicle of the American jeremiad, as described by Sacvan Bercovitch.

# America's Whitmans

# 5

# His America, Our America:
# José Martí Reads Whitman

## SYLVIA MOLLOY

It is good to love a woman; but it may be better to love a man.
José Martí, Letter to Manuel Mercado,
September 14, 1882

An obsessive meditation on male progeniture and filiation runs through
the pages of José Martí. Of his first book of poetry, *Ismaelillo*, celebrating
his three-year-old son, he writes (in French) to his friend Charles Dana,
editor of the *New York Sun:* "I have just published a little book, not for
profit but as a present for those I love, a present in the name of my son
who is my master. The book is the story of my love affair with my son *[mes
amours avec mon fils]:* one tires of reading so many stories of love affairs
with women" (XXI: 253).[1] Even in its more homey aspects, this love affair
appears to be an intensely pedagogical venture. In a fragment of his notebooks striking in its fatherly fetishism, Martí observes that: "When I am
about to store the little straw hat and the booties that my son wore a year
ago, I check to see if what is written in the newspaper in which I am about
to wrap them is the product of men's passions or if it defends just causes.
If it defends just causes, I go ahead and wrap them. I believe in these
contaminations" (XXI: 186). Since I too believe in contaminations, though
probably not in the way envisioned by Martí, I shall proceed to explore
this very fertile conjunction of fathers, sons, and just causes. However, I
shall not forgo "men's passions," as did Martí, but, giving the expression
an additional twist, read it as the adhesiveness (to borrow from Whitman)
that holds fathers, sons, and just causes together.

Intensity of fatherly emotion reverberates throughout *Ismaelillo*. Martí
writes this book about his son, for his son, and, in another example of
contamination between written page and child, refers to the book itself,
with an intensity that goes beyond trite comparison, as his son:

What different shapes this son of mine takes when warmed up by my love! . . . That is why I love this book, because the little one running loose within its pages, now sad, now cheerful, now mischievous, the sim- ple creature whom I, with the potency of my love, turn into my king, my sorcerer, my knight, has really passed before my eyes, airy, shining, bubbling, just as I depict him. I have seen a beautiful little boy, barely clothed in the lightest of shirts, sitting on a very high mound, waving his little pink feet in the air, and I have said to myself: "As this child looks down on those below him, so does he govern my soul. And I have called him my sorcerer." And I imagined him on a throne, humid and fluid as a throne that would shine for Galatea, and myself, coming before him, like a hunter surrounded by his dogs, bringing him, my king and master, my passions for tribute. (XXI: 221)

This fatherly rapture over the "airy, shining, bubbling" little one, in which it is easy to see a prefiguration of that other Latin American lithe spirit and male muse, Rodó's Ariel, is matched, in Martí, by the intensity of filial feeling. As the figure of the son structures affection and desire in Martí's writing, so does the figure of the father. It functions as an allegorical con- struct ensuring historical continuity: "The Father / Must not die till richly armed / Into the fray he thrusts the son!" (XVI: 148). It functions too as a thematic prop, or as a transhistorical principle: "Everything moves toward unity, toward synthesis, essences move to one being; . . . a father is father to many sons; a tree trunk supports many boughs; a sun emits innumera- ble rays. In every case, unity proceeds to multiplicity and multiplicity merges and resolves itself back into unity" (XXI: 52).

This obsession has been diversely commented on, first by Angel Rama and then, most convincingly, by Julio Ramos who reads Martí's insistence on filiation as a way of setting up a new model of affiliation, in Said's sense of the term, as the replacement of one family model by another (184). That women are excluded from Martí's new family model—the "rigid and self-sufficient male couple" that, with a "double outburst of love, success- fully unit[es] father and son in an emotional bond from which all feminine presence, be it maternal or marital, is elided" (Rama 150)—is, of course, quite obvious.

I want to stay for a bit with this notion of a new family model, for it allows me an entrance into Whitman, rather into Whitman as read by Martí. Two observations occur to me, both to qualify and complete Angel Rama's statement. The first is to draw attention to the place of the subject in this new family model—really, family romance—proposed by Martí. Be- tween opposing but reversible male foci of love, the Son and the Father, the "I" operates as a shifter, brokering as it were the relation and effec- tively subverting its rigidity, playing father to the son and son to the father, making the son his father and the father his son. Another fragment from Martí's notebooks addressed to his son, a charming little scene of pedagogy which, in spite of its mocking stance, should be taken at face value, stresses that reversibility: "I see myself playing with you. And in order to make you learn joyfully, I make you a little teacher's hat, and I place my spectacles on your nose, and I sit you down on the highest chair, so that you get used to being big in every way" (XXI: 167). This playful give-and-take assures not so much the presence of a "rigid . . . couple" as the polymorphous, unhierarchical exchange of all-male feeling.

The second important aspect of this intense and polymorphous male bonding is the indubitable *political* significance assigned to it by Martí:

This generous preoccupation *[miedo generoso]*, this care for son and father *at the same time,* this love that encompasses all those who are needy for it, both those who lack it and those who are not even aware of it, this dog-ged vigilance, this labor of preparation, this attention to the substance of things and not to their mere form, this politics that founds instead of fragmenting, this politics of elaboration is the revolutionary. (XXII: 47– 48; emphasis added)

It is in light of these characteristics—the *fluidity* of male-male feeling, the reciprocal learning experience afforded by that exchange, and the *revo-lutionary* value ascribed to that feeling by Martí—that I wish to read his essay on Whitman. Surely one of Martí's most famous pieces, written dur-ing his exile in the United States, it is routinely read and celebrated for its programmatic value as are, unfortunately only too often, most of Martí's works. In celebrating Whitman, such a reading goes, Martí is really cele-brating democracy, is considering Whitman an exemplary influence on the Latin American political project for which he, Martí, is justly famous. This conventional reading of Martí's essay deals less with Whitman himself than with what Enrico Mario Santí has called the *idea* of Whitman (160–61), with what Whitman has finally come to signify, many years after Martí's piece and in part as a result of Martí's piece, in the Latin American cultural imaginary. As such, this reading is anachronistic, yet that is the lesser of its ills. My main quarrel with it is that it is inattentive to detail and inattentive to the dynamics of the essay, replacing process with the end product.

Instead, I wish to look at the process, that is, at how Martí, in a complex series of moves, deals with his personal reactions to the Whitman text and, through those very personal reactions, "packages" Whitman for Latin American consumption. The essay is dated April 19, 1887, that is, four days after Whitman delivered his annual lecture on "The Death of Lin-coln" during what was to be his last visit to New York. Martí's strategy seems, at first view, relatively simple. Resorting to the didactic model he had used successfully in other essays written for a Latin American public, he adopts the role of go-between: Here is the poet (or the event) and here am I, the witness, to interpret him (or it) for you. The Whitman he pres-ents to Latin America is, at first glance, conventionally simple, one more version of the good gray poet: grandiose, prophetic, robust and, above all, *natural*. Martí's elaboration of this notion of the natural is worthy of comment here. How could this astonishing book *not* be prohibited by the short-sighted, Martí asks rhetorically, "when it is a *natural* book?" And he continues:

> Universities and academic knowledge have separated men so that they no longer know one another. Instead of falling into each other's arms *[echarse unos en brazos de los otros]*, attracted by all that is essential and eternal, they draw apart, competing with each other like fish wives *[placeras]*, for purely trivial differences. . . . Philosophical, religious and literary trends restrain men's thinking the way a lackey's body is restrained by his livery. . . . Thus, when they stand before the man who is naked, virginal, amorous, sincere, potent—the man who walks, loves, fights, rows his boat—the man who does not fall prey to unhappiness but recognizes the promise of final joy in the grace and balance of the world; when they stand before Walt Whitman's sinewy and angelic man-father *[hombre padre]*, they flee as if from their own consciences, refusing to recognize in that fragrant and superior humanness the true type of their own discolored, cassocked, doll-like *[amuñecada]* species. (*On Art and Literature* 168–69)[2]

The concept of the natural—or to be more precise, of an American natural—is represented, for Martí, by an ever embracing masculinity ("men falling into each others' arms"), while the fall from the natural—into isolation, into a culture of imitation—is signified by a particularly degraded notion of the feminine, *amuñecada*, diminished by connotations of servility, triviality, and artifice. Whitman, the man-father, a repository of that fragrant and superior male humanness, opens the way, leading his "sons" back to that lost male unity.

It should be remembered that this notion of "the natural," a cultural construct if ever there was one, has illustrious classical antecedents. Indeed, the very same virtues that Martí saw as embodiments of an "American" natural from which men had deviated had already been ascribed, by John Addington Symonds and in strikingly similar terms, to a different "national" tradition: "Hopeful and fearless, accepting the world as he finds it, recognizing the value of each human impulse, shirking no obligation, self-regulated by a law of perfect health, he, in the midst of a chaotic age, emerges clear and distinct, at one with nature, and therefore Greek" (Grosskurth 152n). I shall return to this shifting national attribution, and more particularly to its purported "Greek" origins.

What follows in Martí's essay on Whitman is a fairly extensive web of quotations and near quotations from Whitman, woven with remarkable textual familiarity and rhetorical dexterity into Martí's commentary. Also

notable is the choice of particular texts by Whitman. Martí plunges immediately into "Song of Myself," then goes on directly and unerringly to the
"Calamus" poems:

Since [Whitman's] books and lectures earn him barely enough money for
bread, some "loving friends" see to his needs in a cottage tucked away in
a pleasant country lane from which he rides out in an ancient carriage
drawn by his beloved horses to watch the "athletic young men" busy with
their virile diversions, to see the comrades who are not afraid of rubbing
elbows with this iconoclast who wants to establish the institution of "the
manly love of comrades," to see the fields they cultivate, the friends who
pass by arm in arm and singing, the pairs of lovers, gay and vivacious
like quail. This he relates in his "Calamus," the extremely strange book
in which he sings of the love of friends: "Not the orgies . . . Not the
pageants of you, not the shifting tableaus, your spectacles, repay me
. . . / Nor the processions in the streets, nor the bright windows with
goods in them, / Nor to converse with learn'd persons . . . / Not those,
but as I pass O Manhattan, your frequent and swift flash of eyes offering
me love, . . . Lovers, continual lovers, only repay me." (171–72)

That Martí would gravitate toward the adhesiveness celebrated in "Calamus" where, indeed, men "fall into each others' arms," that he would even
work his way from the poems back to the man who wrote them, making
Whitman, the old "man-father," a son to his "loving friends" and turning
his life into a pastoral, was to be expected. Yet I would suggest that, even
as he openly exalts this male bonding in the spirit Whitman ostensively
wished it to be read—that is, for its political significance, as posited in the
1876 preface to *Leaves of Grass* and in *Democratic Vistas*—Martí is not so sure
of what he is *really* reading. Proof of this insecurity, for instance, are the
changes and the gaps in his quotation of Whitman. The intention of the
opening line of Whitman's poem, "City of Orgies," is clearly laudatory:
"City of orgies, walks and joys." Misquoting, Martí resorts instead to nega-
tion, setting limits from the start: "*Not* the orgies." Maybe this modification
was automatic for Martí, intent as he was on reading the "Calamus" poems
"right," that is, on spiritualizing them. Yet I would argue that if indeed
such cleansing, conscious or not, was at work, the choice of "City of Orgies," a poem so evocative of the male cruising scene, is rather odd. Martí,
the inveterate New York flaneur, perceived the danger of speaking of this
poem even as he was irresistibly attracted to it; in other words, he knew,
or at least intuited, that something more than a Benjaminian auratic encounter was going on in this "frequent and swift flash of eyes." This is
apparent, I think, in a significant elision. After "your frequent and swift
flash of eyes offering me love," Martí suppresses the following line: "Offering response to my own—these repay me." With this suppression, Martí

cautiously removes the first person—Whitman's "I" and/or Martí's own person—from the circulation of desire, denies it an active role in any fecund transaction of male feelings. The city, in the poem that Martí misquotes, acts on the "I," but not vice versa.

Martí's highly circumspect, ambiguous reading—gravitating toward dangerously attractive poems while setting up a distance between them and himself—is particularly obvious in the section of this essay attempting to deal, more or less directly, with sexuality, a section I wish to quote at some length:

> But who can give an idea of his vast and fiercely burning love? This man loves the world with the fire of Sappho. His world is a gigantic bed, and the bed an altar. . . . One source of his originality is the herculean strength with which he flings ideas to the ground as if to violate them when all he wants to do is kiss them with a saintly passion. Another force is the earthy, brutal, and fleshy way he expresses his most delicate ideals. Only those incapable of understanding its greatness have considered that language lewd. With the affected innocence of dirty-minded schoolboys, fools imagine they see a return to the vile desires of Virgil for Cebes, and of Horace for Gyges and Liciscus, when Whitman uses the most ardent images of which human language is capable to celebrate love between friends in his "Calamus." (178)

Why, the reader might ask, begin a paragraph whose principal thrust is to set Whitman "straight" with, as it were, a weak card—the specific mention of Sappho? It might be argued that the mention of Sappho harks back to notions of the natural, of a "Greek" natural similar to the one admired by Symonds, but in all probability the reference is far more complex. By 1887 the mention of Sappho, although susceptible to different interpretations, was surely not innocent. As Joan De Jean has eloquently demonstrated, it was a reference put to active ideological use by nineteenth-century philologists following Winckelmann, usually in connection with, and as a corrective to, implications of sexuality in pederastic relations: "Welcker"—writes De Jean—"posited an essential bond between male physical beauty, militarism, and patriotism on the one hand and Sappho's chastity on the other" (205). And she adds: "The association forged between Sappho and Greek love leads to a double overreaction that eventually cuts off both Sapphism and *pederastia* from sensuality" (211). It is indeed to such a use that Martí resorts: if Sappho's passion is chaste, better yet, sacred (from bed to altar), so then are the "Calamus" poems—ardent, very ardent, but chaste.

Yet one can't help thinking that this model of Sappho, while undoubtedly at play here, was not the only one for Martí; Sappho in this text means the spiritual and the chaste yet also hints at the opposite. A reader of

Baudelaire, Martí surely had other Sapphos in mind, and a passing reference in one of his letters to someone who was living "à la Sappho" gives the reader pause. This affirming-while-denying strategy is reinforced by Martí's other classical allusions, those "vile desires of Virgil for Cebes and of Horace for Gyges and Lyciscus" which merit closer scrutiny. Lyciscus is indeed in Horace an object of love (*Epodes* 11: 110). But Gyges is not, deserving just a passing mention (*Odes*, Book 2, Ode 5: 188) as the conventional pretty boy whose flowing hair makes him sexually ambiguous. If Martí thinks that dirty-minded schoolboys are reading same-sex sex into the "Calamus" poems, guess who is reading it indiscriminately into Horace? A similar overreading may be observed in the reference to Vergil's Cebes, for there is no Cebes in Virgil, at least in Virgil's *text*. Cebes does appear, however, in Vergil's commentators, notably Servius: "Servius proposes that, in Eclogue II, Amaryllis and Menalcas are respectively Leria and Cebes, two slaves belonging to Maecenas whom their master gave to Virgil because he had a fancy for them" (Rose 70). So that we now have a dirty-minded schoolboy not just snooping into Eclogue II—a text that, in its explicit consideration of same-sex love, would have been far too obvious if referred to directly—but into Virgil's life itself. It is precisely this interpretive overkill that undoes the efficacy of Martí's disclaimers for "Calamus," calling attention to them, rendering them suspicious. The overwrought denials betray a preoccupation much more revealing of Martí, and of what Martí was repressing as he read Whitman, than, of course, of Whitman himself.

The intimations of homosexuality in the passage I have read, more reinforced than disproved by Martí's crossed references, generate a compulsively heterosexual justification in Martí's reading of Whitman, the violence of which cannot be ignored. Thus the following description of "Children of Adam" engaged in by Martí immediately after his comments on the "Calamus" poems:

> When he sings the divine sin in "Children of Adam," in scenes which make the most feverish images in *The Song of Songs* seem pale, he trembles, shrivels, swells, and overflows, goes mad with pride and satisfied virility, recalls the god of the Amazons who rode through forests and across rivers sowing seeds of life throughout the land, "singing the song of procreation." . . . [T]o find an appropriate resemblance to the satanically forceful enumeration in which he describes, like a hungry hero smacking his bloodthirsty lips, the various parts of the female body, it would be well to have read the patriarchal genealogies of Genesis in Hebrew, and to have followed the naked cannibal bands of primitive men through the virgin jungle. And you say this man is brutal? Listen to his composition "Beautiful Women," which like many of his poems has only two lines: "Women sit or move to and fro, some old, some young / The

young are beautiful—but the old are more beautiful than the young."
And this one, "Mother and Babe": "I see the sleeping mother and babe—
hush'd, I study them long and long." (178–79)

If, at the beginning of Martí's essay on Whitman, the feminine signified
the trivial, the derivative, the devalued—the "doll-like" artifice as opposed
to the male "natural"—it has escalated, by now, to signify a force to be
destroyed by, and in the name of, heterosexual virility. Whitman's curious
roamer of bodies becomes, in Martí's rendering, a priapic fiend, trembling,
swelling, overflowing, violating ideas and women; a cannibal in a virgin
jungle, "satanically" salivating over female body parts. Additionally, it
should be noted that the only alternative to this bloody celebration that
Martí sees in Whitman is admiration for traditionally nondesiring and non-
desirable forms of the feminine: beautiful old women, a mother with child.
If, in order to correct intimations of deviant male bonding, Martí resorts
to woman, the strategy turns on itself. The truculence attending the feminine, in connection with sexual appetites and procreative urges, makes it a
discordant element, literally an obstacle standing in the way of men.

"It is to the development, identification, and general prevalence of that
fervid comradeship (the adhesive love, at least rivaling the amative love
hitherto possessing imaginative literature, if not going beyond it,) that I
look for the counterbalance and offset of our materialistic and vulgar
American democracy," writes Whitman in *Democratic Vistas* (*PW* 2: 414). In
Whitman's communal masculinity Martí recognizes his own all-male affilia-
tive model, the revolutionary family of sons and fathers confounded in a
continuum of natural, unhierarchical masculine emotion, and he also recognizes the political, specifically *American*, potential of that model,[3] which
he will go on to elaborate in later essays. (I think of course of the discussion
on "natural man" in "Our America.") Whitman, for Martí, is the precursor,
pointing out "to our astonished times the radiant swarms of men spreading
over America's mountains and valleys, brushing their bees' wings against
the hem of freedom's robes" (185). That the intensity of this continental
masculine adhesiveness not only rivaled "amative love" as in Whitman, but
in Martí's case precluded it, may well account for both the fear and the
passion with which he read "Calamus" as a series of poems that needed to
be translated (and to be translated away) in order to function as mirror
texts. To his credit, Martí will have been the only Latin American to consider, in Whitman, the erotic together with the political, and to register his
anxiety, even his panic, before that explosive alliance. Only one year later,
such a combination was unthinkable. In a mediocre, though much-cited
poem of *Azul* (1888), Rubén Darío would congeal Whitman forever in the
Latin American imaginary, totemizing him as the grand old prophet: the
"idea of Whitman" was well on its way. While Martí's reading does not
necessarily give us a new Whitman, I suggest that it gives us, provided we
read it carefully, a new Martí.

## Notes

1. Translations are my own unless otherwise noted.

2. Quotations from this English version have been modified considerably at times for the sake of accuracy. The original Spanish text, "El poeta Walt Whitman," is to be found in *Obras completas,* XIII: 131–46.

3. For an analysis of this model in Whitman which admirably takes into account the interdependence of republicanism, communalism, and sexuality, see Jay Grossman.

# 6

# "In Loftiest Spheres": Whitman's Visionary Feminism

## VIVIAN R. POLLAK

> Of these rapidly-sketch'd hiatuses, the two which seem to me
> most serious are, for one, the condition, absence, or perhaps
> the singular abeyance, of moral conscientious fibre all through
> American society; and, for another, the appaling [sic] deple-
> tion of women in their powers of sane athletic maternity, their
> crowning attribute, and ever making the woman, in loftiest
> spheres, superior to the man.
>
> Walt Whitman, *Democratic Vistas*

This essay describes Whitman's disruption of his own claims to empower
women by reinscribing them within fixed social roles in which they are
always potentially subordinated to men. For complex personal and historical reasons, Whitman tends to collapse the many possibilities contained in
the word "Woman" into the single word "Mother" and then to extol the
preeminence of maternal work in contradistinction to other contributions
that women might make to culture, especially those that depend on self-
determining thought and self-determining language. Consequently, this essay examines both Whitman's feminism and his antifeminism, his resistance
to linguistically totalizing norms, and his reaffirmation of the mid-
nineteenth-century American cult of the mother, which celebrated maternity as any woman's supreme destiny and which, to a significant degree,
depended on a code of women's silence about the unloftiness of the lives
they were in fact living. The tension between Whitman's embrace of the
new (call it the fully audible female voice) and his embrace of the old (call
it the institution and practice of idealizing maternity as a depoliticizing,
universalizing trope) has, I believe, interpretative power for other vexed
issues in Whitman's poetry, all of them having to do with his ambivalence
toward the cultural changes that he himself was helping to inaugurate.

Rather than turning directly to Whitman's biography to explain the personal origins of his discursive practices and to the particulars of his relationship with his much-loved mother, a woman whom he memorably described as "illiterate in the formal sense of the term but strangely knowing" (*WWC* 2: 113–14), I want to begin this discussion of Whitman's identification with women as mothers and his potential cooptation of the role of the woman writer by considering the intersection of race and gender in *Democratic Vistas*, the prose work which is Whitman's postwar sexual manifesto and in which he repeatedly acknowledges the appeal of what another writer, Henry Clarke Wright, called in his 1863 book "the empire of the mother."[1] Participating in the tradition of the American jeremiad that has been eloquently described by Sacvan Bercovitch, Whitman complained of the "absence . . . of moral conscientious fibre all through American society" and of the "appaling [sic] depletion of women in their powers of sane athletic maternity, their crowning attribute . . . ever making the woman, in loftiest spheres, superior to the man" (*PW* 2: 372n).[2] I show that Whitman's ideology of idealizing maternity emerged as a specific response to historically conditioned fears of social and psychological chaos but also that Whitman's magnification of the cultural work of the mother was thoroughly embedded in his original poetic project and not merely the product of his postwar, retrenching middle age. Thus, even in the 1855, 1856, and 1860 *Leaves*, as the poet struggled to articulate a radical social vision in which erotic difference might flourish without destroying his endlessly elaborated fantasy of a national erotic union, his claim to speak *for* women and to understand their experience better than they understand it themselves emerges as the most consistently problematized element of his social, psychological, and political feminist vision.

# I

*Democratic Vistas* was written over the course of several years, beginning in August 1867. Inspired at first by the virulent anti-Americanism of Thomas Carlyle's "Shooting Niagara: And After?", Whitman's own deeply conflicted defense of the theory if not the practice of American democracy was, as he freely acknowledged, a "collection of memoranda . . . open to the charge of one part contradicting another" in whose emotional, moral, and intellectual unity he nevertheless and somewhat miraculously continued to believe (*PW* 2: 362–63). Whitman composed the first part of this strongly impassioned yet disjointed and "wandering . . . argument" (Matthiessen 591n) while on short-term leave from his moderately lucrative job as a record clerk in the Attorney General's office. Transcribing official documents, answering correspondence, abridging and abstracting legal material, he made at least sixteen hundred dollars a year while working intermittently from nine to three in pleasant physical surroundings. This was more money than he had ever made before or was to see again; on a regular basis, he sent some of it home to his mother, who was dependent on him for financial support.

During the unairconditioned Washington summers, when he suffered intensely from the heat—a condition to which, with his strong sense of family destiny, he believed the Whitmans were peculiarly prone—he was able to hire a substitute and to return home for long stays. He could also attend to literary matters. While on an extended vacation in New York in 1867, he wrote back to Ellen O'Connor, the wife of his pen-wielding "champion," William Douglas, "I am well as usual, & go daily around New York & Brooklyn yet with interest, of course—but I find the places & crowds & excitements—Broadway, &c—have not the zest of former times— they have done their work, & now they are to me as a tale that is told." He added, "I am trying to write a piece, to be called *Democracy,* for the leading article in the December or January number of the *Galaxy*—in some sort a counterblast or rejoinder to Carlyle's late piece, *Shooting Niagara,* which you must have read, or at least heard about" (*Corr* 1: 342).

Several months later, Whitman had completed his first "counterblast or rejoinder" to Carlyle's offensive essay, which had condemned the American Civil War as a useless slaughter. "Half a million . . . of excellent White Men," Carlyle wrote, "full of gifts and faculty, have torn and slashed one another into horrid death, in a temporary humour, which will leave centuries of remembrance fierce enough: and three million absurd Blacks, men and brothers (of a sort), are completely 'emancipated' " (7). "Essentially the Nigger Question was one of the smallest," he had written,

> and in itself did not much concern mankind in the present time of strug-
> gles and hurries. One always rather likes the Nigger; evidently a poor
> blockhead with good dispositions, with affections, attachments,—with a
> turn for Nigger Melodies, and the like:—he is the only Savage of all the
> coloured races that doesn't die out on sight of the White Man; but can
> actually live beside him, and work and increase and be merry. The Al-
> mighty Maker has appointed him to be a Servant. (5)

And so on. The language still hurts. Carlyle's diatribe against American democracy had been prompted by the proposed passage of Disraeli's 1867 Reform Bill, which extended the suffrage in Britain to most working-class men. Carlyle likened this extension to "Shooting Niagara," to a headlong leap down Niagara Falls, to cultural suicide.

Whitman, too, had expressed reservations about the politics of the war. In "When Lilacs Last in the Dooryard Bloom'd," his great postheroic vision of American life, "I saw battle-corpses, myriads of them," he wrote,

> And the white skeletons of young men, I saw them,
> I saw the debris and debris of all the slain soldiers of the war,
> But I saw they were not as was thought,

They themselves were fully at rest, they suffer'd not,
The living remain'd and suffer'd, the mother suffer'd,
And the wife and the child and the musing comrade suffer'd,
And the armies that remain'd suffer'd. (*LG* 336)

This is no vision of meaningful personal sacrifice; Whitman specifically withholds the "masculine" consolation of effective military martyrdom. For white women, children, mothers, brothers, and brothers-in-arms, the war's legacy is a "feminized" consciousness of collective futility. Focusing attention on the dramatic and in some ways reassuring binary *life versus death* serves to obscure degrees of vitality and power among the living, as do sentimental appeals to a national family consciousness and to a national family tragedy that suppresses the distinction *North versus South*. Similarly, these depoliticizing tropes function to minimize the importance of race, as well as degrees of whiteness or blackness among persons of the same race (the binary *white versus black* remaining constant). When color is introduced into this scene in the phrase "white skeletons," we tend to experience it as a cliché, but the effect is to reinforce, albeit covertly, the racist status quo. Though it could be argued that whiteness is the universalized color of death, that the human body, deprived of its particularizing fleshly hues, is in fact bleached of its living colors, one contextual effect of Whitman's language is to suppress the contribution of black soldiers and civilians to the war effort.[3] The historian James McPherson observes that without the two hundred thousand blacks who enlisted in the army and navy, thirty-eight thousand of whom were killed, "the North could not have won the war as soon as it did, and perhaps it could not have won at all" (*Negro's* ix-x). According to McPherson, "The enlistment of black soldiers to fight and kill their former masters was by far the most revolutionary dimension of the emancipation policy" (*Abraham Lincoln* 35).

So it may be, as Whitman explained in his 1856 "Poem of the Road," later called "Song of the Open Road," that "The black with his woolly head, the felon, the diseas'd, the illiterate person, are not denied" (*LG* 150). But having lived through the war's bloody confusions, he dreaded further strife. "The fear of conflicting and irreconcilable interiors, and the lack of a common skeleton, knitting all close, continually haunts me," he noted in *Vistas* (*PW* 2: 368). Thus in his war volume *Drum-Taps*, race was designedly not a category to which the poet turned his attention. Preserving American democracy now seemed to depend on this crucial ellipsis, but some of the pressure of racial tension is displaced onto Whitman's unifying sacramentalization of motherhood and of matriarchal families: a displacement already at work in 1855 but more obviously so in subsequent years.

When Whitman revised *Leaves of Grass* in 1871, he added "Ethiopia Saluting the Colors," where race and gender intersect to produce a grotesquely aged Mammy who is explicitly described as "hardly human." Despite the racially and sexually subversive implications contained in the

poem's title and covertly reinforced by the description of her variegated
turban, hers is an eternal curtsy. In naturalizing an African-born, female
figure's sexual and racial subservience, Whitman reverts, appropriately
enough, to the traditional, full end-rhyme closure, internal rhyme, and
stanzaic regularity of his pre-*Leaves* verse. The poem stands out formally
and representationally as a retreat from a more egalitarian social vision.
Composed in 1867, when Whitman tried unsuccessfully to have it published in the *Galaxy*, together with the essay that formed the basis of *Democratic Vistas* (*Corr* 1: 338), "Ethiopia Saluting the Colors," though not initially part of the *Drum-Taps* sequence, became part of that sequence in
1881, where it has remained ever since. Remarkably, "Mammy" is the only
black in this Civil War memorial volume, though there are other mothers,
such as the melodramatically grief-stricken Ohio mother who learns that
her soldier-son is mortally wounded in the conversation poem "Come Up
from the Fields Father," and who then sinks into a suicidal depression because of her desire to "withdraw unnoticed, silent from life escape and
withdraw, / To follow, to seek, to be with her dear dead son" (*LG* 303).
Whitman's postwar project of feminizing race is thus embedded within a
larger project, the creation of a national family romance which is intended
to minimize sectional, racial, economic, and political strife. Mammy appeals, if she does, less as an adult woman with her own sexual history than
as a child-victim forcefully sundered from her parents and from her original African home. After all, with her wagging, "woolly-white . . . head,
and bare bony feet," she asks only to be accepted as human, though it is
not clear that the speaker, depicted as a member of Sherman's army on
the march to the sea, accepts her as such.

"I will not gloss over the appaling [sic] dangers of universal suffrage in
the United States," Whitman explained in his reactive *Vistas*. "In fact, it is
to admit and face these dangers I am writing" (*PW* 2: 363). Universal male
suffrage was a desirable, democratic goal but not yet a practical one, he
believed. Favoring gradual rather than immediate extension of the suffrage to freed*men* (italics mine), Whitman opposed the passage of the Fif-
teenth Amendment (Allen 444–45), which held that "The right of citizens
of the United States to vote shall not be denied or abridged by the United
States or by any State on account of race, color, or previous condition of
servitude" (Zinn 194). And his letters home were peppered with derogatory references to "darkeys." "Dearest Mother," reads one,

> We had the strangest procession here last Tuesday night, about 3000
> darkeys, old & young, men & women—I saw them all—they turned out
> in honor of *their* victory in electing the Mayor, Mr. Bowen—the men were
> all armed with clubs or pistols—besides the procession in the street, there
> was a string went along the sidewalk in single file with bludgeons & sticks,
> yelling & gesticulating like madmen—it was quite comical, yet very dis-

gusting & alarming in some respects—They were very insolent, & altogether it was a strange sight—they looked like so many wild brutes let
loose—thousands of slaves from the Southern plantations have crowded
up here—many are supported by the Gov't. (*Corr* 2: 34–35)[4]

Yet if in the post–Civil War period Whitman's racial prejudice became
more pronounced, he was also becoming more open to the possibility of
arming white women with the vote. As editor of the *Brooklyn Daily Times* in
1858, he had written contemptuously of the view that "woman ought to be
placed politically and industrially on a level with man and to be allowed to
swing sledge-hammers, climb the giddy mast, and hit out from the shoulder at primary elections" (*I Sit* 46). Reporting on "One of the queerest
conventions on record even in this land where all extremes of belief meet
upon a common ground and all sorts of odd-fishes do most congregate,"
he attributed to these antebellum feminists gathered in Rutland, Vermont,
whom he characterized as "amiable lunatics," the view that "The marriage
relation . . . was a detestable humbug" (45, 46). In *Vistas*, however, he had
begun to revise his earlier prejudice against female suffrage. "The day is
coming," he explained, "when the deep questions of woman's entrance
amid the arenas of practical life, politics, the suffrage, &c., will not only be
argued all around us, but may be put to decision, and real experiment"
(*PW* 2: 401). Women might be developed, he affirmed, to be "robust
equals, workers, and, it may be, even practical and political deciders with
the men." But how their potential careers as practical politicians might be
reconciled with "their divine maternity, always their towering, emblemati-
cal attribute" (*PW* 2: 389), Whitman left it to the future to decide.[5]

In the more or less completed essay that was published in 1870, Whitman has little to say about the realities of race in the Reconstruction era.
Instead, as one critic has noted, "he appears to substitute a lengthy discussion of women's elevation for any mention of racial equality" (Weisbuch
85). Searching for "a great moral and religious civilization—the only justification of a great material one," Whitman felt compelled to rehearse his
personal discovery of the tragedy of American culture. "Confess," he
wrote, returning to the world-weary mood of his letter to Ellen O'Connor,

that to severe eyes, using the moral microscope upon humanity, a sort of
dry and flat Sahara appears, these cities, crowded with petty grotesques,
malformations, phantoms, playing meaningless antics. Confess that everywhere, in shop, street, church, theatre, barroom, official chair, are
pervading flippancy and vulgarity, low cunning, infidelity—everywhere
the youth puny, impudent, foppish, prematurely ripe—everywhere an
abnormal libidinousness, unhealthy forms, male, female, painted, pad-
ded, dyed, chignon'd, muddy complexions, bad blood, the capacity for
good motherhood deceasing or deceas'd, shallow notions of beauty, with

a range of manners, or rather lack of manners, (considering the advantages enjoy'd,) probably the meanest to be seen in the world. (*PW* 2: 371–72)

Whitman mentions "the capacity for good motherhood" only in passing, but this capacity is the redemptive focal point of the passage. In the cities, where an "abnormal libidinousness" prevails, colors and forms bleed into each other to produce degeneracy. "Good motherhood" thus functions as a categorical absolute that distinguishes sex from sex and race from race. A return to the traditional preindustrial, rural values signified by this unamplified trope will, Whitman hopes, arrest the unhealthy proliferation of sexualities and the allied hybridizations of race that concern him here. In this urban wasteland, morally astute men such as himself are marginalized, whereas women can still aspire to an indispensable social, economic, and biological role. Perhaps, though, if women return to their destined maternal mission, men too will find meaning in living. In short, "good motherhood," an unamplified and I shall argue unamplifiable trope, is Whitman's solution to the problem of modernity, figured here as the suspension of meaningful sexual, racial, and social norms.

## II

"The capacity for good motherhood" on which so much seems to depend had long been central to Whitman's thinking about women, a subject about which he had once asserted his total ignorance, perhaps in jest. In one of his earliest essays, when he was still Walter Whitman, Junior, the unhappy schoolteacher, he emphasized his desire to write a "wonderful and ponderous book," surveying "the nature and peculiarities of men." But he added, "I would carefully avoid saying any thing of woman; because it behoves a modest personage like myself not to speak upon a class of beings of whose nature, habits, notions, and ways he has not been able to gather any knowledge, either by experience or observation" (*UPP* 1: 37). Subsequently, he made it a point to abandon modesty and to proclaim himself the poet of the woman the same as the man; in his poetry, he engaged in dramatically compelling cross-dressing. But just as Whitman overestimated his access to the experience of blacks—witness "Ethiopia Saluting the Colors," with its embarrassing, highfalutin approximation of pidgin English—so too when he claimed to speak for women, especially in their capacity as racial and sexual gatekeepers or as socially integrating forces, his claims are suspect; for one thing, he slights the importance of agency and negates the free play of female subjectivity. Thus Joanne Feit Diehl reproves him for chauvinist imperialism when she observes that "essential as the Whitmanian Mother may be, she remains an instrument, as through her the poet reaffirms *his* own priority" (11).

When Whitman objectifies women as mothers charged with the burden of achieving social consensus—whether by keeping the races apart or by keeping them together—he feels compelled to represent them as selfless. Two brief examples may suffice. The first, to which I return further on, is a genre portrait of an archetypal mother "quietly placing the dishes on the suppertable." This almost excessively clean white mother, in "There Was a Child Went Forth," has no discontents or dissatisfactions, at least none that Whitman the now-grown-poet-child is willing to pursue. She is apparently fulfilled by what he calls in another 1855 poem "womanly housework," and "the beautiful maternal cares" ("To Think of Time," *LG* 437). This archetypally gratified and gratifying mother, the mother as selfless nurturer, is very different from the love-hungry mother depicted in "The Sleepers." In that episodic 1855 poem, Whitman's own mother, Louisa Van Velsor Whitman, is defined by unsatisfied desire. But here, too, Whitman's mother is presented before she was a mother, when she was still a girl, "a nearly grown girl living home with her parents on the old homestead" (*LG* 429). Haunted by her past, she is a rare figure in Whitman's composite catalog of maternal types, who function in the present as links to the future, their girlhood obscured as completely as Emily Dickinson might have predicted. For unlike Whitman, Dickinson was fascinated by the uncanny eclipse of the girl's life in the life of the wife but had very little to say about the erotics of maternity or about mothers as morally and biologically superior beings. In Whitman's poetry, however, the ideology of woman as mother tends to produce the ideology of woman as Gratified Mother. Whitman, that is, shifts the emphasis from volatile representations of life in process to rhetorical statements designed to arrest further questionings. Morally coercive statements such as "The wife, and she is not one jot less than the husband, / The daughter, and she is just as good as the son, / The mother, and she is every bit as much as the father"—taken from the 1855 poem "A Song for Occupations"—attempt to sum up a subject that has not been carefully examined (*LG* 212). Abstracted from time, "motherhood" functions as premature closure, a resolution to an anxiety that is insufficiently voiced.

In addition to racial restiveness, what might the anxiety be? Lewis Hyde observes that "As in those churches in which sex is tolerated only as an instrument of procreation, it is a persistent quirk of Whitman's imagination that heterosexual lovemaking always leads to babies. His women are always mothers. No matter how graphically Whitman describes 'the clinch,' 'the merge,' within a few lines out pops a child" (185–86). The word "heterosexual" certainly suggests one possibility, namely that Whitman is using maternity as a trope for sexual normality and is mediating personal, psychosexual anxieties, as well as cultural ones, when he describes himself and all men as "Unfolded out of the folds of the woman." Sacralizing female fecundity, he attributes his ethical, psychological, and linguistic virtues to a source common to himself and to all men, an archetypal Poem-Mother who is "brawny," "arrogant," "strong," "well-muscled" and, in a word, mannish (*LG* 391). Infallibly transmitting her earthiest, "friendliest," and most "perfect body" to the speaker, she also transmits such characteristics as superior wisdom, sympathy, and justice. What she does not transmit is an enduring system within which conflicts can be negotiated—conflicts between, say, sympathy and justice, silence and language, imitation and originality.

Sporadically, however, the maternal body, as interpreted by Whitman, has the power to authorize love between men. "Unfolded out of the strong and arrogant woman I love, only thence can appear the strong and arrogant man I love," he writes. "Unfolded by brawny embraces from the well-muscled woman I love, only thence come the brawny embraces of the man." Conventional readings of this highly elliptical 1856 poem, which was then called "Poem of Women," link it to Whitman's interest in eugenics. But as the poet of women, Whitman writes of himself. The utterance of a man caught up in an urgent moral dilemma, his need to affirm what he also denies, "Unfolded Out of the Folds," like other programmatic poems in this apparently sexually explicit, heterosexual genre, makes its strongest claims on us as personal poetry. Beginning in a vaguely pornographic vaginal economy that compels strict obedience to sexual and moral abstractions in which, with his love of shapely particulars, he cannot truly believe, Whitman delivers himself to still other realms of abstraction where, while much is "unfolded," much is concealed.[6]

As my examples are intended to suggest, the life of the mother is not usually a topic that Whitman explores very deeply from the perspective of a particular woman with a personal past whose current consciousness is embedded in specifically recognizable material circumstances. Nevertheless, Whitman believed in his right or rather his obligation to speak for others whom the culture had officially silenced. But he incautiously exaggerated his access to the specific historical experience of groups whose identities and desires he had not fully fathomed but which he claimed to comprehend and to possess. Consider the following famous self-definition:

I am the poet of the Body and I am the poet of the Soul,
The pleasures of heaven are with me and the pains of hell are with me,
The first I graft and increase upon myself, the latter I translate into a new
    tongue.

I am the poet of the woman the same as the man,
And I say it is as great to be a woman as to be a man,
And I say there is nothing greater than the mother of men. (*LG* 48)

Beginning freely and abstractly with an ungendered invocation of body and soul that refuses to acknowledge conventional associations of the body with femininity and of the soul with masculinity, Whitman progressively suggests that self-consciousness, as exemplified by a socially productive relationship to nature and to language, is a male prerogative. Shortly, the opening lines, which are contextually indeterminate, themselves accrue a history; the troubled issue of context reasserts itself. In the first triplet, the botanical metaphors that might further demonstrate the speaker's liberation from time and his inauguration of an ampler, less narrowly realist era produce the opposite effect; the metaphors that enact his spiritual growth cannot be sustained. In the second triplet, we see that Whitman continues to employ neatly organized, oppositional pairings. But they are by now more pronounced, there being more of them. These pairings reinscribe a pervasive nineteenth-century myth that, in identifying women with nature and not culture, limited their access to the male symbolic order. Finally one of the poet's "crudest statements on gender" (Ostriker 227), this potentially visionary passage collapses into praise not just of motherhood but of the mothering of men as the supreme goal of any woman's destiny. The effect of such language is, D. H. Lawrence has apocalyptically contended, to reduce woman to a biological function and to objectify her as a womb (157).

Recently, however, one of Whitman's most astute critics has urged us to consider motherhood as a trope for other forms of creativity, rather than as a purely biological or narrowly familial role. In *Whitman the Political Poet*, Betsy Erkkila writes that

> Although Whitman insisted on the superiority of the mother, he did not limit the female to a maternal *role*, or trap her in what Simone de Beauvoir would later call biological "immanence." . . . Whitman sought to revive the mother not as a biological function only but as a creative and intellectual force. . . . His mothers do not exist as wives in relation to individual husbands, nor are they pious, pure, domestic, or self-sacrificing in any limited sense of the terms. Like feminist works ranging from Margaret Fuller's *Woman in the Nineteenth Century* (1845) to Charlotte Perkins Gilman's *Herland* (1915) to Adrienne Rich's *Of Woman Born: Motherhood As Experience and Institution* (1976), Whitman sought to remove motherhood from the private sphere and release the values of nurturance, love, generativity, and community into the culture at large. Exceeding the bounds of home, marriage, and the isolate family, Whitman's "perfect motherhood" is motherhood raised to the height of solicitude for the future of the race. (258–59)

In one sense, Erkkila is right. For in such lines as "And I say there is nothing greater than the mother of men" there is no husband to whom Whitman alludes directly, unless that husband of the spirit be Whitman himself. And certainly mothers may transmit some of their values to the culture through their sons and daughters, though whether those values can automatically be equated with "nurturance, love, generativity, and community" remains doubtful. Indeed, in a subsequent work Erkkila herself deconstructs this romanticization of womanhood as she challenges the historically neutral, unifying trope of sisterhood. In *The Wicked Sisters: Women Poets, Literary History, and Discord,* she seeks to reclaim "women's literature and women's literary history as a site of dissension, contingency, and ongoing struggle rather than a separate space of some untroubled and essentially cooperative accord among women" (4). But these are precisely the sorts of historical tensions that Whitman's mythicizing motherhood tropes are designed to repress; there are very few internal contradictions by which his "mothers" are discursively constructed. So even though Whitman at one point described himself as the medium for his own mother's (presumably coherent) moral vision and credited Louisa Van Velsor Whitman with generating *Leaves of Grass* (*WWC* 2: 113–14), most contemporary feminist readers will, as Ostriker has done, resist the Whitman who speaks in the passage from "Song of Myself" quoted above.[7]

Both Erkkila and Ostriker would seem to suggest that even Whitman's most problematic statements on gender "are revolutionary compared to the sentimental conventions of his own time" (Ostriker 227). Yet discussions of antebellum and postbellum literary sentimentality within the past decade or so have highlighted the antipatriarchal, matrifocal elements contained within the Cult of True Womanhood itself. Under pressure of such analysis, categorical distinctions between revolutionary, socially subversive, and socially conservative styles tend not to stand up to close scrutiny. Whitman's famously heterodox style, with its extraordinary linguistic, psychological, and intellectual range, makes it even harder to define definitively the shifting relationships between language, on the one hand, and the institutions that regulate social power, on the other, which readers may encounter within any single version of *Leaves of Grass,* let alone within the multiple published versions that constitute his variants.

Contending with these issues, Sandra M. Gilbert, while comparing "The American Sexual Poetics of Walt Whitman and Emily Dickinson," suggests that

> We cannot . . . ignore the fact that both poets assimilated experimental passages . . . into extended sequences whose sexual modalities appear continually to reiterate and reinforce traditional definitions of masculinity and femininity: lapses of gender, indeed, seem to occur because of lapses of genre rather than the other way around. In fact, it is likely that the subversions of stereotypical sexuality which do mark Whitman's and Dickinson's writings are consequences, rather than causes of these poets' mutual disaffections from stereotypical "poetry," specifically from its coherent "voice," its cohesive "form," and its conventional language, rhyme, and meter. It is arguable, in other words, that for both poets the wellspring of all alienation was a profound literary alienation. (130–31)

Gilbert's cogent analysis nevertheless leaves unanswered the question of what, other than literature, motivates literary alienation. And for a poet such as Whitman, who identified his body as his inspiration, literature seems an insufficient (though a necessary) source. Given this much-emphasized relationship between Whitman's body, his gendered subjectivity, and the urgency of his sexual poetics, it seems more likely that Whitman's disaffection from stereotypical poetry was motivated by his erotic disaffections, rather than the other way around. In what follows, I shall continue to suggest that Whitman's poetry was shaped by his gendered ambivalence to personal, political, and literary history, and that the effect of such deeply disturbed, creative ambivalence on women readers, including women poets, has been far from uniform.

## III

To declare oneself the poet of women is one thing; to enact the role of the poet so as to transform that capacious and perhaps not wholly benign desire into performative utterance is another. When Whitman writes, "What exclamations of women taken suddenly who hurry home and give birth to babes, / What living and buried speech is always vibrating here, what howls restrained by decorum" ("Song of Myself," *LG* 36), or when he writes, "My voice is the wife's voice, the screech by the rail of the stairs, / They fetch my man's body up dripping and drown'd" (*LG* 66), is he preempting women's speech or encouraging it? Perhaps, as Adrienne Rich has suggested, "The issue of the writer's power, right, obligation to speak for others denied a voice, or the writer's duty to shut up at times or at least to make room for those who can speak with more immediate authority—these are crucial questions for our time" (Rich, "Eye of the Outsider" 131).[8] The line between sympathetic identification and erasure of the other's irreducible subjectivity is a fine one, as is the line between sympathetic identification and living as another because one cannot or will not live as oneself. Magnificently "Carrying the crescent child that carries its own full mother in its belly" (*LG* 64), the Whitman persona shows off in ways that are rhetorically forbidden to the characters who are his individual creations. As the figure of capable imagination, he necessarily directs the show, however indebted he may be to Nature, the unselfconscious Poem-Mother without whom there would be no show.

Thus despite the fact that Whitman vehemently saw himself as the poet of the woman as well as the man, that he once described *Leaves of Grass* as "essentially a woman's book" (*WWC* 2: 331), and that many nineteenth-century women readers were tantalized, encouraged, and fortified by his writings, there were of course many nineteenth-century women who ignored, rejected, or otherwise problematized his claims.[9] In April 1862, for example, Emily Dickinson told Thomas Wentworth Higginson, an abolitionist activist, women's rights advocate, and literary critic with whom she had just begun to correspond, "You speak of Mr Whitman—I never read his Book—but was told that he was disgraceful" (2: 404). Possibly she was being ironic in representing herself as the docile recipient of received ideas. Possibly not, for she may also have wanted Higginson to know that she was at least somewhat aware of current big-city literary gossip and not nearly as rustic as she was pretending to be. As she continued to play the game of ranking writers in her correspondence with Higginson over the years, other names surfaced. "Of Howells and James, one hesitates," she later wrote (2: 649). This was long after their first meeting in 1870, when she startled him with such comments as "I never had a mother. I suppose a mother is one to whom you hurry when you are troubled" (2: 475), a theme she picked up in a subsequent letter when she explained punningly, "I always ran Home to Awe when a child, if anything befell me. He was an awful Mother, but I liked him better than none" (2: 405). Dickinson, we know, enjoyed being disgraceful herself—or at least playing at disgrace. Possibly this fascination with social, sexual, and linguistic transgression accounts for the emphasis of her Whitman disclaimer to Higginson in 1862. Possibly not.

In addition to Josiah Gilbert Holland, a close family friend who as the editor of *Scribner's Monthly* later rejected Whitman's poems with insulting letters, there were many people who might have cautioned Dickinson against Whitman, including Higginson, a conflicted genteel critic who eroticized his relations with men but who also and not coincidentally repeatedly attacked Whitman's political, sexual, and literary morals in print. So what is surprising here, in April 1862, is that Higginson appears to have been directing Dickinson toward Whitman as the forerunner of a new kind of experimental poetry that she herself was engaged in writing. Higginson also advised her to "delay 'to publish,' " which she did, and when Dickinson's posthumously published poems began to appear in the 1890s, reviewers were somewhat prepared by Whitman's innovations and scandalousness for her deviations from the genteel norm. For all her formal and psychological subversions of the culture's grammar, at least she wasn't Whitman, they thought. Her rhymes might be off-rhymes, but they were rhymes nevertheless (Buckingham 15 and passim).

We don't know if Dickinson ever read Whitman's "Book," though she is likely to have read "As I Ebb'd with the Ocean of Life" when it appeared in April 1860 in the *Atlantic Monthly*, to which she and her family subscribed. There, under the title "Bardic Symbols," she would have encountered that "fierce old mother," the Whitmanian sea, "endlessly" crying for her "castaways," including the corpse of the earlier poet who had believed in his ability to "condense—a Nationality" ("Death of Abraham Lincoln," *PW* 2: 508) regardless of race, sectional and economic difference, sexual orientation, and gender. Dickinson almost certainly read brief excerpts from "As I Ebb'd" and even briefer excerpts from "Song of Myself" in Holland's paper the *Springfield Daily Republican* in 1860, as well as a derisive long column entitled " 'Leaves of Grass'—Smut in Them" (Eitner, Keller). But she never mentioned Whitman elsewhere in her correspondence and so far as we know there were no *books* by Whitman in her library at her death or in the library of her sister-in-law and brother next door.

One of the people who might have warned her against Whitman was her sister-in-law and best friend, Susan Gilbert Dickinson. Sue advocated the passionlessness that enabled American Victorian women not to become the mothers of many children, and erotic demonstrativeness made her nervous. At one point in the early 1880s she cast Dickinson herself in the role of a fallen woman, after having stumbled upon the poet "reclining" at home in the arms of Judge Otis Lord, a widowed male friend. Ironically, Sue warned the sexually venturesome Mabel Loomis Todd to safeguard her husband against the Dickinson sisters, explaining that "They have not, either of them, any idea of morality" (qtd. in Bingham 59). Sue's sense of sexual morality was prudish by modern standards and perhaps even by the standards of her day. But in other respects she was an enlightened woman: a thinker and a doer. She participated in an important nineteenth-century social movement, the movement to limit the size of families, which was crucial in liberating women from motherhood as a totalizing, privatizing, nonaggressive social role. Whitman's poetry is totally insensitive to this issue. More is always better.

All too often, then, Whitman conceives motherhood as a uniform and unifying role, signifying "a vast similitude" (*LG* 1860: 230); mothers do not disrupt, challenge, provoke, or disappoint conventional expectations. They stand reassuringly for continuity and social integration, whereas the Whitman persona stands provocatively for change and intellectual individuation. Fatherhood is a less all-encompassing role and it has a more overtly aggressive marketplace dimension. If these views partly correspond to the political, economic, and social realities of Whitman's time, they also respond to the anxieties of an emerging consumer society in which economic competition between men was so fierce that the prospect of widespread, voluntary participation by middle-class women in the marketplace was intolerable, as David Leverenz and others have shown.

As the self-proclaimed poet of the body, Whitman aggressively endorsed an ideology of Real Womanhood, modeled somewhat after the radical speeches and writings of his firebrand heroine Frances Wright. In her *Views of Society and Manners in America* (1821), Wright had suggested that "The American women might, with advantage, be taught in early youth to excel in the race, to hit a mark, to swim and in short, to use every exercise which would impart vigor to their frames and independence of their minds" (qtd. in Killingsworth 66). In the scandal-producing 1856 "Poem of Procreation," later entitled "A Woman Waits for Me," Whitman characterized the women whom he hoped metaphorically to mate in similar terms:

They are not one jot less than I am,
They are tann'd in the face by shining suns and blowing winds,
Their flesh has the old divine suppleness and strength,

> They know how to swim, row, ride, wrestle, shoot, run, strike, retreat, ad-
> vance, resist, defend themselves,
> They are ultimate in their own right—they are calm, clear, well-possess'd
> of themselves. (*LG* 102)

The Cult of True Womanhood, with its emphasis on the physical, emotional, and mental difference between men and women and the corresponding difference between their social talents and missions, struck him as
an ideological distortion of a healthier natural project.[10] Undraping himself and encouraging his readers to do the same, in his 1856 "Clef Poem"
he had asked, "Do you suppose I wish to enjoy life in other spheres? / I say
distinctly I comprehend no better sphere than this earth, / I comprehend
no better life than the life of my body" (*LG* 1860: 229). To prove the point,
he included the following lines, which he later deleted:

> I am not uneasy but I am to be beloved by young and old men, and to love
> them the same,
> I suppose the pink nipples of the breasts of women with whom I shall
> sleep will touch the side of my face the same,
> But this is the nipple of a breast of my mother, always near and always di-
> vine to me, her true child and son, whatever comes. (*LG* 1860: 229–30)

Proclaiming his freedom from gender anxiety, Whitman seems to authorize cross-generational homosexuality with multiple partners; to authorize
heterosexual relations with multiple partners outside marriage; and then
to privilege a physically and psychologically incestuous relationship with
his own mother. The narrative (if any) that joins these sequential fantasies
is not easily retrieved, but it appears that his mother was the unwitting
partner of his compulsion to substitute physical for verbal expression. Fe-
tishizing his mother's breast, he publicizes their lack of effective verbal
communication. Perhaps this admittedly speculative biographical context
specifies a way in which "Leaves of Grass is the flower of her temperament
active in me." For if not through the body, how could a poet such as Whitman communicate with a mother whom he described as "illiterate in the
formal sense but strangely knowing" (*WWC* 2: 113–14), a mother who also
told a chance visitor, "He was a very good, but very strange boy" (qtd. in
Perry 19)?[11] On still another level, the contextually troubled passage
quoted above may be read as Whitman's attempt to acknowledge and to
exorcise the terrifying (because permanent) infantilization that followed
from excessive dependence on a personal or a cultural mother who, because of the claims made on her by other men and women, young and old,
is unable to respond adequately to the poet's unique sense of personal election, in itself so electrifyingly powerful as to constitute divinity. In any
event, lines such as these produce discomfort because they are the product
of discomfort; Whitman was right to excise them.

Ceding women practical and moral authority within the home as he does in *Democratic Vistas*, Whitman is unwilling to cede them cultural authority in the public sphere. If "the best culture will always be that of the manly and courageous instincts" (*PW* 2: 396), then the best culture will tend to silence women. Ironically, living in a separate sphere called Motherhood drives the Whitmanian mother toward sexual purity, since she is not usually represented as engaged in sexual relations with others or as desiring human contact, though she is always available, at least in theory, to her child. Rather, to the extent possible, the Whitmanian mother is self-dependent. Her alienation from emotionally gratifying relationships with other adults, whether men or women, is reinforced by the fact that Whitman typically erases masculine presence from the home and from his construction of the ideal family. We see this absence of the father in his early fiction as well as in his word portraits of working women in *Democratic Vistas*. When he is willing to represent the lives of adult men and women functioning within the home as he does in the 1855 poem "There Was a Child Went Forth," the results are highly problematic. Here, in the only scene in *Leaves of Grass* in which a married couple with children are up and about and more or less relating to each other within an enclosed domestic space, violence erupts as the archetypal father edges warily into his preordained role as moral monster: "The father, strong, self-sufficient, manly, mean, anger'd, unjust, / The blow, the quick loud word, the tight bargain, the crafty lure, / The family usages" (*LG* 365). The idealized mother and the unidealizable father send each other to extremes. She becomes the selfless Angel in the House, the maternal madonna; a winning icon of wholesomeness, she remains untouched by the vengefulness of her husband's passions: "The mother at home quietly placing the dishes on the suppertable, / The mother with mild words, clean her cap and gown, a wholesome odor falling off her person and clothes as she walks by" (*LG* 365). Children, Whitman implies, need to be protected from unregulated male aggression by their mothers, who participate in asymmetrical power relationships by which they are eerily empowered. So even if the social project is not to keep women confined within the home, the psychological project is to keep men out of it, in part to avoid moral pollution and to keep children safe.[12]

Without intending to silence women, Whitman suggests even in this comparatively fluid 1855 poem that domestic morality is woman's special province and that mild words alone are relevant to her peace-keeping mission. "One genuine woman is worth a dozen Fanny Ferns," he remarked succinctly, after he had quarreled with Sara Willis Parton, who was the first woman to praise *Leaves of Grass* in print. "The majority of people do not want their daughters to be trained to become authoresses and poets," he observed in this same 1857 editorial, while he was arguing against "Free Academies at Public Cost." The majority of people, he added, want for their daughters "only that they may receive sufficient education to serve as

the basis of life-long improvement and self-cultivation, and which will qualify them to become good and intelligent wives and mothers" (*I Sit* 53–54).[13]
He must have been right, but more than a hundred years later, it is distressing to hear this antiprogressive message from the poet of *Leaves of
Grass*.

At the same time, then, that Whitman was actively championing economic equality for women, deploring their low wages, and representing
them in a variety of economic roles in his journalism, in his poetry this
larger social context tends to drop out. Except for those rare moments
when he identifies with women artists and with women as frustrated lovers,
the life of women as he imagines it is simply less various than that of men.
They contain fewer multitudes economically, intellectually, and psychologically, though on them, granted, the future of the race is said to depend.
Challenging the nineteenth-century cult of domesticity and the allied doctrine of separate spheres, Whitman also tended to reinscribe it. Of such
fundamental contradictions is his poetry made.

As we have seen, throughout his life as a poet, Whitman identified linguistic creation with the disruption of conventional gender rules and roles. In
that sense, he projected himself as an antinatural poet, for there was little
doubt in his mind about nature's normative social text: it was originally
heterosexual. Fracturing and multiplying this text almost beyond recognition so as to destabilize the sexual binaries on which the erotic myths of his
culture depended, the poet nevertheless adhered to a maternal ideology
that tended to subordinate women to men. Inspired initially by a strong
mother who accepted him uncritically and categorically, the subsequent,
less "natural" Whitman listened carefully to the voices of other women,
thwarted as his mother had been by marriage, who wished to be heard in
their own right and not merely as instruments of the male symbolic order.
Because of the power imbalance between his parents—his mother psychologically strong, his father psychologically weak—Whitman experienced
himself as having been subjected to "the empire of the mother," though at
the same time he was also painfully conscious of his mother's thwarted
aspirations for a more self-determining life. Here was a woman, he knew,
who might have been happy, who had a gift for happiness, and who succeeded in preserving some semblance of family unity despite powerful
pressures to dispersion. Here was a woman, too, who drained his energies,
who misunderstood him (to the extent that she understood him at all), and
who was not shy about voicing her needs. Walt, she wrote, was her "good
old standby" (qtd. in Walt Whitman, *Faint Clews*). Walt, she wrote, was the
son she trusted.

Given this biographical paradigm, Whitman the social visionary found
himself in a classic double bind which may be summarized as follows. On
the one hand, he wished to reinscribe the role of the mother as an enduring archetype of personal and national strength; on the other hand, he
wished to liberate women from the inevitable confinements of this role,

just as he sought to liberate himself from the confinements of his role as dutifully successful son. This situation of ambivalence toward the mother and toward the social and economic obligations of the son proved discursively productive. At one end of the spectrum, the mother, for Whitman, came to represent "the origin of all poems" rather than a fixed social identity. At the other end of the spectrum, the mother represented a social and biological fate. At the heart of his poetic project, then, lay a complicated relationship to a personal mother, to the social institution of motherhood, and to the literary institution of sentimental domesticity by which "motherhood" was discursively constructed. Critiques of Whitman as a woman-identified, feminist poet have traditionally failed to accommodate the complexity of his interventions in this cultural conversation.

## Acknowledgment

I am grateful to Carolyn Allen, Calvin Bedient, Paula Bennett, Margaret Dickie, Betsy Erkkila, Jay Grossman, Caroline Klumpar, and the anonymous referee for this volume for insightful criticisms of drafts of this essay. Their diverse and probing commentary reaffirmed my sense of the complexity of the subjects I had chosen to discuss and helped me to think through some of the issues and assumptions that I had initially deployed more casually. In some instances, they vigorously dissociated themselves from my conclusions, which is as it should be. "Whitman" truly *is* large and does contain multitudes.

## Notes

1. As the feminist historian Mary Ryan explains in her book of the same title, *The Empire of the Mother: American Writing about Domesticity 1830–1860,*

Despite the incongruity between the domestic mystique and the realities of an industrializing society, the cult of the mother's empire continued to gain converts during the 1850s. Even the fledgling women's rights movement succumbed to its seductions. This process is illustrated by the women's rights journal founded by Amelia Bloomer and titled, ominously, *The Lily.* In its early issues, *The Lily* printed adamant proposals for sexual equality, and sarcastically reviewed the "namby pamby sort of articles on women and wives." By the mid-1850s, however, *The Lily* enthusiastically endorsed a thoroughly domestic image of woman: "Not in the whole world . . . is there a character as heroic as the home mother." While she was to remain in her isolated domestic sphere, the ideal woman was invested with incomparable power. *The Lily* maintained that "Without home, without the domestic relations, the love, the cares, the responsibilities which bind men's hearts to the one treasury of their precious things, the world would be a chaos, without order, or beauty; without patriotism, or social regulation, without public or private virtue." (111–12)

2. Bercovitch refers to *Democratic Vistas* as Whitman's "towering state-of-the-covenant address," yet he argues that the work "has proved disappointing as political or social commentary because it is a work of symbolic interpretation. Its terms are doomsday or millennium." He further notes that a "determination not to surrender the dream, because the dream was the only option to despair, informs Whitman's work" (198).

3. For a reading of this passage that draws attention to its historical evasiveness but that concentrates on the decomposing materiality of the (presumably white) corpse, see Sweet 75–76. He observes that the scene "is conceived in such a way as to demonstrate that effacing the history of death in war and achieving the ideological significance that makes sense of death in war are a single operation."

4. Several years later he was to break with his champion William Douglas O'Connor, author of the pugilistic "Good Gray Poet," over just this issue. During the heated presidential campaign of 1872 in which Horace Greeley vied openly for the black vote, O'Connor accused Whitman of bigotry; Whitman, who was supporting Grant, responded recklessly; and the damage was done. The friends did not speak again for more than a decade, though Whitman extended his hand when they met by chance on the street the following day. For the most thorough study of the Whitman-O'Connor relationship, see Loving, *Walt Whitman's Champion;* for the view that erotic complications determined the rupture, see Cavitch 173–85.

On slave-owning in Whitman's family background, see Justin Kaplan 131–32; and Allen 15. On family attitudes toward blacks, see also George Washington Whitman 4–5, 127, 156, and passim. In the late 1880s, when Horace Traubel was questioning him about his racial attitudes, Whitman conceded, "After all I may have been tainted a bit, just a little bit, with the New York feeling with regard to anti-slavery" (*WWC* 3: 76).

5. Needless to say, women today continue to negotiate these issues. In my own state of Washington in 1992, Senator Patty Murray was elected as "just a mom in tennis shoes." She proudly adopted this slogan after it had been derisively coined by a male colleague in the Washington legislature. But when it was announced early in her Senate term that Murray had canceled her appointments for a day to stay home with a sick child, many of my own hardworking feminist colleagues were indignant. They didn't cancel classes when their children had the flu; why should she?

6. For a reading of this poem that places it in the context of nineteenth-century eugenics, see Killingsworth 62–65. He suggests that "Enfolding and effusing—the actions of the female genitalia—become the model for ideal creative power," but does not fully persuade himself that this is the case. More generally, in "Procreation and Perfectibility: 1856," in *Whitman's Poetry of the Body,* he argues that "Whitman's woman—rather than developing fully as the archetypal model for creative power—becomes something of a cog in the eugenic machine" (73).

7. See also Michael Moon's superb reading in *Disseminating Whitman,* which emphasizes Whitman's nongeneric use of the word "men" (78), as well as his devaluation of women who are not mothers.

8. The context for her remark is a critique of Elizabeth Bishop's "Songs for a Colored Singer."

9. The classic nineteenth-century feminist appreciation of Whitman is by Gilchrist—his most influential, enthusiastic, contemporary woman reader. For a fine study of Gilchrist's often tormented life, see Alcaro.

10. The classic account of this ideology is Welter. The opposing ideology of Real Womanhood is set forth in Cogan.

11. For another view of Louisa and literacy, see the fine essay by Eve Sedgwick and Michael Moon in this volume.

12. Both Erkkila (*Whitman the Political Poet* 257–59) and Ceniza ("Walt Whitman" 51–52) implicitly and explicitly describe Whitman's women as moving out of the home rather than remaining confined within it. Erkkila further describes the conflict between Whitman's emphasis on the power of motherhood and his admiration for women such as "Frances Wright, George Sand, Margaret Fuller, Anne Gilchrist, Lucretia Mott, and Delia Bacon—all women who had challenged traditional women's roles" as "a contradiction at the root not only of nineteenth-century American culture but of feminism itself" (*Whitman the Political Poet* 315–16).

13. For an account of Whitman's quarrel with Fern, see Warren. For a critique of this account, see Ceniza, "Review."

# 7

# Whitman's "Whoever You Are Holding Me Now in Hand": Remarks on the Endlessly Repeated Rediscovery of the Incommensurability of the Person

## ALLEN GROSSMAN

*Whoever You Are Holding Me Now in Hand*

Whoever you are holding me now in hand,
Without one thing all will be useless,
I give you fair warning before you attempt me further,
I am not what you supposed, but far different.

Who is he that would become my follower?
Who would sign himself a candidate for my affections?

The way is suspicious, the result uncertain, perhaps destructive,
You would have to give up all else, I alone would expect to be your sole
    and exclusive standard,
Your novitiate would even then be long and exhausting,
The whole past theory of your life and all conformity to the lives around
    you would have to be abandon'd,
Therefore release me now before troubling yourself any further, let go
    your hand from my shoulders,
Put me down and depart on your way.

Or else by stealth in some wood for trial,
Or back of a rock in the open air,
(For in any roof'd room of a house I emerge not, nor in company,
And in libraries I lie as one dumb, a gawk, or unborn, or dead,)
But just possibly with you on a high hill, first watching lest any person for
    miles around approach unawares,

Or possibly with you sailing at sea, or on the beach of the sea or some
  quiet island,
Here to put your lips upon mine I permit you,
With the comrade's long-dwelling kiss or the new husband's kiss,
For I am the new husband and I am the comrade.

Or if you will, thrusting me beneath your clothing,
Where I may feel the throbs of your heart or rest upon your hip,
Carry me when you go forth over land or sea;
For thus merely touching you is enough, is best,
And thus touching you would I silently sleep and be carried eternally.

But these leaves conning you con at peril,
For these leaves and me you will not understand,
They will elude you at first and still more afterward, I will certainly elude
  you,
Even while you should think you had unquestionably caught me, behold!
Already you see I have escaped from you.

For it is not for what I have put into it that I have written this book,
Nor is it by reading it you will acquire it,
Nor do those know me best who admire me and vauntingly praise me,
Nor will the candidates for my love (unless at most a very few) prove victo-
  rious,
Nor will my poems do good only, they will do just as much evil, perhaps
  more,
For all is useless without that which you may guess at many times and not
  hit, that which I hinted at;
Therefore release me and depart on your way. (*LG* 115–17)

It seems to me that all valid poems begin at the moment when speech of
the poetic kind is seen to be the only recourse of the speaker—when, therefore, the criterion of speech of the poetic kind is seen to be "your sole
and exclusive standard"—all other means of response being exhausted or
unavailable (among which exhausted means may be poetry itself, before
the revolution intended by *this* poet). It is in this sense—as the last means
available for the disclosure and grounding of the incommensurability of
the person, (the residual function of poetry as Whitman understands it)—
that I take up and "hold" Whitman's poem ("Whoever you are holding me
now in hand"), and find myself addressed by it as in a primal schoolroom
of moral courtesy, like a knight upon whom a lady has laid the obligation—
the decorum—of an ordeal, or like any novice in the service of the master
of a practice.

Whoever you are holding me now in hand,
Without one thing all will be useless,

I give you fair warning before you attempt me further,
I am not what you supposed but far different.

This poem (the third of the "Calamus" sequence) presents the problem of its own use (the "holding" of it) as the discipline of the meaningful "use" of a person. What voice, then, do I hear when I hear the voice in this poem? I hear the startled outcry ("Whoever you are holding me now in hand") of the half-blind master (he cannot quite *see* you, "whoever you are")—*a master but also one who speaks with the irascibility of a subjected will, a will suddenly at the end of its resources*—precisely the "companion," certainly not in the ordinary sense a hero—an instrument, rather, a *metier,* the lyre, the book: very small, capable of being taken up and secreted about the person ("Or if you will, thrusting me beneath your clothing"), a body that cannot choose to signify or not, that speaks poetically because it has no means other than the poetic to regulate the outcome of an occasion it did not elect. The occasion being, let us say, the inevitable self-presence of the body.

"Hit on," taken up, touched on his blind (his corporeal) side, he (or she, the gender is indifferent) pronounces nonetheless, as an archlover, that is to say as a master of representation (after the manner of Christ speaking to his apostles in preparation for the *transfiguration:* "If any man would follow me, let him deny himself and take up his cross. . . ." [Matt 16: 24ff])—pronounces a stern *ars amatoria*—the "art of love" of the body of the book considered as a person ("Who is he that would become my follower? / Who would sign himself a candidate for my affections? / The way is suspicious, the result uncertain, perhaps destructive, / You would have to give up all else, I alone would expect to be your sole and exclusive standard / Your novitiate would even then be long and exhausting," etc.) Thus speaks the book of the Whitmanian nomothetic or disciplinary master of love—*the esoteric carpenter of a new mediation,* "*love of comrades,*" and of a new institution, "the institution of comrades"—uttering the iron law of the person in relationship: "I am not what you supposed, but far different."[1]

The "result is uncertain" because the *incommensurability* criterion required by "the love of *comrades*" ("comrade" being the mediation that specifies equality) paradoxically entails *invisibility.* There is no image of the incommensurable, as there is no actual social formation characterized by equality, and therefore there is no image of the person. But the sufficient condition of any *actual* state of affairs ("the *love* of comrades") is *visibility;* and the principle of the institution of visibility is *commensurability* which entails hierarchy (the principle of institution, just so), and hierarchy (the defeat of equality) is the sufficient condition of (poetic) representation, as it is of any *actual* state of affairs (social, linguistic, or perceptual). Thus, the way becomes dangerous; and the only commissioned guide is the esoteric master of representation (poetic knowledge) who keeps the secrets of his art. What are those secrets? They are the terms of the enigmatic negotiations between *the absolutely contradictory requirements of human value:* friendship based in equality (comradeship), and human presence based in representation (love). The "enigmatic negotiations" of which I speak are the new inactual poetics of the Whitmanian "greatest poet."

Let me put the matter in another way: equality, as Aristotle made clear in his complex theorization of the relationship of comrades (e.g., *Nicomachean Ethics* VIII, vii), is the only sufficient condition of comradeship or friendship, because it is the only just response to the claims of persons in relationship; but equality (which does not mean that persons are of the same specifiable value, but that persons are all possessed of the same incommensurable value-bearing nature) cannot be an actual state of affairs, as the framers of the American Constitution found when they undertook to *institute* the Declaration of Independence. Whitman was well aware that "to be in any form" was to be a represented image to another, and that to *be* in any form—including the human form—implied a judgment as to what could occupy the finite space of appearance. The "prudence" of the "greatest poet" is to mediate this problem. Hence the greatest poet "judges not as the judge judges but as the sun falling around a helpless thing" (*LG* 713). This is, however, a paradox since *to be in human form* (the only state in which justice is meaningful) requires hierarchy (injustice). All appearance casts a shadow (a "dark patch"). To be just, therefore, requires disappearance from the finite space of the actual such as Whitman's speaker (his book, presenting the greatest poet) enacts and laments. To go the way of the greatest poet (the "equable" one) is precisely uncertain of result, a dangerous way, suspicious, perhaps destructive, presided over by the subjected master (at the edge of actuality) of a paradoxical art which is at once the sufficient condition of universal justice (appearance) and is also by its nature unjust (appearance precludes other appearance): hence, an impossible art or craft, at best the exploit of a few, esoteric.

Accordingly, Whitman's "Calamus" is an *esoteric* pastoral, a narrowing of the genre of the pastoral text toward the problematic of its fundamental motive, knowledge of other minds, or more precisely, *instruction* in the knowledge of other minds.[2] But what would such knowledge be like? Like touch? Like reading? Like sleep? Or would it be, as William James proposes, somehow (poetic) knowledge of the unknowable ecstasy of others leading to the valorization of all mind? Would it be, therefore, justice at last? The pastoral is, in any case, the schoolroom of poetic representation of the *hetairos*, the *alter*, the other—the comrade—as a speaker.

Schoolrooms and poems are alike in that both are sites on which instruction is reproduced, and also the possibility conditions of the reproduction of instruction—both the effects of literacy (for example) and the social formations in which literacy can be transmitted. Or, in the case of the poem, it is the site on which instruction is conveyed by a particular poetic text, and the means (as craft, for example) by which texts of that kind can be reproduced, poems made. This functional likeness of poems to school-rooms predicts that poems will be found in schoolrooms, and that in poems (such as Whitman's *Leaves of Grass*) schools are found. And as in every schoolroom a schoolmaster, so in every poem the master of poetic knowledge.

Hence, every school is both an exoteric (public) *and also an esoteric* (se-cret) institution. In a certain sense, schools are always exoteric, and instruc-tion always conducted in the public light of day, *the agora*, the marketplace. But schools are also, at all times, secret, esoteric, conducted in the dark—never other than the schoolroom of the unsearchable, the most passionate *transference* which is also the most Egyptian (occult, Harpocratic) wisdom, the source of justice because the beginning in the person of (social) con-sciousness altogether. In Whitman's pastoral of "Calamus" *(the pastoral of the enigmatic invisibility of the person: highest value, the "life that does not exhibit itself"),* the transference—that esoteric power of explanation for which the speaker in this poem speaks—is constituted of the primal scene of repre-sentation itself. More precisely, it is constituted of the logic of the primal scene on the basis of which representation is put in question.

Indeed, the Whitmanian talent, exhibited in the originality of his struc-tures, his "free" verse, consists in the capacity to scrutinize the logic of representation as he received it. This capacity takes the form of an ex-treme, interrogatory, phenomenological innocence: "This then is life . . . How curious! how real!" (as in "Starting from Paumanok," *LG* 16). Such is the primal scene in the light of which Whitman views all experience ("the wide flat space," where rises the live oak of Louisiana). In the light of that "space," Whitman undertakes that revision of the fundamental logic of representation (his new poetics, his cure of poetry by poetry) and therefore of the logic of love (since the logic of representation prevents the truth of love for the same reason that it prevents, as we have seen, the actuality of justice). Whitman's reinstauration of love by poetic means is the new thing for which we value him. Such working at (human) value, Whitman reminds us, is the basis of (poetic) value, the value of the poem and the value of the poet.

The speaker in the poem, "Whoever you are holding me now in hand," is to be accounted for as follows: at the moment when (and this is the effective moment of the Whitmanian practice) the material instrument of our discourse, which is *the person*, remembers suddenly *the logic of its own function, and ceases* to carry *our* messages, our own mystified reports of de-sire, into the world ("For it is not for what I have put into it that I have written this book") and at that moment begins *as an artifact which is also a person, to speak for itself on behalf of its own histories*—what does it say? It restates *the esoteric terror of its own making as the discipline of access to its nature.* "You would have to give up all else . . . / Your novitiate would even then be long and exhausting, / The whole past theory of your life and all confor-mity to the lives around you would have to be abandon'd."

To hold the "poet" in hand ("Whoever you are holding me now in hand") *as poet* (and not another thing)—*the poet whom you love as poet*—is to acknowledge that *the ethical logic of the man/book* to whom you have (because you love him) transferred the otherwise unsecured, secret logic of the intelligibility of your cosmos ("the whole past theory of your life") *is the same as the logic of representation, by which persons appear or do not to one another. In effect, the story of the love of the person who is known by reason of representation (because he or she appears) will be already written as the history of representation itself. Why? Because the story of love always has the same structure as the representations which manifest the lover, so that the healing of the story of love consists of the overcoming of the structure of representation—the freeing of the person from slavery to representation. Such slavery is exemplified by the enforced manifestation of the slave body in parts 7 and 8 of "I Sing The Body Electric"* (LG 98, 99). *Insofar as the representation is of a new kind, just so far the love of the poet as poet—which is to say the love of the other as comrade, as an agent of my representation—will be love of a new kind. And the coherence of the world—its poetry—will be of a new kind—perhaps just.*

*All of which is to say that when you "hit on him"—take him in hand, hold him— the one who is the companion utters the laws of his own making:* not the laws of procreation (the laws, by and large, of the "Children of Adam"), but the laws of representation or, more precisely, the laws of the instrument of representation as the principle of life. The soul of the carpenter is the statute of his rule, the "calamus." In Virgil's *Eclogues*, where the calamus is at home—"Pan was the first to make many reeds *[calami]* one with wax. / Pan cares for the sheep and the shepherds of the sheep" (*Eclog.* II, 34, 35). The making of many into one (*calamos . . . coniungere pluris*), of nature into representation, kills in one sense and quickens in another. In rhetorical terms, our poem—"Whoever you are holding me now in hand"—is an *ekphrasis* upon Whitman's book as a whole: "These leaves conning you con at peril." In the *ekphrasis* on the artifact, the artifact utters *laws*—always: "You must change your life" (Rilke), "Beauty is truth" (Keats), "Death is now the Phoenix nest" (Shakespeare).[3]

Indeed, the originary moment of Whitman's new pastoral—his new genre ("paths untrodden") exploratory of presence unmediated by representation and therefore appropriate to the celebration of the "need of comrades," acknowledged now for the first time as the vocation of the poet hitherto concealed even from himself ("clear to me now . . . that the soul of the man I speak for rejoices in comrades")—lies deep in the prehistory of poetry in the West. It is identical with the prehistory of the practice of any poetic speaker as such, any speaker whom we love *as poet* and not as any other thing, any messenger whom we value not for *this* message or *that* one, *but for the possibility of all messages.* Consider, for example, Hermes's salutation to the tortoise in the "Homeric Hymn to Hermes" (the earliest text in Western poetic theory) as it supplies the paradigmatic structure of the mediation signified as "comrade," and tells *the tragic history of which I speak*. In the hymn, the *hetairos* (the comrade) is none other than the musical instrument carved from the shell of a living tortoise, the lyre, at the moment of its first making. Hermes greets the tortoise whom he is about to destroy in order to make the first lyre in these words: "Hail comrade of the feast *(daitos hetaire)*, lovely in shape, sounding at the dance. . . . Living you will be a spell against deceptive witchcraft. But if you die, then you will make sweetest song" (11.51ff.).

Whitman's companion-master (*hetairos*, lyre, book) who speaks by the convention of the artifact in *ekphrasis* and says, "Whoever you are holding me now in hand," remembers the first making of the instrument of representation itself and is a singer (always) of inveterate, tragic histories structured hypotactically upon the violent constraints of exclusive "or," this but not that, *life or sweetest song*—the monologic rhetoric of the master who must be a "sole and exclusive standard." You will notice that Whitman's characteristic *parataxis* signified by the inclusive "or"—"Or else" (1.13); "Or possibly" (1.18); "Or if you will" (1.22)—is suspended in our poem like a dream in school *within* the hypotaxis of the tragic story (that is to say, between 11.1–12 and 11.27–37). How then (since his syntax of justice, paratactic order, is still captive within the hypotaxis of exclusion) can Whitman's song be new?

The originality of Whitman consists of a poetic discourse which presents itself as none other than the speech of the principle of representation which, casting off all other messages, utters in the uncanny language of liminality (Whitman's "free verse" considered as unmeasured, neither unmanifest nor manifest: subvocal, as it were virtual) the logic of its own history (life of one sort in place of life of another sort). In effect, the Whitmanian *poetry of last recourse undertakes what can only be done by poetic means, the cure of poetry by means of poetry of another kind*, the reinvention of representation through the overcoming of representation with the intention of producing by poetic means a "human form" that is truly human because free.

The speech of the esoteric master (we now see) is the speech of the founder by new poetic means of the institution which is the "institution of comrades," the successor institution to the institution of representation: "I hear it was charged against me that I sought to destroy institutions, / But really I am neither for nor against institutions . . . / Only I will establish . . . the institution of . . . comrades" (*LG* 128). "The institution of comrades" is intended to satisfy the equality criterion of the Declaration of Independence. *The originality of the companion as "greatest poet" is the articulation of the structural possibility-conditions of equality.*

Entrance into the institution of comrades—the polity of "love"—occurs by way of interrogation of the *askesis* (discipline) of representation, the logic of which is specified in the story of the construction of the lyre: "But if you die, you will make the sweetest song." The comrade is the principle of song—not the song of *Love*, but insofar as it is a case of representation, the song of all the love there is—the principle, in effect, of access to *you*. The "long-dwelling kiss"—the kiss prolonged—is the loving acknowledgment of another, acknowledgment which has been made free (or as free as poetic originality can make it—"long-dwelling," not eternal) of the tragic implications of appearance.

To obtain such access ("kiss") is to throw oneself upon the represented body (the nature of which as representation is the esoteric knowledge of the master) as if it were a vital afterlife (a secular eschatological sleep with death left out) of which the dream is "touch" (as in the playing of an instrument). "For thus merely touching you is enough, is best, / And thus touching you would I silently sleep and be carried eternally." This is the dream in the schoolroom dreamed by the esoteric master, the master of representation who is also a master of love.

The poem disseminated ("carried eternally") shows us what it might mean to "throw oneself upon the represented body" with the confidence of one who understands its terrors and by understanding would defer forever its fatality: "And thus touching you would I silently sleep and be carried eternally." But this "sleep" is also a death, for life in representation other than which there is no life is death-in-life (cf. "Song of Myself," stanza 50).

Who, then, is the follower of this master? Only the ascetic poet, strong enough to enter into the logic of his metier (and, by refraining from representation, live on) can hear this speaker, the schoolmaster of the schoolroom of the esoteric pastoral. ("The way is suspicious, the result uncertain, perhaps destructive.") What then, when it speaks on its own behalf, having put off the mystifications of our messages, does Whitman's book teach? What is the one thing without which all this will be useless? It is in a sense the esoteric truth (continually rediscovered, and hidden again, throughout the history of the world, and throughout the history also of every day, hour, and minute of human intercourse)—the truth of the incommensurability of the highest value—that is to say, *the truth of the incorporeality of corporeality as corporeality enters into the construction of human presence* which is what erotic love means to Whitman, the truth of it.

I will express this discovery as a set of *four Whitman principles:*

*The first Whitman principle* is that the person is the esoteric, that the esoteric is love which exacts acknowledgment of the invisible ("I am not what you supposed, but far different"), and that the school of the person is the esoteric school of the blind mirror of radical transference by which the invisible comes to be acknowledged as source, as first experience. The enactment of this acknowledgment is "the long-dwelling kiss" of the new husband, the comrade, which is prolonged within the context of the grammar of *scarcity:* the syntax of parataxis and inclusive "or" suspended within the syntax of hypotaxis and exclusive "or."

How is this "long-dwelling kiss" extricated from the actual state of affairs? By means, as I have indicated, of the paratactic countergrammar (or logic) of infinite resource—of which the determinator is the inclusive "or"

("Or else," "Or possibly," "Or if you will") which supplies the structure of the parataxis—the dream in school of that counterinstitution—the institution of comrades which is constructed by the speaker, the companion, the *metier* personified, the lyre, *the voice you hear.* The inclusive "or" is the signature in Whitman of the subjunctivity (counterfactuality, virtuality) of the discourse which takes itself into consideration as capable of justice and puts in question the fatality of representation.

*The second Whitman principle* is that all mediation is hierarchical (whether open or closed, free or bound, paratactic or hypotactic). "Nor will the candidates for my love (unless at most a very few) prove victorious." The book as speaker—stern master of the esoteric truth of the invisibility of the person—*is also unmistakably the archetypal erotic subordinate*, the one who is taken up and held, the lyre, the lover carried by the grace of the other into the absence of the other ("Carry me when you go forth over land or sea"), the beloved *hetairos* who dies, departs as air, waits patiently.

*The third Whitman principle* follows: All mediations are *techne* and all *techne* is nonethical, or (as Whitman prefers to express it) symmetrically ambivalent more or less: "Nor will my poems do good only, they will do just as much evil, perhaps more." Therefore representation, like all *techne*, in order to be put in service of the person, requires regulation. The regulative mimesis of this poem (it is after all a lecture), and the source of the speaker's despair ("Put me down and depart on your way," "Therefore release me and depart on your way"), is the always questionable problematic of the school: instruction considered as the paradoxical teaching of the regulative principles of nonethical representational technology: *what to do with what you hold in hand*—an ambiguous lesson in courtesy.

Whether you understand it to be the lyre, the calamus, or the book, there must be a regulative principle to contribute the *wisdom*, the ethical destination and the deeply Whitmanian courtesy of the *techne,* the sexual delicacy of the new husband, his human form: "Here to put your lips upon mine I permit you." The regulative principle, the *wisdom*, is exoteric and public, as the *techne* is Hermetic and esoteric. The former (the exoteric, the public, the ethical) dwells within the latter (the esoteric, the secret, the nonethical) in Whitman's text. That is, the Whitmanian paratactic reconstruction of public culture in the interest of abundance and intersubjectivity dwells structurally within, and is dependent on *the equally Whitmanian hypotactic culture of scarcity and monadological solitude.* Further, the hypotactic is prior—that kingdom of scarcity, that "wide flat space" in which is found the live oak of other mind.

*The fourth Whitman principle* is, in fact, the impossibility of teaching these principles ("Therefore release me and depart on your way")—these principles of the esoteric master, in whose school of love the instruction (by the nature of the lesson) *always* concludes with the sentence: "I am not what you suppose but far different." Such is the unassimilable lesson—desolate and fruitful—of the incommensurability of the person, the esoteric lesson, impossible to learn, and taught if at all by the esoteric master who is impossible to satisfy, which produces, nonetheless, the silent moment—the silence of unanswerability—to which I referred as the valid moment of the poetic intervention at the beginning of these "remarks" when I said: "It seems to me that all valid poems begin at the moment when speech of the poetic kind is seen to be the only recourse of the speaker—when, therefore, the criterion of speech of the poetic kind is seen to be 'your sole and exclusive standard.' " That standard—the poetic standard—establishes the difference of the person which is in the end always "far different." A difference by its nature always too far. But what is the insatiate *logic* that grounds and impels the Whitmanian confrontation with the impossibility of which the poem speaks? It is, perhaps, none other than the logic of the desire to prolong *this kiss*.

# Notes

1. Whitman's sense of the word "companion" derives, by whatever route, from Greek, *hetairos*, fundamentally the subject-other who dies—as in the case of Achilleus's Patroklos, or Gilgamesh's Enkidu, or Hesiod's tortoise in the "Homeric Hymn to Hermes" (see discussion later in this essay), but also Dante's Beatrice or James's Milly Theale. This "companion" figure is in the position of the discursive other, the other by reference to whom (and as a consequence of whose death) the self becomes real. The companion *(hetairos)* of tradition may be either male or female. The "carpenter" is of course a reference to Whitman's pictured self-image placed (instead of a signature or printed authorial name) opposite the title page of the first edition of the *Leaves of Grass*. Christ, like Whitman, was a (part-time) carpenter.

2. "Calamus" as a whole book within Whitman's Book is a reinvention of the genre of pastoral within the epic-scriptural discourse of *Leaves of Grass*. Pastoral, from Virgil's time at least, presents the relationship of two at the moment of the loss of the social conditions which make "comradeship" actual, that is to say at the moment of any person's entrance into history—*comradeship* being the just mutuality of two, sufficient knowledge of another mind; and *history* being the state (in representation) which renders comradeship unjust and therefore impossible, the state of representation as such. Whether the actual is figured as imperial appropriation (e.g., Virgil, *Eclogue* I), or as the death of Lycidas which the muses cannot prevent, because that death is the shadow entailed by representation itself which the muses signify, in either case, in pastoral *one person of two in relationship* has always already been displaced or destroyed. Whitman's "new" pastoral is an effort to return out of history to the prehistoric pastoral *topos* reconstructed as the life rid of the fatality of appearance—reconstructed, that is to say, as "Escaped from the life that exhibits itself" (*LG* 112). In effect, the pastoral is a schoolroom of the recovery *per impossibile* of knowledge of the friend.

3. *Ekphrasis*. A poem about an artifact in which (in the end) the artifact

declares by speaking (somehow) the rules of its own making *as if they were ethical imperatives*. Modern examples are: Keats's "Ode on a Grecian Urn" ("Beauty is truth, truth beauty, That is all / Ye know on earth, and all Ye need to know."); Rilke's "Archaic Torso of Apollo" (*Du must dein Leben ändern* / "You must change your life"); Shakespeare's "Phoenix and the Turtle" in which the emblem speaks the meaning of its construction, "Death is now the Phoenix nest." Whitman produces this poem ("Whoever you are holding me now in hand") constituted entirely of the speech of the artifact (his book, *Leaves of Grass*) personified as the masterwork which knows the rules of its own construction and promulgates them. Since in Whitman's poem the book is personified, such rules are rules of access to the meanings ("I am not what you supposed, but far different") and the incommensurable value ("already . . . I have escaped from you") of other persons. The artifact may of course signify sexually (cf. Rilke's "Archaic Torso"), but is not gendered (as artifacts are not). Anyone may join (of whatever class, sex, or gender) the institution of comrades provided they can endure the abstractness of the discipline which promulgates the principle— not freedom but justice. The abstractness of the discipline of just personal presence is what makes the way "suspicious," "uncertain," "perhaps destructive." Such is, in fact, Whitman's "breakthrough."

# 8

# Errata sobre la erótica, or the Elision of Whitman's Body

## JORGE SALESSI and JOSÉ QUIROGA

> "[A]nd believe it, gentlemen, or believe it not, when I got up next morning I had no more *slept* with Socrates, within the meaning of the act, than if he'd been my father or an elder brother. You can guess what I felt like after *that.* I was torn between my natural humiliation and my admiration for his manliness and self-control, for this was strength of mind such as I had never hoped to meet."
>
> Alcibiades in *The Symposium* (104)

*The voice in italics is Argentinean,* the second voice may be Cuban. The first voice will narrate an erotic encounter mediated by a book.

*It was Petronius's* Satyricon, *a scholarly reference at this point and in this context, but at that time a handbook of amatory desire between men, read for different literary values than the ones we might speak of in this essay.* But maybe not. *Then as now, Petronius was the intertext of dreams, the replication of an unending sexual urge that I* (that Argentinean I) *was desperate to share with schoolmates, especially with my "best (male) friend," the Giton of my Argentine Rome* (Giton, the lover). *But the reaction of my native Giton disappointed me. "You are funny" he said, and maybe it was true, sharing Petronius under Perón* (Perón, Evita's husband). *But I* (that Argentinean I) *persisted, and wanted to look for a way out of this more than textual* impasse. *Then I found Whitman* (one always finds Whitman at this time), *and invited my friend for a textual romp in a tree house. There, fondling and embracing* more than Whitman *over* Leaves of Grass, *but also above them, it worked. "I celebrate and sing myself," he said, and I said* (he said). *"And what I assume you shall assume." Line by line, a double voice emerged,* Whitman a duo, translating, *resurrecting,* eroticizing, *a certain Whitman* (Walt, the hemispheric poet). *The body of Whitman* (the body of the father figure called Whitman) *was the body that we could imagine being seduced by.*

These *Argentine* bodies implicitly asked a question about Whitman; they assumed a certain knowledge of their body and of their desire by the mediation of a book, by a "Song of Myself" reterritorialized into something else. As the performance continued, inhabiting a space of open doors (a tree house), Whitman's voice receded and the imaginary created the democratic lack of self that Whitman also desired. As with all fantasies, the unexamined is what gives this one a certain weight, allowing us to ponder a series of questions raised by a translated Whitman, loved as the possibility of a modern body—*a democratic nobody, to paraphrase Borges* (more on that later). Gay desire *(above all, gay adolescent desire)* turns Whitman into a textual erotic machine; it always rewrites his body in order to allow the subject to disappear and give way to the very mechanism of seduction. It is significant how, in that *Argentine* Rome, only Whitman—that ruddy internationalist with no cosmopolitan affectations—could carry the weight of erotic pleasure: it was a voice imported from another milieu that promised eros itself as salvation, beyond the liturgy of the church, beyond the dogmas of the military.

This scene of instruction appears as a biographical example, a personal history to be added to the already illustrious account of Whitman's reception in Latin America.[1] For it is well known, *at least to us,* that a poetical battle over Whitman has taken place in the "other" America *(Our America, said Cuban patriot José Martí).* The "conquest" of Whitman has enlisted the most celebrated figures of Spanish-American poetry: Martí himself, Rubén Darío, Jorge Luis Borges, and Pablo Neruda all read, misread, desired, repressed, had to come to terms with Whitman. The body of Whitman desired by love, negated by panic, framed by ideology, that arises out of these visible and invisible translations commands an already considerable bibliography in Latin America, for Whitman's promise was international in a curiously specific way. His use of *America* at times seemed to defy cultural insularity by ransacking all borders: the geographical border of the Rio Grande *(Rio Bravo)*, the linguistic border *(that of the langue)*, and the artificial and somewhat bureaucratized borders between certain states. Because what Whitman at times seems to promote is a continental panegyric where all questions are resolved by the sheer force of a will *(in the doubled sense of legacy and of self)*, his example shades imperceptibly into an imperial relation of cultural and political dominance as policy. Not wanting to add another biographical or bibliographical account to the story, we should say at the outset that the process of translation, as it is explored in this essay, entails its own particular version of economics: the object is not to rescue some pristine original, forgotten and elided, from a "target" language, but to look at how the original has been controlled to the point of defacement, and how this defacement negotiates love and eros by substituting, metaphorically, the machine for the body.[2] In other words, this essay wants to revisit the critical reception of Whitman in order to underscore the homoerotically repressed scenes of instruction that may lie at the root of the Whitman question in Latin America.

# I

Perhaps we should look into the translations of Whitman that were available in Argentina under Perón, in order to provide some sense of how Whitman's flesh may have been literally sublimated. To do so, we will put the translated machine first:

Tu jadeo y tu gruñir rítmicos, que ora se agrandan, ora decrecen a la distancia;
Tu gran reflector fijado en medio de tu negro frontal;
Tus oriflamas de vapor que flotan, largas y pálidas, ligeramente purpuradas;
Las densas nubes negras que vomita tu chimenea;
Tu osatura bien ligada, tus resortes y tus válvulas, el vértigo de tus ruedas temblorosas. (Whitman, *Poemas* 56–57)

This is a fragment of "To a Locomotive in Winter," and these panting, rhythmic gyrations, these dense and black clouds, spurt from a locomotive "chimney" that needs to be read as the body of Whitman and also as the sensual body of a locomotive of 1876. Translated by the Uruguayan poet, Armando Vasseur, in 1912, Whitman's locomotive is turned into an erotic manifesto that is already not without a certain Marinettian flair. In the original, the body is more mechanical:

Thy metrical, now swelling pant and roar, now tapering in the distance,
Thy great protruding head-light fix'd in front,
Thy long, pale, floating vapor-pennants, tinged with delicate purple,
The dense and murky clouds out-belching from thy smoke-stack,
Thy knitted frame, thy springs and valves, the tremulous twinkle of thy wheels. (*LG* 472)

The space of this reverential *thy* of the yanquee Whitman becomes the familiar and intimate "tú" of a Hispanic Whitman—"tu jadeo," "tu gruñir." But Vasseur's body-machine is always on the verge of collapse, convulsive and ecstatic: if Whitman's headlight merely protrudes, Vasseur's "reflector" illuminates but also reflects, imitating something situated not merely "in front" but "fixed" (fijado) on a black surface that resembles a forehead. We could say that in bridging the distance between the human, animal, and mechanical, Vasseur opts to bring the object closer to a living thing, with a closeness signaled by the familiar "tú." But the different registers of affect operating in Whitman's original and in Vasseur's translation are found when Whitman's murky clouds that belch out of a smokestack are transformed into equally dense, black clouds that a chimney vomits: "Thy dense and murky clouds out-belching from thy smoke-stack" is transformed into "Las densas nubes negras que *vomita* tu chimenea." Vomit always heightens the melodrama of an intensely visceral reaction evoked and provoked within the body as if some foreign agent had made its way through the hidden tracts of the body, and which only the body as a whole can expel as an animal would. Sentiment, for Vasseur, is already Nietzschean: it is melodrama, feeling, but a feeling that comes into contact with a resistant surface.[3] It is on this surface that we see Whitman's inscription, for Whitman can only be Vasseur's lover through the mediation of the machine, through the desire for the machine. For Vasseur to love Whitman, he can only manifest his love for a machine that rhythmically pants and roars.

The locomotive, with its never-ending cycles of appropriation and expulsion, can serve as an emblem of the literary and critical reflection on Whitman. In contrast, let us consider the marked change in tone, the more attenuated desire of the most quotable lines from Whitman's work:

> Me celebro y me canto
> Lo que me atribuyo también quiero que os lo atribuyáis
> Pues cada átomo mío también puede ser de vosotros, y lo será. (*Poemas* 115)

Vasseur's translation of the famous beginning lines of "Song of Myself" sounds hygienic, for the English "you" is always rendered into a plural "os." Unlike Spanish, English makes no distinction in its second person plural or singular, but Vasseur's choice of the plural has Whitman speaking not to an other, but rather to others that have to assume their very individuality by joining Whitman. If Whitman played, in his second-person address, with the singular and the collective, with a subject that may also become a nonsubject, a democratic *en masse,* Vasseur decides to meet Whitman from a collective mode of address that can only aspire to a personal engagement with Whitman by negotiating itself *out* of the collective: from plural to singular.

"My tongue, every atom of my blood, form'd from this soil, this air, / Born here of parents born here from parents the same, and their parents the same" (*LG* 29). For the son of a family of Italian immigrants, living under the Argentinean nationalist Peronist regime and reading in a tree house, these lines could only produce a certain unease, especially when Vasseur renders them in a tone full of nationalistic resonance: "Mi lengua, cada molécula de mi sangre emanan (notice the change: *emanate,* not *formed*) de esta tierra (*tierra: earth,* not *soil*) de este aire, / Nacido aquí, de padres cuyos abuelos y bisabuelos también nacieron" (119). Whitman's positing of a generational continuity, grounded in the American soil, contrasts with the social fabric of an Argentina composed of a considerable number of immigrants. The translation operates from the *you* to the formal *vuestro* in a tone of messianic fervor, not unlike a political harangue. "The leveling idea," Vasseur wrote in his introduction to the translations of 1912, "the love for common men, the ennobling of all the varieties of the *profanum vulgus,* the passion for Nature and for human liberty . . . the apotheosis of fecund sensualism and of physical beauty, shine in [Whitman's] poems like the Sword of the Archangel at the entrance to Milton's *Paradise Lost"* (48; our translation). According to Vasseur, what shines in these poems is of such a seductive force that sensualism, physical beauty, and passion itself are at the limit of an unknown that does not live in the future, but rather in some past to which we no longer have access. The poems are the very sword of the Archangel: they promise something that we can only remember, and mourn, as a loss. Lest any reader think of Whitman as a decadent poet, writing about the narcissistic and solipsistic self, Vasseur rewrites Whitman's song as an inaugural epic, a tale of forgotten origins whose reading carries a redemptive message for humanity.

Vasseur's comments reveal something of the anxiety that the translator must feel in presenting his original for a different public. Seen from this angle, it is curious that, in searching for a precedent for Whitman, Vasseur names no English Romantic, but rather Milton (perhaps a Blakean Whitman?). But the connection is explained by Vasseur's choice of "fecund sensualism" to describe Whitman, as if "fecund" itself needed to be underscored in order to repress the fact that Whitman may not be talking about Adam and Eve but rather, to put it bluntly, Adam and Steve. In order not to pass Whitman off as some kind of Wildean *maudit,* the cliché of Anglo-Puritanism needs to be invoked. Once the ground has been settled, once Whitman's name is affixed to an eminent tradition of morality, his message can be remotivated as Nietzschean ecstasy.

With morality's claims met, the space where the *you* (tú) appears, where the "fecund sensualism" can manifest itself, is within the glorious corporeality reserved for the ecstatic locomotive, the pulse of wheels and axles, the rhythmic frenzy of desire. If Vasseur desired Whitman's body, the translated love is sublimated into the machine. But a curious machine at that, one that withholds, represses, and can only expel whatever is inside as vomit. Perhaps we can say that Latin American poets under Whitman's spell rewrite Alcibiades's story in *The Symposium.* They would all sleep with their Socratic Whitman, but they find that the Socrates of this particular demos wants to sleep with them. Their flight into panic turns them into perverse Alcibiades inverting their desire for the master, turning his eminent sensuality into the flaming sword at the entrance of a paradise that they fear is but a more insidious version of an uncanny platonic cave.

## II

These mechanical tropes of inversion, repression, and elision that may be seen in Vasseur and throughout Spanish-American translations are predicated on the erratic and erotic encounters—the accidents—that lie over and under Whitman's Latin American literary body. Erratic because of the erotomania disguised by Whitman's Latin American incarnations, erotic precisely because of the erratic nature of this desire, one in which the vocabulary of literature threatens to be "contaminated" by a language of affection over and around Whitman's body. In order to address this, we need to revisit this structure as it is written and codified in the texts of Jorge Luis Borges and Pablo Neruda. We shall concentrate, in particular, on two of the most important essays on Whitman and Latin America that have been published recently: Doris Sommer's "Supplying Demand: Whitman as the Liberal Self" (1986), and Enrico Mario Santí's "The Accidental Tourist: Walt Whitman in Latin America" (1990). Sommer's essay deals with the imaginary reception and relationship that is called forth by Whitman, and through Whitman by his Latin American readers; Santí's essay concentrates on the biographical and bibliographical aspects of these Latin American readings of Whitman by considering a series of accidental revisions that account for the uncanny mode in which Whitman was received by poets as varied as Neruda, Borges, and Paz. In order to explore Whitman's visitations in the Spanish-American milieu, both essays engage two sides of a common narrative—one where bibliography and the imaginary coalesce. We shall use these essays as a point of departure for creating a kind of fantastic bibliography of the imaginary that would give an account of the erratic and erotic encounters this essay is interested in—erratic in terms of the accidental visitations narrated by Santí, erotic in reference to Whitman's body as the locus of a particular supply and demand narrated by Sommer. Bibliography, as we shall demonstrate, is always bound up with acts of imaginative, erotic, and necessarily cultural, intervention.

Doris Sommer sees Whitman as supplying his own demand, by offering a tantalizing, fragmentary totality of the self. Santí, on the other hand, explores how the imaginary relationship between Whitman and his translators arises from the mediated reception of texts. Both Sommer and Santí examine (and these are Santí's words) "the *erratic* relationship between Latin American poets and Whitman." This relationship "appears to be constituted by the disparity between what Whitman actually was and what they *imagined* he was and wrote" (161). Whitman forms, as Santí points out, a body of information that is filtered through the language of another removed from the original. The translations of Whitman confirm the alienated, second-order quality of this discourse. In the case of Vasseur, Santí shows how Whitman is received from Italian sources that are also intertextually contaminated by Nietzsche; Vasseur's voice negates temporality by working through a projection of the imaginary, and ultimately succeeds in presenting, in Santí's terms, a rhapsodic but not ecstatic voice. Following the injunction that Whitman also preached, and that was later learned, modified, and adopted by Borges, in order to *be*, one could neither translate nor imitate the voice. Or, as Whitman himself wrote: "He most honors my style who learns under it to destroy the teacher" (*LG* 84).

Carefully measuring the possible erotic exchanges between the poet's life experience and his poetry, Doris Sommer refers explicitly to the difficult negotiation of Whitman as homoerotic poet, a point that Santí alludes to at various points in his essay but does not openly address. Sommer explains that "[t]he scandal of displacing heterosexual love with homoeroticism is obviously related to Whitman's appeal for the reader's surrender, to the socially equalizing quality of his free verse. . . . Homosexual love, then, becomes an allegory for a nonhierarchical and truly democratic relationship" (80–81). She adds: "I doubt that Whitman's democratic ideal preceded or conditioned his sexual preference; but I am convinced that his homosexuality allowed him to feel what a radically democratic relationship would be, one that overcame both masculine domination and feminine coyness" (81). One could say that in her decision not to elude Whitman's biography, Sommer may herself project utopian fantasies of a radical gay democracy, while at the same time she points out Whitman's imagination of democracy as a homogeneous community and not as a community of differences. Sommer carefully reads this difficulty as originating in Whitman's homoeroticism, and as soliciting a reader's surrender, a point which Santí implicitly alludes to when he explores Borges's and Neruda's anxious and oscillating acceptance and rejection of Whitman. Nevertheless, it is unclear whether Latin American poets read the utopian projection of homosexuality as democracy in Whitman, or whether this substitution of the democratic polis for Whitman's supremely embodied homoerotics is instead simply another instance of a heterosexual imaginary's projection on homosexuality. We should turn now to Santí's narrative, in order to ground the terms for a future exploration of the mechanisms that Sommer writes about.

In "The Accidental Tourist," Santí explains how Neruda first wrote about Whitman at the age of eighteen under the pseudonym "Sachka," in a review of a translation of *Leaves of Grass* published in 1923. Neruda admonished in that review that "each poet will sing whatever he wishes without caring about Whitman's hygienic precepts" (qtd. in Santí 166). Thus, in a language couched in the "hygienic" Latin American discourse that, during the first decades of the twentieth century, mediates the translation of cultural and aesthetic models used for the construction of "healthy" Latin American nationalities, Santí points out how Neruda simultaneously accepts and rejects Whitman's influence. This ambivalence, Santí explains, becomes more telling when compared with another piece Neruda wrote the same year, but this time about the poetry of Carlos Sabat Ercasty, an Uruguayan poet who has been called "Whitman's apostle" in Latin America. Neruda's rave review of Sabat Ercasty (Santí calls it "sycophantic") demonstrates the extent to which the Chilean poet absorbed the Whitmanian influence he resisted in Whitman himself. Soon after, in 1923, Neruda began writing in the so-called "Sabat Ercasty mode" *El hondero entusiasta*, a book that would be published later with a preface in which Neruda admits that Sabat Ercasty's influence led him to suppress the book for *ten* years, and furthermore that the published work was, according to Neruda, "the document of an excessive and burning youth" (10).

Neruda's excessive ardor was part of the quest to create a "poesía aglomerativa"—a quest that he defers in order to publish, in 1924, his *Veinte poemas de amor y una canción desesperada (Twenty Love Poems and A Song of Despair)*. With this book Neruda achieved the renown that he wanted as a poet. As Santí correctly states, only by repressing Whitman's voice in himself could Neruda find his first (published) poetic voice, that of the melancholic lover of the *Veinte poemas*. What needs to be underscored here is the economy of desire and repression, the sexual link that Neruda feels in terms of a rambling *poesía aglomerativa*, somehow out of control, as if the body itself were to collapse by overexposing itself. It is obvious that Neruda felt that to import Whitman's style entailed some kind of masculine negotiation that needed to be sublimated as a difference between form and content. One could have either one or the other, but not both: one could employ the Whitmanian long line, imitating the precursor's cumulative poetry, or one could take Whitman's subject matter and write of intense desire and passions in the *Veinte poemas*. But it was to be always either one or the other. If we may take Santí's narration one step further, it seems that Neruda's sensuous desire needed to find another object: it could not allow *for itself* the desire *for the self* as a desired body, freely available to a supposed Whitmanian democracy of desirous subjects.

Neruda became one of the most important Latin American *love* poets of the twentieth century, but he could never be a poet of *desire*. Unlike Paz, for example, Neruda's body is only available as the lover of another object that is gendered as a Woman, as America, as History. The true poetry of desire had to wait for the patient elaboration that Octavio Paz was effecting throughout the 1940s, as he was also negotiating the influence of Whitman on his work.[4] What these Latin American negotiations suggest is that this literary process is eroticized by permanently displacing a repressed desire that is at once erotic and stylistic and "self-disciplinary." Young poets cap an "excessive and burning youth," finding their first poetic voice by avoiding any and all sexual and erotic manifestations of the desire that awakens it. Whitman becomes a kind of *pharmakon*, wanted and rejected at the same time.

The economy of desire and repression also works for Borges, who first encountered Whitman's verse in Geneva in 1917, while he was reading German Expressionist poetry. In his "troubled kinship" with Whitman—his desire to be, and not merely to imitate, the American bard—Borges had to negotiate between writing like Whitman, attacking Whitman's followers in Argentina in the 1920s, and finally reinventing Whitman as the desired (no)body. If Neruda's repression entailed pairing down a certain style, Borges's complex repression of Whitman sublimates the erotic call of the precursor by means of a wholesale eroticization, not of the body of Whitman, but of literature itself. Borges changes the object of that desire

(Whitman and his self) into an erotic relationship with literature. Hence the particular eros of Borges's very persona: the lover of books, the one who was able to transform Whitman's "infecund" sensualism into the "fecund" sensualism of the literary.

The telling avoidance of (or at least the negotiation with) Whitman's homosexuality is an important element of a translating machine that needs to internalize and withhold the sensualist Whitman, for this figure always demanded a convergence of the erotic and literary aspects of a work. Where we would undertake a revision of the bibliographical and critical work on Whitman in Latin America at this point is by opening up the closet of literary and critical representation. What this closet hides or uncovers is a critical machine where questions as to personal and "objective" readings are eluded and elided, where the body is always sublimated into the machine itself. The mere fact of translation, with its implications as to choice, renders useless the very distinction between personal and objective readings, for translation operates in a different space—with controls, valves, shifts, and pulleys all its own. Read this way, Whitman's influence on the twentieth-century Latin American lyric arises out of the continuous fabrication of the translating machine. Whatever it is that drives some poets and not others to Whitman needs to be explored by combining both the erratic and the erotic, if Whitman's polemical shadow is to be understood.

In terms of the choice of precursors, it is significant that these acts of difficult negotiation occur in poets who may not be classified as gay.[5] For a corrective and competing alternative version to this critique one might look at the very different reception accorded to Whitman within certain gay Latin American circles. When asked about Walt Whitman back in the 1930s, the openly gay Mexican poet Xavier Villaurrutia (one of those whom Neruda attacked while he was Chilean consul in Mexico), replied, perhaps with not uncommon prescience, that he was a poet for Boy Scouts.[6] The seductions of the translating machine obviously work in different ways and different modes. But the story of the gay nonreading of Whitman in Latin America still needs to be told. For the fact that Whitman appealed to "straight" poets already implies a particular mode of reading. "Gay" poets knew their Verlaine, their Nerval, and, like Villaurrutia, their Cocteau. Whitman's eros must have already reeked of campfires, of insect repellents, of wilderness trails, of boys who really liked orderly marches through insufferably ambivalent terrain.

## Notes

1. See, for example, Santí's "The Accidental Tourist: Walt Whitman in Latin America," discussed below, as well as Alegría's already classic *Walt Whitman en Hispanoamérica*.

2. An excellent example of this mode of critique may be found in Molloy's

"Too Wilde for Comfort: Desire and Ideology in Fin de Siècle Spanish America," which is in many ways the point of departure for this essay.

3. As Santí points out (163–64), Vasseur's translation owes a great deal to a growing Nietzschean cult in Latin America; on Nietzsche's gradual assimilation into Spanish, see Sobejano. It should also be pointed out that Emerson was increasingly translated into Spanish in the late nineteenth and early twentieth centuries, such that it is difficult to distinguish and separate out the common cluster formed by Nietzsche, Whitman, and Emerson at this time. For a further elaboration of this translation cluster and its effects on the transition between Spanish-American Symbolism and the Avant-garde, see Quiroga.

4. "The Accidental Tourist" opens with considerations of Paz's notions of hemispheric compositions mediated by Whitman during the 1940s. See also Paz's *Primeras letras (1931–1943)*.

5. This lack of appeal may be traced in part to the appropriation of Whitman by poets like Neruda who transformed Whitman into a powerful source for a critique against "cosmopolitan" or "elite" (read: gay) Latin American poets.

6. See Paz's *Hieroglyphs of Desire* 99.

# Whitman's Americas

# 9

# Homosexuality and Utopian Discourse in American Poetry

TOM YINGLING

with an Introduction by

ROBYN WIEGMAN

## Introduction

When Tom Yingling writes in the following essay that "No text exists before history," he is speaking of the way that textuality has no existence apart from or prior to the cultural contexts and historical contingencies that frame its potential meaning. In varying degrees, this statement accounts for Yingling's sense that the utopian gesture in American poetry is one of limits, and it is the particular contribution of his essay to this volume that he demonstrates the changing shape of these limits for poets in both the nineteenth and twentieth centuries. In doing so, his essay is an important commentary on the seemingly incommensurate relationship between those entities his title forthrightly couples, "Homosexuality and Utopian Discourse in American Poetry."

As he points out, the utopian is as central to the cultural rhetoric of "America" as homosexuality is antithetical to it. And yet, American poets beginning with Whitman, who is for many scholars the most important and most adhesive of them all, repeatedly set a utopian homoerotic unity against the *im*perfections of America. In this way, they unsettle those normative evaluations that cast homosexuality's eradication as the necessary preamble to America's utopian fulfillment, finding in this strange and seemingly unimaginable wedding something of America transcendent enough to claim. This is a far cry from the popular discourses of the contemporary era which, as Yingling mentions, continue to read homosexuality as the failed and faithless partner in America's democratic attainment.

But why invest, critically speaking, in the details, failed or revisionist, of this partnership? What constitutes the history that exists before this text? After all, in his gesture of reading the utopian Yingling participates in the critical project of those poets he examines—in the variously celebratory and condemning portraits provided by Whitman, Crane, and Ginsberg. Or perhaps I should say here that Yingling *begins* to participate, since his text, you will undoubtedly notice, never completes the argument it sets for itself. This, we might say, is symptomatic of the very encounter between homosexuality and the utopian that Yingling hopes to trace. This essay's form, in other words, plays out the incomplete and increasingly problematic relationship which Yingling asserts is characteristic of homosexuality and utopian discourse in American poetry itself.

According to this argument, the ontological status of both America and homosexuality undergoes increasing specification in the twentieth century, so much so that Crane and Ginsberg will have to grapple, as Whitman did not, with the dystopian rhetoric of homosexuality that comes to dominate a variety of cultural narratives of sexuality. Following Michel Foucault's work on the history of sexuality and Michael Lynch's delineation of its impact for and in American culture, Yingling believes that in Whitman we can recognize how "there was as yet . . . no language secure enough for the delimitation of homosexuality." It is this that makes possible the semiotic uncertainty that allows Whitman to wed homosexuality with the utopian, and it is the impossibility of maintaining such uncertainty under the historical conditions of early- and late-twentieth-century sexual formations that accounts for accusations against America's failure in the poetry of both Crane and Ginsberg. But in forging this distinction, Yingling is not saying that homosexuality was once utopian and now it is not; he is not lamenting a past that promised America as the land of homosexual fulfillment; he is not reading Whitman as making a claim for homosexuality as the "center for future social perfection." He is not making the past more complete, more historically or politically sufficient than the present.

Instead, Yingling interprets Whitman's poetry as functioning as a political strategy of displacement, in his words "a strategy not of replacing heterosexual with homosexual institutions but of rethinking altogether the notion of patriarchal institutions and their control over the individual." Such a rethinking leads to a more powerful and in many ways more utopian gesture on Yingling's part: that homosexuality can be read, in Whitman if nowhere else, as "the institution which ends institutions." There are many reasons why this is an important political strategy for the critic. Most crucially, it evinces his resistance to those discourses of identity that have underwritten the construction of homosexuality as an ontology since the late nineteenth century. Identities are not, for Yingling as for those critics he cites, liberatory categories that can be invoked for democratic inclusion by the excluded at will. As witnessed in the writings of Crane and Ginsberg, the emergence of a discourse of homosexual identity complicates the political terrain in which the utopian can be imagined, giving rise to this and other meditations on the institutional structure and force of America itself.

There is, of course, something else that must be said here, something not about Whitman, Crane, and Ginsberg, the trinity of poets culled together by the critic to explore an American history of homosexual and utopian affinities and disidentities. What of the trinity of critics—Foucault, Lynch, and Yingling—all of whom contributed in their own ways to the contemporary elaboration of the politics of sex and sexuality, all of whom are now dead of AIDS? The incompletion of Yingling's discussion marks the historical contingencies that frame these and other lives—the material limit, one might say, of coupling homosexuality and the utopian at the end of the twentieth century. When the critic writes, "no text exists before history," we must take him at his word.

R.W.

The political discourse in American literature has not always been utopian, but it has almost always had to take into account what America is, was, or might be, and that "might be" has always included a legacy of utopian promise. Similarly, homosexuality has always had to imagine the world other than as it is, reorganized socially, politically, and (sometimes) economically in order to award centrality and significance to the terms of the lives of gay men and women. This has not always led the homosexual writer into utopian questions, but in the case of American poets, where the utopian promise of America is a standard topos, the collision of the two has been remarkable. As Sacvan Bercovitch points out in *The American Jeremiad*, the term "America" has connotations of the national, spiritual, and ideological that do not obtain in other geopolitical labels like "France" or "England." Bercovitch writes that the term "America"

> bespeaks an ideological consensus—in moral, religious, economic, social, and intellectual matters—unmatched in any other modern culture. . . . Only in the United States has nationalism carried with it the Christian meaning of the sacred. . . . Of all the symbols of identity, only *America* has united nationality and universality, civic and spiritual selfhood, secular and redemptive history, the country's past and paradise to be, in a single synthetic ideal. (176)

This essay will look at the problem that arises for American poets like Whitman, Crane, and Ginsberg when homosexual desire becomes an important issue in the figuring of this utopian promise of America since homosexuality is usually held to be at odds with "moral, religious, economic, social, and intellectual" consensus. Because it has more generally been considered a social ill to be "corrected" than a factor that might contribute positively to utopian social organization, homosexuality is not part of the usual discourse of Utopianism, and we need only recall today's headlines to see how it still figures in patriotic rhetoric of a certain variety as an unAmerican activity, a practice threatening to the very fabric of our nation. Nor is America unique in this marriage of homophobia and nationalism. Homophobia and xenophobia were colateral signs in Regency Britain, as Louis Crompton's *Byron and Greek Love* points out; and the later nineteenth-century British empire feared homosexuality as the end of the race, as attacks on Wilde make clear.

Not so surprising is the fact that utopian discourse has often made an issue of gender and sexuality as a more general (i.e., heterosexual) problem. From the Shakers (religious celibates of the nineteenth century whose communities were separated along gender lines), through the nude-culturalists from the turn of the century to the twenties who were inspired by both anarchist political philosophies and philosophies of sexual liberation, to the commune experiences of the sixties and seventies (which seem to have been similarly inspired), American utopias have always had to imagine sexual relations and a sexual division or nondivision of their communities as one of the things that defined them as different from the dominant culture, as one of the terms of contest for utopia. Roland Barthes claims that "utopia begins" when "meaning and sex become the objects of free play . . . liberated from the binary prison" (Barthes, *Roland Barthes* 133), in this particular case the binary prisons of linguistics and gender. But most utopian communities have not been able to suspend the heterosexual binary so easily, and most communities have not been formed with a guarantee of free sexual practices (much less free homosexual practice) as one of their founding tenets. In fact, most have repressed sexual activity. Utopian anarchists after the turn of the century should not form colonies, one writer warned, because "if the colony is based on economic or political unorthodoxy it will be destroyed by the sexual radicals. That is to say, the economic and political radicals who are not also sexual radicals will not permit freedom of speech and life in sexual matters, and so disruption ensues" (Walker).

If we consider homosexuality not as a genital sexual behavior, however, but as a mode of social organization and interaction, then we can see that homosexuality is a social question of some urgency for utopian discourse *beyond* the relatively simplistic question of whether or whom to fuck. If we think of Foucault's work on the history of sexuality, it is easy to see homosexuality deployed across social space in patterns that make it either a refusal of or a submission to modes of social organization and control, a deployment, resistance, and submission in which are implicated not only the more obvious modes of patriarchal repression but also more subtle questions of capital, social bonding, and institutional allegiance. It is my contention that Whitman, Crane, and Ginsberg (each in a different socio-historical milieu) ground their poetry in a homocentric vision of unity and transcendent possibility against which they test an imperfect "America," what Ginsberg calls "the lost America of love" (Ginsberg, *Howl* 24). It would be well to decide whether in this context "utopia" is merely a euphemism for "genderless" society, and whether "genderless" is itself a euphemism for "male"—whether the male homocentric vision of utopia is based on an elimination of the female, and whether the gay male vision of the good life is merely an orgy of male bodies.

It is necessary to ask this because it is certainly one of the forms of expression seen in gay male media and fantasy. And, unfortunately, these cultural practices might be more relevant to the "real" than the relatively theoretical literary utopias this essay engages. But for Ginsberg, Crane, and Whitman, while none of them is without his misogynistic moments, the desire for utopia is *not* exactly akin to the heterosexual male desire to escape, control, or eliminate the female; it involves a rethinking of social organization on a scale that includes a rethinking of the question of woman (although it seems not often to include a rethinking of the question of the lesbian). We do have examples of women's texts that depict utopia, if not strictly as the absence of men, then as a site where the absence of men contributes to gynocentric possibility. Charlotte Perkins Gilman's *Herland* (1915) is perhaps the classic example of this since it so clearly partakes of utopian conventions. But there are other, perhaps more familiar, texts such as Adrienne Rich's *The Dream of a Common Language,* the very title of which points toward a u-*topos* or non-site of transparent speech; in "Natural Resources," Rich confronts in only slightly mocking form this question of a unigendered world:

*Could you imagine a world of women only,*
the interviewer asked. *Can you imagine*

*a world where women are absent.* (He believed
he was joking.) Yet I have to imagine

at one and the same moment, both. Because
I live in both. *Can you imagine,*

the interviewer asked, *a world of men?*
(He thought he was joking.) *If so, then,*

*a world where men are absent?*
Absently, wearily, I answered: Yes. (61)

Rich's dream of a common language founders, if it does, on the mythological dimension of its desire—it is perhaps only a dreamed utopian landscape. But I want to use her text to return to the question of gay utopia because Rich more explicitly than the gay men I am interested in here is aware that the problem of gender, the problem of sexuality, and the problem of utopia are all more properly the problem of language.

Joel Barlow is a name no one would expect to find in this essay. But Barlow, Connecticut Wit, good Federalist, and later anti-Federalist American that he was, begins an important topos for American poetry (especially American epics, which more properly engage the question of political and social formations and which Whitman, Crane, and Ginsberg all considered themselves to be writing), a topos that continues through Adrienne Rich. He sees that the "problem" of America (for him, the problem of bourgeois democracy) is involved with the problematic of language. He sees (although he does not see that he sees) that representation (political and linguistic) will not work. Long before Pound, in a lengthy footnote inspired no doubt by Leibnitz, he solves this by appeal to the ideogram as a writing that refers directly to the real; but he is condemned to write in English, and he does so (by all accounts) rather badly.

*The Columbiad* (1807), however, established two interesting motifs that are helpful in thinking through this problem of homosexual utopia in America: one, "America" is actually for Barlow an unwritten text, an entity that exists only as promise, a literally uninscribed wilderness that cannot yet be articulated—"America" is unnamed space; two, there will be a future moment in which the legacy of Babel will be reversed—all peoples of the earth will be educated to democracy, one transparent language of unlimited capacity will replace all others simultaneously and there will be no more linguistic deferral, duplicity, or difference. In the end, wars will cease and suffering end because utopian "America" *will* be a literalized second coming of the word.

It is helpful to see that the first of these motifs partakes of what Bercovitch has suggested is the rhetorical function of "America" as a sign; "America" works as that space of perfection to which reformists can call the nation in the name of its own best intentions. It is, therefore, always empty, ready only to be called to that perfection and utopia it is. Although a deist, Barlow evidently still needed this vision of a millennium; he was one of four Americans considered radical enough to be awarded honorary citizenship by the Revolutionary government in France.

I turn now to another, more recent French connection, Roland Barthes, for whom the text, being of the "order of the signifier" produces an opposite utopian configuration of language; for Barthes, the text participates in its own way in a social utopia; before History (supposing the latter does not opt for barbarism), the Text achieves, if not the transparence of social relations, then at least that of language relations: the Text is that space where no language has a hold over any other, where languages circulate

(Barthes 1973, 164).[1] No text exists before history, of course; all reading, all desire is historical, and this textual dream of something beyond history is a phantom of Barthes's most elegant desire. His contention is somewhat similar to Barlow's in that whether one considers it conventionally as a threshold of transparency or from a poststructural point of view as an opaque textuality where signifiers refuse any hierarchy, law, or order, the utopian is what it has always been—that which does not yet and never will exist (something like "America").

But if Barthes's contention is somewhat similar to Barlow's, its difference is more significant for my purposes, for Barthes sees utopia as a strategy and not as a deferred result, place, or goal; utopia is for Barthes a way of reading that refuses the canons of law. And Barthes, also a homosexual, finds in the figure of the wandering signifier the perfect synecdoche for gay utopia: the subject loosed of its social respectability, its required or expected meaning, allowed to circulate at will and even perversely among its fellows. Gay utopia is, in this case, an orgy, an instance of pleasure and bliss; the body—Whitman's body electric, Ginsberg's shocking anatomy, Crane's "diaphanous body of the world"—each is the site of textual *jouissance*. Men become, in each of these four texts, signifiers freed of their "souls" and allowed to point horizontally at other men, referring freely, promiscuously, polymorphously to one another.

If America never exists, and utopia is a problem of language—what are we to make of homosexuality? Does it exist? Many of us seem to think so. But does it exist outside language, outside of thinking it as a relation among other discourses and practices? Of course not, and because of this, it is itself always a sign of a deferred state, a political and rhetorical construct. This is the burden of Whitman's "Calamus," and the reason why, I would claim, all three of these issues (America, utopia, homosexuality) come together in the work of other poets as well; Whitman can make homosexual cities the center of his continental vision because both homosexuality and America have no ontological status beyond that of being textual, utopian effects. I will not have time to go deeply into this, but the claim about Crane and Ginsberg would be that they are thrown into increasing tension on this because both "America" and "homosexuality," as they become signs for distinct geopolitical and social entities, lose the elasticity that allowed Whitman to make them utopian. Indeed, both participate in dystopic rhetoric. Crane agonizes over the failures both of America and of his homosexual "lust." Ginsberg (in the role of prophet) blasts America for its failure, and of the three he is the most resolute in locating a restored utopian potential of America in a liberated erotic community that seems quite specifically (but not limited to the) homosexual. Whitman's vision, however, seems untarnished by any reality whatsoever. He writes:

Come, I will make the continent indissoluble,
I will make the most splendid race the sun ever shone upon,

I will make divine magnetic lands,
  With the love of comrades,
    With the life-long love of comrades.

I will plant companionship thick as trees along all the rivers of America,
  and along the shores of the great lakes, and all over the prairies,
I will make inseparable cities with their arms about each other's necks,
  By the love of comrades,
    By the manly love of comrades.

For you these from me, O Democracy, to serve you ma femme!
For you, for you I am trilling these songs. (*LG* 117)

Whitman does not turn here from the subject of homosexuality to the more significant subject of democracy, as critics have been quick to claim; only for those critics is democracy a displacement of homosexuality. For Whitman democracy is the mother of homosexuality, that matrix from which it springs.

But clearly this is not far from standard rhetorics of American perfection—only now the "paradise to be" will include (at its center perhaps) a place for homosexuals ("inseparable cities with their arms about each other's necks"), and this rhetoric of a perfectly homocentric world reappears ironically as the epigraph to Ginsberg's *The Fall of America* (1972), a text that all too clearly sees the failure of that democracy Whitman championed:

> I confidently expect a time when there will be seen, running like a half-hid warp through all the myriad audible and visible worldly interests of America, threads of manly friendship, fond and loving, pure and sweet, strong and life-long, carried to degrees hitherto unknown. . . . I say democracy infers such loving comradeship, as its most inevitable twin or counterpart, without which it will be incomplete, in vain, and incapable of perpetuating itself. (*Democratic Vistas* [1871]; qtd. in *The Fall of America*)

It is interesting that when Crane defends Whitman to Allen Tate as something other than an enthusiastic Americanist, it is to this text that he too points.

Another poem from "Calamus," however, appears to participate just as fully in this dream of a new continent founded in homosexual attachment:

> I dream'd in a dream I saw a city invincible to the attacks of the whole of the rest of the earth,
> I dream'd that was the new city of Friends,
> Nothing was greater there than the quality of robust love, it led the rest,
> It was seen every hour in the actions of the men of that city,
> And in all their looks and words. (*LG* 133)

Whitman finally goes so far as to claim that homosexuality rather than democracy is in a cosmic sense the calling of the United States: "I believe the main purport of these States is to found a superb friendship, exaltè, previously unknown, / Because I perceive it waits, and has been always waiting, latent in all men" (*LG* 134).

Just as America remained a future and unlimited possibility because one of its codes was "the-as-yet-unwritten," there was as yet ("Calamus" was written around 1857–60) no language secure enough for the delimitation of homosexuality (Michael Lynch's essay on the gradual delineation of homosexuality as a pathology in the nineteenth century is interesting on this point); although he borrowed the term "adhesiveness" from phrenology, and this had connotations of its own, the desire Whitman was interested in could be represented in almost any fashion he desired. This is part of what makes his text "scandalous"—that he writes of not just what cannot be politely written of, but what in some sense cannot be written of at all because it does not yet exist. His text continues to seduce, I would claim, precisely by virtue of its namelessness, its uncertainty, its ability to entertain meanings not dependent upon fixed semiotic practices. Whitman's text demonstrates an uncanny homosexual ability to identify a "same" by attention to the different, an ability to cruise its reader skillfully:

> Ah lover and perfect equal,
> I meant that you should discover me so by faint indirections,
> And I when I meet you mean to discover you by the like in you. (*LG* 135)

Whitman never seems in need of an adequate vocabulary for the representation of homosexuality; he insists rather that homosexual moments are remarkable only in that they are exceptional:

> What think you I take my pen in hand to record?
> The battle-ship, perfect-model'd, majestic, that I saw pass the offing to-day under full sail?
> The splendors of the past day? or the splendor of the night that envelops me?
> Or the vaunted glory and growth of the great city spread around me?—no;
> But merely of two simple men I saw to-day on the pier in the midst of the crowd, parting the parting of dear friends,
> The one to remain hung on the other's neck and passionately kiss'd him,
> While the one to depart tightly prest the one to remain in his arms. (*LG* 133)

It is important to see in this last example that the male bonding depicted by Whitman is not exemplary of the homosocial bonding of which Sedgwick has written. This is, rather, a vision of relations between men where no middle term representative of exterior forces of power intrudes; this is

desire without triangulation, or with no triangulation other than the triangulation of language, textuality, and readership (no mean set of triangula-
tions, granted). But if all desire is mediated, if neither internally nor exter-
nally is the object of desire pure or purely itself, what nevertheless makes
Whitman's text so radical is precisely its ability to imagine relations between
men as not based on commercial, sexual, or racial exploitations. Male
bonding in Whitman is not based on a displacement of desire but on its
enactment freely and openly between two men whose sexuality requires no
mediating other. (It is, as this essay has not yet suggested, a truly utopian
text.)

As this would imply, what is truly radical about Whitman's vision of
homosexual utopia is its relation to the issue of institutions; what is often
not immediately clear is that the homoerotic vision of "Calamus" actually
rejects any futuristic "America" as a utopian site for homosexuality. Perhaps it does not do so as rigorously as one would like, so that Ginsberg is
led to question Whitman's interest in and allegiance to America as bank-
rupt. "A Supermarket in California," which establishes homosexuality as its
moral center, ends, for instance:

> Ah, dear father, graybeard, lonely old courage-teacher,
> what America did you have when Charon quit poling his ferry
> and you got out on a smoking bank and stood watching the
> boat disappear on the black waters of Lethe? (*Howl* 24)

Just as the rest of *Howl and Other Poems* rejects a dystopian "America" and
its Cold War version of reality for a consciously marginal (if not suicidal)
utopia of pleasure, "A Supermarket in California" suggests that one might
have better things to do with one's time than invest in an illusory
"America." But this is exactly what "Calamus" also suggests, for it finds
that a strategy of marginality (like Roland Barthes's practice of reading) is
the only effective means toward the reimagination of social organization
and symbolic orders. The more superficial textual claim for homosexuality
as a center for future social perfection masks a conception of utopia as a
political strategy of displacement, a strategy not of replacing heterosexual
with homosexual institutions but of rethinking altogether the notion of patriarchal institutions and their control over the individual:

> I hear it was charged against me that I sought to destroy institutions,
> But really I am neither for nor against institutions,
> (What indeed have I in common with them? or what with the destruction
>     of them?)
> Only I will establish in the Mannahatta and in every city of these States in-
>     land and seaboard,
> And in fields and woods, and above every keel little or large that dents the
>     water,

Without edifices or rules or trustees or any argument,
The institution of the dear love of comrades. (*LG* 128)

Here homosexuality becomes the institution which ends institutions; it is
without patriarchal "edifices or rules or trustees or any argument," the
displacement of all cultural centers rather than a replacement for oppres-
sive ones. We see this as well in the descriptions Whitman offers of homosexual bonding. Each man becomes the center for the other, but they
admit of no law outside the desire in which their lives are centered. Nor is
this center a fixed place or purpose; its only principle is movement:

We two boys together clinging,
One the other never leaving,
Up and down the roads going, North and South excursions making,
Power enjoying, elbows stretching, fingers clutching,
Arm'd and fearless, eating, drinking, sleeping, loving,
No law less than ourselves owning, sailing, soldiering, thieving, threat-
     ening,
Misers, menials, priests alarming, air breathing, water drinking, on the turf
     or the sea-beach dancing,
Cities wrenching, ease scorning, statutes mocking, feebleness chasing,
Fulfilling our foray. (*LG* 130)

Certainly this could be made to sound suspiciously like an adolescent desire, and certainly these activities are coded and emblematic of a free existence only within certain historical moments and under certain conditions.
But Whitman's vision of this lawless life need not be inclusive in order
still to participate in the utopian; the terms it chooses displace the cultural
authority of existing centers and therefore extend their significance beyond what this one couple is capable of achieving in the way of masculine
play.

Whitman's text finally witnesses to the fact that utopian schemes are
moments of vision in which is imagined an alternative social organization.
And he sees this not only as an implicit critique of the social order already
in place nor only as a replacement for that order, but as the beginning of
a continual questioning of the dominant orders of social control, as the site
for questioning and contesting any number of symbolic orders that do not
initially seem relevant to the question of homosexuality. This is achieved
through identification with and seeking out a position of marginality from
which dominant practices may be critiqued (thus the strategy of cataloging
"others"—slaves, prostitutes, syphilitics—who are culturally invisible or dismissed). Within the marginality that "Calamus" enacts, there is "a glimpse
through an interstice caught," a moment when Whitman imagines himself
seated on the margins of a roomful of working-class men whose behaviors
he and his lover neither reject nor mirror: rather than boisterous words

being their connection to one another, they sit silently and hold hands, "content, happy in being together" (*LG* 131–32). It is a remarkable moment in "Calamus," that moment when Whitman confronts both the textual nature of his vision of utopia, and its radical limitation for replacing the existing order.

Rather than an alternative vision of the world, which seems rejected as a mere dream of a city of friends, "Calamus" becomes a text that seeks and celebrates moments within dominant culture that subvert its values, conventions, and control. Whitman discovers that homosexual utopia is not a place but a practice; and if homosexual utopia is a strategy of displacement rather than a future site of social perfection, "Calamus" demonstrates that one of the things that needs to be displaced is "America." . . .

## Notes

1. In cases where we have been unable to track down the exact source of Yingling's reference, we have left his original citation intact.

# 10

# America on Canvas, America in Manuscript: Imaging the Democracy

## ELIZABETH JOHNS

In 1871 in *Democratic Vistas* Walt Whitman dismissed American drama, verse, and art in no uncertain terms: "Do you [call] that perpetual, pistareen, paste-pot work, American art?" (*PW* 2: 388–89) When several years ago I considered this snub in the context of evidence in the popular anthologies in the Library of Congress, I appreciated his disdain for much of his era's literary production. I already knew from years of looking at storerooms of museums and old exhibition catalogs that many bad pictures had been relentlessly exhibited during the years that ambition exceeded training. However, because I admired many strong paintings created during even the early years of Whitman's career, I wondered if there were not an underlying reason for his contempt for images that would tell us something about the very relation in cultural production between "canvas" and "manuscript." Could there even have been a "Whitman" in paint in the 1850s and 1860s—at least one artist who would have evoked Whitman's admiration? This essay offers some thoughts on the question.

Near the heart of the matter may be the different social "work" taken up by journalists and image makers across Whitman's lifetime, missions fundamental to the nineteenth-century nature of print and images and their publics. The very function of the printed text, especially in journalism, was to unite the reader with the writer and thus with other readers as well (in recent terms, to interpellate the reader in the same relation to the material as the writer constructs). Much of the population at midcentury shared at least an intuitive grasp of verbal rhetoric and felt at home with words. They did not feel this way about images, however. Because pictures were associated with an elite tradition, the very nub of the relationship between painter and patron complemented the special "taste" of clients. Unlike readers' "natural" ability to respond to verbal rhetoric, viewers' appreciation of images came from education, experience, and self-cultivation, all of which enabled patrons to join painters in setting themselves apart from other members of the constituency.

With none of this exclusivity, Whitman's poetry flowed from his assumptions as a journalist. Highly attuned to the power of the rhetoric of commonality, he knew how to gather a community around the printed word, to extend the imagination of readers eager to include themselves in the social world of language, and to pull the reader out of the present into a new future. In the fevered language of *Leaves of Grass,* Whitman created a society in which differences between northerner and southerner, easterner and westerner, workman and stockbroker, slave and freeman, male and female, would be healed—first in the imagination and then in action. Repressed in this vision were the political, economic, and social differences that had strained the capacity of individuals across the nation to think of American society as a single national body.

Unlike Whitman, antebellum image makers did not see their mission in terms of healing the cracks in the body politic; they had no program to promote collectivity. From the earliest Colonial settlements, painters were commissioned to make portraits of the ambitious and the successful. In the early nineteenth century artists in the Northeast tapped the rising interest in regional tourism to market landscape paintings, and they appealed to New Yorkers' political investments with comic scenes of the constituency outside the city. No single artist made visual inventories of American geography, citizens, and occupations as did Whitman, nor did a group of artists do so, or even a random assortment of artists. No artist would have dreamed, much less said, as Whitman did, that "the genius of the United States is . . . always most in the common people" ("Preface," *LG* 1855: 5–6). It was not until photography and lithography democratized the distribution and apparent readability of images after the Civil War that visual texts can be assumed to have functioned in common experience like verbal texts.

Although the appropriate visual comparisons with Whitman's mission come from the 1830s, '40s, and '50s, one finds the establishment of a pattern of exclusivity early on even in works other than portraits. The ambitious painter John Trumbull found in the 1790s, for instance, that he could not raise a subscription audience along the entire Atlantic seaboard for a series of historical images about the Revolution. A typical part of this series is his *The Death of General Warren at Bunker Hill,* 1786 (Yale University Art Gallery), which dramatizes the martyrdom of the General in a scene that both celebrates Colonial victory and laments the cost of it. Even in the flush of the Revolution's success Trumbull could not market his projected series about military and political turning points because these crucial events implicated only specific regions in the constituency. Another such example of the narrow social definition that fueled images is that would-be landscapists in the Federal period gained patronage only for views of estates and townscapes. Thomas Birch and others like him found their business through the ambitions of the new American "gentry" to show their resemblance to English counterparts with impressive houses and gardens. Similarly, Birch could interest Philadelphians, but not Bostonians or New Yorkers, in such depictions as *The Upper Ferry Bridge, Schuylkill River,* 1815 (Historical Society of Pennsylvania), which flattered those who had invested in the development of the city.

A telling contrast to Whitman's project in 1855 to enfold American humanity into one body was the program of artists who created a market in New York in the 1830s for scenes of ordinary people carrying out their activities (Johns, *American Genre Painting,* passim). These painters, like their artistic predecessors, worked to inscribe increasingly important differences among members of the social body. With New York as the center of art exhibition, patronage, and criticism, the prejudices of New Yorkers called the tune. In this climate artists depicted citizens disdained by urban New Yorkers as the "others" in the democracy—Yankee farmers, westerners, blacks, women, and the urban poor. Painters produced an inventory of images quite different from Whitman's. Instead of farmers of "wonderful vigor and calmness and beauty of person" (*LG* 1855: 118), as Whitman put it, William Sidney Mount painted awkward, scheming yokels in such works as *Bargaining for a Horse,* 1835 (New-York Historical Society) (Fig. 10.1). In this image, Mount pokes fun at the stereotypical whittling New England farmers who, both old and young, carry out economic and political

**Fig. 10.1** William Sidney Mount, *Bargaining for a Horse,* 1835. Oil on canvas, 24 x 30 in. Courtesy New-York Historical Society, New York City.

"horsetrading" while their barns lie empty. The speculation that had resulted in the economic and political havoc in the 1830s was by and large carried out by urban citizens, but in jokes, plays, and in this picture, city dwellers and patrons laid the obsession with trading rather than production at the feet of the rural "Yankee." Much the same process of projection marked New Yorkers' myths about western frontiersmen. On the one hand seen as hardy and courageous, such figures were also deemed as potentially savage, undisciplined, and socially unacceptable because of their environment. Thus Brooklyn painter Charles Deas, who had traveled briefly in the West, produced the painting *Long Jakes, Mountain Man,* 1845 (Manoogian Collection, Detroit), to be interpreted according to the prejudices of the viewer. "Long Jakes" controls his horse and seems at ease in a vast, strange landscape, yet he wears a somewhat foolish-looking hat and his reddish nose would have been to many viewers of the 1840s a telltale sign of alcoholic indulgence. Extensive reception indicates that this frequently reproduced image symbolized for many anxious East Coast viewers westerners' lack of urban preparation for their growing political power.

Such setting apart of portions of the population was a major function of other images as well. No artist celebrated the "negro [holding] firmly the reins of his four horses" (*LG* 1855: 35), to use Whitman's language, but for a large and appreciative audience Eastman Johnson created *Old Kentucky Home,* 1859 (Fig. 10.2), originally entitled *Negro Life at the South,* which associated a range of black characters with a rundown house, dead hearth, and barren yard. In this picture, which was popular both before and after the Civil War, two black men devote themselves to idle leisure, one in courting and the other in playing the banjo. As African-American males, they are thus associated with laziness, music, and sexuality, while the black women in the picture assume the roles of caring for the children. To secure the point about the meaning of the black social body, a sturdy house can be seen next door, from which a young white woman enters the scene. Presumably she is the "mistress," come to oversee these "children." The reception of the painting reveals that before the war, the image overtly justified slavery; after the conflict, it was retitled with the name of Stephen Foster's nostalgic song "My Old Kentucky Home" to lament the earlier golden days.

Unlike Whitman, painters were not "the poet of the woman the same as the man" (*LG* 1855: 44). Not only did they not paint the "clean-haired Yankee girl [working] in the factory or mill" (*LG* 1855: 38), but few artists painted women in scenes of everyday life at all. When women did appear in images, they were conspicuously sidelined or even behind barriers, as in Mount's *Bargaining for a Horse,* in which the presumed wife of the older farmer looks on the scene behind the fence that separates the farmhouse from the barn area. Whitman saw the exercise of voter sovereignty as having awesome significance, but George Caleb Bingham found it ironical, even amusing, and cataloged the scheming, rowdiness, and ignorance of the voters in his *County Election,* 1852 (Boatmen's National Bank of St.

**Fig. 10.2** Eastman Johnson, *Old Kentucky Home (Negro Life at the South)*, 1859. Oil on Canvas, 36 x 45¼ in. Courtesy New-York Historical Society, New York City.

Louis). In this image, voters variously politic, drink, and look stupified against an ironic backdrop of an orderly townscape and serene blue sky. The final touch of irony is a banner prominently propped against the porch on which votes are being recorded that reads "The will of the people, the supreme law." Indeed, genre painting as a whole expressed the very opposite of Whitman's willed confidence in the democracy, in no works more so than in paintings by Pittsburgh artist David Gilmore Blythe, who about 1859 in his *The Post Office* (Fig. 10.3) critiqued the democracy for the greed, shabbiness, and self-interest that swept across social class, gender, and age at midcentury. A group of figures push each other at the delivery window while others on the porch are snooped on and pickpocketed by almost inhuman-looking urchins. The crowd is presided over by a classical bust in the niche above the post office window that makes the scene a parody of the republic that the founding fathers had envisioned.

So uncomfortable were most art patrons with the general masses and the "lower orders" that in the 1840s and '50s they hailed landscape painting rather than scenes of the common people as *the* national visual expression. But landscapes defined the body politic as well, although more subtly than genre painting. Thomas Cole began what later was called the Hudson River School with scenes of elite tourist attractions in the Catskill moun-

**Fig. 10.3** David Gilmour Blythe, *The Post Office*, 1859–1863. Oil on canvas, 24 x 20 in. The Carnegie Museum of Art, Pittsburgh.

tains, such as his *Kaaterskill Falls,* 1826 (Warner Collection of Gulf States Paper Corporation, Tuscaloosa, Alabama), that hid the accessories of viewing platforms and sluice gates with which the proprietors marketed the falls. This and other landscapes presented nature's bounty as available to those with the economic resources to visit it and the social and intellectual resources to reconceive it in their imaginations. Landscapes on exhibition walls, such as Asher B. Durand's *The Beeches,* 1844 (Metropolitan Museum of Art), and Frederic Church's *Mt. Ktaadn,* 1853 (Fig. 10.4), were of New

**Fig. 10.4** Frederic Edwin Church, *Mt. Ktaadn*, 1853. Oil on canvas, 36¼ x 55¼ in. Yale University Art Gallery, New Haven, Connecticut, Stanley B. Resor, B. A., 1901, Fund.

153

York and New England, not Georgia, not the Carolinas (original colonies though they were), not Ohio, not the Mississippi River valley, and not, typically, even Virginia. National identity, for the patrons, painters, early dealers, and exhibition coordinators who dominated art production, meant the racial stock, the agriculture and commerce, the religion, and the contemporary politics of the Northeast. *Mt. Ktaadn* is particularly forthright in holding up for admiration for Church's typically New England and New York patron a scene that combines domestic settlement and the early technology of a mill with the abiding benediction of the region's tallest mountain, still wild. When Western landscapes became popular in the 1860s, "national" scenes such as Albert Bierstadt's *The Rocky Mountains, Lander's Peak,* 1863 (Metropolitan Museum of Art) were interpreted as land completely open to development, and thus as a statement of the philosophy of manifest destiny that ambitious easterners saw as the individual and social purpose of settlement and expansion. The mountains in the background of this painting are a composite that presents a fantastic beauty; although across the foreground groups of Native Americans are camped and prepare meals in family and other groups, at least one reviewer claimed that the Indians were mere accidents on the face of nature. Even the establishment in 1839 in New York of what became the American Art Union, a popular patronage organization that sold memberships and distributed engravings and paintings by lottery from Savannah to New Orleans and St. Louis to Detroit, did not result in a conception of the nation's land and the nation's people in terms anywhere near the breadth of Whitman's. The members of the American Art Union were recruited with rhetoric that complemented their taste for the exclusive rather than a platform that urged the cohesiveness of the social body.

In contrast to painters, the printmakers who developed their businesses in the 1850s and came into major prominence after the Civil War would seem to have acknowledged an increasingly diverse society. They marketed their product, of course, for a much larger class base. However, whereas Whitman embraced differences with a unifying voice, Currier and Ives, who called themselves "Printmakers for the American People," conspicuously marketed images to separate constituencies. There were "Catholic images" and "domestic" images, scenes of famous horse races, scenes of sporting animals, pictures of firemen, views of cities, and caricatures of politicians. Images that the firm *did* advertise as national had an obvious ideological bias. One such slant was provided by the series of prints on homes and families, as "The Cottage Dooryard: Evening," 1855 (Peters Collection, Smithsonian Institution), showing the happy ideal American family in their rural cottage (the architecture and the topography and flora very much inspired by English nature), boy children playing in the front yard, mother with girl child on the porch, benign father overseeing his kingdom. The image was pitched to the domestic audience, to middle-class women eager to assert the importance of the family. The firm's "Home to

Thanksgiving," 1867 (Peters Collection, Smithsonian Institution), produced soon after the official establishment of the national holiday, is another case in point. A snow-covered rural landscape, sleigh, extended family, and farm animals, defined the American home as associated with New England, by implication the locus of American morality and probity. Other issues of national identity were given sanction by Currier and Ives in the hand-colored lithograph "Washington at Mount Vernon, 1797" (Peters Collection, Smithsonian Institution), which was produced in 1852, soon after the Compromise of 1850. The print is a vision of a paternal and benign president who, standing appreciatively at the edge of his fields watching his happy slaves at work, sanctions slavery as paternal and benign. And the West, too, got its facile treatment by Currier and Ives. Such tributes to manifest destiny as "Across the Continent" of 1868 (Peters Collection, Smithsonian Institution) condenses the vast continental expanse into a prairie being crossed by a train, the land itself already the site of a model town with a prominent schoolhouse in the foreground. The Rocky Mountains in the distance seem to be a minor obstacle to this cheerful, inexorable progress westward. Images, in short, were nurtured by the resilient exclusivity of their patrons, who were concentrated in the urban Northeast. The very cultural activity of image making before the war mitigated against any artist assuming the point of view of Whitman.

But after the war, the artistic milieu shifted dramatically. When Whitman took a backward look in 1871, was he disappointed in the very mission of the images that he had seen so often as a New York journalist? Did the social smugness of earlier landscapes and genre painting annoy him, along with the pat sentimentality of most Currier and Ives images? Or was the object of his disdain the frequently dismal quality of the style and technique of so many of the pictures? It is difficult to know the degree of connoisseurship Whitman had for what we might think of as "strong" pictures. One comment that he made about pictures, however, seems to me to suggest an answer. He lauded the rather pedestrian painter Walter Libbey's picture *Boy Playing the Flute* because Libbey depicted the boy as classless (Bohan 11). Is it not the case, then, that Whitman's tirade against visual art came from the failure of American artists to create a visual community? Was he disgusted that American painters did not choose topics and scenes that would urge the body politic toward a democratic future?

At the very time of Whitman's public explosion of rage and grief at what Americans had permitted themselves to become, the painters Winslow Homer and Thomas Eakins had just come into artistic maturity. They and their viewers were to have a considerably more cosmopolitan, indeed transatlantic, assessment of the function of painting, and American society had grown considerably beyond the relatively simple divisions between class and region of the prewar years. Homer and Eakins stood in a relationship to market forces substantially altered from that of their earlier counterparts—indeed, Eakins, with a small independent income, was virtu-

**Fig. 10.5** Winslow Homer, *Veteran in a New Field,* 1865. Oil on canvas, 24¹/₈ x 38¹/₈ in. The Metropolitan Museum of Art, New York. Bequest of Miss Adelaide Milton de Groot, 1967.

ally free from them—and both could take a stance somewhat independent of their viewers' prejudices. Over careers of more than four decades, these artists were to create visual counterparts to Whitman's community of the American body. There is no evidence that they took Whitman's preaching as their model; rather, out of their own psychic needs and the cultural milieu in which they situated themselves and their viewers, they combined the poet's affection for the human being with his subtle destabilizing of individual identity. Their paintings are not buoyant, not even cheerful, but measured and steady. This phenomenon, which strikes me afresh even now, seems to illustrate Robert Frost's observation that art comes not from grievances but from grief—grief that in Homer and Eakins was for both self and the larger society. Some years after his tirade in *Democratic Vistas,* Whitman came to know Eakins and to admire his work. Although he never commented on the significance of Homer's achievements, I believe by 1890 he could have found both artists to have assumed his mantle, both artists to have projected his vision of humanity, albeit a darker one.

From the end of the Civil War, Homer created images of a common person—a generic American, we might say, incarnated in children, women, and laboring men. Although he placed them in New England, the figures transcend class, occupation, religion, or politics. In *Veteran in a New Field,* 1865 (Fig. 10.5), for instance, a farmer harvests grain that stretches across and into the depth of the canvas. His back to the viewer, the farmer devotes himself to the task, a union cap and other military details in the foreground the sole signifiers of the earlier gruesome field in which he had worked. Playing on a prominent metaphor for the conflict, Homer creates here an American Everyman who returns after the bitter war to harvest what nature has provided, putting behind him the war's horrible harvest of bodies. In other pictures as well he drew profound metaphors about the social body. In *Dad's Coming*, 1873 (Fig. 10.6), a young boy, mother, and baby wait at the edge of the sea, each in his or her own world of age, gender, and potential future. In this deceptively simple image, Homer raises the most profound questions: Will the father return? Will the social body be drawn together? Are not they—are not we—ominously subject to the unexpected, as uncontrollable as the sea? In *The Cotton Pickers*, 1876 (Fig. 10.7), Homer depicts two young black women stopped momentarily from their work in the fields. They seem, like other members of the body politic, to be in an ambiguous relation to their previous defined status, self-aware and guarded in their relationship to the viewer, and both participating in and yearning to be distinct from their labor. Do they not stand before the viewer in a vivid humanity? And in another picture in which the person close to nature becomes an archetype for the groundedness of each of us in natural forces, *Fog Warning* of 1886 (Museum of Fine Arts, Boston) presents a fisherman rowing desperately against a rising sea and ominous fog. Leading the viewer to suspect that the fisherman may not be able to row back to the distant ship from which he had launched his dory, Homer evokes the terrible vulnerability of human beings that Whitman, too, cherished and mourned.

**Fig. 10.6** Winslow Homer, *Dad's Coming*, 1873. Oil on panel, 9 x 13¾ in. Collection of Mr. and Mrs. Paul Mellon, Upperville, Virginia.

**Fig. 10.7** Winslow Homer, *The Cotton Pickers*, 1876. Oil on canvas, 24¹/₁₆ x 38¹/₈ in. Los Angeles County Museum of Art.

Whereas Homer painted about the social body with the figures of rural and coastal humanity, Eakins concentrated on urban persons, mostly Philadelphians. Even more intensely than the work of Homer, that of Eakins partakes of the passion about humankind and the love of the physical body that marks Whitman's work. In his paintings, Eakins created portraits of people whose work he admired; in his photographs, Eakins made images of male beauty and companionship that, like some of Whitman's poetry, probed the homosocial body as a metaphor for the ideal society (Johns, "An Avowal of Artistic Community"). In fact, although Whitman and Eakins came eventually to know each other, even before they met the two shared a commitment to the communicative power of the body itself. Whitman's companion Bill Duckett served as Eakins's principal photographic model for a series of pictures in the mid-1880s about the beauty of the male body. These photographs, in which Duckett posed as a meditative odalisque whose passive beauty was to be enjoyed by the viewer, are homoerotic but they also confound the categories of gender much as Whitman had done—insisting that what we share is more important than what separates us (Fig. 13.10).

After Eakins actually met Whitman, the relationship between poet and artist developed almost mystically, as the men seemed to recognize in each other what they most cherished or yearned for in themselves. Although Eakins claimed that he initiated the friendship to paint Whitman's portrait, he returned to visit many times, sometimes with paints and sometimes with the camera. In admiration of Eakins's intensity Whitman came to call him a "force" (Homer 89). The portrait that Eakins painted of the poet (*Walt Whitman* [Fig. 10.8]) is not at all flattering. Much as Whitman's eyes and mouth hint that he is about to issue a sparkling witticism, his body slumps into old age. Taken aback by what he called its "Rabelaisian" character, Whitman admitted that it was the best likeness anyone had made of him (Homer 89).

In the Whitman portrait as in his other work, Eakins used the physicality and the psychological fragility of his sitters to break down artificial dis-

**Fig. 10.8** Thomas Eakins, *Walt Whitman*, 1887–88. Oil on canvas, 30⅛ x 24¼ in. Pennsylvania Academy of the Fine Arts, Philadelphia.

**Fig. 10.9** Thomas Eakins, *The Champion Single Sculls (Max Schmitt in a Single Scull)*, 1871. Oil on canvas, 32¼ x 46¼ in. The Metropolitan Museum of Art, New York. Purchase 1934, Alfred N. Punnett Fund and Gift of George D. Pratt.

**Fig. 10.10** Thomas Eakins, *Amelia Van Buren*, c. 1891. Oil on canvas, 45 x 32 in. The Phillips Collection, Washington, D.C.

tinctions between human beings—to, as he put it, "peer deeply into the heart of American life" (Johns, *Thomas Eakins* 168). His sitters are middle class—rower, singer, surgeon, physicist. But as he did with Whitman, Eakins leveled professional distinctions by making his sitters subject to nature's process, giving them skin that ages, eyes that reveal doubt and caution, and shoulders that slump to betray the agonies of disappointment. In one of his earliest portraits, *Max Schmitt in a Single Scull,* 1871 (Fig. 10.9), he placed human achievement in the flow of time, making the face of the champion rower, half hidden by shadows, a subtle undercutting of the victory the painting purported to celebrate. He infuriated photographer and painter Amelia Van Buren, who was also his student, by presenting her body almost overwhelmed by the chair in which she poses and her expression melancholic to the point of exhaustion (*Amelia Van Buren,* 1891 [Fig. 10.10]). The artist was no easier on himself than on his sitters: grief and wariness pervade the *Self-Portrait* that he presented to the National Academy of Design when after three decades of artistic practice he was finally elected to membership (1902, National Academy of Design).

In imaging the body politic, the genre painters and landscapists of the 1830s into the 1860s focused on the separations in the citizenry, both explicit and implicit. And events did reveal that such divisions were not only permanent but powerful. In the wake of the Civil War, as though only after the most profound grief could connectedness even be posited, Homer and Eakins searched out the physical and psychic being that all shared. One might say that their work—especially Eakins's unforgettable faces—urges Whitman's plea: "What is it then between us? . . . Whatever it is, it avails not—distance avails not, and place avails not, I too lived . . ." ("Crossing Brooklyn Ferry," *LG* 162).

# 11

# Whitman's Lesson of the City

## ALAN TRACHTENBERG

"The chief street of a great city," wrote Whitman in 1856, "is a curious epitome of the life of the city; and when that street, like Broadway, is a thoroughfare, a mart, and a promenade all together, its representative character is yet more striking" ("Broadway"). In his poems Whitman's city shares these representative features of Broadway, the conjunction of thoroughfare, promenade, and marketplace: a place of passage, movement of people, goods, and useful knowledge, and a place of display and spectacle, of things in the guise of goods in shop windows and of persons in the guise of exchangeable social identities. "An endless procession," as he writes in the 1856 article, his city is at once material place and mode of perception.

What we seek is that nexus, the rapport between procession as Broadway life and procession as a way of taking life in, processing and representing it. How does the city's materiality, its hidden or obscurely visible political economy and its economy of social relations, figure itself in the tapestry of perception Whitman invents as he sets out to model the city as poetry? Passage from street to poem, itself an endless and intricate procession, is the issue at hand.

Broadway persists in Whitman's memory as the archetypal place of urban instruction, its "representative character" implying but also withholding a pedagogy. In a late poem (1888) he addresses the great city's "chief street" as "portal" and "arena," salutes it as "Thou visor'd, vast, unspeakable show and lesson!" (LG 521). What is the visor'd lesson, and why unspeakable? Epitomized by its greatest thoroughfare, Whitman's city brings people together in countless varied and fluid transactions, unutterable in their variety and veiled in their changeableness. People pass blindly and mingle unknowingly with others who are their immanent "you." The street instructs the poet to interrupt the flow without dispersing it, to seize "whoever you are" as the necessary occasion for "my poem," for my coming to be myself.

163

Whoever you are, now I place my hand upon you, that you be my poem,
I whisper with my lips close to your ear,
I have loved many women and men, but I love none better than you.

O I have been dilatory and dumb,
I should have made my way straight to you long ago,
I should have blabb'd nothing but you, I should have chanted nothing but
   you. ("To You," *LG* 233)

The audacity of "That you be my poem" confirms the extremity of need:
only You gives voice to I, only the fusion of I and You which is the poem
brings me to myself, and you to yourself. Whitman's city is the imaginative
space where such things happen—not a place he represents but a process
he enacts. The lesson of Broadway, its instruction in the mutuality and
interdependence of I and You, constitutes Whitman's poesis: not a speak-
able lesson but a continuing process, the originating event of his discourse.

A process undertaken and undergone, moreover, as William James understood, not for the sake of sensation alone, the quivering touch or ecstatic vision, but for the sake of a state in which self and other fuse into a
new sensation of being, quivered into new identities. Whitman cruises the
city in search of significant others—as James will put it, "the significance of
alien lives"—and finds his "You" in every encounter. "You have waited,
you always wait, you dumb, beautiful ministers. . . . Great or small, you
furnish your parts toward the soul" ("Crossing Brooklyn Ferry," *LG* 165).
The poet interpolates the other, whether person or thing, as "soul," the
You which realizes the I. Soul names the ground on which enactments of
new identity occur. James called this way of being in the city "rapture,"
and in a popular lecture in the late 1890s, "On a Certain Blindness in
Human Beings," he recruits Whitman's rapt attention to the city as exem-
plum of a vision he too wishes to promulgate.

According to James, Whitman "felt the human crowd as rapturously as
Wordsworth felt the mountains." James portrays Whitman as "rapt with
satisfied attention . . . to the mere spectacle of the world's presence"
(James 122–24) and presents this open-eyed receptivity to "mere spectacle"
as an antidote to that "blindness," as he puts it, "with which we all are
afflicted in regard to the feelings of creatures and people different from
ourselves." We cannot see beyond the horizon of the "limited functions
and duties" of our practical lives, our "single, specialized vocation," and
in that private darkness we nourish our own "vital secrets," blind to "the
significance of alien lives" and thus to the fullest significance of our own
(James 113). Calling this a certain blindness in human beings, James seems
to assert its universality as an existential, transhistorical human condition.
Without diminishing the general character of the condition—and James
speaks of a person's unknowing relation with her or his dog to underscore
that dimension—he also localizes a present version of this blindness with

pointed allusions to a common predicament shared by his audience. And he alerts us to seek similar evidence of a historical social condition and predicament in Whitman's rapture and raptness.

James gave his lecture on "a certain blindess" principally at women's colleges in the late 1890s, but his address embraces a larger range of middle-class citizenry, the "we of the highly educated classes (so called)," that is, specialized professionals or students looking forward to academic or professional or corporate careers. Perhaps he chose this theme to perform before young women aspiring to professionalism because he deemed women, for whom professional and academic careers were still novel and scarce, more sympathetic than college men to the insight that the highly educated have drifted "far, far away from Nature."

> We are trained to seek the choice, the rare, the exquisite exclusively, and to overlook the common. We are stuffed with abstract conceptions, and glib with verbalities and verbosities; and in the culture of these higher functions the peculiar sources of joy connected with our simpler functions often dry up, and we grow stone-blind and insensible to life's more elementary and general goods and joys. (James 126)

Whitman doubtless helped James write such lines, emboldened him to prescribe that we "descend to a more profound and primitive level," that we learn from "the savages and children of nature, to whom we deem ourselves so much superior" (James 126–27).

This agitation toward a more vigorous, natural, emotional, and risk-filled life signals a distinct motif of the middle-class nineties, a yearning for revitalization, a protest against a metropolitan malaise of conformity and repression among white-collar workers, the new managerial-professional class of incorporated urban America that James addressed. "Deadness" toward the world of others is "the price we inevitably have to pay for being practical creatures," which is to say, incorporated creatures. James tells his young women listeners that it is all right, it is healthy, it is tonic, to go sensuous, savage, and irrational. "The holidays of life are its most vitally significant portions, because they are, or at least should be, covered with just this kind of magically irresponsible spell" (James 129).

Holiday of course grates, seeming to trivialize alien lives by offering touristic excursions to their significance. Diction like "magically irresponsible spell" must have embarrassed James himself, for when he published the lecture in a volume in 1899, he noted in the preface that "it is more than the mere piece of sentimentalism which it may seem to some readers." Those who have read his philosophic essays, he wrote, will recognize the essay's seriousness as an expression of "the pluralistic or individualistic philosophy." By pluralistic universe he means that "truth" being "too great for any one actual mind," we need to learn to see through many lenses, multiple perspectives. "The facts and worths of life need many cognizers to take

them in. There is no point of view absolutely public and universal. Private
and uncommunicable perceptions always remain over, and the worst of
it is that those who look for them from the outside never know *where*"
(James vi).

This authorial gloss on the underlying philosophical argument of the
essay also glosses the role of Walt Whitman as James's rapturous city poet.
Without saying so, James portrays a Whitman who intuits pragmatism, the
view that truth is plural and partial, subjective, fragmented, scattered.
James alerts us to the presence of "many cognizers" in Whitman's domain,
to the significance of scale of perspective, shifts of point of view, positions
of the moving eye. As an instance of Whitman's rapt attention toward the
crowd and its otherness, James inserts in his lecture a passage from an
1868 letter to Pete Doyle which James found in what he called "the delicious volume" published as *Calamus* in 1897. It is Whitman of the omnivo-
rous and voracious eye describing a ride atop a Broadway omnibus.

> You know it is a never ending amusement and study and recreation for
> me to ride a couple of hours on a pleasant afternoon on a Broadway
> stage in this way. You see everything as you pass, a sort of living, endless
> panorama—shops and splendid buildings and great windows . . . crowds
> of women richly dressed continually passing . . . a perfect stream of peo-
> ple . . . and then in the streets the thick crowd of carriages, stages, carts,
> hotel and private coaches . . . and so many tall, ornamental, noble build-
> ings many of them of white marble, and the gayety and motion on every
> side: you will not wonder how much attraction all this is on a fine day, to
> a great loafer like me, who enjoys so much seeing the busy world move
> by him, and exhibiting itself for his amusement, while he takes it easy
> and just looks on and observes. (James 123–24)

It's not so much what or how Whitman sees here that so captivates James,
not the city's great promenade and marketplace taken in as a panoramic
spectacle, but the flow of the passage, the speaker's taking it easy, his guilt-
less loafing while life passes by, "this mysterious sensorial life, with its irra-
tionality," as James says later in the lecture.

As urban loafer, flaneur of Broadway coaches and Brooklyn ferries, the
Whitman James stages for us plays a crucial demonic role in the argument.
Of all the literary authorities James raises in support of his argument
(Wordsworth, Emerson, Stevenson, Tolstoy), Whitman looks most the part
of disreputable tramp, "a worthless, unproductive being." By his very otherness he demonstrates James's point that you don't have to go to such
extremes of errant behavior, that vacations from the office might suffice to
see the world in a new, nonhabitual light. The letter to Doyle and the
Brooklyn ferry poem show the antithetical conception of productivity and
worth which James argues alone makes ordinary everyday conceptions tol-
erable. Feeling "the human crowd as rapturously as Wordsworth felt the
mountains, felt it as an overpoweringly significant presence," Whitman says

in effect that "simply to absorb one's mind" in the crowd "should be business sufficient and worthy to fill the days of a serious man" (James 122). For James's Whitman the mere seeing of things means serious business, yielding profits of a different order from those recognized by the practical, productive, specialized world: "To be rapt with satisfied attention, like Whitman, to the mere spectacle of the world's presence, is one way, and the most fundamental way, of confessing one's sense of its unfathomable significance and importance" (James 124–25).

This term, rapt, calls for closer attention. Whitman himself understood the arrogant impropriety of his stance, the insult to the ideology of private ownership in what he found sufficed, his satisfaction in saying "I see, dance, laugh, sing." In the passage which follows in section 3 of "Song of Myself," Whitman acknowledges the voice of the bourgeois superego by asking, in regard to the hugging bedfellow who withdraws at the peep of day leaving behind swelling baskets covered with white towels:

> Shall I postpone my acceptation and realization and scream at my eyes,
> That they turn from gazing after and down the road,
> And forthwith cipher and show me to a cent,
> Exactly the value of one and exactly the value of two, and which is ahead?
>   (*LG* 31–32)

The eyes gaze after, naturally rapt; the antithetical condition is to cipher and count, to apply the calculus of ownership to an incalculable act of love.

Rapt attention, then, stands opposite conventional forms of possession, ownership, property. Mulling over the mystery of private property in the years just before 1855, Whitman noted that "the money value of real and personal estate in New York city is somewhere between five hundred millions and a thousand millions of dollars." What does this mean, he asked?

> It is all nothing of account.—The whole of it is not of so much account
> as a pitcher of water, or a basket of fresh eggs,—The only way we attach
> it to our feelings is by identifying it with the human spirit,—through love,
> through pride, through our craving for beauty and happiness. (*NUP* 119)

He might have said through our rapture. In another notebook entry in the same years he wrote: "What is it to own any thing? It is to incorporate it into yourself, as the primal god swallowed the five immortal offspring of Rhea, and accumulated to his life and knowledge and strength all that would have grown in them" (*NUP* 113). In "There Was a Child Went Forth," one of the originally untitled 1855 poems, going forth means swallowing the world: "And the first object he look'd upon, that object he became" (*LG* 364). To be rapt in attention toward someone or something, in Whitman's presumed gloss on James's figure, is to become that person or thing, to incorporate it as nourishment, knowledge, strength.

Yet, to be rapt also says to be seized, carried off, taken from one place to another, transposed, perhaps by force or by emotion, a state of transport, ravishment: James's terms project an excess beyond the figure of exultant poet for whom the city stands in for Wordsworth's "nature," source of ultimate refreshment, verification, and meaning. Rapt and rapturous, with hidden kinship to rape, convey an inchoate sense on James's part of a violence immanent in Whitman's version of the city, in his crowds, in his apparent surrender as passive panoramist to their inducements and promises. Indeed, if we think of "City of Ships" and especially the haunting "Give Me the Splendid Silent Sun," Whitman's Civil War city is filled with the clamor and agitations of war, but signs of siege appear even earlier, a discordant note at the deeper frequencies of his urban vision.

Consider the first appearance of a distinctively urban place in "Song of Myself," the initially untitled opening poem of the 1855 edition. It occurs in what would later become section 8 and presents not an entirely heartening picture: a kaleidoscopic display of colliding images, visual and aural, fragmented narrative shards composing a tableau of untold stories, "living and buried speech" echoing from "impassive stones." An hallucinatory air hovers over this Broadway passage, which seems more typical of Baudelaire or Eliot than the Whitman of William James:

> The blab of the pave, tires of carts, sluff of boot-soles, talk of the prome-
> naders,
> The heavy omnibus, the driver with his interrogating thumb, the clank of
> the shod horses on the granite floor,
> The snow-sleighs, clinking, shouted jokes, pelts of snow-balls,
> The hurrahs for popular favorites, the fury of rous'd mobs,
> The flap of the curtain'd litter, a sick man inside borne to the hospital,
> The meeting of enemies, the sudden oath, the blows and fall,
> The excited crowd, the policeman with his star quickly working his passage
> to the centre of the crowd,
> The impassive stones that receive and return so many echoes,
> What groans of over-fed or half-starv'd who fall sunstruck or in fits,
> What exclamations of women taken suddenly who hurry home and give
> birth to babes,
> What living and buried speech is always vibrating here, what howls re-
> strain'd by decorum,
> Arrests of criminals, slights, adulterous offers made, acceptances, rejections
> with convex lips,
> I mind them or the show or resonance of them—I come and I depart.
> (LG 36)

The scene verges on an implosion into private rage and pain, into passionate disorder. In its fragmented inventorial form the passage resembles a newspaper page, a reenactment of such a page with juxtaposed accounts of riots, street fights, sudden illness, criminals apprehended. What does the poet make of this spectacle in which rich and poor, over-fed and half-starved, fall together in sunstroke or fit? How does the poet relate to the policeman with his star, the figure of coercive authority who pushes his way to the center of the crowd, indeed at the exact center of the passage itself? What does "come and depart" in the closing line (in 1855, "I come again and again") reveal about the poet's place in the scene, the speaker's way of being in such a city place?

The concluding line retrospectively discloses the presence of the poet in a curiously paradoxical posture of minding (in both senses of watching and caring about) and not-minding the scene, gripped yet independent of it: an oddly tentative closure swinging between coming and going, staying and leaving, turning toward and turning away. What can we make of this alternating motion in Whitman's relation to the crowd? James might say that the poet's rapture demands the freedom from practical commitments, from family and job, which coming and going imply. To enjoy the pleasure of merely watching life go by, to stay open to what James calls the "vital secrets" of other people's lives, you had better not make a profession of it.

This pragmatic explanation has merit, for it reminds us that Whitman's posture is that of a person with a definite calling, a vocation of his own to avoid vocations which entrap one within fixed identities. But we seek a formal explanation as well, an account of the form or typical forms of Whitman's representation of his poet in the city: a formal account, moreover, through which we might better understand Whitman's response to the pressures and opportunities of the historical moment.

Perhaps the coming and going or ebb and flow pattern provides an enabling condition for Whitman to confront the crowd in the first place, to confront it "face to face" as a condition of his own being, as the "dumb, beautiful ministers" which minister to harmony with the world at the close of "Crossing Brooklyn Ferry." Section 42 of "Song of Myself" restates the earlier dynamic relation of poet to crowd in somewhat more opaque but paradoxically illuminating terms:

A call in the midst of the crowd,
My own voice, orotund sweeping and final. (*LG* 76)

A voice heard from without yet recognized as originating from within— "my own voice" as "a call" heard from within "the crowd." Whitman's speaker makes the ecstatic claim of the mystic, that he stands at once inside and outside himself, within the crowd which comprises the city, part of it yet detached enough to hear his own voice. The poet minds his own voice calling at once to the crowd and to himself, calling himself through or by means of the crowd: an act of self-interpolation, himself as the "performer" in the following lines:

Come my children,
Come my boys and girls, my women, household and intimates,
Now the performer launches his nerve, he has pass'd his prelude on the
    reeds within.

And a few lines later, in an ecstatic fit:

My head slues round on my neck,
Music rolls, but not from the organ,
Folks are around me, but they are no household of mine. (*LG* 76)

The poet comes to himself through the intermediary of the crowd; the call
emerges from and expresses the oneness of being close and being distant.
Coming and going define a mode of acceptance, Whitman's way of placing
himself in the crowd yet holding (or withholding) himself free and aloof
from it, far enough away to witness it, to discern its patterns, to re-create
it as an element of his own being, what he calls "soul," as in the final lines
of "Crossing Brooklyn Ferry": "You furnish your parts toward eternity, /
Great or small, you furnish your parts toward the soul" (*LG* 165).

"Crossing Brooklyn Ferry" recapitulates the ebb and flow pattern in the
representation of crowd and the self's relation to the crowd. The capacious,
vehicular structure of that poem invites the epithet processional, a form of
movement, in this case stately, majestic, with great formal feeling, though
in the case of the kaleidoscopic panorama in section 8, agitated, uncertain,
edgy. In "There Was a Child Went Forth," "Broadway Pageant," "City of
Ships," and "Give Me the Splendid Silent Sun," whatever the emotional
tonality of the procession its effect is to produce an idea of a totality, an
assembly of parts constituting an immanent even if not yet present whole.
Processional form signals a hope of unity at the site of difference and conflict: it is Whitman's crowd control, we might say, his way of subduing
and containing recalcitrant particulars within his dream of an American
oneness—his answer (in the sense of equivalence) to the cop's star or club
at the center of the crowd.

We can better approach the problem of dissonance in Whitman's city,
then, by looking at his compositions. When Whitman writes to Doyle, "You
see everything as you pass, a sort of living, endless panorama," he is being
serious about the worth and value not just of seeing but of this particular
mode of urban perception, a moving mode of dynamic panorama, the
mode of procession. It constructs itself as a recounted movement through
city space, a passage which attempts to comprehend a whole in its parts, to
create an impression of a totality out of disparate, disjunctive parts.

A mode of this sort had arisen in the popular press of the new industrial
metropolises of Europe and the United States in the 1830s and 1840s, and
Whitman took as if naturally to the emerging conventions of moving panorama as early as his 1840s newspaper accounts of life in the burgeoning

city (*Walt Whitman of the* New York Aurora). As a visual and kinetic form
the panorama-procession occupied theatrical space within the city; as a
written form in the penny press and periodicals it developed out of the
"ramble" familiar to London readers in the late eighteenth century, drew
upon the "city mysteries" genre of Sue and Lippard and Poe, and in Whitman's city poems takes a new turn as a nuanced method of structuring and
comprehending urban experience. "Crossing Brooklyn Ferry" is Whitman's most exquisitely realized work in the processional mode, but we find
it in much of his journalism and incidental prose and in other poems of
passage through city space.

James doesn't comment on the formal composition of Whitman's rapturous utterances, except to remark dimly and perhaps archly that "his
verses are but ejaculations—things mostly without subject or verb, a succession of interjections on an immense scale." But had he examined the structure within which these interjections performed their work, he might have
found in Whitman's processional order evidence of something he evokes
earlier in the lecture. Speaking of that moment of swiftly changing consciousness, as when "the common practical man becomes a lover," and "the
hard externality give[s] way," illuminating us by "a gleam of insight into
the ejective world," James wrote that "the whole scheme of our customary
values gets confounded, . . . our self is riven and its narrow interests fly
to pieces, then a new centre and a new perspective must be found"
(James 118).

New center and new perspective offer a clue to the radically urban mental configuration embodied in Whitman's processional form. It allows the
speaker of his poems access to ever changing perspectives from a flexible
point of view because it understands the constancy and thus inevitable in-
completeness of its need, a permanent, agitating need, for the other, for
You. A common pattern in the poems is the idle saunter unexpectedly
ruptured, and then a zoom-like shift from wide-field panoramic perspective to close-up scrutiny:

> By the city dead-house by the gate,
> As idly sauntering wending my way from the clangor,
> I curious pause, for lo, an outcast form, a poor dead prostitute brought,
> Her corpse they deposit unclaim'd, it lies on the damp brick pavement,
> The divine woman, her body, I see the body, I look on it alone,
> That house once full of passion and beauty, all else I notice not. (*LG* 367)

The shift in perspective away from the clangor of the main thoroughfares
to the "outcast form" produces the poem's most dramatic perspectival shift,
from within the clangor which knows the prostitute as outcast, to the poet's
own outcast act of looking alone on the dead body, the wondrous but ru-
ined house of the corpse, a look in which the surrounding city of substance
and power—"the rows of dwellings . . . Or white-domed capitol with ma-

jestic figure surmounted, or all the old high-spired cathedrals"—loses its priority and its reality: "That little house alone more than them all—poor, desperate house!"

A similar pattern of a turn in space and a constriction of perspective, a narrowing and sharpening of focus, occurs in "Sparkles from the Wheel":

> Where the city's ceaseless crowd moves on the livelong day,
> Withdrawn I join a group of children watching, I pause aside with them.
>     (*LG* 389)

And as in the dead-house poem, this turn is followed by an obsessive close-up and an attendent shift in the long view of the enclosing city space: in this case, the city vastness rising up as if newly perceived from the perspective of the small group of children, poet, and knife grinder, "an unminded point set in a vast surrounding." Moreover, the sparkles from the wheel suggest a new perception, of city substance collapsing into mere sensation: "Myself effusing and fluid, a phantom curiously floating, now here absorb'd and arrested." The effusion and the arrest suggest a pattern of distintegration of substance into sensation, of matter into light, which elsewhere—"There Was a Child Went Forth," for example—accompanies doubts about the reality of appearance:

> The doubts of day-time and the doubts of night-time, the curious whether and how,
> Whether that which appears so is so, or is it all flashes and specks?
> Men and women crowding fast in the streets, if they are not flashes and specks what are they?
> The streets themselves and the façades of houses, and goods in the windows,
> Vehicles, teams, the heavy-plank'd wharves, the huge crossing at the ferries,
> The village on the highland seen from afar at sunset, the river between,
> Shadows, aureola and mist, the light falling on roofs and gables of white or brown two miles off,
> The schooner near by sleepily dropping down the tide, the little boat slack-tow'd astern,
> The hurrying tumbling waves, quick-broken crests, slapping,
> The strata of color'd clouds, the long bar of maroon-tint away solitary by itself, the spread of purity it lies motionless in,
> The horizon's edge, the flying sea-crow, the fragrance of salt marsh and shore mud,
> These became part of that child who went forth every day, and who now goes, and will always go forth every day. (*LG* 365–66)

An astonishing and immeasurably beautiful enactment of dematerialization, the very condition, in Whitman's processional mode, for fusion of I and You, for integration into a new identity and achievement of the soul.

The very energy of Whitman's processional lines in such a passage, and throughout the majestic "Crossing Brooklyn Ferry," invokes in us a sense of the fragility of the triumph of such lines. They are won against forces of distintegration which Whitman may have understood less gothically than Poe and Melville but with an equal sense of their menace to the integrity of selfhood. But Whitman, like James, also sensed a promise within the decentering forces of the market and of modernity in general, the promise of new registers of selfhood achieved in relation to the "significance of alien lives." He invented his urban processional as a way of moving through the city, through its encountered others, directly to the soul, Whitman's great trope for communal love, labor, and spirit, the only means of attaching the city's incalculable collective wealth, "the money value of [its] real and personal estate," to human experience. Is this not the office of those "dumb, beautiful ministers" in "Crossing Brooklyn Ferry," those persons and things encountered in the crossing no longer alien, who always wait until "[w]e receive you with free sense at last, and are insatiate henceforward" (*LG* 165)?

This receiving of the world with free sense is exactly the function of Whitman's processionals. Procession dissolves the world into sensation in order to accomplish this reintegration. It is a lesson in a mode of being, a way of remaining within the float even while disentangling oneself from it. No wonder James saw within it, saw even further than he may have realized, a remedy for a certain blindness. Seeing processionally is Whitman's most radically urban way of seeking the soul, a way of freeing people from the hold of money and ownership to seek possession of themselves, in Karl Mannheim's terminology, through the ecstasy (ex-stasis) which comes with recognition of oneself in others. Whitman's lesson of the city, his vision of ecstatic community, lies in the turn in consciousness which the unspeakable life of the street brings home.

# 12

# Making Capital: War, Labor, and Whitman in Washington, D.C.

## KATHERINE KINNEY

I begin with the question many, perhaps all, critics have asked when considering Whitman's relation to the Civil War: "What is to be done with the bodies?" Whitman's literal handling of soldiers' bodies, his rendering of them in poetry and prose, and the reader's response to the textual specificity of wounds, dismemberment, disease, and death have posed a critical crux for understanding the poet of the body and the Union. In his reading of *Drum-Taps*, Michael Moon connects these levels of bodily contact, arguing that the "proximity of the writing to the kinds of bodies it tries to incorporate . . . frequently renders the relations of these bodies to each other and to the reader uncanny" (173). In this essay I want to consider the perhaps even more pressing significance of this proximity within Whitman's wartime prose, particularly his *Memoranda During the War* and its later incorporation into *Specimen Days*, and to expand this consideration to a second level of proximity, one generating equally uncanny relations: the presence of the wounded and writing in the nation's capital city.

In early 1863, Whitman wrote a letter to Emerson announcing his intention to write "a little book" about the war and emphasizing the significance of the capital in his design. The familiar quote, "America, already brought to Hospital in her fair youth—brought and deposited here in this great whited, sepulchre of Washington itself—" (*Corr* 1: 69), begins a dramatic, even melodramatic description of Washington city as a corrupt political space redeemed by the presence of sacrificial youth:

> Capital to which these deputies, most strange arrive from every quarter,
> concentrating here, well-drest, rotten, meager, nimble, full of gab and
> their thrice accursed *party* . . . —while by quaint Providence come also
> sailed and wagoned hither this other freight of helpless worn and
> wounded. (*Corr* 1: 69)

The archaic, epic language all but obscures the physical presence of the wounded.

It is only when the letter announces a turn to the personal, "I must abruptly say to my friends," that Whitman begins to narrate events in the particularized manner characteristic of his war prose, evidently speaking of specific cases as literally rather than symbolically representative of the various states and thus the nation. Washington is no longer the "great white sepulchre" but whitewashed hospital barracks of particularized height and length and provisions. Whitman ends the letter with a description which is much closer to the book as published.

> As I took temporary memoranda of names, items, &c of one thing and another commissioned to get or do for the men—what they wished and what their cases required from outside, &c—these memoranda grow bulky, and suggest something to me—so now I make fuller notes, or a sort of journal . . .—This thing I will record, it belongs to the time and to all the States—(and perhaps it belongs to me). (*Corr* 1: 70)

In this description the local grows into the national, but Washington as a preconceived, symbolic national space is no longer at issue in the writing.

It is significant that not only the capital but the conception of an engendering plan for the book falls out of Whitman's introduction to *Memoranda* and *Specimen Days*, and I would argue that this significance is not merely coincidental but can be read as a reaction, whether conscious or not, to the symbolic capitalizing of and on the bodies within the national space of Washington during and following the war. In the opening of *Memoranda During the War* Whitman effectively denies any literary self-consciousness in its composition, presenting instead what began as an account of the origins of the text in the letter to Emerson as the text itself, highlighting, even literalizing, the sense of proximity described by Michael Moon.

> From the first I kept little note-books for impromptu jottings in pencil to refresh my memory of names and circumstances, and what was specially wanted, &c. In these I brief'd cases, persons, sights, occurrences in camp, by the bedside, and not seldom by the corpses of the dead. Of the present Volume most of its pages are *verbatim* renderings from such pencillings on the spot. . . . I have perhaps forty such note-books left, forming a special history of those years, for myself alone. . . . I leave them just as I threw them by during the War, blotch'd here and there with more than one blood-stain, hurriedly written. (*Memoranda* 3)

The authority of the memoranda rests not in Whitman's agency as poet but in their proximity to the wounded. And while the notebooks are certainly not "left just as [Whitman] threw them by," the rhetoric of the memoranda works to close the space between the event and its representation with a sacramental offering of the literal trace, the blood, of the bodies there described.

In *Traces of War*, Timothy Sweet takes this offer literally, arguing that the notebooks "bear traces of the violated human body which cannot be represented and thus must fail to become part of the public record of the war. The very presence of the 'blood-stain[s]' prevents Whitman from representing them; their reality thwarts textualization" (48). Sweet here assumes that the bodily "trace" is literally present in the notebooks; that it signifies without textualization; and that this signification would in some way challenge "the public record of the war." But rather than desiring a representation of the war which would somehow (re)produce the bodies of the dead and wounded as an ultimate artifact or relic, it is also possible and useful to see in these bloodstains the invocation of Whitman's own laboring body. These traces, textual rather than literal,[1] mark the memoranda's original, functional role in Whitman's nursing as notes to remind him of soldiers' names and desires while in active service to them and not only in the retrospective mode they are given in published form. The memoranda are not simply about Whitman's work in the hospital, they were part of it.

The bloodstains direct us not simply to the historical fact of wounding but to the intimate proximity of these bodies, the soldiers' and Whitman's, as well as the closeness of his labor and the writing. As Michael Moon has eloquently argued in *Disseminating Whitman*, and most especially in "Memorial Rags," the intimate handling of bodies and the revealing of wounded and "shattered flesh" in the war texts are "highly erotically charged" ("Memorial Rags" 11). Moon uses this reading of "The Wound-Dresser" to illustrate his search for new forms of mourning to meet the pressing needs of gay men facing the terrible losses inflicted by AIDS. Rejecting homophobic constructions of homosexuality based on "physiological deficiency or abnormality," Moon argues instead for an idea of "bodily abundance and supplementarity" in relation to mourning. The erotic attachment to the shattered flesh of the wounded, dying, and dead is thus neither pathologized as "necrophilia" nor denied as in the traditional critical constructions of Whitman's sublimation of desire through his hospital work. Instead, possibilities for "rememberment" are created—a relation to the dead in which "loss is not lost" (12).

This idea of a "bodily abundance" revealed under the sign of the erotic carries possibilities not only for transforming individual psychic processes, but also for challenging "the public record of the war" which Timothy Sweet invokes. The "bodily abundance" which so marks Whitman's war prose exceeds the institutionalization of memory which the capital comes to embody. If Timothy Sweet is right to argue that "the labor of the soldier does not produce material value; his body is expropriated and exchanged by the state for the maintenance of its ideology" (33), the possibility of the erotic, particularly the homoerotic, allows the soldier's body to exceed this appropriation at some level. (The recent hysteria over gays in the military, especially the insistence on continuing some form of official monitoring of behavior, suggests this quite clearly.)

Again, as Moon argues, the meaningful effect of proximity is ultimately not practical or literal, but uncanny. Whitman insists that the notebooks carry the power to bring back the war and the bodies in material form.

> Out of them arise active and breathing forms. They summon up, even in this silent and vacant room as I write, not only the sinewy regiments and brigades, marching or in camp, but the countless phantoms of those who fell and were hastily buried by wholesale in the battle-pits, or whose dust and bones have been since removed to the National Cemeteries of the land, especially through Virginia and Tennessee. (*Memoranda* 3)

What is striking is not simply the supernatural presence of the past, but the tension between the "active and breathing forms" and the dead, buried, disintegrated bodies which are evoked at the end. The movement from the notebooks as physical artifacts from the war, to Whitman's withheld, "special history of the war," to the war dead's final, public, and symbolic burial in national cemeteries, of which Arlington is the most prominent, suggests a powerful ambivalence about the textualizing of the war's casualties, leading finally to a very suggestive refusal to organize his own record of the soldiers' bodies.

This refusal is more rhetorical than actual. As published in both *Memoranda During the War* and *Specimen Days,* the hospital accounts differ from the notebooks and from each other.[2] In a line which appears at the beginning of the *Memoranda* and at the end of his account of the Civil War in *Specimen Days* Whitman writes, "In the mushy influences of current times . . . the fervid atmosphere and typical events of those years are in danger of being totally forgotten" (*Memoranda* 5; *PW* 1: 116). As a goad to public memory, Whitman describes sitting by the deathbed of a soldier who "recurr'd to the cruelties on his surrender'd brother, and the mutilations of the corpse afterward" (*Memoranda* 5; *PW* 1: 116). The language here is typical—specific yet generic, perhaps referring to a particular case or offering a composite. But the image of mutilated corpses spurs another example, the vengeful execution of seventeen Confederate soldiers at Upperville. Set off in parentheses, Whitman refers us back (or forward in the *Memoranda*) to his description of "A Glimpse of War's Hell-Scenes" but then narrates what he left out before: "(the seventeen kill'd as in the description, were left there on the ground. After they dropt dead, no one touch'd them—all were made sure of, however. The carcasses were left for the citizens to bury or not, as they chose)" (*PW* 1:116–17). These are the things Whitman wrote that "it was best the public should not know" and the things he makes public. In the war prose it is dangerous to forget and dangerous to remember.

This profound ambivalence regarding memory and memorialization centers again and again on the handling of bodies—the responsibility to give proper burial and the loss associated with it. Whitman does not say whether the citizens of Upperville buried those dead. In his account the bodies of the past confront a forgetful present, but the text does not offer any sure mediation of these two states; it neither stabilizes public memory nor closes the book on the past. The most significant change in this section from the *Memoranda* to *Specimen Days* is the inclusion of the line, "The real war will never get in the books"—a statement whose rich ambiguity ironically named more than one book about the Civil War.

This ambivalent attitude toward definitive memorializing gestures can be located at least in part in Washington. Whitman's haunting description of the Patent Office Hospital offers a suggestive place for considering the ways in which the proximity of Whitman's writing to the wounded was shaped by the presence of both in the capital (Fig. 12.1).

A few weeks ago the vast area of the second story of that noblest of Washington buildings was crowded close with rows of sick, badly wounded and dying soldiers. . . . Two of the immense apartments are fill'd with high and ponderous glass cases, crowded with models in miniature of every kind of utensil, machine or invention, it ever enter'd into the mind of man to conceive. . . . Between these cases are lateral openings, perhaps eight feet wide and quite deep, and in these were placed the sick, besides a great long double row of them up and down through the middle of the hall. Many of them were very bad cases, wounds and amputations. Then there was also a gallery running above the hall in which there were beds also. It was, indeed, a curious scene, especially at night when lit up. The glass cases, the beds, the forms lying there, the gallery above, and the marble pavement under foot. . . . (*PW* 1: 39–40)

Whitman refuses to comment on the nature of the curiosity here, ending only with the remark that "such were the sights but lately in the Patent-office" and the information that the wounded have since been removed. The most obvious level of curiosity would seem to be the juxtaposition of broken bodies and machines, suggesting a prophetic judgment of the modernity of the Civil War's confrontation of mass armies. Whitman's description of the Patent Office eerily suggests Stephen Crane's metaphor in *The Red Badge of Courage:* "The battle was like the grinding of an immense and terrible machine to him. . . . He must go closer and see it produce corpses" (158). In the Patent Office the historical connections underwriting the power and terror of the metaphor of "the war machine"—a metaphor which gains increasing currency from the Civil War to the Vietnam War—become visible.

In 1862 the Patent Office Building presented a more general significance as one of the few complete Federal buildings and as one of the most

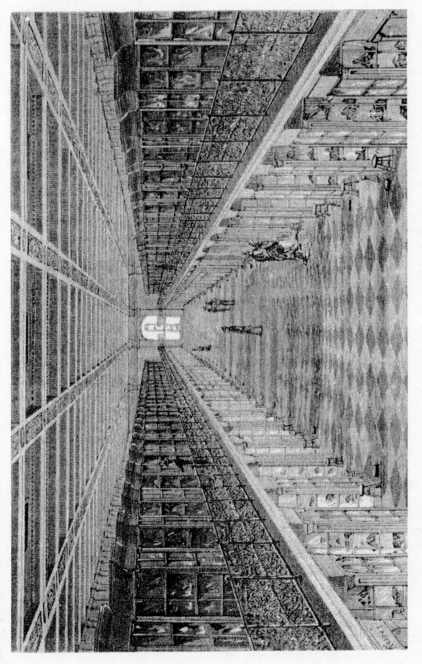

**Fig. 12.1** The Model Room of the Patent Office, reprinted from Mary Clemmer Ames, *Ten Years in Washington* (1875: 438). Ames's caption reads: "This room contains the fruits of the inventive genius of the whole nation. More than 160,000 models are deposited here." Following the battles of Second Bull Run, Antietam, and Fredericksburg, the hall was filled with wounded and dying soldiers.

admired architecturally with its Doric facade of white granite modeled on the Parthenon. Architecturally and functionally, the Patent Office represented the classicism of L'Enfant's original plan for the capital city and the rational humanism of the mechanical, manufacturing base of the northern antebellum society, as suggested by the display of Ben Franklin's printing press at the main entrance. Home to the Department of Interior as well as the Patent Office, the building housed an important scientific library and was a central meeting place for scholars and scientists, offering public lectures and programs in addition to the historical displays. The social and cultural significance of work regarded as important and progressive taking place in a structurally significant and complete space can perhaps be suggested by the reminder that the Capitol itself was without a complete dome at the outbreak of hostilities, and the Washington Monument had stood at one-third its completed height since 1856. Washington was in a very real sense unfinished in 1862.

At the outbreak of the war the Patent Office presented a physical embodiment of the republican, artisan activities and instruments which typify so many of Whitman's poetic catalogs, such as section 15 of "Song of Myself." If the Patent Office celebrated machines as signs of individual creativity and social progress, the Patent Office Hospital suggests the factory moving irrevocably toward Fordism in which bodies are placed indiscriminately into the available places between machines. This may be one of the reasons that so few of the *Drum-Taps* poems contain extended catalogs in which the poet's vision and the use of parallelism and repetition creates unity in multiplicity. "First O Songs for a Prelude" most fully uses the catalog in this way, but to attest to the war's, rather than the poet's, unifying power as Manhattan is put on the march.

In "The Wound-Dresser" the speaker moves from case to case, conveying the sense of the hospital as a kind of terrible catalog, but his presence, like that of the wounded, is embodied in a specific time and place. He cannot be everywhere and with everyone at once as he does to "weave the song of myself" (*LG* 44); "To each and all one after another I draw near, not one do I miss" (*LG* 310). The task of individuation is made more pressing and more difficult in the face of "The crowd, O the crowd of the bloody forms" by both the formlessness of inhuman violence and violated bodies and the regimentation of a "march in the ranks hard-prest" (*LG* 305). Modern war, like the factory which it mimics, has appropriated the poet's vision of simultaneity, shaping multitudes of bodies into indistinguishable spaces, gestures, and costumes. Whitman's claim that *Drum-Taps* was more aesthetically unified than *Leaves of Grass* is in many ways the obverse of his claims of informality in the war prose, both marking the way in which the war strained his previously privileged forms of order and unification.

Later in *Specimen Days* Whitman recounts a return to the Patent Office on the occasion of Lincoln's Second Inaugural Ball, and here uses an abbreviated catalog of impressions in addressing the contrast between the ball and the "different scene" presented by the wounded from Second Bull Run, Antietam, and Fredericksburg.

> To-night, beautiful women, perfumes, the violins' sweetness, the polka and the waltz; then the amputation, the blue face, the groan, the glassy eye of the dying, the clotted rag, the odor of wounds and blood, and many a mother's son amid strangers, passing away untended there, (for the crowd of the badly hurt was great, and much for nurse to do, and much for surgeon. (*PW* 1: 95)

Here "the great white sepulchre of Washington" has been uncannily realized, not an analogy driven by an archaic, epic design, but a vision of death. The death of the soldiers is figured but Whitman's, in his absence from the scene of suffering, is as well; there are too many to be attended, his work remains undone. Behind the celebration of Lincoln's reelection and the assurance that the war would end, that the Union would survive, remains the vision of corporal and perhaps constitutional dismemberment. The war remade the nation, circumscribing the power of the states into Federal domination.

The capital had to make room for the bodies, a literal as well as figurative gesture. Whitman describes the simultaneous way in which the wounded fill the hospitals and the hospitals fill the city:

> Here in Washington, when these army hospitals are all fill'd . . . they contain a population more numerous in itself than the whole of the Washington of ten or fifteen years ago. Within sight of the capitol, as I write, are some thirty or forty such collections, at times holding from fifty to seventy thousand men. Looking from any eminence and studying the topography in my rambles, I use them as landmarks. (*PW* 1: 66)

Whitman's visual survey enacts a gesture key to the capital city's Enlightenment plan. The scale of buildings and the arrangement of avenues was intended to provide a variety of disparate civic and governmental centers which would be connected through vistas, avenues, and promenades. Whitman continues, "Through the rich August verdure of the trees, see that white group of buildings off yonder in the outskirts"; he points to another, and then another. The "white group of buildings" mimics both the white granite and marble facades of the federal buildings and the pastoral vision of the American town, but Whitman reminds us, it "is indeed a town . . . of wounds, sickness, and death" (*PW* 1: 66).

Public gestures of memorializing, like Lincoln's Gettysburg Address or Arlington National Cemetery, seek to control these uncanny inscriptions of death on the symbolic topography of the capital. One of the most overt attempts to make a place for the dead in postwar Washington can be found in the Army Medical Museum. Opened in 1867 in an appropriately morbid and dramatic space—Ford's Theater—the museum put on display the "pathological specimens" which the War Department had ordered the medical corps to collect. According to illustrations in Mary Clemmer Ames's *Ten Years in Washington* (1875), these specimens were displayed in glass cases very similar to those in the Patent Office, fulfilling the eerie sense of the wounded as part of the technological display hidden in Whitman's description of the hospital (Fig. 12.2).

The "curious scene" of the Patent Office, with its spectral, nighttime suggestiveness, is here brought into the open scrutiny of objective display. Gone is the fleshy, tactile, sentient, and sensual presentation of the handling of bodies which Whitman performed and recorded. Ames's book includes a catalog illustration of eight of the museum's "curiosities" (Fig. 12.3). The first specimen, "A Withered Arm," carries this explanatory note: "Skin, flesh and bones complete. Amputated by a cannon shot on the battle field of Gettysburg. The shot carried the severed limb up into the high branches of a tree, where it was subsequently found completely air and sun-dried." The arm stands as a metonym, not for the soldier's body of which it was once a part, but for the cannon shot's capacity for injury. The freakish process of mummification belies amputation's literal and figurative claim as the mark of the war's irredeemable violence. The arm presents instead the essence of reification, in which, according to Marx, "reality, what we apprehend through our senses, is understood only in the form of the object of contemplation, but not as sensuous human activity" (Porter 191). The withering of flesh and the objective display of the museum mark precisely this loss of sensuality—a loss countered by the "bodily excess" of Whitman's war prose in which injury and his response to it, including writing, remain "sensuous human activity." In the Army Medical Museum the body parts are presented through the language of empiricism but ultimately speak in their hideous autonomy as alienated commodities and spectacles of mass culture which owe more to Barnumism than to principles of scientific classification.

If, as Carolyn Porter argues, "sensuous human activity" is "the referent for 'history,'" then the display of pathologized body parts in Ford's Theater symbolizes the alienation of history in postwar commodity culture (195). In the note accompanying the illustration of "All that remains Above Ground of John Wilkes Booth," it is designated a "strange freak of fate that these remains of Booth should find a final resting place under the same roof and but a few feet from where the fatal shot was fired." But it seems less a function of fate than of the marketplace as the increasingly imperial power of the capital city feeds the economy of the tourist trade. Relics of the Civil War share the stage with relics of the Indian Wars, as North and South are joined together in the imaginative and military push West. The "Skull of an Indian" precedes the "Skull of a Soldier" and the "Skull of Little Bear's Squaw" precedes the "Skull of a Man." In spite of

**Fig. 12.2** The Main Hall of the Army Medical Museum. The display of injured body parts mirrors that of the "fruits of the inventive genius of the nation" in the Patent Office (Ames 476).

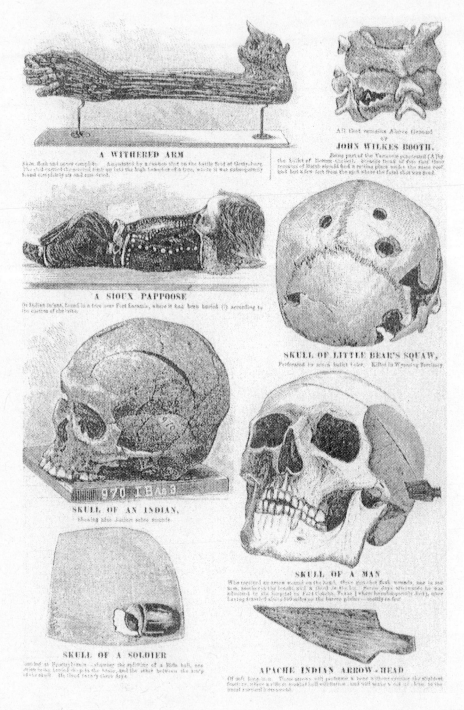

**Fig. 12.3** "Curiosities from the Army Medical Museum." War's violence contained and displayed as a tourist attraction (Ames 482).

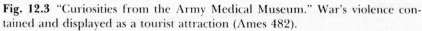

the informal social Darwinism which segregates "Indian" from "man" and "squaw" from "Indian," these skulls are united by the dramatic extent of their injuries. The injuries to Indian bodies are simply counted, "nine distinct sabre wounds" and "seven bullet holes," foreshadowing the future body counts of the Indian Country of Vietnam. Offered as objective description, the numbers supplement the image of U.S. military power and suppress the agency of Indian bodies and cultures. In contrast, the injuries of the "man" and "soldier" are narrated. These "American" skulls tell stories of powerful if perverse resistance measured still in numbers of days or miles and not the individualized pains, fears, and desires of Whitman's cases. History here is literally the abstraction of bodies into processes of power, production, and consumption. Carnage and assassination are comprehended and displayed as a tourist attraction. Ames notes that more than twenty-five thousand people visited the Museum annually (476).

Whitman's memoranda were composed, collected, and prepared for their various printings within a culture actively seeking literal and figurative ways to contain the sheer physical presence of the war's wounded and dead. The crude example of the Army Medical Museum proved itself to be only a curiosity. It may perhaps have been an intermediate gesture, a necessary demonstration of the government's ability to control, order, and enumerate the wounded and the dead in the immediate aftermath of the war. But it offers at least a suggestive explanation for why Whitman would claim again and again that his war prose was without literary design. These memoranda are not formal systems, he insists, but haphazard, random jottings, without any of the mediating gesture of poetry or narrative. With this language of informality, Whitman blunts the taxonomic associations of his own scientifically borrowed language of catalog, type, case, specimen, and collection. Whitman is not finally resisting art, but seeking to counter the techniques of categorizing and abstracting the bodies produced by the war.

The defining gesture of abstraction as the essence of public memorialization can be found in the Washington Monument. When it was completed in 1884, the Washington Monument established the identity of the Mall as a national memorializing space. The Robert Mills design originally called for the obelisk to be surrounded by a portico at the base which would tie it architecturally to the style of the great public buildings, but would also hold burial vaults for public figures. Structural problems forced the base to be redesigned when construction was resumed in 1877 and the burial vaults and porticoes were never built. Thomas Casey, the engineer who completed the memorial, praised the simplicity of the monument's "great abstraction," but the decision to remove literal bodies from the site of the memorial which named and centered the capital city seems at least suggestively related to the recent memory of Washington as all too literally filled with bodies. The bodies disappear in one of the most perfectly phallic representations of power ever conceived.

L'Enfant's diversified conception of the city sought unity through the movement of people from one public building to another, each situated so as to present a different aspect or view line. Whitman's memoranda, often presented as sights viewed from his room or encountered on his walks through the city, present Washington as a series of aspects, one often awash in the blue of soldiers, on parade, or more often, eating, sleeping, or waiting on the streets of the city. The Washington Monument centers this orientation by providing the ultimate vista for the city—a single place from which the whole can be comprehended. In getting above this level, the Washington Monument testifies to the ultimate sublimation of the bodies into a centralized vision of the nation, capital, and history. As Betsy Erkkila has argued, "By the end of the war, republican idealism had itself taken a strong economic and material turn as the concepts of liberty, equality, individualism, and laissez-faire were put in the service of one of the most aggressive capitalist economies in history" (*Whitman the Political Poet* 243). The centralizing of Federal power in the Capitol during the war enabled the consolidation of economic capital on an unprecedented scale.[3]

As Timothy Sweet argues, the soldier's body is always already sublimated into such national capital. The uniform marks the state's power to expropriate individual will and desire and commandeer the body for the collective corps. But Whitman describes again and again the ways in which soldiers in Washington literally occupy a space greater than that contained by ranks, barracks, battles, or orders.

> *The Blue Everywhere:* The city, its suburbs, the capitol, the front of the White House, the places of amusement, the Avenue, and all the main streets, swarm with soldiers this winter, more than ever before. Some are out from the hospitals, some from the neighboring camps, &c. One source or another, they pour plenteously, and make, I should say, the mark'd feature in the human movement and costume-appearance of our national city. (*PW* 1: 85)

In "The Eighteenth Presidency!" Whitman envisioned the orderly entrance of working men into the capital, tan and bearded, fresh from their tools, who would fill the offices of Congress and the presidency and make good the promise of a government of the people. The soldiers do not fill the offices of power, but in fact mark a distance between governmental power and their bodies which carries at least an implicit critique. But the "human movement" of these soldiers does animate the capital, uniting its various Federal and civic sites into a common, "national" space. These unmarshaled troops "swarm" and "pour," preserving in their very excessiveness the democratic vision of that space which can only be seen when moving through the city on its streets and promenades rather than from the seats of power.

This embodied movement carries with it the possibility of the erotic.

Whitman records that he took long walks out of Washington in the company of Peter Doyle, reversing the soldiers' journey into the city: "Fine moonlight nights, over the perfect military roads, hard and smooth—or Sundays—we had these delightful walks, never to be forgotten," noting that the roads "made one useful result, at any rate, out of the war" (*PW* 1: 111). This reversal of direction rewrites the purpose and efficacy of the military presence in the capital. Rather than further centralizing Federal power and domain, the "perfect military roads" open the possibilities for individual pleasure and unauthorized unions.

Following World War II, the Mall took its present form, cleared of obstructing buildings and opening a view line from the Capitol unequivocally centered by the Washington Monument and anchored to the west by the Lincoln Memorial. But in true Whitmanian fashion the banished bodies uncannily returned as the Mall became the premier national site for civil protest. Civil Rights, anti–Vietnam War, Pro-choice, and lesbian and gay pride marches have all drawn crowds in the hundreds of thousands. As bodies fill the Mall, the Washington Monument serves as a marker for measuring crowd size, a measurement repeatedly in dispute as participants and organizers have in every case charged that the National Park Service grossly underestimated turnout. The number of bodies, it seems, routinely exceeds what the government views as officially possible for the space to contain.

But two more recent features of the Mall deserve special comment: the Vietnam Veteran's Memorial and the fall 1992 display of the NAMES Project AIDS Memorial Quilt. Near the end of the war writings in *Specimen Days* Whitman writes, "Even the typical soldiers I have been personally intimate with,—it seems to me if I were to make a list of them it would be like a city directory" (*PW* 1: 111). The Vietnam Veteran's Memorial features exactly such a directory, a guide book to the location of names on the wall. Here Whitman's catalogs of the dead and wounded are institutionalized in granite, but the memorial does not repeat the sublimating gesture of the Washington Monument. It carefully names the dead and the missing and offers the bereaved the tactile satisfaction of touching a name and rubbing a copy of its recessed letters. The memorial is further marked by an intimate proximity similar to that of Whitman's war writings; built not by the government but by veterans, the memorial works to construct a space for the shared experience of the living and the dead. As Charles Griswold notes, while all of Washington's other war memorials are dedicated to the honored dead, the Vietnam Veteran's Memorial is dedicated to all those who served in Vietnam.

In October 1992 the *Washington Post* featured a striking photograph of the AIDS Memorial Quilt covering the Mall's memorial space (Fig. 12.4). The Washington Monument towers awkwardly in the background as the camera focuses on the quilt at ground level. The quilt, like the Vietnam

**Fig. 12.4** The 1992 display of twenty thousand panels of the NAMES Project AIDS Memorial Quilt on the Capital Mall. The Quilt returns perspective to ground level as the Washington Monument recedes into the background.

Veteran's Memorial, enumerates the dead. But even more powerfully than the memorial, it textualizes the intimacy of the labor which produced it. If the quilt's shocking size (twenty thousand panels, fifteen acres at that time) can in fact cover the national space of the Mall, it remains, like Whitman's memoranda, relentlessly localized as well. Sewn by friends, lovers, and families of the dead, it speaks most powerfully to the bodily abundance Moon describes by invoking not simply the dead but those who mourn. The quilt preserves at the individual and collective levels the work of remembering those who have been lost, actively resisting the sublimation of the body and desire represented by the Washington Monument where loss is ultimately lost.

Whitman's memoranda offer, more provisionally perhaps, this same resistance. As in the photograph of the AIDS Quilt, the capital city falls into the background of Whitman's war writings—the proximity of its capitalizing structures comes to carry too much of the imprint of the war's specter of death and dismemberment. Instead Whitman gives us his writing as a function of his work: touching, sitting, waiting, kissing, cheering, feeding, remembering—labors which are not ultimately translatable into Capital.

## Notes

1. It does not finally matter, at least for my argument, whether the bloodstains are actually on the notebooks or not. They function textually if not literally as a mark of proximity and from all accounts of Whitman's hospital service he was close enough to the wounded to make such stains possible.

2. In *Whitman the Political Poet*, Betsy Erkkila notes the textual discrepancies in Whitman's account: "Whitman's Civil War diaries and notebooks may have been written on the spot, and some of them do appear to be blood smeared, but there is little correspondence between them and his published *Memoranda*. That is, his *Memoranda* is not a 'verbatim' rendering of his Civil War notebooks, but a remembrance and reinvention of the war written a decade after its close" (207).

3. See Erkkila: "The gravitation of power from the periphery to the center during the Civil War represented a radical shift from the state-centered union of the past: America was no longer a union of states but a national union. Without the opposition of the South during the war years, government power was exercised increasingly in the interests of the urban and industrial North; economic legislation of the period—a protective tariff, a national banking system, railroad subsidies, and the release of national resources—reflected the new nationalism and the entrepreneurial interests of an industrial, capitalist class" (*Whitman the Political Poet* 246).

# Legacies

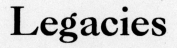

# 13

# Whitman's Calamus Photographs

## ED FOLSOM

I then realized that there was a sort of link (or knot) between
Photography, madness, and something whose name I did not
know. I began by calling it: the pangs of love.
                    Roland Barthes, *Camera Lucida* (116)

The 130 extant photographs of Walt Whitman form the most extensive
photographic record of any American writer who lived and died in the
nineteenth century, but there are some surprising absences among this
abundance of images. While most of the photos, as we would expect, are
images of himself alone, in fourteen cases Whitman appears with someone
else. As we consider these photos of Whitman with others, it is instructive
to think about those people with whom he does *not* appear: he never appears with any member of his family, for example, though he had many
opportunities to be photographed with, especially, his brothers George,
Jeff, and Eddie, and with his beloved mother, Louisa Van Velsor Whitman.
We can imagine that Whitman might have desired some lasting visual me-
mento of his deep affection for Louisa (he always displayed a photo of her
in his bedroom), or of his relationship with Jeff, partner on his New Orleans sojourn; or with George, the brother he traveled to the Fredericksburg battlefield to nurse and with whom he lived for years in Camden; or
with Eddie, his retarded youngest brother, whom Whitman slept with and
cared for. But, in the visual record of Whitman's life, his family is entirely
absent.

There are other strange absences. There is no photograph of Whitman
with Horace Traubel, his devoted friend and amanuensis who visited him
virtually daily for the final years of his life, and who had countless photos
of himself taken with many of Whitman's friends, but, oddly, never with
the poet himself. Missing, too, are the photographs we might expect of him
with friends and disciples like Richard Maurice Bucke, William Douglas
O'Connor, Thomas Harned, John Burroughs, and Edward Carpenter.
These remarkable absences all suggest that Whitman did not view his accumulating photographic record as a documentary archive or visual biogra-

phy. Rather, as Michael Davidson contends in his essay on Whitman's cross-dressing elsewhere in this volume:

> It is hard to think of another writer of his era who so thoroughly exploited the possibility of the camera for staging versions of self, from Broadway dandy to rough-hewn outdoorsman, from kindly preceptor to visionary sage. In all of these representations, clothing, props and body language are important adjuncts to the effect desired. (223)

In his photographs with other people, Whitman used the others as props in the staging of radically new versions of the self, new subject positions that destabilized traditional categorizations of human relationships and that portrayed alternative familial and social bonds that he knew an emerging democracy would demand.

Instead of documenting his biological family, then, Whitman chose to construct an evocative visual record of a very different kind of family, one in which he could coterminously occupy the place of father and mother, wife and husband, lover and friend. His photographs with others record an alternative affectional family, one that recasts traditional gender roles and allows him to be, at once, lover/mother/father/brother. Whitman's subject position in these portraits is unstable and shifting, representing him as a "fluid, vast identity" (*LG* 514), as "the fluid and attaching character" (*LG* 154) he sought to vocalize in his poems. On three different occasions, Whitman was photographed with the children of friends (Figs. 13.1– 13.3).[1] In these tender portraits, Whitman—the childless man who nonetheless once claimed to have fathered six children—appears with seven different children, embracing them in something between a maternal and grandfatherly way, his body language collapsing the usual gendered distinctions, just as his poetry often did when his "I" spoke as father and mother:

> O the old manhood of me, my noblest joy of all!
> My children and grand-children, my white hair and beard,
> My largeness, calmness, majesty, out of the long stretch of my life.
>
> O ripen'd joy of womanhood! O happiness at last!
> I am more than eighty years of age, I am the most venerable mother,
> How clear is my mind—how all people draw nigh to me! (*LG* 180)

In the snapshot of Whitman with the family of his playwright friend Francis Howard Williams (taken in Williams's backyard), Whitman's large hand easily holds little Aubrey Williams, who just as easily rests her arm and tiny hand on Whitman's thigh (Fig. 13.3). As if to underscore his unsettling new subject position as mother man, Whitman has apparently effaced the real mother from the only surviving copy of the photograph,

**Fig. 13.1** Whitman with Kitty and Harry Johnston. Photographer: William Kurtz. 1879. Courtesy of Gay Wilson Allen.

**Fig. 13.2** Whitman with Nigel and Catherine Cholmeley-Jones. Photographer: George C. Cox. 1887. Courtesy of Library of Congress.

scratching Mrs. Williams's face off the photographic surface, a final editing of the image that completes the transformation of a nuclear family into a more fluid democratic and egalitarian one, where the maternal and paternal, the tender and the strong, mix in the new coalescent figure of Whitman "the tenderest lover" (*LG* 122), the maternal father of a nation. The effacing of Mrs. Williams removes the only adult woman ever to appear in a photograph with Whitman and allows Whitman to occupy not the expected role of emblematic father but the transgressively blended role of father/mother: he replaces the absent father in this photograph and displaces the present mother. As with the other photographs of him with children, we are presented here with the conventions of a posed family portrait where the "family" has to be construed outside traditional definitions, even while familiar and comforting "family" emotions are triggered by the careful staging and posing.

Whitman never had his picture taken with anyone who was remotely his contemporary in age. The only other photographs of Whitman with others are a series of revealing images of him with four young male friends—Peter Doyle, Harry Stafford, Bill Duckett, and Warren (Warry) Fritzinger (Figs. 13.4–13.9). One way to describe Whitman's photos with others, then, would be to say that he shared photographic space only with children (the informal snapshot of the Williams family, with Mrs. Williams expunged, underscores his prohibition of adults). But, while Whitman referred to Peter Doyle, Harry Stafford, Bill Duckett, and Warry Fritzinger as "darling boy" or "my son," and while in his letters he often constructed them as children, they were in their late teens or early twenties at the time the photographs were taken. They do not appear in these photos as symbolic children; they occupy a different and far more intimate relationship with the poet. Their age moves them into an even more unstable relational realm than was the case with the younger children.

This series of photographs of Whitman with his young male friends forms a revealing subgroup of Whitman photos. Spanning the last twenty-five years of his life, they were taken in four different decades: the late 1860s with Doyle (the first photos in which Whitman appears with anyone else); the late 1870s with Stafford; the mid-1880s with Duckett; and the early 1890s with Fritzinger. Punctuating Whitman's post-Civil War life, they become visual representations of the poet's "Calamus" relationship.[2] They were all taken after the appearance of his "Calamus" poems in 1860, and they manifest his decision, announced at the opening of that cluster, to "proceed for all who are or have been young men, / To tell the secret of my nights and days, / To celebrate the need of comrades" (*LG* 113). These photographs represent and document Whitman's involvement in "[t]he institution of the dear love of comrades" (*LG* 128). In 1876, shortly before he had his photo taken with Harry Stafford, Whitman wrote that,

**Fig. 13.3** Whitman with the family of Francis Williams (Aubrey, Marguerite, Churchill). 1888? Courtesy of Library of Congress.

**Fig. 13.4** Whitman and Peter Doyle. Photographer: M. P. Rice, Washington, D.C. c. 1869. Courtesy of William R. Perkins Library, Duke University, Trent Collection.

important as they are in my purpose as emotional expressions for humanity, the special meaning of the *Calamus* cluster of LEAVES OF GRASS, (and more or less running through that book, and cropping out in *Drum-Taps*,) mainly resides in its Political significance. In my opinion it is by a fervent, accepted development of Comradeship, the beautiful and sane affection of man for man, latent in all the young fellows, North and South, East and West—it is by this, I say, and by what goes directly and indirectly along with it, that the United States of the future, (I cannot too often repeat,) are to be most effectually welded together, intercalated, anneal'd into a Living Union. (*LG* 753)

**Fig. 13.5** Whitman and Peter Doyle. Photographer: M. P. Rice, Washington, D.C. c. 1869. Courtesy of Ohio Wesleyan University, Bayley Collection.

**Fig. 13.6** Whitman and Harry Stafford. Photographer unknown. Late 1870s. Courtesy Sheffield [England] Library, Edward Carpenter Collection.

Given such a political agenda for "Calamus," we might expect that Whitman would have published and distributed the photos of himself that documented such a "sane affection," but it was not until after Whitman's death that any photos of the poet with his young male friends (or those of him with the younger children) were published. When, in the decade following his death, they began to appear, they were accompanied by commentary that sometimes illuminated but often blurred the revisionary and transgressive nature of the images. Eager to protect Whitman from the taint of homosexuality, his most powerful disciples tried to stifle the poet's radical intersecting of sex, gender, and democracy by simply dismissing as calumny any suggestion of Whitman's sexual transgression. Controlling access to the Calamus photos was part of their strategy, and they were wary of any attempts to distribute the photos widely.

In *Walt Whitman: A Study* (1893), John Addington Symonds included the first sustained public discussion of Whitman's "Calamus" emotions as suggestive of a physical love of man for man, and he included in his book as an illustration the photograph of Whitman with Warren Fritzinger (Fig. 13.9), an informal portrait taken in 1890 by Whitman's English admirer John Johnston (who would later publish the picture in his *Diary Notes of a Visit to Walt Whitman and Some of His Friends in 1890* [1898]). Johnston's Calamus photo captures Walt and Warry on the Camden docks, with the poet in his wheelchair, attended to by the young man he called his "sailor boy" (Elizabeth Keller 124), who served as Whitman's nurse and companion during his final three years: "I like his touch," Whitman said in 1889; "he has that wonderful indescribable combination—rarely found, precious when found—which, with great manly strength, unites sweet delicacy, soft as a woman's" (*WWC* 6: 83). Just as in these photos Whitman poses in such a way as to cross gender distinctions, so does he admire in his young comrades their ability to transgress such boundaries as well, to "unite" a "sweet delicacy, soft as a woman's" with "great manly strength." It is to that rare and "precious" and "indescribable combination" that he sought to give voice in his "Calamus" poems and to envision in his Calamus photos.

Symonds was anxious to have this photo when he first saw it, and he wrote to Johnston immediately, asking for a copy. In an 1891 letter to Horace Traubel, Symonds referred to his own lover, the Venetian gondo-

**Fig. 13.7** Whitman and Bill Duckett. Photographer unknown. Camden, New Jersey. 1886. Courtesy of Ohio Wesleyan University, Bayley Collection.

**Fig. 13.8** Whitman and Bill Duckett. Photographer unknown. 1886. Courtesy of Ohio Wesleyan University, Bayley Collection.

lier Angelo Fusato, as "my Italian 'Warry'" (Symonds, *Letters* 599). Traubel, the self-appointed keeper of Whitman's reputation, was clearly alarmed by Symonds's implication and quickly began to distance himself and the Whitman establishment from Warry: when another English admirer, J. W. Wallace, praised Warry's intimate service to Whitman, for example, Traubel's protective armor went up: "You have in some respects made too much of Warry, and given to his work for Walt meanings and associations which are not properly a part of the picture."[3] Something in Warry's relationship to the poet clearly unsettled Whitman's literary disciples, and Symonds's inclusion of the Warry photo in his book was therefore an incendiary event, especially given Symonds's accompanying commentary on Whitman's "Calamus" emotions, emphasizing precisely the fluid boundaries between masculine and feminine that Whitman so admired in Warry:

In his treatment of Love, Whitman distinguishes two broad kinds of human affection; the one being the ordinary sexual relation, the other comradeship or an impassioned relation between man and man. The former he describes as "amativeness," the latter as "adhesiveness." There is no reason why both forms of emotion should not co-exist in the same person. Indeed, Whitman makes it plain that a completely endowed individuality, one who, as Horace might have said, is "entirely rounded and without ragged edges," will be highly susceptible of both. (*Whitman* 75)

Symonds celebrates Whitman's "high pitch of virile enthusiasm, which, at the same time, vibrates with acutest feeling, thrills with an undercurrent of the tenderest sensibility" (*Whitman* 87), but he delicately sidesteps the

**Fig. 13.9** Whitman and Warren Fritzinger. Photographer: John Johnston. On the Camden wharf, 1890. Courtesy of Charles E. Feinberg. (There is another similar photo of Whitman and Fritzinger, not reproduced here, taken by Johnston moments after this one; see Folsom, *"This Heart's Geography's Map"* 37.)

issue of Whitman's outright endorsement of male-male sex, nonetheless noting that, "human nature being what it is, we cannot expect to eliminate all sensual alloy from emotions raised to a high pitch of passionate intensity" (*Whitman* 91–92). Finally, Symonds allows Whitman an eloquent silence on the question of male-male sex: "Like Plato, in the *Phaedrus*, Whitman describes an enthusiastic type of masculine emotion, leaving its private details to the moral sense and special inclination of the individuals concerned" (*Whitman* 90)—this despite the fact that Whitman wrote to Symonds the much discussed "I have had six children" letter, denying the "morbid inferences" that Symonds drew from *Leaves of Grass* about "the possible intrusion of those semi-sexual emotions & actions which no doubt do occur between men" (*Corr* 5: 72–73).[4] In his book, Symonds acknowledges Whitman's denials but lets the reader know he suspects that the poet was disingenuous:

> Had I not the strongest proof in Whitman's private correspondence with myself that he repudiated any such deductions from his *Calamus*, I admit that I should have regarded them as justified; and I am not certain whether his own feelings upon this delicate topic may not have altered since the time when *Calamus* was first composed. (*Whitman* 93)

His inclusion of the Fritzinger/Whitman photo served Symonds as visual proof that the poet's Calamus emotions in fact extended to the end of his life; when he wrote to Johnston asking for the photo, he indicated that he had a special insight into the meaning of the image: "I am trained to see, an artist of any kind sees more than the uninitiated can" (Symonds, *Letters* 531).

Three years later, in 1896, Thomas Donaldson in his *Walt Whitman, the Man* published another Calamus photo—the image of Whitman and Bill Duckett in Whitman's phaeton (Fig. 13.7). Donaldson captioned the photo "Mr. Whitman in his buggy—Bill Duckett, his boy friend, with him. Camden, October 1886." The ambiguity of the term "boy friend," signaling at once a friend who was but a boy and an intimate male partner, is simply allowed to stand with no gloss. The photo—fuzzy and taken from some distance—seemingly implies nothing more than a driver-passenger relationship: Duckett often served as Whitman's driver. But the relationship echoes in suggestive ways the Whitman-Peter Doyle relationship, which began, of course, as a conductor-passenger relationship on a streetcar. Doyle's own recollection of his first encounter with Whitman was, as he said, a "curious story":

> We felt to each other at once. I was a conductor. . . . Walt had his blanket—it was thrown round his shoulders—he seemed like an old sea-captain. He was the only passenger, it was a lonely night, so I thought I would go in and talk with him. Something in me made me do it and

something in him drew me that way. He used to say there was something in me had the same effect on him. Anyway, I went into the car. We were familiar at once—I put my hand on his knee—we understood. He did not get out at the end of the trip—in fact went all the way back with me. (Bucke 23)

Doyle's recollection comes from an interview that appeared in Richard Maurice Bucke's 1897 book, entitled *Calamus,* a collection of Whitman's letters to Pete. For the frontispiece to this book, Bucke arranged to have an engraving made of one of the two photographs of Whitman with Doyle (Fig. 13.4). This engraving, appearing five years after Whitman's death, was the first public appearance of any of his formal Calamus photographs, those in which the poet joins his young male comrades in something like a wedding pose: the comrade's hand is always on the shoulder of the poet, who, seated, appears as elder comrade, father figure, and bride. Whitman's subject position is unstable enough here to allow him spatially to occupy the position of bride but temporally (given his age and stature) to play the groom's role, too. While Whitman never cross-dressed in his photographs, he did cross-pose, and these traditional wedding poses of an old man/bride/ groom and young man/groom/bride have some of the effects of cross-dressing: gender and sex and even generation lose their categorical status as Whitman and his comrades stage unnamed identities and relationships.

It was not until 1905 that the second Whitman/Doyle photo was published (Fig. 13.5). It appeared in Eduard Bertz's *Walt Whitman: Ein Charak-terbild,* the German work that inflamed the controversy about Whitman's sexuality; in it Bertz mounted an extended argument asserting that Whitman was homosexual, and offered the Whitman/Doyle photo as one prime piece of evidence (281–86). Traubel (who had given Bertz a copy of the photo) and other American Whitman defenders relentlessly attacked Bertz's book, which to this day (despite its relevance to much Whitman criticism) remains untranslated. The other Calamus portraits, including the formal portraits with Stafford and with Duckett (Figs. 13.6 and 13.8), re-mained unpublished until quite recently; they were circulated only among Whitman's close friends and their families. The Calamus photos, then, re-mained esoterica for many years after Whitman's death.

While we cannot be sure just what significance these photos had for Whitman, we do know that he valued them and that he showed them to an intimate group of friends. Roland Barthes, in his essay on photography, notes that to be photographed is to experience "a micro-version of death," a sense of "becoming a specter," for "the Photograph . . . represents that very subtle moment when, to tell the truth, I am neither subject nor object but a subject who feels he is becoming an object" (*Camera Lucida* 14). Whit-man was well aware of the death-objectification built into any act of repre-sentation, and *Leaves of Grass* was his attempt to heroically withstand that inevitable process, to create the illusion of a living representation, of a book as a man. The photographs and engravings of himself that he wove into the various editions of *Leaves* were part of his desire to merge into print, to plant a living identity into the pages of his book, to keep alive and make perpetually elastic that transitional moment of subject becoming object.

With his Calamus photos, however, Whitman resisted the process of objectification in a different way, remaining reluctant to have the photos replicated, even while he kept them close at hand and shared them with his friends. Barthes observes that "Society is concerned to tame the Photograph, to temper the madness which keeps threatening to explode in the face of whoever looks at it" (*Camera Lucida* 117). Whitman, too, was aware of the culture's power to tame what it found potentially crazy, and his decision not to publish these photos indicates his awareness that, were they to become common objects, society would temper them (as in fact happened when Bucke had the Doyle/Whitman photo transformed into a subdued line engraving for the frontispiece to *Calamus*). Whitman's friends who saw the photos sensed the power, even the madness, in the representations of a male-male affection that as yet had no genre of representation. The "look" in these photos greatly disturbed some of Whitman's disciples, even if they could not precisely name the quality that most agitated them. These Calamus photos jostled traditional photographic representational genres, opening the space for a new kind of subjectivity, but a subjectivity that could initially be made available only to a restricted public, lest the photos slip into the common currency of images, their marginality, madness, and pangs of love turned mainstream, safe, and sane. While Whitman often published images of himself that swept everyone into his gaze, he secluded those images of himself in which his gaze is shared with or focused on others; his books were built on self-representations that were inclusive in their outlook, but his exclusive gazes were preserved in portraits unpublished during his lifetime. His "Calamus" poems, distinctive in tone from the rest of *Leaves*, remained all the more inscrutable because none of the portraits that accompanied Whitman's various books and editions ever represented the new relationship.

Their obscurity and encrypted quality, then, rendered these Calamus photographs hieroglyphs in an emerging sign system of male-male desire. Eve Kosofsky Sedgwick has suggested how "Photographs of Whitman, gifts of Whitman's books, specimens of his handwriting, news of Whitman, admiring references to 'Whitman' which seem to have functioned as badges of homosexual recognition, were the currency of a new community that saw itself as created in Whitman's image" (*Between Men* 206). And Richard Dellamora has extended this suggestion into an analysis of what he calls "the Whitmanian signifier," discovering in the late nineteenth century a striking "use of his name as signifier of male-male desire during the period" (86). The Calamus photographs were a key part of this new code, becoming a kind of black-market currency set up by a coterie of Whitman's friends and followers for those who did not deal in the mainstream heterosexual economy. Because he did not publish them in any of his books or include any in his widely circulated groups of reproduced photographs, these images remained sequestered signs of a Whitman who was "not what you supposed, but far different" (as he described himself in the "Calamus" poems [*LG* 115]). The Calamus photos, again like the "Calamus" poems, represent a self located not on the open road but "In paths untrodden, / In the growth by margins of pond-waters, / Escaped from the life that exhibits itself" (*LG* 112). Public photos of such marginalized territory could not exist, because once such images became public they could be co-opted and tamed by the heterosexual majority (just as for decades the dominant readings of "Calamus" were simply as friendship poems).

This sequestered life escaped exhibition except to the initiated few, for whom the Calamus photos—rare and intimate—became talismans. Characteristically putting his faith in a transformed future, Whitman wrote in "Calamus" that it would only be the "Recorders ages hence" who would be able to see "down underneath this impassive exterior," who would be able finally to "Publish my name and hang up my picture as that of the tenderest lover, / The friend the lover's portrait, of whom his friend his lover was fondest" (*LG* 121–22). Whitman left behind a small group of portraits that he knew would eventually be appropriate for such a display, portraits that signaled a self beneath the "exterior" of his widely distributed self-sufficient portraits. We have already seen how John Addington Symonds procured a copy of the Fritzinger/Whitman photograph, an image that he knew he was "trained to see" in ways the "uninitiated" never could. Similarly, soon after the Doyle/Whitman photos were taken, members of Whitman's circle began vying for their own copy of that significant image; Edward Stewart—in an 1870 letter to Whitman in which he expressed longing to join in the "gay times" that he knew Whitman, Doyle, and the other "old Covies" were enjoying, and in which he told Whitman that he had rejected "some very flattering valentines" from women because the invitations "came from wrong quarter"—requests photos, especially "a double one of yourself & Peters I would like very much to have that" (Shively 110–11).

This "double photograph" (Fig. 13.5) of Whitman and Doyle was clearly considered a dangerous representation by some of Whitman's friends and admirers. We have already noted that, by 1905 (when the image first became public), it was used by Eduard Bertz as an obvious sign in the emerging semiotics of homosexuality. We can perhaps get the best sense of how explosive the photo seemed by observing how it struck Thomas Harned, Horace Traubel, and William Douglas O'Connor, the three main keepers of Whitman's reputation (two of whom became the poet's literary executors and thus had a heightened sensitivity about Whitman's public image). One day in Whitman's room, in 1889, Traubel picked up the picture (which Whitman kept close by), examined it, and described it as "a rather remarkable composition: Doyle with a sickly smile on his face: W. lovingly serene: the two looking at each other rather stagily, almost sheepishly." What then happened in the room as Whitman and his friends looked at the photo is extraordinary: Whitman, Traubel tells us, "laughed heartily the instant I put my hands on it," and Harned began to mimic and mock the look on Doyle's face, causing Whitman to retort: "Never mind, the expression on my face atones for all that is lacking in his. What do I look like there? Is it seriosity?" Harned's answer is astonishing: "Fondness, and Doyle should be a girl." Clearly, Harned has sensed a homoerotic quality in the photo that he finds perverse and very discomfiting. Whitman shakes his head at Harned's remark and laughs, defending Doyle as "a master character": "Tom, you would like Pete—love him: and you, too, Horace. . . . you, Horace, must particularly make it your point to come in relations with him" (*WWC* 3: 542–43).

The next year, Traubel finds the picture again (now on the floor by Whitman's chair) and this time describes it as "the two sitting l͟o͟o͟k͟i͟n͟g gazing into each other's eyes"; Traubel's emendation is telling, for he clearly sees more than a look, something intimate, intent, expressive of desire, requiring him to alter the neutral "looking" to the more suggestive "gazing." Traubel then writes that it is "a picture which O'Connor described to me as 'silly-idiotic,' " though Whitman continues to call it "first-rate." Whitman then exclaims, according to Traubel, "Dear Pete! Many's the good day (night) we have known together!" (Traubel MS; see *WWC* 7: 265). Traubel's parenthetical "night" is also suggestive; since Traubel in this manuscript is recording Whitman's spoken words, he almost never uses parentheses, and it is difficult to imagine how Whitman could utter a parenthetical word (this is the only time in Traubel's vast record of Whitman's conversations that I have found such a use of parentheses). It is probable that Whitman said "night," but that Traubel thought he had better record "day" and at least contemplate for a while which way he should present the statement when he published it (since Traubel did not live to publish these notes, it is impossible to say). Traubel apparently is uneasy about the implications of Whitman's many good nights with Doyle, just as he is about the "sheepish" look on Whitman's and Doyle's faces, and he is struck by how negatively Harned and O'Connor react to the photo.

Some of Whitman's most influential friends, then, obviously felt that the photo—as an icon of male-male affection—was too dangerous to be made public; they feared that it would confirm what others already suspected of Whitman—that his "Calamus" poems spoke of a physical as well as a spiritual union between males. Were such a suspicion to become generally acknowledged, Whitman's hopes of entering the canon of great American writers in an increasingly homophobic culture would be doomed (thus his disciples' outrage at Bertz's avowal of Whitman's homosexuality, with the photo offered as evidence, and thus their efforts to keep Bertz's argument safely distanced in the German language). The photograph, as a trace of reality, seemed to Whitman's friends *too* physical, too telling in the bodily proximity (a love-seat pose) and erotic gaze that it staged and recorded.

So, after Whitman's death, when Bucke issued his *Calamus* collection of Whitman's letters to Doyle, he carefully chose the *other* photograph of the two friends—the safer, more casual one—to be engraved as the frontispiece, presenting the book as the record of a loving but spiritual friendship. And, as often happens when photographs are engraved, H. D. Young's frontispiece portrait softened the photo—stylizing it so as to strip it of its immediacy and charged physicality, and deadening Whitman's gaze at Doyle.

Though Whitman's associates were alarmed by the poet's gaze turned privately onto another male, they realized that his intense, absorptive, democratic gaze was the key to his poetic vision. They celebrated the democratic gaze, and their dilemma was that this affirmative public gaze seemed somehow to be inextricably bound to the forbidden private one. Many of his disciples, in other words, were "afraid of the merge" (*LG* 1855: 31), unwilling to go as far as Whitman insisted in the breaking of bounds between the public and the private. For Whitman, the love of comrades was not an emotion marginal to a democracy, but central to it; his faith was in a future of "manly affection": "It shall be customary in all directions, in the houses and streets, to see manly affection, / The departing brother or friend shall salute the remaining brother or friend with a kiss" (*LG* 609). As Dana Brand has noted in his study of Whitman's "imaginative interaction with the city" (156), Whitman developed a new kind of urban affection based on the propagation of this gaze into a crowd, discovering that "urban spectatorship magnified with affective energy" (183) might create a "new city of Friends" (*LG* 133), a revolutionary Calamus love that would transform the nation:

> When "Calamus" lovers do have some form of physical contact, . . . they generally hold hands or place arms around each others' necks. . . . To place an arm around the neck of a lover, or to walk hand in hand with him, is to join gazes, to look out at the world from a joined perspective. Even if such contact differs from gazing into the eyes of the lover, it is still a form of love experienced in a shared gaze. (183)

This is one source of power in the Calamus photos—Whitman and his male companions share gazes. In the case of the Doyle photos, Whitman's gaze is directed at Pete, and in the photo that most disconcerted his friends, Whitman and Doyle are lost in each other's gazes. Instead of seeing signs here of a new kind of affection that could redefine America, Whitman's official disciples could only respond homophobically by seeing such images as a perversion of the heterosexual norm ("Fondness, and Doyle should be a girl," as Harned expressed it). Not unreasonably, they feared the Calamus photos would be swallowed up into the emerging medical discourse of "homosexuality" as a pathology (thus their disgust at Bertz).

We have no record of Whitman's disciples' reaction to the photograph of Harry Stafford and Whitman (Fig. 13.6), but they must have recoiled at least as much at it as they did at the image of the poet with Doyle. Taken in the late 1870s, this photo is the most vivid marriage pose. In 1876 Whitman had entered an intense and stormy relationship with young Harry, and he gave him a ring to symbolize his affection; it is visible in the photo on Harry's right hand. Over the next few years, the ring was taken back and regiven several times; Harry's and Walt's letters to each other record the 'til-death-do-us-part intensity of their involvement: "You know when you put [the ring] on," Stafford wrote in one letter, "there was but one thing to part it from me and that was death" (qtd. in Shively 160).

I discovered this striking photograph in the Edward Carpenter papers in the Sheffield, England, library; it was sent to Carpenter by Harry's sister Ruth, along with a letter recalling Carpenter's visit to the Stafford farm in 1877 (where, according to Gavin Arthur—one of Carpenter's lovers—Carpenter experienced fellatio with Whitman [Katz 636]). It is fitting that Carpenter ended up with the photo; he himself lived with a young working-class man and was a pioneer in writing about homosexuality. He propagated the exchange of visual tokens of male affection among those in the Whitman circle, as when he wrote the poet in 1880: "When you see Harry Stafford give him my love and say I am going to send him a photo: and hope he will send me one." A couple of months later Carpenter wrote again to Whitman, telling him of his own young Calamus lover: "I am living with a man—the best friend I ever had or could think to have—an iron worker. . . . He often says 'I wish Walt Whitman would come over here.' "[5]

The Stafford/Whitman photo was thus as meaningful a token for him as the Fritzinger photo was for Symonds, one that he shared privately among his friends. Like many of Whitman's disciples, Carpenter was concerned and ambivalent about how to publicly present Whitman's sexuality. In his book about Whitman, Carpenter quotes the poet's famous self-description: "There is something in my nature *furtive* like an old hen!" (43). This furtiveness caused Carpenter to always hedge his bets when he tried to define Whitman's sexual nature: "Both sexes seem to come equally within the scope of his love" (151), he wrote in his essay on "Walt Whitman's Children," but in the manuscript of this essay, we find that his sentence originally continued on: "Both sexes seem to come equally within the scope of his love, whether physical or spiritual."[6] The last phrase is heavily crossed out and, like the Stafford photo, was never published. There was a conspiracy of silence about the physical side of Whitman's love, and Carpenter's excised comment worked much like the Calamus photo that he possessed and preserved but did not publish. Instead of confronting the political implications of same-sex love, Carpenter chose finally to present Whitman's Calamus-emotion as safely cleansed of physical passion and sublimated into a spiritualized communal concern.

In some ways, the most mysterious relationship recorded in the Calamus photos is that between Bill Duckett and Whitman (Fig. 13.8). Of the four

young men with whom Whitman was photographed, we know least about
Duckett: as a teenager, he lived on Mickle Street and was taken in by Whitman's housekeeper, Mrs. Davis; he lived in Whitman's house as a boarder
at various times in 1886. At this time, Whitman wrote one of his stranger
documents—a two-page reminiscence about Duckett's life with Whitman,
written as if told by Duckett! Whitman seems to have been trying to prime
the young man to write a saleable set of notes, but Bill was slow to pick up
on the project and wrote only a few cursory entries before giving up (see
White 21–22). Whitman hired him to drive his buggy and wrote letters of
reference to help him get other jobs. Duckett accompanied Whitman on a
trip to New York for the poet's April 1887 Lincoln lecture. But the two
had a falling-out, and by early 1889, Mrs. Davis went to court to collect on
Duckett's unpaid boarding bill. Whitman was horrified to learn that at the
trial Bill suggestively testified that he owed no money since Whitman had
invited him into his home as his guest. As evidenced in the photo of the
two of them, they were close friends; Whitman recalled several occasions
on which he and Bill had traveled together (on one of which, no doubt,
the photo was taken): "he was often with me: we went to Gloucester together: one trip was to New York: . . . then to Sea Isle City once: I stayed
there at the hotel two or three days—so on: we were quite thick then:
thick: when I had money it was as freely Bill's as my own" (*WWC* 4: 65).
Duckett continued to ask Whitman for money as late as 1889, after which
he disappears from Whitman scholarship.

Duckett shows up again in a remarkably explicit photograph (Fig. 13.10)

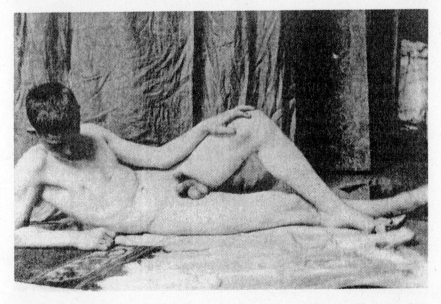

**Fig. 13.10** Duckett at Philadelphia Art Students League Rooms. Photographer:
Thomas Eakins. 1886–92. Metropolitan Museum of Art, David H. McAlpin
Fund.

taken by Thomas Eakins, who had painted and photographed the poet
during the 1880s and 1890s. Duckett apparently became one of the models
for Eakins's erotic male nude photographs (see Hendricks 6, 141; Johns,
"Avowal" 78–80). Eakins, of course, took many photographs and did many
paintings of nude males and females, and his images of nude males wrestling, swimming, or loafing together serve to document the emergence of
what Betsy Erkkila calls Whitman's "homosexual republic" ("Whitman and
the Homosexual Republic" 153).

Over the years, poets and critics have speculated about the possibility
that there might have been an Eakins painting or photograph of Whitman
in the nude. The poet Philip Dacey, for example, in "Thomas Eakins: The
Secret Whitman Sitting," offers a dramatic monologue in which Eakins tells
about the imagined time he painted Whitman nude: "I helped him / out of
his robe and shawl-like blanket, feeling / the while like a nurse about to
bathe a patient." Even naked, Whitman manages to strike a pose, construct
an identity:

> He was giving me The Good Gray Poet down
> to his last disguise. Even the face he showed
> was itself a mask, formal, hieratic,
> as if he meant to say, "Even while you should
> think you caught me, behold, I have escaped you."

And then, just when Whitman seems most revealed, stripped of disguise,
he becomes for Eakins the impossible cross-gendered mother man:

> . . . I kept myself as composed as any
> of my paintings, letting myself be moved
> by what I saw, but never giving in.
> Until I focussed on his old man's dugs,
> or they focussed on me. Those centers burned me,
> like eyes themselves, pitiful blind eyes
> that saw everything. I had the thought—
> or it had me, seeming to pierce me from
> all sides at once—"This is my father, this
> is my mother," and with that thought sank
> like Whitman, from my reserve into my weeping.
> What the words meant I didn't know.

Dacey's Eakins never finishes his portrait, knowing he could never fully
accomplish the painting he wanted:

> the one in which Whitman's nakedness doesn't
> challenge us, like a hat worn indoors or out,
> but enters us like words whispered at night,
> some message about our secret parentage—

"I am your father, I am your mother"—
what a sleepy child might vaguely hear
and never—never fully—understand. (6–9)

What if Whitman actually did pose naked for Eakins's camera? What would we make of a photograph of Whitman "undisguised and naked" (*LG* 29)? Such an artifact may in fact exist. Among the series of photographs of nude men and women that Eakins left behind—what he called his "naked series"—is one that is now simply labeled "old man" that bears a striking resemblance to Whitman (Fig. 13.11). The date of the multiple photo is uncertain—sometime in the 1880s. If the "old man" is not Whitman, Eakins clearly found a model who was a ringer for Whitman, a stand-in who could serve Eakins as Whitman's body-double for his form studies. If this multiple photograph is of Whitman, it would have been taken sometime between 1882 and 1886;[7] it clearly had to have been taken before Whitman suffered a severe stroke in June 1888. In the early and middle 1880s, Whitman was in relatively good health (following his recovery from an earlier stroke) and was busy posing for several artists, including Eakins, Gilchrist, Sidney Morse, and J. W. Alexander.

In fact, in the late 1870s and early 1880s, while recovering from his first stroke, Whitman often shed his clothes and was very comfortable being naked around friends and acquaintances. The poet who portrayed himself in "Song of Myself" as "hankering, gross, mystical, nude," often swam naked as a young man (in scenes like those later made familiar in Eakins's "Swimming Hole" painting and photos), but his most extended descriptions of nakedness came when he was in his late fifties and early sixties. In *Specimen Days* ("A Sun-Bath—Nakedness"), Whitman tells of his days spent in the nude by Timber Creek in the late 1870s, when he would take an "Adamic air-bath" and enjoy "two or three hours of freedom, bathing, no talk, no bonds, no dress, no books, no *manners*." "Nature was naked, and I was also," wrote Whitman, arguing that "nakedness" was not "indecent," that he experienced "moods when these clothes of ours are not only too irksome to wear, but are themselves indecent." Sounding like a supporter of Eakins's controversial insistence on the undraped figure as essential for an artist's training, Whitman celebrated the "purity" of nakedness, and he suggested that those "many thousands" who had not experienced "the free exhilarating extasy of nakedness" could not know "what faith or art or health really is," for "the whole curriculum of first-class philosophy, beauty, heroism, form" derived from the "natural and religious idea of Nakedness" (*PW* 1: 150–52). Around this time, in 1879, as Whitman turned sixty, Herbert Gilchrist sketched him naked (except for hat and shoes) by Timber Creek. (Fig. I.2) As late as the summer of 1881, Whitman records a joyous "naked ramble" on the beach at Far Rockaway, as he playfully shouts Homer to his friends who watch from a nearby boat (*PW* 1: 273).

It is fitting, then, that Whitman would have been photographed in the

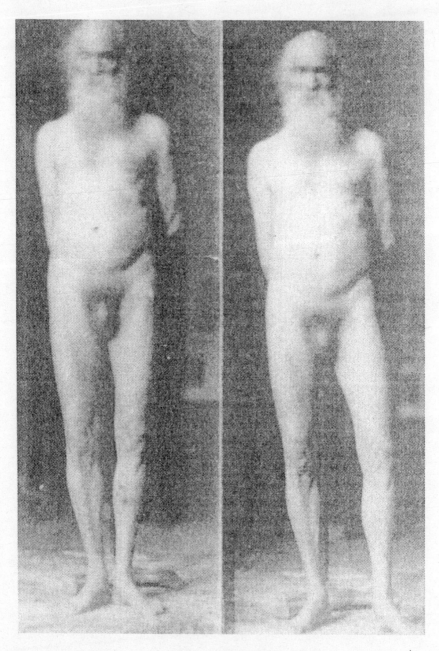

**Fig. 13.11** Old Man (Detail). 1880s. Photographer: Thomas Eakins. Albumen, 3³/₁₆ x 7⁵/₈ in. The Collection of the J. Paul Getty Museum, Malibu, California.

nude by Eakins, but several factors need to be considered in trying to de-
termine whether or not this image is indeed Whitman's. The date generally
cited for Whitman's and Eakins's first meeting is early 1887; this is based
solely on Whitman's 1889 recollection, reported to Horace Traubel, that
his first meeting with Eakins occurred when the artist "came over with
Talcott Williams" and then returned to Camden a couple of weeks later,
carrying "a black canvas under his arm" to begin painting Whitman's portrait. "After that," Whitman said, "he came often—at intervals, for short
stretches" (*WWC* 4: 155). Since we know that Eakins painted Whitman's
portrait in 1887, it has seemed reasonable to assume that the first meeting
between the two men was early that year. If the date of this first meeting
is accurate, and if all the "naked series" photos were taken before Eakins
left the Pennsylvania Academy in 1886, and if Eakins was indeed the photographer for the entire "naked series" (unlikely, since he is the model for
one of the multiple photographs), then the "old man" in the photograph
could not be Whitman. If, however, Whitman's recollection is faulty (or
if he was hiding a fact of an earlier meeting with Eakins) or if Whitman posed for another photographer (one of Eakins's associates), then the
"old man" could be Whitman. The evidence seems to point to most of
these "naked" photos having been taken around 1883, a date that, for a
number of reasons, is feasible for a first meeting between Whitman and
Eakins.

Talcott Williams, the man who accompanied Eakins to Whitman's house
in 1887, would have been the likely connection. Williams, a reporter and
then editor for the Philadelphia *Press,* was a good friend of Whitman's. He
and Whitman had been in touch before Williams even moved to Philadelphia in 1881; Whitman's daybooks record his sending books to Williams
in Springfield, Massachusetts (where Williams worked for the *Springfield
Republican*), as early as March 1880. After he moved to Philadelphia, he
quickly turned the *Press* into one of Whitman's most vigorous supporters;
he also published Whitman's poems in the paper and paid him hand-
somely. By 1882, Whitman considered Williams "an ardent friend," especially for his editorial support of the poet in the Boston censorship controversy over the 1881 edition of *Leaves* (see *Corr* 3: 296–97, 378–79). By
1884, Whitman was frequenting Williams's home, and he and Williams met
often throughout the 1880s. Williams, who would later become director of
the Columbia University School of Journalism, was a remarkable journalist,
known for his liberal views and often unorthodox methods (he once accompanied Weir Mitchell, one of Whitman's physicians, to a brothel to see
what it was like [Dunbar 185]).

After settling in Philadelphia, Williams also quickly became good friends
with Eakins, whom he knew well during the artist's often stormy years at
the Academy (1882–1886), where his controversial teaching methods (including removing the loincloth from a male model with female students
present, having female students work with male cadavers, having female

students pose in the nude for him at private sessions, and photographing
his students in the nude) continually got him in trouble and led to his
dismissal in 1886 (see Foster and Leibold 69–79). As he did with Whitman,
Williams firmly supported Eakins in the *Press* and fought the public's prud-
ishness about sex and nudity: Whitman's explicit portrayal of the body in
his poetry was for Williams the verbal equivalent of Eakins's explicit portrayal of the body in his paintings and photographs. Only months before
Williams defended in the *Press* Whitman's inclusion of explicit bodily and
sexual descriptions in his poetry, Whitman published his *Specimen Days* account of the exhilaration he felt when he ran naked on the beach the previous summer. By 1882, then, Williams would have been well aware of Whitman's comfort in stripping off his clothes in front of others, and he would
have read Whitman's other celebrations of "Sweet, sane, still Nakedness"
in *Specimen Days* (*PW* 1: 152). At this time, Whitman was in good health
again, strong enough to swim in the sea and run in the sand, and it would
have been during these years (1882–1886) that Eakins took the "old man"
photo. Just as Williams brought Eakins out to Camden in 1887 to begin
painting Whitman's portrait, so, four or five years earlier, he may have
brought Whitman into Philadelphia to pose for Eakins's camera, the two
artists of the naked human body brought together in one lasting representation.

Eakins was a great admirer of Whitman. We don't know when he first
read Whitman, but we can be sure that Williams, who often wandered the
streets of Philadelphia with Eakins in the early 1880s (see Dunbar 184),
would have talked to him about the poet. By the 1890s, Eakins and his
friends referred to each other as "all us Whitman fellows," and they did so
in the context of their belief that the human body was beautiful and should
be studied without shame (Foster and Leibold 179). Eakins, of course, went
on to photograph Whitman in the final years of the poet's life, and he
brought his associates to photograph him as well (see Folsom *"This Heart's
Geography's Map"* 38–41, 61–62; Homer 85–98). As for Whitman's views
on Eakins, it is important to note that he admired the painter most of all
for his ability, unique among artists, to "resist the temptation to see what
they think ought to be rather than what is" (*WWC* 1: 41). Eakins's photographic sense of reality—his ability to open himself fully to the physical
world like a treated photographic plate (see Folsom, *Native Representations*
99–126)—led Whitman to conclude that "Eakins is not a painter, he is a
force" (*WWC* 1: 284). Whitman particularly delighted in a story that
Traubel once told him about Eakins "of a girl model who had appeared
before the class, nude, with a bracelet on—Eakins, thereupon, in anger,
seizing the bracelet and throwing it on the floor." Hearing this story, Whitman laughs and exclaims, "It was just like Eakins—and oh! a great point is
in it, too" (*WWC* 5: 499). Whitman celebrates Eakins for his insistence on
getting rid of any distracting ornament, on turning our sight full force on
the naked form. As Kathleen A. Foster notes, "Together, these men define

a zone at the edge of late-nineteenth century Anglo-American culture where art and sexuality struggled for fresh expression" (Foster and Leibold 116). It would seem appropriate, then, that these mutual admirers should have met in the early 1880s to preserve in a series of photographs their unashamed celebration of nakedness.

This photo of the confident and proud old man stripped but, as Dacey suggests, still giving us the Good Gray Poet down to his last disguise, recalls the opening of Whitman's first self-review of *Leaves of Grass:*

> Very devilish to some, and very divine to some, will appear the poet of these new poems, the "Leaves of Grass;" an attempt, as they are, of a naive, masculine, affectionate, contemplative, sensual, imperious person, to cast into literature not only his own grit and arrogance, but his own flesh and form, undraped, regardless of models, regardless of modesty or law, and ignorant or silently scornful, as at first appears, of all except his own presence and experience. (*LG* 777)

This Eakins photo was not published until this past decade; like the Calamus photos, it existed out of the public realm during the century in which the Whitman-myth was developed that canonized a more conventional and less unsettling national poet than we should have had. Whitman has always been read as the poet of the body and the poet of comradeship, but his photographic texts encourage us to read his written texts in far more transgressive and explicit ways than we usually have. In deciding not to publish these photos and also not to destroy them (as he did other photos of himself that he found problematic for various reasons), he left them for posterity, once-secluded images that are only gradually flowering into public meaning, staging possibilities for a radically democratic and egalitarian set of affections.

## Notes

1. At least two "family group" photographs were taken in the 1879 session with Kitty and Harry Johnston at the William Kurtz studio in New York. Kitty and Harry were the children of Whitman's good friends, the New York jeweler John H. Johnston and his wife Amelia F. Johnston. The children called the poet "Uncle Walt," and, in 1888, Kitty wrote to "My dear Uncle Walt": "We . . . need one dear person to make the family complete; this person is a Grandpa; won't you come and be one to us? we would all be so happy if you came" (see *Corr* 5: 254n). At least four group photos were taken in the 1887 session with Nigel and Catherine Cholmeley-Jones at the George C. Cox studio in New York. Nigel and Catherine were the nephew and niece of Jeannette Gilder, editor of *The Critic*, who accompanied Whitman to Cox's studio; Cox

saw the children as "soul extensions" of the poet (Folsom, *"This Heart's Geography's Map"* 58). For reproductions of all the extant photos in these series, see Folsom, *"This Heart's Geography's Map"* 23, 33–34.

2. I use the terms " 'Calamus' relation" and " 'Calamus' emotions" throughout this essay. Such terms have become contested territory in Whitman criticism, and they are often used to refer specifically to the period of the late 1850s, when Whitman clearly experienced a relationship with a male that led to the composition of what became in the 1860 edition of *Leaves of Grass* the "Calamus" cluster of poems. My use of these terms indicates a more extended and protean set of relationships throughout Whitman's life. It is sometimes forgotten that Whitman kept returning to and redefining the term "Calamus" after its initial appearance in print in 1860. In this essay, I quote his extended rewriting of "the special meaning of the *Calamus* cluster" (*LG* 751) in 1876. He would continue to come back to and rethink the implications of the term throughout his life. Even as late as 1890, when confronted with the charge that "the subject of 'Calamus' " might be understood as "verging upon the licentiousness of the Greek," Whitman's response was to once again reconstruct the meaning of the term:

> Yes I see! and indeed I can see how it might be opened to such an interpretation. But I can say further, that in the ten thousand who for many years now have stood ready to make any possible charge against me—to seize any pretext or suspicion—none have raised this objection; perhaps all the more reason for having it urged now. "Calamus" is a Latin word—much used in Old English writing, however. I like it much—it is to me, for my intentions, indispensible—the sun revolves about it, it is a timber of the ship—not there alone in that one series of poems, but in all, belonging to all. It is one of the United States—it is the quality which makes the states whole—it is the thin thread—but, oh! the significant thread!—by which the nation is held together, a chain of comrades; it could no more be dispensed with than the ship entire. I know no country anyhow in which comradeship is so far developed as here—here, among the mechanic classes.

Horace Traubel, who records this statement, notes that Whitman spoke "with a great vehemence as if it came of deep and long rumination" (*WWC* 6: 342–43). Without denying the homosexual interpretation of "Calamus," Whitman deftly dilates its meaning into a wide social realm and insists that it is essential to his entire poetic project. In this essay, then, I use the term "Calamus" to suggest Whitman's evolving construction of male-male affection; the Calamus photographs are one expression of the range of implications inherent in Whitman's extended use of the term (see Folsom, *Native Representations* 166–71).

3. Traubel's letter (May 4, 1893) is in the Whitman Collection, Bolton (England) Metropolitan Library. For more on Traubel's relationship with Warry Fritzinger, see Krieg. Robert Peters, in what is apparently a spoof, claimed in 1984 to have discovered a cache of love letters and love poems from Whitman to Fritzinger (including photos of both men); see Peters 254–58.

4. Whitman's letter to Symonds has occasioned a substantial amount of commentary. For three of the most illuminating recent interpretations of Whitman's motives in writing the letter, see Lynch 92–94; Erkkila, "Whitman and

the Homosexual Republic" 166–68; and Martin, "Whitman and the Politics of Identity" 172–74.

5. Both of Carpenter's letters to Whitman are in the Sixsmith Collection, John Rylands University Library of Manchester, Manchester, England. The first letter is dated Easter Sunday, 1880, the second July 1, 1880.

6. Carpenter's manuscript is among the Edward Carpenter Papers in the Sheffield, England, central library.

7. Eakins's photograph of the old man appeared in an exhibition catalog called *Photographer Thomas Eakins* (Philadelphia: Olympia Galleries, 1981: 33) and was reprinted in Parry 63. Eakins photographed many men and women of various body types, almost always posing them in the same seven postures. Many of the models were Eakins's students at the Pennsylvania Academy; Eakins himself posed for one series. This group of photos furnished him with a storehouse of accurate representations of the human body for use in his paintings and art classes. Eakins also used the photos to illustrate "the general axes of weight and action" and "the centers of gravity" of the human figure. He began taking the "naked series" in 1882, mounting each multiple photograph on a piece of light blue textured cardboard. Sometime after he resigned under pressure from the Pennsylvania Academy in 1886, a package of the "naked series" photographs (including this one) ended up in the hands of Edward H. Coates, Chairman of the Committee on Instruction; the images remained in Coates's safe deposit box and resurfaced only in the late 1970s (see Parry 53–62; Goodrich 1: 246–48; and McCauley 36–45).

It was difficult to get nude models in Philadelphia in the early 1880s, and Eakins resisted using drifters who picked up money for posing nude (see Foster and Leibold 75). Since in the "naked series" he set out to catalog various body types for the use of his students, Eakins needed a large number of models. So he convinced his students to pose, and he and his soon-to-be wife Susan Macdowell led the way by serving as models. It is important to note that of the more than fifty models Eakins managed to recruit for this series, only one is an old man and only one a young boy (interestingly, both the unidentified boy and old man seem to have been photographed on the same day or at least in the same setting and same light; see Parry 58). There are many intriguing questions here, but for our purposes the most intriguing is this: who is this single old man, and why would he be part of the series?

# 14

# "When the World Strips Down and Rouges Up": Redressing Whitman

## MICHAEL DAVIDSON

Another self, a duplicate of every one . . .
Under the broadcloth and gloves, under the ribbons and arti-
  ficial flowers,
Keeping fair with the customs, speaking not a syllable of itself.
                    Walt Whitman, "Song of the Open Road"

So we are taking off our masks, are we, and keeping our
mouths shut? as if we'd been pierced by a glance!
                    Frank O'Hara, "Homosexuality"

I always say you're born naked and the rest is drag.
                    RuPaul

## I

In his speech to the Republican Convention in August 1992, Patrick Buchanan described the previous month's Democratic Convention as "that
giant masquerade ball up at Madison Square Garden where twenty thousand liberals and radicals came dressed up as moderates and centrists—in
the greatest single exhibition of cross-dressing in American political history."[1] On one level, Buchanan's invective was addressed to what he perceives as the liberal platform of the Democrats—their inclusion of abortion
rights, health care reform, and environmental issues at the convention. On
another level, it was addressed to the increasing presence of gay and lesbian issues in American political life—AIDS research, domestic partners legislation, job protection, artistic censorship—which challenge the Family
Values agenda of the religious right. By regarding Democrats as political
transvestites, Buchanan may link sexual and political identities such that
(so-called) perversity in one sphere may be read as corruption in another.
    It is worth keeping Buchanan's rhetoric in mind as we consider Walt
Whitman's legacy to later poets if only to remind ourselves of the continu-

ing and virulent strand of homophobia that permeates our current political debate.[2] When identity is regulated according to a heterosexual norm, when gender is policed by rigid binaries, then Whitman's radical view of the self as ensemble is jettisoned. It might also be worth keeping Buchanan's trope of cross-dressing in mind as we consider the ways that contemporary gay male poets have appropriated Whitman's sexual politics to speak for social identities that even the good gray poet could not have envisioned. Whitman's "glorious mistake," as Robert Duncan called it, is not that he believed in America but that he envisaged it as a nation of others—a queer nation—where private and social bodies could be linked under a common law.

Duncan, like many poets of his generation, understood that there was a price for linking the private and the social:

> I too
> that am a nation sustain the damage
>     where smokes of continual ravage
> obscure the flame.
>         It is across great scars of wrong
>     I reach toward the song of kindred men
>     and strike again the naked string
> old Whitman sang from. (64)

Duncan recognizes that in order to identify with Whitman, he must "sustain the damage" of a society in which he is not allowed to participate. The price of nonparticipation, for both Duncan and Whitman, is painful vision, an ability to see "always the under side turning, / fumes that injure the tender landscape" (64). Whitman anticipated such mediated relations to the social body by describing himself perpetually "aft the blinds of the window," gazing out at forms of nakedness and mutuality for which "democracy" was the most available term but for which "adhesiveness" proved the most potent. When he becomes the woman who "hides handsome and richly drest" to watch the twenty-eight bathers or when he asserts that he is "the poet of the woman the same as the man," readers have heard a sensible appeal to pluralism. The gay or lesbian poet, however, might hear in such lines not simply identity within difference but identity within identity, the adoption of one role to articulate another. Finding their literary and sexual identities in the years following World War II, gay writers addressed Whitman by re-dressing his problematic of identity in specifically gendered terms. Thus the perennial topic of Whitman's influence must take into consideration not only the "outsetting bards" he produced but the multiple identities from which he was productive.

## II

Before considering Whitman's direct influence on subsequent writers we should consider the validity of using cross-dressing to describe his performance of gender. After all, there is no indication that Whitman crossed Brooklyn ferry in drag or even addressed the social practice of transvestism. I am using cross-dressing as a sign of what Marjorie Garber calls a "category crisis" in which the deliberate confusion of gender markers confuses definitional distinctions (male/female, subject/object, poet/reader, gay/straight) (16). According to Garber, cross-dressing is a pervasive phenomenon in social life, ranging in its forms from businessmen who wear women's underwear beneath their three-piece suits to gender-bending rock stars like Michael Jackson and Madonna to full-scale drag balls. Its appearance threatens to disrupt narratives of gender and sexual differentiation not because it reverses roles but because it foregrounds gender and sex *as* roles. Far from representing the desire of one gender to reveal its "true" identity through the garb of the other, cross-dressing foregrounds the performative character of identity itself. The eternal debate over Whitman's "object-choice" has been framed narrowly within an identitarian (and heterosexist) logic—if interested in stevedores and boat captains, therefore not interested in women—thus limiting the poet's many claims to be "untranslatable" (*LG* 89).[3]

As Garber points out, the presence of transvestism in literature represents a "category crisis elsewhere" (17) in society, a displacement of tensions in culture at large onto the normative logics of gender differentiation. As I will point out in the case of Frank O'Hara, images of cross-dressing in his poetry often articulate racial and national crises during the Cold War period. In Whitman, the adoption of female personae signals the emergence of new sexual categories in the postbellum period that were beginning to be defined in medical and psychological literature. These categories, especially those defined in phrenological and mesmerist tracts, challenged definitions of masculinity and homosociality that were part of America's expansionist development. But such displacements of crisis from one sphere of society onto the sex/gender system needn't result in a strict binarist conception. In Jennie Livingston's film about African-American drag balls, *Paris is Burning* (1991), what is revealing is not so much the presentation of males dressed up as women (in high style fashions or Las Vegas chorus line gear) but men dressed up as men in a variety of professional roles, from military cadet to professional executive in three-piece suit. The sheer range of cross-dressed styles, across genders, classes, professions, races, and attitudes in this film provides the best optic on how limited the term "cross-dressing" can be when confined to a simple replacement of one gender with its putative opposite. Although Livingston's film depicts a distinctly postmodern version of gender confusion (one dependent on the existence of large urban populations of African-Americans and Latinos), it expands the possibilities of what transvestism *might include* as identity performance.

The most common gender-crossing scenario in Whitman is that in which, like the twenty-eight bathers section of "Song of Myself," the poet adopts a feminine position in order to participate erotically with other males. Sexual and textual acts interlink in ways that force the reader to become, as it were, a third participant in Whitman's mediated desire. Michael Moon describes such moments as those in which "[w]oman and (male) speaker meet in the 'unseen hand' which is also a sign of the substitutive relationship in which the poem *makes* seen what is unseen (hidden or proscribed desire) through the substitution for it of language and writing" (*Disseminating Whitman* 47). This materialization of unspeakable identities in the text is often figured through a rhetoric of dressing and undressing in which the act of removing clothing reveals an identity hidden beneath. "Undrape! you are not guilty to me" (*LG* 35) is Whitman's most characteristic appeal to authenticity, yet such invocations of nakedness are framed by the clothing that must be removed. "Agonies are one of my changes of garments" (*LG* 67) Whitman acknowledges in section 33 of "Song of Myself," and elsewhere he speaks of "thrusting [himself] beneath . . . clothing" (*LG* 116) or of seeing "through the broadcloth and gingham" (*LG* 35) in order to reveal the body underneath. He notes "The little plentiful manikins skipping around in collars and tail'd coats," but he acknowledges in them, "the duplicates of myself" (*LG* 77). For every claim that "What is commonest, cheapest, nearest, easiest, is Me," there is the countervailing awareness that the poet must "[Adorn himself] to bestow [himself] on the first that will take [him] . . ." (*LG* 41).[4]

Whitman adorned himself in much more immediate ways than in poetic figures of speech. In daguerreotypes and photographs taken throughout his life, Whitman constructed versions of himself to present to the public and to introduce each successive edition of his poem. As Alan Trachtenberg notes, his "pictures took on epithets of their own—'The Christ likeness,' the 'Quaker picture,' 'my sea-captain face,' the 'Lear photo,' the 'Laughing Philosopher,' and, inevitably, 'the mysterious photograph' " (67). It is hard to think of another writer of his era who so thoroughly exploited the possibility of the camera for staging versions of self, from Broadway dandy to rough-hewn outdoorsman, from kindly preceptor to visionary sage. In all these representations, clothing, props, and body language are important adjuncts to the effect desired. And he compounded this visual self-presentation with a series of reviews and publicity blurbs of his own work, written by himself, in which the "myth" of Walt Whitman was created for the public. What is remarkable about all such performances is that Whitman saw them as serving an essential authenticity, analogous to the poetry which, as he wrote in one unsigned review, becomes "his own flesh and form, undraped, regardless of models" (*LG* 777). If *Leaves of Grass* was to be an "indirect epic" of the American Adam, Whitman's self-conscious reinvention of himself may have been the poem's most indirect feature.

Perhaps the most famous moment of cross-dressing, aside from the twenty-eight bathers passage mentioned above, is that in "The Sleepers" where Whitman as dreamer becomes both female lover and male beloved, as well as the surrounding darkness:

> I am she who adorn'd herself and folded her hair expectantly,
> My truant lover has come, and it is dark.
>
> Double yourself and receive me darkness,
> Receive me and my lover too, he will not let me go without him.
>
> I roll myself upon you as upon a bed, I resign myself to the dusk.
>
> He whom I call answers me and takes the place of my lover,
> He rises with me silently from the bed. (*LG* 426–27)

In the passage's opening lines, the speaker is female, but genders quickly change place as the darkness is invoked. By asking that the darkness "double" itself, the speaker demands both obscurity as well as duplicity in the erotic scene about to take place. By doubling the darkness, she/he may be released from all boundaries and "resign" her/himself to whatever happens. Robert K. Martin notes that the " 'I' of these lines is both active and passive" (*The Homosexual Tradition* 10); the speaker desires both to "receive" as well as to "roll myself upon you as upon a bed." But Martin sees the female voice as a "pretense" which Whitman eliminates as the passage moves toward its sexual apotheosis, whereas I see the constant shifting of positional relations between woman, lover, and darkness as the displacement of a unitary voice released by sexual excitation and reenacted in the dream.

This reading is supported by the subsequent section, omitted in the final 1881 edition of *Leaves of Grass*, in which the complex deixis in the lines above is replaced by a series of metonymic substitutions for a sex act of an indeterminate nature. The speaker finds him/herself naked and vulnerable: ". . . no one must see me now! my clothes were stolen while I was abed, / Now I am thrust forth, where shall I run?" (*LG* 626). Revealed (and aroused) the speaker is now subject to (or the subject of) a sexual act that, however explicit, is also wildly indeterminate with reference to the specific event taking place:

> The cloth laps a first sweet eating and drinking,
> Laps life-swelling yolks—laps ear of rose-corn, milky and just ripen'd;
> The white teeth stay, and the boss-tooth advances in darkness,
> And liquor is spill'd on lips and bosoms by touching glasses, and the best liquor afterward. (*LG* 627)

Critics have regarded these lines as representing fellatio, through the phallic images of corn and the ejaculatory "spill'd" liquor. But the very ambiguity of "laps" as noun and verb, as protective covering and oral stimulation,
makes placing this act extremely difficult. What seems considerably more
important than defining the ways Whitman's figuration "hides" a given sexual act is the way that it "reveals" the multiplicity of erotic possibilities
made possible through the shifting of roles. These lines should be read in
terms of the larger poem: a dream fantasy in which subject and object shift
positions, leaving the speaker caught among multiple personae: "I am the
actor, the actress, the voter, the politician" (*LG* 426). When in the second
section, Whitman, imagining himself dead, says "It is dark here under
ground, it is not evil or pain here, it is blank here, for reasons" (*LG* 427),
he is speaking as much about the ambiguities of sexual identity as he is
about mortality. It is precisely this "blank . . . for reasons," a sexual and
textual surd, that subsequent writers have tried to fill in.

# III

Most theories of influence explain Whitman's mediated relations to identity
as an oedipal struggle with strong literary precursors. Harold Bloom's influential version of this model points to a tension between expansive acceptance and evasiveness, but he can only explain such vacillation as a sign of
Whitman's filial anxiety over the dominating presence of Emerson. Hence
the following passage exemplifies a rhetorical *clinamen* or "reaction formation against his precursor":

Apart from the pulling and hauling stands what I am,
Stands amused, complacent, compassionating, idle, unitary,
Looks down, is erect, or bends an arm . . .
Looking with side-curved head curious what will come next,
Both in and out of the game. . . . (*LG* 32)

By reading this passage as a conflicted response to Emerson's "Experience," Bloom avoids a more profound critical *clinamen* that would histori-
cize this alienation (249). Whitman's "what I am" stands "apart from the
pulling and hauling" not simply to defend himself from Emerson's authority but because he is institutionally prohibited from entering categories of
self-presence which Emerson subsumed under the Transparent Eyeball. It
was for Hart Crane to recognize the social stakes of Whitman's mediated
gaze and begin a process of homosexual response that has continued into
the recent period.[5]

I have characterized this response by the term "redress" to speak of at
least two ways in which poets have "talked back" to Whitman, each of
which is based on homosexual desire.[6] The first usage refers to the mode

of redress as corrective or remedy by which modernist poets acknowledged
Whitman's importance while attempting to neutralize his excesses. This is
the mode of Ezra Pound, T. S. Eliot, and many New Critics who saw Whitman as an embarrassing American relative complicating their project of
cultural risorgimento. "Mentally I am a Walt Whitman who has learned to
wear a collar and a dress shirt" (*Selected Prose* 145) says Pound, and in his
"A Pact" we hear the young expatriot strike a grudging truce with his stub-
born literary father:

> I make a pact with you, Walt Whitman—
> I have detested you long enough.
> I come to you as a grown child
> Who has had a pig-headed father. (*Personae* 89)

What remains unacknowledged in Pound's response may be his discomfort
over Whitman's importance for those British poets of the 1890s—Robert
("foetid") Buchanan, John Addington Symonds, Algernon Swinburne, William Rossetti—with whom he was anxious not to be confused. Since several
of these poets—Symonds, most famously—identified with Whitman's particular homosexual meanings, we may insinuate in Pound's swaggering
posture a gendered male alternative to what he perceived as an effeminate
British affectation.[7]

Whitman's excesses, so embarrassing to an earlier generation, became
his virtues for poets who came of literary age in the 1950s and 1960s. His
direct address, sexual themes, and open forms offered a salutary alternative to literary and social formalisms. Taking Whitman's personal address
to heart, young poets "redressed" him in contemporary garb, the term now
used to mean "dress again." One can see the range of such appropriations
in the anthology edited by Jim Perlman, Ed Folsom, and Dan Campion,
*Walt Whitman: The Measure of his Song,* in which the poet is presented in
a variety of contemporary settings: Whitman playing baseball (Jonathan
Williams), selling hot dogs at a beach concession stand (Larry Levis), working as Native American ecologist (Joseph Bruchac), languishing in rush-
hour traffic (William Heyen), and arm wrestling with Louis Simpson (Dave
Smith). And in perhaps the best-known version of this "redressed" Whitman, Allen Ginsberg discovers him "poking among the meats in the refrig-
erator and eyeing the grocery boys" (qtd. in Perlman 123). In Ginsberg's
vision, Whitman is brought directly into consumer society, a ghostly shop-
per searching for images of American plenitude. The contemporary supermarket, with its "peaches" and "penumbras," becomes the reified version
of that "lost America of love" Whitman envisioned through comradeship.
In all these refashionings, Whitman is a figure of loss whose historicity,
ironically enough, lies in his ability to transcend his historical moment and
reinvigorate the present. By redressing him as "our contemporary," poets
have measured the failings of American political and social life and have

created a space for themselves as, in Lawrence Ferlinghetti's phrase, "Whitman's wild children" (qtd. in Perlman 204). Whitman's legacy, in this reading, is based on a hearty spirit of masculine comradeship that both excludes women and reinforces homosocial community.

There may be a third way in which Whitman is recovered, this time shorn of all ontological supports and invested with those gender-bending tendencies excoriated by Patrick Buchanan. It is this considerably transformed mode of redress that we find in the work of Frank O'Hara who often invokes Whitman as a sign of American resilience and energy but whose chatty, cosmopolitan tone seems the very opposite of Whitman's bardic celebrations. O'Hara acknowledges Whitman in numerous poems and essays, but I am interested less in the earlier poet's direct appearance than in his absence—the ways Whitman's afflatus is ventriloquized through O'Hara's flexible, often theatrical voice. When O'Hara says that "only Whitman and Crane and Williams, of the American poets, are better than the movies," he is setting a standard for poetry based upon Hollywood, not tradition and the individual talent (498). It is by this (however parodic) standard by which O'Hara's poetry achieves its particular relevance for homosexual identity insofar as it constructs its most profound moments of self-revelation through public figures like Lana Turner, Billie Holliday, and Norma Shearer or by means of the signage of modern urban life.

O'Hara's desultory, "I do this I do that" mode offers a plastic vehicle for addressing positional relations. As Bruce Boone points out, O'Hara's camp tone, far from trivializing homosexual identity, represents its presence as communal possibility, even its potential for opposition and transgression. Furthermore, the discursiveness of this style undercuts the bardic, testamentary features of the "new American poetry" with its faith in the redemptive powers of the (masculine) voice and body, and creates the possibility of a presence formed out of feminine as well as masculine identities.

If Whitman's "voice" does not seem immediately evident in O'Hara it may be because of the persistence of a certain identitarian logic that limits influence to thematic or tonal parallels. Robert K. Martin, for example, does not include O'Hara in his important book, *The Homosexual Tradition in American Poetry*, because the poet does not "use his homosexuality as an element of self-definition in the way that Whitman or Crane does" (xix). This seems an unnecessarily narrow definition of both sex and self, one that presupposes a unitary and recuperable identity not unlike the one upon which Harold Bloom bases his theory of influence. The self of which O'Hara sings is a good deal more fluid:

My quietness has a man in it, he is transparent
and he carries me quietly, like a gondola, through the streets.
He has several likenesses, like stars and years, like numerals.
My quietness has a number of naked selves,

so many pistols I have borrowed to protect myselves
from creatures who too readily recognize my weapons
and have murder in their heart! (252–53)

Any celebration of multiplicity here is less a sign of self-revelation than it is an indicator of vulnerability.[8] When each proposition of self comes with its own weapon, then the single voice—what O'Hara calls the "serpent" in his midst—remains locked in infinite reflexivity. Once the self is recognized as a "likeness," however, it can be manipulated to accommodate any occasion. And while this may offer a degree of control in a homophobic environment, it may also lead to a sense of rootlessness and despair. O'Hara's only defense is to regard dispersion and change as a kind of grace:

to be born and live as variously as possible. The conception
of the masque barely suggests the sordid identifications.
I am a Hittite in love with a horse. I don't know what blood's
in me I feel like an African prince I am a girl walking downstairs
in a red pleated dress with heels I am a champion taking a fall
I am a jockey with a sprained ass-hole I am the light mist
                                    in which a face appears
and it is another face of blonde . . .
and I've just caught sight of the *Niña*, the *Pinta* and the *Santa Maria*.
              What land is this, so free? ("In Memory of My
              Feelings," 256)

These "identifications" may be sordid to the individual seeking a unitary center or ground, but for the gay poet in 1956, they may be necessary for survival. O'Hara opposes the totalized frame of the masque to the allegorical representations within it, the "cancerous statue" of the self to the multiple "ruses" it adopts. In Whitmanian terms the opposition is that between the "word En-Masse," with its spatial image of linguistic colonization, and the particularity of individuals listed in his catalogs. O'Hara inflects Whitman's national allegory and its manifest destiny overtones, with a postcolonial narrative of domination, cultural fragmentation, and crisis. "What land *is* this, so free?" O'Hara asks, speaking not from the explorer's ship but from the about-to-be colonized shore. By staging an elegy for his feelings in terms of colonization, O'Hara signals the limits to Whitman's expansive self and the barriers to truly democratic vistas. At the same time, he extends Whitman's logic of identification in which, by refusing to be contained by any single self-definition, he becomes a series of theatrical roles.

"In Memory of My Feelings" offers an interesting corrective to Patrick Buchanan's association of national and private identity. Whereas the spokesman for the Moral Majority thinks of America as having a continuous, national self whose autonomy is threatened by multiple others, O'Hara identifies the nation as a series of "ruses," the proliferation of which refuses a continuous narrative history. O'Hara suggests that, like sexuality itself, nationhood is unstable as a category. It posits a uniformity of values that cannot be extended to the multiple others who live within the borders of Times Square, not to mention the United States. Eve Sedgwick makes this point by speaking of the variety of ways in which national identity is formed, based on the "others" who are excluded:

> Far beyond the pressure of crisis or exception, it may be that there exists for nations, as for genders, simply no normal way to partake of the categorical definitiveness of the national, no single kind of "other" of what a nation is to which all can by the same structuration be definitionally opposed. ("Nationalisms" 241)

Since Whitman's poetry is part of a national cultural experience as well, invoking him often legitimates this "categorical definitiveness" by excluding his more subversive meanings. By acknowledging both national and personal self as "selves" or "transparencies," O'Hara redresses a certain valedictory treatment of Whitman's democratic ethos and refigures it as gender trouble.

This synthesis of nationalism and sexuality is the subject of O'Hara's most open invocation of Whitman, "Ode: Salute to the French Negro Poets," a poem that imitates the earlier poet's rhetoric and lineation. Like "Out of the Cradle, Endlessly Rocking," O'Hara finds himself on the margins of the continent, reflecting on the origins of his poetic vocation:

> From near the sea, like Whitman my great predecessor, I call
> to the spirits of other lands to make fecund my existence. (305)

This rhapsodic apostrophe and its celebration of democratic participation are swiftly undercut by a more jocular tone. O'Hara is "trying to live in the terrible western world"

> . . . where to love at all's to be a politician, as to love a poem
> is pretentious, this may sound tendentious but it's lyrical

which shows what lyricism has been brought to by our fabled times. (305)

When "love" is reduced to formulaic homilies in political speeches, when the lyric sustains rhymes like "pretentious/tendentious," then the force of Whitman's experimental epic is neutralized. For among other things, O'Hara's "Ode" is about genre: the ability to write in private forms like the lyric or more public forms like the ode. To some extent Whitman represents a heroic moment in American poetry when each genre (and its corresponding rhetoric) could accommodate both kinds of love: love of country and love of person. In order to heal the distance between these two forms of love O'Hara appeals to Afro-Caribbean poets like Aimé Césaire for their alternative visions of what it means to live "in the terrible western world." The legacy of Césaire and Whitman is not a vision of consensus and synthesis but of the "love we bear each other's differences / in race which is the poetic ground on which we rear our smiles" (305).

Written in 1958 at the height of the Algerian war (and during the U.S. Civil Rights movement), O'Hara's ode celebrates a "poetic ground" that refuses categories of nationhood or race:

> the beauty of America, neither cool jazz nor devoured Egyptian heroes,
>   lies in
> lives in the darkness I inhabit in the midst of sterile millions
>
> the only truth is face to face, the poem whose words become your mouth
> and dying in black and white we fight for what we love, not are. (305)

In these last lines, "the beauty of America" (or for that matter France) cannot be defined in terms of cultural artifacts (cool jazz), sheer size (millions) or essentialized categories (what we are). Rather, beauty lies in a struggle for "what we love" among differences. O'Hara appropriates "darkness" as a space in which the racial and sexual other lives "in the midst of sterile millions." By linking Whitman and Césaire, O'Hara suggests a bond between American romanticism and Negritude surrealism that refigures the cultural character of the Americas. Both represent literary traditions that attempt to join words and physical acts. When O'Hara says that in such immediacy "words become your mouth," he implies that words are no longer empty signifiers, incapable of expression, but are one with the persons who speak them. At another level, O'Hara asserts that words are becoming to your mouth, in the way that lipstick enhances facial features.

Such sentiments are repeated in his mock manifesto, "Personism," where O'Hara advocates placing the poem "squarely between the poet and the person, Lucky Pierre style" (499). Poet and reader are thus "face to face" with the medium of poetry between them. Gregory W. Bredbeck reminds us that "Lucky Pierre" is gay slang for the person in the middle of a homosexual threesome, and is like the text itself, "both receptive and piercing" (272). In this context, the text is an active participant in the interchange between poet and reader, and since O'Hara often addresses his poems to specific lovers and friends, private address and public acknowledgment of affection create an odd pact with the general reader. It is much like Whitman's ability to address his reader through the mediating frame of his material book. Staring at his reflection from the deck of the Brooklyn Ferry, Whitman sees us as well, "face to face," between the pages of a book.

O'Hara similarly suggests that future generations will read this "mes-

sage / of our hearts" but must do so "in adolescent closets who once shot at
us in doorways" (305). The furtiveness of such reading partly refers to the
risks taken by youths who read the subtexts of marginalized literatures,
whether sexually explicit (as Whitman's work was thought to be) or subversive of Western imperialism (as in Césaire's). Despite this Whitmanian faith
in the reader, difference "in the terrible western world" continues to be
treated as division and threat, enacted through violence. Brad Gooch
points out that the reference to being shot at in doorways refers to an
incident when O'Hara was mugged in the doorway of his apartment building. When the poet ignored the demand for money and continued to walk
up the stairs, he was shot by his assailant (251). Although the race of the
mugger is not stated in the poem (nor in Gooch's account) it is clear that
for O'Hara, the bridge across differences is still broken and the doors to
sexual and racial closets remain closed.

O'Hara's deliberate appropriation of Whitman's idiom in "Ode: Salute
to the French Negro Poets" is part of a larger strategy of tonal variation in
which the voice becomes not the medium for expression but the site of
contestation.[9] "It is the law of my own voice I shall investigate," (182)
O'Hara says in "Homosexuality," a poem that directly confronts the performative character of idiolect in gay subculture. This is not the bardic
"afflatus" many of his generation inherited from Whitman, but a voice conscious of its own contingent character, its own status as social discourse.
Where others are, as he says in the same poem, "taking off [their] masks"
in gestures of authentication and revelation (Allen Ginsberg might be the
model), O'Hara studies the social sites of speaking.

The critical possibilities of exploring the "law" of voice are very much
at issue in "For Bill Berkson (On Again Looking Into *Saturday Night*),"
where tone is used to deflect an overheard homophobic remark while representing one's powerlessness in the face of it:

"who did you have lunch with?" "you" "oops!" how ARE you

>      then too, the other day I was walking through a train
>      with my suitcase and I overheard someone say "speaking of faggots"
>      now isn't life difficult enough without that
>      and why am I always carrying something
>      well it was a shitty looking person anyway
>      better a faggot than a farthead. (441)

Tone is everything in this passage. The affected speech with which it opens
("'oops!' how ARE you") is itself a defense against distraction, a way of
countering the implicit accusation of having forgotten a recent luncheon.
In the incident that follows the voice continues in the same tone parodied
as specifically homosexual speech. O'Hara's comedic response to the over-

heard remark ("speaking of faggots") deflects its violence by reducing it to
adolescent badinage. But the violence that undergirds such verbal fisticuffs
is made explicit:

> or as fathers have often said to friends of mine
> "better dead than a dope" "if I thought you were queer I'd kill you"
> you'd be right to, DAD, daddio, addled annie pad-lark (Brit. 19th C.)
>
> > well everything can't be perfect
> > you said it. (442)

The genealogical origins of social stereotypes and name-calling are ex-
posed as O'Hara acknowledges their paternal source. He counters the authority of this imperative by turning "Dad" into the hipster's "daddio," thus
deflating the threat involved. By participating in several rhetorical
frames—camp banter, adolescent one-upmanship, paternal homilies—
O'Hara may investigate gay identity both from the standpoint of the object
of derision as well as the subject of new verbal and oppositional strategies.

This example suggests some of the costs of Whitman's participation
ethos—costs that D. H. Lawrence could only interpret as Whitman's longing for death. But O'Hara sees Whitman's desire to merge with others as
a way of confronting the static character of modern urban life, of making
personal an otherwise threatening landscape. The phantasmagoria of New
York becomes accessible as a heteroglossia of potential conversations. So it
is for Whitman:

> I too knitted the old knot of contrariety, . . .
> Saw many I loved in the street or ferry-boat or public assembly, yet never
>     told them a word,
> Lived the same life with the rest, the same old laughing, gnawing, sleeping,
> Play'd the part that still looks back on the actor or actress. (*LG* 163)

This is Whitman the flaneur who sees every social type but cannot act on
his own furtive looks and averted glances. O'Hara replaces those silences
with signifying speech acts that testify not by any truth value in the statements themselves but by their character as social discourse.

It is this Baudelarian Whitman that provides me with my title, taken
from O'Hara's "Easter," a long quasi-surrealist poem which, although
Whitman never appears, foregrounds a kind of urban incarnation similar
to "Crossing Brooklyn Ferry" and portions of "Song of Myself." The poem
plays variations on a motif of cross-dressing in which nakedness is replaced
by cosmetic renewal: "When the world strips down and rouges up / like a
mattress's teeth brushed by love's bristling sun" (97). Here the modernist
imperative to make strange is countered by an aesthete's imperative to
make cosmetic. O'Hara is not interested in paring away the familiar to

reveal the primary ideograms of cultural order but in eroticizing the surfaces of an edifice that has become transparent—or invisible. The distinction may seem slight—that between "stripping down" and "rouging up"—but it marks a transition from a modernism of miraculist unities to one of constructed differences.

If the title of this poem is operative, it refers to an apotheosis from a transcendental to a secular plane. The word made flesh is literalized in a night of cruising, analogous to Whitman's rambles around New York but now invested with new dangers and excitements:

> it's the night like I love it all cruisy and nelly
> fingered fan of boskage fronds the white smile of sleeps. (97) [10]

The surreal catalogs that make up the bulk of the poem are like the ornate rhetoric of this couplet—attempts at creating a textual surface as sensual as the night itself. But there are risks to cruising in alternate identities, the possibility of encountering a "pubic foliage of precarious hazard / sailors / Silent ripples in a bayou of raffish bumpkin winks" (97) or of meeting the "black pirate whose cheek / batters the heavenly heart" (99). Erotic potentiality mixes with corruption and decay; boundaries between seductiveness and repulsion merge as the poem cruises among unmoored signifiers:

> a marvellous heart tiresomely got up in brisk bold stares
> when those trappings fart at the feet of the stars
> a self-coral serpent wrapped round an arm with no jujubes
> without swish
> without camp . . .

> I supplicate
> dirty blonde mermaids leaning on their elbows
> rigor mortis sculpting the figure of those iron tears. (97)

Marjorie Perloff has linked such lines to Dada and Surrealist poets like Tristan Tzara and Benjamin Péret for the way that they subvert causality and analogy through catalogs of dissimilar materials. (66). What links "Easter" to Whitman, however, is the way that this linguistic subversion derives from a social and sexual logic of "bold stares" and camp duplicity. O'Hara's juxtaposition of dissimilar (or exotic) images is a kind of verbal drag in which a world "drowned in flesh" is dressed up in "trappings" that deflate the presence of an informing Logos. Even the serpent in the garden is a kind of ornament, "wrapped round an arm / with no jujubes." This secularized Eden offers no rewards in the afterlife; its trappings "fart at the feet of the stars," declaring a kind of independence through sumptuary display. The pun on "stars" as both heavens and Hollywood celebrities merges the two realms of this cosmopolitan incarnation and gives to

O'Hara's surrealist surface a distinctly American character. O'Hara, like Whitman in "The Sleepers," casts himself as an expectant lover for whom wandering and waiting in Gotham City promise renewal through dispersion. O'Hara extends such merging, in a "sleep trooped about by paid assassins mad for kisses," bringing Whitman's homoerotic poetics of longing into a contemporary world of cross-dressed identities.


## IV


My permission to use cross-dressing as a trope for the textual performance of identities is partially granted by Whitman who, in a letter to Emerson included in the 1856 edition of *Leaves of Grass*, used the term "dressed up" to describe (and dismiss) the dandified literature of his era:

> There is no great author; every one has demeaned himself to some etiquette or some impotence. There is no manhood or life-power in poems; there are shoats and geldings more like. Or literature will be dressed up, a fine gentleman, distasteful to our instincts, foreign to our soil. Its neck bends right and left wherever it goes. Its costumes and jewelry prove how little it knows Nature. Its flesh is soft; it shows less and less of the indefinable hard something that is Nature. (*LG* 736)[11]

The language of castration here notwithstanding, Whitman worries over a literature that is "dressed up" and therefore "foreign to our soil." Sartorial and national metaphors link misogyny and xenophobia in a letter designed to extend fellowship among like-minded males. The presence of unlike-minded males helps Whitman mark his difference from those soft-fleshed types who have not been kissed by the rough beard of masculine friendship.

At the same time, Whitman recognizes the close relationship between men who feminize their identities and writing which creates identities by dressing up. His feeling that such writing is "foreign" perhaps betrays its own form of homosexual panic, one that O'Hara dispels by indulging its theatrical possibilities. O'Hara acknowledges his "foreignness" to Whitman's discourse of nature ("I can't even enjoy a blade of grass unless I know there's a subway handy, or a record store or some other sign that people do not totally *regret* life" [197]), but he discovers another nature within the city, a nature fabricated out of the passing parade. Cross-dressing becomes a figure for the multifariousness of that parade, its existence as a series of costumes, attitudes, and positions. For every hearty assurance that "What is known I strip away" (*LG* 80), there is the countervailing knowledge that what is revealed is a blank, a conceptual chasm for which language is inadequate: "I do not know it—it is without name—it is a word unsaid" (*LG* 88). It seems less important to "name" it as his homo-

sexuality, as many critics have done, than to see it as an identity in formation, an identity in drag.

The Family Values ideologues of the religious right have, of course,
"named" this identity and have sought thereby to restrict it from public
view. Under their platform Whitman continues to stand indicted since although he celebrated, in "Song of the Exposition," "the same old human
race, the same within, without," he also confessed a "queer, queer race, of
novel fashion" in adjacent lines (*LG* 199). No wonder he was offended at
Symonds's attempt to bring him "out" in one form when, under his own
terms, he was already out in a number of others. For poets like Frank
O'Hara who took Whitman at his word—a word "unsaid"—stripping the
world of its illusions also meant dressing it up as illusion.

## Notes

1. *Los Angeles Times*, Aug. 18, 1992, A 10. The radical right has used the
charge of transvestism to impugn liberals before. In the 1988 presidential elections, the Moral Majority's Jerry Falwell propagated a comic book, distributed
by his son and drawn by a "Christian cartoonist," depicting Democratic presidential candidate Michael Dukakis in a wig and dress. Responding to the potentially libelous nature of the representation, Falwell said, "It portrays the
person in the context of what he is for or against" (Garber 54).

2. Nor is homophobia restricted to campaign rhetoric. Oregon's 1992 Initiative 9, the "Abnormal Behaviors Initiative," proposed to amend the state constitution to deny minority status to gays and lesbians and to restrict state funding
or jobs to anyone who treats homosexuality as anything other than "abnormal,
wrong, unnatural and perverse."

3. There are obvious risks to using cross-dressing as a term for textual practice, not the least of these being that it erases specific political and social meanings of transvestism within gay and lesbian society. As social practice, transvestism functions as a critique of gender stereotypes or as a provocative attack on
the sex/gender system. A great deal of queer theory (including Garber's book)
and popular journalism has seized upon drag as a significant form of cultural
production, but these venues often fail to acknowledge the milieu in which
cross-dressing has the most dramatic social effects. The gay and lesbian community has long understood the subversive and oppositional possibilities of
drag and has used them to confront homophobic society. It has debated the
limitations of drag—its reinforcement of gender stereotypes and heterosexual
roles—in forging a political movement. But cross-dressing involves the warping
of codes that inhere on many levels, from the sartorial to the rhetorical. If a
poet like Emily Dickinson adopts, as she often does, the role of a male when
she wants to describe conditions of power unavailable to women in the 1860s,
she is extending the possibilities of transvestism into a textual form that may
or may not have implications for her own sexuality. Similarly, in 1855, Whitman's desire for other men literally had no name, in our contemporary psychological sense, and thus had to be represented through scenarios that did.

4. One could regard Whitman's catalogs as vast explorations of multiple
identities in which the poet becomes so many things that the very unity to
which his listings aspire is negated. Not only does Whitman identify with "the
woman the same as the man" (*LG* 48), but he also identifies with cities, mountains, animals, and gods. If a catalog represents an attempt to enumerate for
the purposes of cultural renewal, Whitman's catalogs, by their sheer diversity,
call attention to the theatrical nature of identification. Although the poet may
walk "with perfect ease in the capitol," he is not so much representative as a
"representation":

> Then the mechanics take him for a mechanic,
> And the soldiers suppose him to be a soldier, and the sailors that he has follow'd
>     the sea,
> And the authors take him for an author, and the artists for an artist,
> And the laborers perceive he could labor with them and love them. (*LG* 168)

5. In this essay I am using the term "homosexual" to refer to same-sex
relations among males. While not denying important influences by Whitman
on both heterosexual women and lesbians, I want to limit my discussion to one
specific form of identity construction involving masculine identity. In fact, it is
because Whitman's ideal of same-sex relations is so specifically gendered as
masculine that I want to study how later poets used him to confuse gender
positions in their own work. On Crane's use of Whitman to develop his own
homosexual text, see Yingling, *Hart Crane* 4–7, 211–13.

6. I derive this phrase from Ed Folsom's excellent survey of literary tributes
to Whitman, "Talking Back to Walt Whitman: An Introduction."

7. The mode of redress that I have identified with modernism does not end
with Whitman's rediscovery in the late 1950s. Louis Simpson, in an essay setting out to "honor" Whitman, spends most of his time explaining how embarrassed he has been as a poet by Whitman's "whooping it up," his "use of big-
sounding words," his visionary tendencies, and his desire that "young men . . .
throw their arms about his neck" (qtd. in Perlman 257–61). It is not that Simpson and his modernist forebears do not claim Whitman as a source for their
poetry, only that in order to do so, they must bring him down a peg, displaying
their own good sense at Walt's expense.

8. Whitman's variation on O'Hara's lines could be those in section 28 of
"Song of Myself" in which the speaker's masturbatory fantasy is staged in terms
of a rape in which his "fellow-senses" are taken away and replaced by unnamed
new identities:

> On all sides prurient provokers stiffening my limbs,
> Straining the udder of my heart for its withheld drip,
> Behaving licentious toward me, taking no denial,
> Depriving me of my best as for a purpose,
> Unbuttoning my clothes, holding me by the bare waist. . . . (*LG* 57)

9. Whitman's most thorough explanation of the variable voice is "Song of
the Answerer" where the poet describes himself as a translator rather than an

inspired author, one who responds rather than inaugurates. The human condition which he witnesses speaks in a variety of idiolects:

> Every existence has its idiom, every thing has an idiom and tongue,
> He resolves all tongues into his own and bestows it upon men, and any man translates, and any man translates himself also,
> One part does not counteract another part, he is the joiner, he sees how they join.
> (*LG* 168)

10. According to Brad Gooch's biography, O'Hara did love to cruise the bars, parks, and public spaces for casual (and promiscuous) sex (194). The potential for violence, whether from plainclothes police in the bars or "rough trade" encounters, informs much of the disjunctiveness of this poem and qualifies the traditional view of O'Hara as happy peripatetic stroller.

11. This passage is discussed at length in Fone (27).

# 15

## "For America—For All the Earth": Walt Whitman as an International(ist) Poet

### WALTER GRÜNZWEIG

**I**

Walt Whitman's international reputation was carefully mapped out by the author himself. He saw his work as standing in an international context and himself as an international poet and cultural figure. Thereby he broke, from an American as well as a European point of view, yet another bound: that of the national—and at times nationalistic—bias frequently informing literature and the construction of the literary canon. Although Whitman is frequently said to be the first *American* poet, his work simultaneously reaches beyond the very national literary boundaries he himself is credited with having established.

In a programmatic statement on "Poetry To-day in America," he explained his wish to bind nations closer together through poetry: "I would inaugurate from America, for this purpose, new formulas—international poems. . . . I have thought that both in patriotism and song . . . we have adhered too long to petty limits, and that the time has come to enfold the world" (*PW* 2: 484). Thus, at a time when the definition of a nationally independent American literature was still new and far from being universally accepted, Whitman, through his poetry, wanted to push beyond the "petty limits" of a national literature.

This program was clearly politically motivated. In his 1889 address to the German-speaking readers of the first German edition of *Leaves of Grass,* he claimed: "I did not only have my own country in mind when composing my work. I wanted to take the first step towards bringing into life a cycle of international poems. The main goal of the United States is the mutual benevolence of all of humanity, the solidarity of the world. What is lacking in this respect may be supplied by the art of poetry, by songs radiating from all countries in the world" (*Grashalme Gedichte* xii).[1] Similarly, in his address to Russian readers, he claimed: "my dearest dream is for an internationality of poems and poets, binding the lands of the earth closer than all treaties and diplomacy" (Letter to anon., December 20, 1881, *PW* 2: 512). This message goes beyond the harmless and mostly ineffective humanistic truism that art—unlike politics—has a universal(ist) appeal. Treaties and diplomacy in the nineteenth century, especially among European kingdoms and empires, *excluded* their citizens. For a revolutionary spirit like Whitman, diplomacy amounted to a conspiracy against the masses.[2] Thus, an international network of poetry *and* poets is posited as a positive cultural-political force against a treacherous diplomacy.

The central addressee of *Leaves* is indeed the common people throughout the world:

> For America—for all the earth, all nations, the common people,
> (Not of one nation only—not America only). ("L. of G.," *Complete Poetry*
>     1275)

For that purpose Whitman would, as he announces in "Starting from Paumanok," "trail the whole geography of the globe and salute / courteously every city large and small" (*LG* 19). But Whitman did not only want his oeuvre to *serve* the internationalist idea. His work itself, poetry as well as prose, poetics as well as politics, reflects an internationalist, intercultural poetics. Inclusiveness and universality, prominently noted characteristics of his poetry, are expressions of this poetics.

The main task of a poet is, Whitman claims, to project "cosmic brotherhood, the dream of all hope, all time" ("The Bible as Poetry," *PW* 2: 548) into the world. This is "the thought of the solidarity of nations, the brotherhood and sisterhood of the entire earth" ("Ventures, on an Old Theme," *PW* 2: 520). The notions of internationalism and democracy are intertwined:

> democracy . . . alone can bind, and ever seeks to bind, all nations, all
> men, of however various and distant lands, into a brotherhood, a family.
> It is the old, yet ever-modern dream of earth, out of her eldest and her
> youngest, her fond philosophers and poets. Not that half only, individu-
> alism, which isolates. There is another half, which is adhesiveness or love,
> that fuses, ties and aggregates, making the races comrades, and fraterniz-
> ing all. (*Democratic Vistas*, *PW* 2: 381)

How could this truly radical internationalism be compatible with Whitman's often acclaimed Americanness? The solution to this seeming paradox lies in Whitman's interpretation of America and American culture: even Whitman's American nationalism can be interpreted *internationally*. He saw himself, as he put it, as "One of the Nation of many nations" (*LG* 44), and developed this point in a variety of ways. In speaking of Whittier,

Whitman claims that while the New England poet is "rather a grand figure," he is also "pretty lean and ascetic," "not universal and composite enough . . . for ideal Americanism" ("Old Poets," *PW* 2: 659–60). This "composite" quality is what Whitman admires most in American culture: "British, German, Scandinavian, Spanish, French, Italian—papers published, plays acted, speeches made, in all languages—on our shores the crowning resultant of those distillations, decantations, compactions of humanity, that have been going on, on trial, over the earth so long." ("The Last Collective Compaction," *PW* 2: 540)

A universal, composite culture, distillations, decantations, compactions of humanity—Whitman's images and rhetoric grow bold and enthusiastic when speaking of American society in the nineteenth century. America's superiority is founded on its inclusiveness: "European [and] Asiatic greatness are in the past. Vaster and subtler, America, combining, justifying the past, yet works for a grander future, in living democratic forms" ("Monuments—The Past and Present," *PW* 2: 536). "America, combining" Europe and Asia, goes beyond national achievements to a new "composite" culture which today would be referred to as multicultural. Art, culture, and poetry thrive best, if not exclusively, in the "multitudinousness" of America:

> Think, in comparison, of the petty environage and limited area of the poets of past or present Europe, no matter how great their genius. Think of the absence and ignorance, in all cases hitherto, of the multitudinousness, vitality, and the unprecedented stimulants of to-day and here. It almost seems as if a poetry with cosmic and dynamic features of magnitude and limitlessness suitable to the human soul, were never possible before. ("A Backward Glance O'er Travel'd Roads," *LG* 565–66)

Repeatedly, he wants to go beyond even the boundaries of the planet: "If there can be any such thing as a kosmic modern and original song, America needs it, and is worthy of it" ("An Old Man's Rejoinder," *PW* 2: 657). This is a rhetoric largely without material foundation in the nineteenth century but it lays the groundwork for Whitman's continuing relevance and presence beyond his own time.

## II

From the point of view of the international reception to his work, "Salut Au Monde!" initially published in 1856, is Whitman's most successful individual poem. Its references to all imaginable locations on the globe have a "natural" and emotional appeal to international readers. After all, how often has the Styrian farmer (*LG* 146) been addressed by an American poet?

Foreign fascination with this poem, however, is explained not only by the poem's personal appeal but also by its deep roots in history. Whitman's rhetoric in "Salut Au Monde!" can be placed in the specific context of the European revolutions of 1848. The American poet shared his enthusiasm for the midcentury revolutionary movements with the European (as well as American) left and creatively reworked its international rhetoric into some of his poetry. This was the reason why Whitman was later so easily adopted by the international left.[3]

In 1848, Karl Marx had concluded the *Communist Manifesto* with the battle cry "Working Men of All Countries, Unite." In his analysis, "national differences and antagonisms between peoples are daily more and more vanishing, owing to the development of the bourgeoisie, to freedom of commerce, to the world market, to uniformity in the mode of production and in the conditions of life corresponding thereto" (*Marxism* 36). In 1850, the Italian revolutionary Giuseppe Mazzini (1805–1872), one of the founders of the internationally oriented revolutionary movement "Young Europe," had described his "concetto non-nazionale, ma inter-nazionale" (not a national, but an international conception) for a new Europe (Mazzini, "Organizzazione della Democrazia" 202). Such internationalist models for revolutionary change were in fact one of the most significant results of the failed revolutions of 1848, and they fell on fertile ground in the United States. Along with Lajos Kossuth, whose impact was heightened by his much-publicized presence in the New World, Mazzini was a prominent figure in the American discussion about possible U.S. intervention to assist the European revolutionaries. The *Democratic Review* of 1852, preparing the ground for U.S. elections that year, hailed Mazzini and Kossuth as international heroes of the revolution.

Whitman was well aware of Kossuth and Mazzini's importance, and his poem "Salut Au Monde!" reflects this discussion in the United States.[4] The lyrical persona hears the "fierce French liberty songs" (*LG* 138), sees the "battle-fields of the earth" (*LG* 142), and sends his "Health to you! good will to you all, from me and America sent!" (*LG* 147). Human beings from every part of the globe are equally represented, a technique which has frequently been taken as proof of Whitman's international orientation. But few critics have attempted to explain the organization and structure of the poem as a whole. Whitman's most interesting contribution to a lyrical internationalism emerges in the light of an observation by Mazzini that Whitman may have known:

> Take the map of Europe. Study it synthetically in its geographical structure, in the great indications furnished by the lines of mountains and rivers, in the symmetrical arrangements of its parts. Compare the previsions of the future which this examination suggests, with the existing collocation of the principal races and idioms. Open the page of history, and seek for the signs of vitality in the different populations, resulting from the *ensemble* of their traditions; listen, in short, to the cry which rises from the conscience of these populations through their struggles and their

martyrs. Then observe the official governmental map, such as has been sanctioned by the treaties of 1815 [dictated by Metternich]. In the contrast between the two, you will find the definitive answer to the terrors and complaints of diplomatists. Here is the secret of the *conspiracy* which they are endeavouring to destroy, and which will destroy them. Here also is the secret of the future world. ("Europe: Its Condition" 292–93)[5]

What is important here is not so much the geopolitical argument but Mazzini's use of the map. The point of Whitman's frequently misunderstood lists in "Salut Au Monde!" is precisely to render insignificant the "official governmental map." Oceans, mountains, rivers, and peoples form natural entities reaching beyond and thus ignoring political borders and institutions. Borders play no role whatsoever; the world in Whitman's poem is a liberated one.

It is not surprising that the world reacted with the greatest enthusiasm to this lyrical strategy. One of the most interesting authors who followed Whitman's internationalism in the spirit of "Salut Au Monde!" was the German expressionist poet Armin T. Wegner (1886–1978). Like many other artists and intellectuals, Wegner entered World War I as a medic—a decision in which he was probably influenced by the example of Whitman's wound-dresser. In the course of the war, he developed a broad internationalist vision. Later, this bold author faced up to Hitler. A few months after the Nazi takeover in 1933, he wrote an open letter to Hitler in which he asked him to respect human rights in Germany. After having been incarcerated for a time, he left Germany and lived until 1945 as an exile in Italy.

Wegner's attempt to combine an enlightened Marxist ethos with a Whitmanesque vision produced a series of remarkable internationalist poems. One of the most interesting is "Funkspruch in die Welt" (Radio Message to the World) written at the close of World War I:

To All, All, All! To the peoples of Europe and the peoples of America!
To the steppe tribes of Asia, to the rice farmers of India and the peoples
    of the South Sea!
To the stony jungles of the cities,
To the loneliest of camel herdsmen, who prays in his tent!
I lift my heart out of a buried well calling out to you: Drink! Drink! . . .

Let me approach you with bared head, you peoples, touch your hands,
Look into the eyes, deep, deep, like lovers after long separation,
You lonely ones, who are buried, broken by silence,
Who, exiled, roaming around the alien earth,
You one-eyed, you mothers weakened by tears! You all, who were obsessed
    and lied to—
O the smell of the scenes of carnage of this earth,

Which rises through the filter of your hearts, you Reconverted ones, is
    sweeter than the smell of paradise.
And you, most loved ones, from the prisons of all countries,
Whose chains we loosened from the pale stalk of your hands,
Must I not kneel down, to kiss your loins with tears of joy?

O arms, embracing the globe!
Love radiates from my ten fingertips.
And the hair on my head, still, is a flame of love. (117)[6]

This poem is a strange mixture of Lenin and Whitman. "To All" refers to
Lenin's famous call to all peoples and governments to end World War I
and to enter into negotiations for a just and lasting peace. But only the
beginning of the poem is Leninist, and it soon changes into a Whitmanesque catalog addressing the disadvantaged of this world. Unlike Lenin, Wegner's ultimate aim is not social emancipation but a new union and
internationalist unity of the world on a nonintellectual, sensual basis: "O
arms, embracing the globe! / Love radiates from my ten fingertips."

The unique internationalist rhetoric of Whitman's work has led his followers around the world to construct Whitman as an internationalist poet
and to emulate his poetry. It has also brought about what I like to call the
international Whitman movement. A map of the world that recorded contacts between Whitmanites would reveal a dense network of relationships
around the globe.

The first attempts to establish an *international* Whitman Society had already occurred during Whitman's lifetime. It is characteristic that this effort was undertaken by a person with a tricultural background, a German-
Japanese-American. Sadakichi Hartmann (1867–1944), who later became
an artist working in a variety of fields, was a disciple of Whitman. He believed that Whitman's message needed to be heard throughout the world
and that this goal could only be realized through an international organization. However, the project exceeded young Hartmann's financial and orga-
nizational capabilities and had to be discontinued.[7]

The second project, Horace Traubel's organization, significantly called
*Walt Whitman Fellowship International*, was far more successful. The *Fellowship* was more than just one of the many commemorative societies designed
to further the memory and popularity of the poet's work; it was supposed
to transport a leftist and internationalist ideology. Among those associated
with it were Emma Goldman and Eugene V. Debs in the United States,
Léon Bazalgette in France, and the German-Scottish anarchist poet John
Henry Mackay.

In the late 1980s, Horace Traubel's papers became accessible to the public. The list of his correspondents reads like a Who's Who in international
radicalism around the turn of the century. Homosexual activists, anarchists, socialists, early conservationists, women's liberationists, are all repre-

sented in Traubel's correspondence relating to Whitman. Through his journal, *The Conservator*, which was meant to conserve and further radical traditions, Traubel put himself in touch with groups in virtually every European country and with quite a few Japanese and Latin American "comrades."

Although the *Whitman Fellowship* was open to non-U.S. citizens, some Europeans thought a special European organization was needed. Documents relating to the attempted creation of a European Whitman Fellowship were found at an unlikely place: at the castle of the city of Querfurt, until recently in the German Democratic Republic. There, among the papers of Johannes Schlaf, the German naturalist poet, Whitmanite, and Whitman translator, is correspondence from various European Whitmanites, including Whitman's French translator and biographer, Léon Bazalgette. Bazalgette wrote to Schlaf in 1905: "I wonder whether we could not, one day, attempt to found a Whitman society in Europe—like the *Fellowship* of which H. Traubel is secretary."[8]

Bazalgette's characterization of Whitman as a "poet-prophet whom humankind, in a few centuries, will count among its Gods"[9] shows the spirit in which these European Whitmanites pursued their work. Among those involved in these efforts were Stefan Zweig, Emile Verhaeren, Romain Rolland, Francis Vielé-Griffin, Jules Romains, and the little-known French writer Henri Guilbeaux. Guilbeaux, Romain Rolland's secretary and a personal friend of Lenin's, ultimately became a follower of Mussolini. It is unclear why the project finally failed—possibly logistical reasons played a role, possibly the worsening of the international climate in Europe. But it was a forceful attempt reflecting the sense of community shared by Whitmanites of several countries.

Stefan Zweig corresponded about Whitman with Romain Rolland, and so did Hermann Hesse. In 1919, an antiwar book with poetry and prose by Whitman entitled *The Wound-Dresser* appeared in Switzerland. It was edited by the Alsatian expressionist René Schickele with translations by the Franco-German poet Ivan Goll and the German-Jewish writer, translator, and mystic, Gustav Landauer.[10]

These connections also extended eastward. Given the lack of Whitman texts in the original, Schlaf's translation served as a basis for Whitman's reception and popularity in the Slavic nations. Slav writers such as Oton Župančič, the Slovene author, and Jaroslav Vrchlický, the Czech poet, were connected with modernist developments in poetry by way of Whitman and Schlaf. Emanuel Lešehrad's Czech translation of Whitman was inspired by an early German Whitmanite, Alfred Mombert. Young representatives of the Slavic avant-garde, among them Antonin Svova and Otokar Březina, exchanged their ideas on Whitman with such authors as the Bohemian-Jewish expressionist poet Franz Werfel.

Moreover, these intercultural relationships were not limited to the turn of the nineteenth century. By 1868, Whitman's very first German translator, the revolutionary German poet Ferdinand Freiligrath, then exiled to Britain, had learned about Whitman through foreign sources, namely William Rossetti. Freiligrath's introduction to Whitman, published in a leading German daily, was translated into English and used propagandistically by American Whitmanites and by Whitman himself.[11] The first book-length translation into German was the result of a collaboration between two men Whitman knew personally. One of them was Thomas William Rolleston, an Irishman who hoped that, by Whitmanesque infusions of democratic spirit, the Germans would be sufficiently strengthened to weaken Britain, thereby securing Irish independence. The second, Karl Knortz, was a German-American, who believed that Germans in the Old *and* the New World needed to become acquainted with and internalize Whitman's democratic ideology.

The intercultural connection also went far beyond Whitman's death in 1892 and Traubel's in 1919. Exiled German communist writers learned about Whitman in Russia. Here the first Soviet Commissar of culture, Anatoly Lunacharsky, along with Cornel Chukovsky and others, had firmly established a Soviet tradition of Whitman reception in the 1920s and '30s. Erich Arendt, an important East German poet with expressionist beginnings, was responsible for a fine and voluminous translation of Whitman in the German Democratic Republic. He learned about Whitman in Latin American exile, mostly from Whitmanite Pablo Neruda, and brought this Latin Whitman back to a slightly gray postwar East Germany. In 1955, the International Peace Council, frequently regarded as a Communist front organization, decided to stage an international celebration in honor of the first centennial of *Leaves,* a recommendation that was dutifully followed in most Eastern European countries. Whitman's photograph, strongly reminiscent of Karl Marx anyhow, was enlarged to poster size and carried through the streets of Moscow, Warsaw, and Sofia.

This intercultural collaboration also spilled over into the other arts. A book of woodcuts by Frans Masereel, the Flemish graphic artist, was introduced by his friend Stefan Zweig, the nexus between them being Whitman. A number of German and Austrian composers such as Kurt Weill, Paul Hindemith, and Ernst Toch picked up on Whitman during their exile in the United States, very consciously emphasizing his international theme.

Whitman's internationalist appeal translated into intercultural collaboration. For a large group of writers, politicians, and artists identifying themselves as Whitmanites, American culture stood for global culture. Klaus Mann, Thomas Mann's son, speculating about his new identity as an exile, wrote in 1940: "I am no longer a German. Am I still an exile? It is my ambition to become a Citizen of the World, of American nationality. . . . (The spirit of Walt Whitman, whom I am reading again: with greater joy than ever)" (Mann, *Der Wendepunkt* 399).

Yet Mann, an intellectual of the first order, also raised some disconcerting questions. Where do we draw the line between internationalism and colonialist hegemony? More troublesome still: Can such a line be drawn? In his essay "The Present Greatness of Walt Whitman" published in the exile journal *Decision* in 1941, Klaus Mann wrote:

> The very term "interest" has a double connotation: it may be interpreted as a purely altruistic approach, or it may imply a very different sort of attitude—selfish, utilitarian, aggressive. Both patterns are one-sided and therefore insufficient. . . . In many cases both elements—the spirit of nationalistic expansion and the spirit of universal solidarity—overlap or interfuse altogether. ("The Present Greatness of Walt Whitman" 27)

Mann suggests that universal love is often associated with universal egotism and that active solidarity can often be fatal for its recipients. To him, Whitman's poetry contains troubling reminders of other ideologies:

> One might object that the Christian message has been exploited and misused through the centuries for imperialistic purposes, and that Whitman's "loving aggressiveness" could easily serve as an ideological excuse for similar aims and tactics. This may be so, and would be ugly and deplorable. All we can do to forestall such a development is to stress and clarify the real sense and impact of his vision, which is (at least consciously and subjectively) infinitely remote from any scheme of nationalistic or capitalistic greed. ("The Present Greatness of Walt Whitman" 28)

Mann's fear is justified in view of some of the political developments of our day. Internationalist rhetoric abounds in Europe when the rich Western European nations celebrate their new European Union, but their policy toward East-Central and Eastern Europe suggests a more hegemonic internationalism, an exclusive rather than an inclusive concept.

On the other side of the political spectrum, those European leftists who had turned internationalism into a religion during the 1960s and 1970s, have withdrawn to positions of quiet nationalism at times disguised as "regionalism." The confusion surrounding internationalist models and positions has contributed to the general political failure to come to terms with nationalist horrors in what used to be Yugoslavia. The question of whether to intervene in Bosnia and whether such intervention would amount to friendly assistance or would further complicate the situation, proves the ever increasing ambiguity of internationalism in the contemporary context.

This ambiguity of the internationalist spirit itself has been present since the beginning. It was also present in Whitman's poetry. In "Years of the Modern," Whitman explicitly connects colonialism with globalist internationalism. The outcome is an interesting piece of "imperialist" poetry:

> His daring foot is on land and sea everywhere, he colonizes the Pacific, the
>     archipelagoes,

With the steamship, the electric telegraph, the newspaper, the wholesale en-
gines of war,
With these and the world-spreading factories he interlinks all geography,
all lands;
What whispers are these O lands, running ahead of you, passing under the
seas?
Are all nations communing? is there going to be but one heart to the
globe? (*LG* 490)

As imperialist as this passage may sound, it retains a characteristic ambiguity. The "daring foot" is that of the "average man" (*LG* 489). This 1865
poem, with its promise to break "frontiers and boundaries of the old aris-
tocracies" (*LG* 489), thus also continues the rhetoric of the 1848 revolutions
(and, of course, the radicalism of the French revolution).

Whitman's "globalist" poetry is at times also fairly eurocentric. In "Passage to India," Whitman's lyrical persona appeals to "history," which, not
surprisingly, is associated with colonialism:

Along all history, down the slopes,
As a rivulet running, sinking now, and now again to the surface rising,
A ceaseless thought, a varied train—lo, soul, to thee, thy sight, they rise,
The plans, the voyages again, the expeditions;
Again Vasco da Gama sails forth,
Again the knowledge gain'd, the mariner's compass,
Lands found and nations born, thou born America,
For purpose vast, man's long probation fill'd,
Thou rondure of the world at last accomplish'd. (*LG* 414)

When Whitman attempts to create a spiritual quasi-religious superstructure
for modern technology, science, and communication, his metaphorical use
of Vasco da Gama reveals the difficulty of the undertaking. If the mythical
passage to India, which had long informed American thinking, can be related to classic European colonialism represented by the Portuguese explorer, the spiritualization of the enterprise is less than convincing. Even
"Salut Au Monde!" with its "tracks of the railroads of the earth" or "the
electric telegraphs of the earth" in section 5 implies a Western bias in favor
of expansion, economic exploitation, and technology.

### III

The reception to Whitman at the University of Pennsylvania, which houses
important Whitman materials and has traditionally focused on Whitman
studies, shows us that the nexus between internationalism and imperialism
was a natural one some eighty years ago. In a letter dated May 23, 1907, a

professor of English at the University of Pennsylvania wrote to Horace
Traubel:

> My dear Mr. Traubel:—
>
> In reply to your request I gladly write the following:
> It may interest the members of the Walt Whitman Fellowship to know
> that the students of the University have been lectured to specifically on
> Walt Whitman every year for the last ten years, that they have been in-
> structed fully to recognize the importance of Whitman from a historical
> point of view and for the intrinsic nobility of his opinion and broad and
> liberal art. *Of late I think we have laid especial stress on the fact that Mr. Kipling
> in his imperialism, his sense of expansion and his large treatment of large issues
> is, when all has been said, a disciple of Walt Whitman.*
>
> It is the contemporaneousness of Whitman that made him the man
> that he was and will long remain. It was a great truth to be told that in
> literature we must not dwell wholly in the past.
>
> Expressing my deep sympathy with the noble ethics, the high aims,
> the liberality that knew no bounds, all of which were so distinctively char-
> acteristic of the great poet, I greet this meeting with the hope that the
> Fellowship may long continue and make more widely and better known
> the work of this great man.
>
> > Sincerely yours,
> > Felix Schelling[12]

The writer, Felix Emanuel Schelling (1858–1945), professor of English,
was not an expansionist politician but an honest philologist. A member of
the National Institute of Arts and Letters, the American Philosophical Society, and the Modern Language Association, he did much of his work in
Elizabethan literature.[13] Traubel had obviously requested information on
the state of Whitman activities at the University of Pennsylvania so he
could give a report at the reunion of the *Fellowship* convening annually on
Whitman's birthday. Whether Traubel had expected this sort of a reply
from Schelling and announced it over the *Fellowship* dinner, and whether
he agreed with it or not, remains unknown.

What emerges from the letter, however, is a reading of Whitman which
is, at least from our point of view, rather unusual. Far from criticizing
Whitman's "imperialism," Schelling views it as a natural phenomenon
which has its rightful place in American thinking. He connects imperialism
with attitudes of "intrinsic nobility," "noble ethics," and "high aims."
Through Kipling, he connects it to the mission, indeed burden, of the
white man. Schelling's political naiveté reveals the implicit dangers of Whitman's internationalism. A "liberality which knows no bounds" may simply
be too aggressively liberal. Breaking bounds seems like an optimistic project, but in a completely boundless world, humanist values may at times be

lost and human identity threatened. The recent discussion surrounding the next stage of European integration ("Maastricht") has revealed just such fears.

Whitman's self-construction as a poet, his work, his reception, and the construction of his person by others all testify to the pervasiveness of the internationalist message carried back and forth between America and the rest of the world. Whitman is the earliest, most vocal, and most outspokenly "internationalist" poet in world literature. But his version of internationalism, both as produced and received, carries with it the questions internationalism raises, questions with which those trained in Whitman's political spirit need to come to terms.

## Notes

1. The English original of this text is lost; this is a retranslation into English. All translations from the German in this essay are my own.
2. See Giuseppe Mazzini's critique of diplomacy below.
3. For Whitman's reception by the German political left, both Marxist and anarchist, see my books *Walt Whitmann: Die deutschsprachige Rezeption als interkulturelles Phänomen*, 100–18, and *Constructing the German Walt Whitman*.
4. Although the poem was initially published in 1856, Grier has shown that Whitman's ideas for "Salut Au Monde!" go at least as far back as 1854 (*NUP* 1: 138, 147).
5. The essay was first published in the *Westminster Review*, April 2, 1852.
6. In the original German version of "Funkspruch in die Welt," the passage reads:

An alle, alle, alle! An die Völker Europas und die Völker Amerikas!
An die Steppenhorden Asiens, die Reisbauern Indiens und die Völker der Südsee!
An die steinernen Dschungeln der Städte,
An den einsamsten Kamelhirten, der in seinem Zelte betet!
Aus verschüttetem Brunnen hebe ich mein Herz und rufe euch zu: trinkt! trinkt!
[. . .]

Laßt mich herantreten zu euch mit entblößtem Haupte, ihr Völker, die Hände berühren,
Euch in die Augen schauen, tief, tief, wie die Liebenden nach langer Getrenntheit.
Ihr Einsamen, die ihr verschüttet lagt, die das Schweigen zerbrach,
Die ihr vertrieben über die Fremdheit der Erde irrt,
Ihr Einäugigen, ihr von Tränen geschwächten Mütter! Ihr alle, die ihr besessen und belogen wart—
O der Geruch der Leichenfelder der Erde,
Der durch das Filter eurer Herzen steigt, ihr Wiederbekehrten, ist süßer als Paradiesesduft.
Und ihr, Geliebteste, aus den Gefängnissen aller Länder,
Denen wir die Ketten vom bleichen Strunk ihrer Hände lösten,
Muß ich nicht niederknien, in Freudentränen eure Lende zu küssen?

O Arme, die den Erdball umspannen!
Liebe strahlt aus meinen zehn Fingerspitzen.
Und noch das Haar auf meinem Haupte ist Flamme der Liebe.

7. See Sadakichi [Hartmann].
8. Bazalgette to Schlaf, January 18, 1907. Schlaf papers, Querfurt, Germany. The original is in French.
9. Bazalgette to Schlaf, March 29, 1906. Schlaf papers, Querfurt, Germany. The original is in French.
10. Walt Whitman, *Der Wundarzt. Briefe, Aufzeichnungen und Gedichte aus dem amerikanischen Sezessionskrieg.*
11. Ferdinand Freiligrath, "Walt Whitman," 257–59. Translation in various American magazines including *The New Eclectic Magazine*, July 1868, 325–29.
12. Felix Schelling to Horace Traubel, Horace Traubel Papers, Library of Congress. Italics mine.
13. See *Encyclopedia Americana*, 1948 edition, vol. 24, 365.

# Epilogue: Whitman's Centennial and the State of Whitman Studies

## JAY GROSSMAN

### I

*Breaking Bounds* is a project, a conference, and a collection of essays that has been in diverse ways influenced by the presence and the eloquence of Tom Yingling. This is the case not only because this volume is dedicated to his memory—Yingling died of complications associated with acquired immune deficiency syndrome on July 27, 1992—or because it places into circulation an excerpt from one of his unfinished essays as a place-holder for the paper he did not live to deliver at the University of Pennsylvania conference that was this volume's origin. Rather, *Breaking Bounds* can be said in a most literal sense to grow out of the same engaged scholarly tradition that lay at the core of Yingling's own work as an academic and activist, an engagement emblematized well by a seminal sentence from the first chapter of his *Hart Crane and the Homosexual Text:*

> The power to claim a proper textual strategy, of course, always highlights cultural values and taboos, and the way in which Whitman's corpus has been divided and aligned into a canon that emphasizes his American qualities and de-emphasizes his erotic and homoerotic ones speaks to the manner in which critical evaluations may mirror cultural values while masking themselves as transparent to the text, as natural rather than produced. (7–8)

Among a range of goals, *Breaking Bounds* has from its inception sought to intervene in the critical processes that Yingling here identifies, in order to render what appear self-evident or merely salutary as instead contingent and culturally-produced arrangements that impose order rather than simply clarifying or highlighting. The conferences in relation to which "Breaking Bounds: A Whitman Centennial Celebration" sketched out its parameters for examining Whitman's canon and career were held at the University

of Iowa and at the Museum of the City of New York during 1992, the year
that marked the one hundredth anniversary of Walt Whitman's death. A
single phrase from Yingling's explanation—"the way in which Whitman's
corpus has been divided"—serves well as an introduction to the section
headings that structured the scholarly investigations at these events: "The
Biographical Whitman," "The Political Whitman," "The International
Whitman," "The Historical Whitman," "Whitman as Reporter," "Whitman
and Popular Performance," "Whitman and Popular Religion," "Whitman
and Photography," "Whitman and Language," "Whitman and the Aesthetic Life," "Whitman and Science," "Whitman and Sexuality." There is
of course much to be said for these structuring paradigms, not the least of
which is perhaps the pragmatic recognition that the sheer multiplicity of
Whitman's prolific textual production fairly demands an entrance into his
writings by means of some delimiting scheme or plan; as the poet himself
warned: "I am large . . . . I contain multitudes" (*LG* 1855: 85).

Nevertheless, I want in the following pages to concentrate upon one
particular aspect of this volume's bound-breaking objectives, and to consider a bit more fully Yingling's suggestion that these seemingly commonsensical divisions enable the exclusion of the homosexual dimension of
Whitman's life and writings.[1] Toward that end, I shall offer a modest genealogical inquiry by means of a long-forgotten article by Malcolm Cowley,
published in *The New Republic* in April 1946. Entitled "Walt Whitman: The
Secret," the article contains this rather resonant anecdote in its opening
paragraph:

> Long ago a critic I greatly admired, and still admire, invited John Wheel-
> wright and me to have lunch with him at his club. We talked about Whit-
> man. I don't remember whether it was Wheelwright or I who said, over
> the entrée, "Of course you know that Whitman was a homosexual."—
> "Oh, no," the critic said; and a moment later he left the table, not angrily,
> but with the deeply troubled look of one just told that he had been be-
> trayed by his dearest friend. Wheelwright and I waited a long time, un-
> able to order coffee or dessert and feeling that the elderly club members
> were staring at us; then we got our hats from the cloakroom and wan-
> dered into the street. Later I heard that the critic had been planning to
> write a biography of Whitman, but it never appeared. (481)

The first thing we might notice about this episode is its clear depiction
of what Eve Kosofsky Sedgwick has helped us to see as the homosocial/
homosexual continuum. Under this dispensation, the revelation about
Whitman (who, prior to the declaration, is himself, seemingly, a potential
club member) brings to the fore the inherent instability of the binary that
would distinguish between the luncheon club's sanctioned all-male interac-
tions (within which "greatly admiring" a critic is perfectly acceptable), and
some other unspeakable realm within which males also interact. The passage leaves fruitfully open the question of just who has transgressed—espe-

cially in its description of the "deeply troubled look" with which the unnamed critic leaves the table—even as Cowley's ambiguous pronouns leave unclear what exactly has happened: has Whitman as "dearest friend" betrayed the trust of this critic because he (Whitman) is a homosexual, or has the interest in Whitman betrayed the critic's own homosexuality, in which case Cowley has given us one of the first (anonymous) "outings" in American literary history and American gay history?

Implausible at first glance, "outing" suddenly seems to be the passage's open secret, and everywhere we look in the passage we find the fear of homosexual contagion: not simply in the unnamed critic's reaction (whose anonymity registers as this contagion's surest symptom), but most palpably in the reaction of "the elderly club members." Having themselves overstepped some invisible boundary, Cowley and Wheelwright banish themselves and "wander" away from this all-male enclave, guilty somehow by association, and for associating with both the unnamed critic and with Whitman. Of course, the theme of banishment registers even more resonantly in the critic's disappearance and the "biography" that "never appeared."

Cowley, for his part, ends the article with what he believes to be all the necessary disclaimers; he has written, he says, "not in any sense as an attack on Whitman, but simply as a step toward laying the foundation for the revaluation that must soon be made": "I detest the sort of people who say that Poe was impotent, that Grant was a drunkard, that Franklin Roosevelt had the sort of optimism that is a clinical symptom after infantile paralysis" (484). The morally and medically inflected dictions of innocence and abnormality give the lie to Cowley's claims that he means only to prepare some neutral ground for a wholesale reappraisal; the die is cast for something quite different, among other places, in the very terms of the analogies to Poe's impotence and to Grant's drinking and to Roosevelt's "clinical symptom." Cowley's article actually carries out an even more insidious method of dealing with Whitman's homosexuality, however, by means of a strategy of containment that returns us to the notion of those seemingly benign divisions with which I began. "What was extraordinary about [Whitman]," Cowley writes, "was simply his poetic genius, which existed apart from the rest of his character" (483). Cowley may seek to reevaluate (not now, but "soon"), though not before the poetry has been secured away from the fear of contagion, from the taint of the abnormal. Not before Whitman has been dismembered, while at the same time rendered impotent, intemperate, and pathological. Reevaluation indeed.

*Breaking Bounds* is not an antidote to these cultural and critical practices, but with regard to the categorizing scheme that it puts into play—"Genealogies," "America's Whitmans," "Whitman's Americas," "Legacies"—Betsy Erkkila and I hope that one of its most important aspects will be to provide viable and vibrant alternatives whose repercussions and ultimate efficacies cannot be fully known in advance. This is to say that within these categories, what also cannot be known in advance are the parameters within which Whitman's "sexual" and "homosexual" representations—or any other dimension of his writings—may elicit their fullest critical and cultural meanings and ramifications. It is hoped that this deliberate un-knowing and not-knowing can be the strength of this collection not only in its multifarious relations to a range of readers, but also to the burgeoning field of cultural studies named in its subtitle.

## II

*Breaking Bounds* is also—and not by any means incidentally—framed by a pedagogical imperative linked to other questions raised by the divisions that have come to structure the scholarly appraisals of the writings of Walt Whitman. For when, in the public service announcement that Betsy Erkkila considers in the introduction to this volume, the young man wishes aloud that "they" had told him in school that Walt Whitman was gay, I cannot help but wonder how we as teachers, scholars, intellectuals—or more generally, as citizens interested in furthering a multifaceted antihomophobic project—are interpellated and challenged by that pronoun. In taking as a point of departure a public service announcement that was never permitted to appear over the (so-called) public-serving airwaves in Philadelphia, I am wondering what the impact of such a refusal might be on some of the most vulnerable among us—young gay and lesbian teens. Motivated here by that young man's wish, I want to explore in particular how "we" as "they"—and, in particular, how we who are teachers—might be implicated in all of this.

The next question might be simply put: who is the Whitman that is disseminated in college and university classrooms? A reader's report I recently received may provide the framework of an answer, and set out the terms of what I and a number of other contributors to *Breaking Bounds* might be said to be arguing against. "From what I have seen of Whitman scholarship in recent years," this reader wrote, "it's the political/sexual Whitman that scholars focus upon today. Scholars (and a fair number of teachers, too) now are more likely to examine the "Children of Adam" and, especially, "Calamus" groups than the big democratic chants favored a decade or two ago." On the one hand, according to this reader, one can teach the "sexual poems," and on the other, decades ago, "the big democratic chants"—but there is no sense that the two ever do or ever can be made to meet. If there's the possibility of a conjunction in the composite adjective "political/sexual," it is also true that the "democratic" chants are oddly separated out from the "political." Within this scheme, a poem is "political" or "sexual" or "democratic," but not all three, and certainly not all three at the same time.

I am assuming here that some students may never read scholarly journals or full-length works of cultural and literary criticism, though some of them are doubtless being taught by scholars whose pedagogy has been influenced by the full range of criticism working through the historical nuances of Whitman's sexual representations. At the same time, these undergraduates may be much more likely to use overview literary histories, works like Robert Spiller's 1948 *Literary History of the United States,* and one of the most recent entries to the shelf, the 1988 *Columbia Literary History of the United States,* edited by Emory Elliott. Available in library reference rooms, these texts present themselves as embodiments of cultural consensus about the figures and the histories they delineate.[2] Their very titles confidently assert cultural power and cultural capital, and the material characteristics of these heavy, sometimes multivolume works fairly announce their unequivocal status as History, as Truth (or at least as something manifestly different from what may seem the more ephemeral musings of a professor about his or her personal interest). Consequently, I want to sketch out briefly how Whitman and the questions raised by his sexuality sit in these two texts.

Contrary to what we might expect, the Spiller history's chapter on Whitman—written by Henry Seidel Canby—provides more that a student might find encouraging or useful if he or she were looking to Whitman for some kind of gay history or gay lineage. Canby's Whitman retains a certain, determinate nonconformity, carried along in part by two parenthetical characterizations that occur very near the start of the chapter.

As a reporter (and Whitman both in prose and in verse was always a reporter), he left daily his pleasant stall in Brooklyn to roam New York, to frequent its theaters in the years of great Shakespearean actors, and to drink in its operatic music while he watched the capture of vast audiences by the art of poetic oratory. As a Bohemian (and Whitman, who seldom lived with his family and never married, was always a Bohemian), he delighted in the crowds of Broadway, studied the "en-masse," as he called it, without prejudice, preferring workmen, farmers, the vitality of the common people, to the static and the complacent in American society. (473)

Whitman as Bohemian permits at least a space for unconventionality; indeed, in Canby's references to opera and Broadway, we may even find the traces of a modern, now-more-legible, postwar, gay male persona. But I am also thinking here analogously of Henry Abelove's recent suggestion that Thoreau's retreat to Walden might be seen as a "queer action" insofar as it figures what Abelove calls "life outside the discourses of domesticity, romantic love and marriage, and the white bourgeois family" as "valuable and vivid" (23). Perhaps these lines from Canby's portrait of Whitman can be said to point to something similar.

Now there can be no denying that Canby's denunciation, when it comes, is adamant, and yet even in its very extremity, I think, a space is opened out for what is being so vehemently excluded:

This ruddy body of Whitman's, with its electric senses, and its quick perception of passion, was not the body of an average man. Sexually, it and
he (for his imagination of course was involved) belonged in the vague
regions that lie in the hinterland of what a doctor or a psychiatrist would
call a normal man or woman. He was physically sympathetic, mentally
interpretive, for both sexes, richer perhaps than either taken alone.
There is not one particle of evidence that he was actively homosexual,
and when he was challenged in old age he recoiled from the idea with a
horror whose sincerity is convincing. Yet from the records of his life and
the testimony of the imagery of his poems, it is clear that his love went
out more readily, more frequently, though not more passionately, to men
than to women. With the boys he loved and cared for in the Civil War
hospitals, and with young friends like the streetcar conductor, Pete
Doyle, this love seems paternal. But there was often a perturbation, as he
called it, a sexual arousing that does not differ from the passion between
man and woman. . . . Yet his love poems to women are too aglow with
fervor to let one doubt that he knew also the love of women, and here in
full sexual release. (484)

One can hardly help wondering which "particle of evidence" for ascribing
"active" homosexuality would be sufficient, though it seems certain that the
four same-sex "marriage" photos (or the Eakins nude) discussed by Ed
Folsom in this volume must go a very long way indeed toward meeting this
long-held demand of Whitman scholars. But these observations aside, it
needs to be admitted that Canby's account itself exhibits a certain frank-
ness, as well as an earnest attempt to characterize specifically where and
how the evidence seems to point. For example, while it may not at all be
the reading we would support, the suggestion that Whitman "recoiled . . .
with a horror whose sincerity is convincing" in response to John Addington
Symonds's probing questions, is, nevertheless, one possible reading of
Whitman's famous reply.[3] By the time we get around to the would-be clari-
fication that Whitman experienced "a sexual arousing that *does not differ*
from the passion between man and woman," or that he "knew *also* the love
of women" it is hard to say just what is to be inferred, although by the
logic of the passage and its strenuous attempts to draw distinctions, it certainly must depend upon something more than simply "full sexual release."
I would not want to presume that my imaginary undergraduate reader
could necessarily work out of this passage the nuances I have just suggested, but I am nevertheless heartened to find these spaces of possibility.
    One gets as well, in a concurrent passage, some alignment of the politi-
cal and the sexual:

[Whitman's] sexual oversensitiveness is supernormal rather than abnormal. It made him a writer of great love poems. It made him an apostle
of the love of comrades, which he believed alone could insure a durable
democracy. It made it easy for him to dramatize himself as a symbol of

the lusty vigor of expansionist America and of a sexuality fully developed
and expressed and indispensable to the growth of a perfect society. It
made it fatally easy for him to carry his sexuality beyond the bounds of
reason and good taste. (485)

If we are at the last constrained between the "the bounds of reason and
good taste," somewhere in the middle we have been given the possibility
of reckoning the specifically political consequences of Whitman's sexual vision, and in decidedly Whitmanian language: "a sexuality fully developed
and expressed and indispensable," with its adjectives piled upon adjectives,
is a line that could easily have come out of Whitman's own long reply to
Emerson in the 1856 edition of *Leaves of Grass*.[4]

A single passage from Jerome Loving's chapter on Whitman for the
*Columbia Literary History* severs precisely this vital link between the political
and the sexual:

> In the third edition of *Leaves of Grass* the poet who felt divine "inside and
> out" in 1855 admits "that the soul of the man I speak for rejoices in
> comrades." It has been argued that a "religious purpose" lay at the heart
> of Whitman's best poetry, but the evidence for this assertion is generally
> limited to the poet's retrospective statements about his art. Later he
> would adopt the pose of the more conservative "Emersonian" poet and
> seek "a passage to more than India!" but in "Calamus" we find him on a
> passage to nowhere except the doubts and fears of personal—and very
> possibly homosexual—love. (456)[5]

Here, ostensibly, is an avowal of the possibility of homosexual content and
context, but one that reads more like a stinging rebuke than Canby's own.
"A passage to nowhere except the doubts and fears of personal—and very
possibly homosexual—love." But just a line or two from "Calamus" calls
into question at once such a hyperpersonalized, quasi-pathologized reading, because Whitman refuses to keep separate, private, or hidden what
Loving would keep from view. Instead, the poet overtly names what he
calls "the main purport of These States" ("Calamus 35") and *visibility* is
its keynote:

> It shall be customary in all directions, in the houses and streets, to see
>    manly affection,
> The departing brother or friend shall salute the remaining brother or
>    friend with a kiss.
> . . .
> The most dauntless and rude shall touch face to face lightly,
> The dependence of Liberty shall be lovers,
> The continuance of Equality shall be comrades. ("Calamus 5," *LG* 1860:
>    350–51; ellipsis added)[6]

Loving's "road to nowhere" is to lead to a unified Republic and a secured Union, literally a queer nation, which means we are here facing the distinct possibility that one person's "nowhere" is another's utopia. But that does not, I think, sufficiently explain the curious anachronism we have uncovered, one in which the more recent account of Whitman's sexuality and its significance seems really to be caught in a kind of 1950s time warp. This has much to do, I think, with the current visibility of homosexuality in the public sphere—for why else does Loving denominate "private" what is everywhere appearing since the 1980s as the very public, sometimes shouting, and increasingly angry proclamations of a queer love that had previously, even recently, dared not speak? And how else explain Canby's comparatively carefree recognition of this homoeroticism's public "purport" when juxtaposed first against Loving's erasure, and then against the absence of a public celebration of Whitman's centennial at the Library of Congress in the District of Columbia where he nursed his Civil War soldiers, and which houses the largest publicly-owned archive of materials and memorabilia by and about "America's Poet" in the world? The bounds between "sexuality" and "democracy" and "politics" are still policed in these post-Stonewall, postliberation days, these days of (always relative) "queer" visibility, even as a recent *Newsweek* cover queries "the limits of tolerance," as if some elusive destination called "tolerance" had already been reached.[7]

Loving writes that "Whitman's ultimate theme in 1860 is the fusion of Love and Death" (456), but we may be left wondering where the comrades and the Republic have gone in that summary; where is Whitman the Bohemian, where the ineluctable but inexorable links between the poetry and the politics? Elsewhere Loving calls Whitman a "lifelong bachelor in both the literal and the literary sense" (450), and while this may be strictly true, it is also the case that such a characterization propagates what can only be called a hetero-normative account of this poet's life and works, an insistence that these are the terms (married versus bachelor) within which Whitman is best understood, when he is himself searching out and shaping alternatives. And what of the students who turn to this chapter in this "updated" *Columbia Literary History of the United States*, looking for some clue from Whitman, some possibility?

Perhaps more than anything else, Loving's account of Whitman's "Calamus" series reminds us how the public dimension of Whitman's sexual representations needs constantly to be rediscovered. In contradistinction to the speaker's insistence in "Calamus" that the most overt implications of these bonds between men will be at the macro level of the nation-state, one finds instead the critical insistence that Whitman's sexual writings need to be separated out from his stance as a public poet, from his place as America's Poet of Democracy. It is a familiar pattern. As Jonathan Goldberg has concluded in an incisive bit of criticism about even the dissenting opinions in the watershed case *Bowers v. Hardwick* (1986), in which the U.S. Supreme Court refused to find any constitutional protection for private, consensual sexual activities between adults of the same gender, "to protect homosexuality through arguments about the right to privacy offers no safeguards for homosexuality as a social identity—it assumes that homosexuals are defined solely by private sexual acts. . . . [B]oth majority and minority views . . . agree that if homosexuals have any place at all it is the closet. (The majority would have that closet barred and padlocked, of course.) Both views would keep homosexuality and homosexuals invisible. Public space is presumptively heterosexual" (10–11). These justices and many of their fellow citizens cannot imagine that the significance of, or the protections for, homosexuality (in *Bowers*, anomalously reduced to an incoherent category called "sodomy") could possibly be extended to include a public sphere where it might be safe for two men to walk hand-in-hand through public streets saturated with the markings and productions of an omnipresent heterosexual majority. But Whitman could imagine exactly such a world; indeed, he writes in *Democratic Vistas* (1871), "democracy infers such loving comradeship, as its most inevitable twin or counterpart, without which it will be incomplete, in vain, and incapable of perpetuating itself" (*PW* 2: 415)— and we owe it to our students, especially our gay and lesbian students, to tell them about it.

I return us, then, to the question of our responsibilities as teachers— formal and informal, inside the classroom or beyond it. Many of the essays in *Breaking Bounds* seek to place Whitman's queer nation and our own in dialogue, partly as a means of demonstrating to gay students that they do indeed have a place in this ongoing literary—but not only literary—history. The recognition in our classrooms, our homes, our public halls, and private sanctuaries, of these still unfolding histories could mark a passage to somewhere even more expansive (internationally, intranationally) than the Walt Whitman Bridge that spans the Delaware.

## III

As I have attempted to find a form for this epilogue that would contain not only my admittedly—and deliberately—circumscribed assessment of the other Whitman centennial conferences of 1992, while at the same time bringing this volume to its close, I found myself turning to another place in Tom Yingling's work. Reading his essay "AIDS in America: Postmodern Governance, Identity, and Experience," I have found myself pondering the word homology—even though Yingling never uses the word—because it accurately depicts the structures that seem to me to be in place and that force the alignment between Yingling's subject there, and mine here.

The analogy emerges, I think, in relation to Yingling's justification of ACT-UP's disruption of Health and Human Services Secretary Louis Sullivan's speech at the Sixth International AIDS Conference in San Francisco in June 1990:

the point in that intervention, [Yingling writes,] was multiple, but among the strong reasons for pursuing it was the continuing non-representation of those most directly affected by the epidemic in the very apparatuses (such as that convention, such as the Department of Health and Human Services) supposedly designed to address their needs, and supposedly doing an admirable job in that. The "game" in this case had failed to include all of its players, and some of those players—the ones with less power in the situation—decided to halt the game. (309 n19)

I have become preoccupied with the word homology—which my dictionary defines as "a similarity often attributable to a common origin"—because that is the word that registers the interconnectedness of the methodologies and institutional structures that render homosexuality invisible or inapplicable across the range of these cultural scenes—the AIDS conference in San Francisco and the yes, *different*, but homologous centennial conferences on Walt Whitman.

For, as Betsy Erkkila makes clear in this volume's introduction, the conference and the volume called *Breaking Bounds*, unlike the two other major centennial events held in New York City and in Iowa City, were brought forward without the grant assistance of the United States government. And while NEH insisted it was for other reasons, she and I have a difficult time crediting the rationale they gave for our proposal's rejection, because what linger in our ears are the words of the NEH program officer who asked before he could comment upon the proposal's viability: "Does it matter to you that Whitman was gay?" That question took different forms at the other centennial conferences I attended, but its resonance was unmistakable: one very well-known American literary historian insisted, for example, that he still did not know of any "proof" that Whitman was "active homosexually"; another respected Whitman scholar suggested that Whitman's relationship to his mother could best be explained by calling up the truism that male homosexuals are often more attached to their mothers. But the erasure took other forms as well: in the insistence, for example, that Whitman was first and foremost an aesthete, his poems, first and foremost, like all great art, separate, to revisit Cowley's words, from the rest of his "character." Yet Katherine Kinney and Michael Warner—to name only two—demonstrate with compelling insights in their contributions to this volume the ways in which the perimeters between some realm called "the literary" and another and somehow antithetical realm of "the political" mutually interpenetrate, even as Sylvia Molloy, Michael Davidson, and Jonathan Arac separately remind us that the interpretation—one might almost call it, at the behest of Jorge Salessi and José Quiroga, the "translation"— of artistic productions is itself always structured by the cultural and temporal frames within which the act called reading (and so, writing) necessarily occurs. These are among the deliberate recastings of *Breaking Bounds*.

The various erasures that I have been enumerating—the deployments at scholarly and public health conferences alike of a kind of ignorance that is not simply the obverse to some enlightenment, but is more properly seen as power in another form[8]—are not by any means uniformly homologous, but, I would insist, they are no less substantial or significant for being less than uniform. And I cannot help taking this opportunity to recount the urgency of the project, for there is most assuredly a connection between those agencies in Washington, D.C. so clearly wanting us to be "troubled" by the issue of Whitman's homosexuality and its propagation at a literary conference, and other institutions in that same city that continue to make invisible the suffering and the bravery of a pandemic of colossal proportions. (Even under a new administration, we are being asked to submit to the fundamentally anti-intellectual regime of "Don't ask, don't tell." And only days before this essay was submitted for copy editing, almost two-thirds of the U.S. Senate voted to deny funds to school districts that attempt to acknowledge the presence of their young gay and lesbian students through curricular or extracurricular activities.[9]) As if the facts of gay teenage suicide were not real, as if deaths from AIDS were not mounting, and as if the omission of Whitman's homosexuality or its being made marginal did not evince real consequences in the sequence of consequences that result in macro genocide or micro despair. So, homologous.

After quoting the opening lines of a poem that first appeared in the 1860 *Leaves of Grass* as "Calamus 30"—

A promise to California,
Or inland to the great pastoral Plains, and on to Puget Sound and Oregon,
Sojourning east a while longer, soon I travel toward you, to remain, to
    teach robust American love—

Malcolm Cowley writes, "[a]t this point, we first perceive that Whitman is trying to identify, or at least confuse, homosexuality with Americanism" (483). Confusion, again, and the breaking of bounds. Fifty years after Cowley wrote, and one hundred years after Whitman died, the work of productively confusing Whitman's "homosexuality" with "Americanism" continues. For it is not simply the case that Whitman's sexuality intrudes upon other dimensions of his work: in these lines from "Calamus," for example, Whitman gives us his political project, securing the bonds of the union by means of his celebration and institutionalization of the love between comrades. But I ask you: under which category should this poem be included? The Political Whitman? Whitman and Sexuality? The Influential Whitman? The Topographical Whitman? These three lines demonstrate in an instant the inability of a series of divided Whitmans fully to account for the fluidity of Whitman's work, a fluidity that the contributors to *Breaking Bounds* investigate and interrogate, often with breathtaking insight and innovation.

It is not the case that we should absorb a new version of Whitman Our

Contemporary—in the guise, perhaps, of a post-Stonewall gay liberationist. Indeed, it may turn out that the least of our difficulties in this regard is the fact that the word "homosexual" does not appear until 1892, the year of Whitman's death. What is necessary, however, is a certain candor—not to declare Whitman a homosexual on our terms so much as to discuss, and to take account of, commonly, regularly, and especially with our students, Whitman's "queerness." From *Breaking Bounds,* by breaking bounds, we might begin to propagate new Whitmans, ones who—essentially, if you like—break down categories, and who insist that we do the same.

Not every essay in *Breaking Bounds* addresses directly the questions raised by Whitman's multivalent sexual (self-)representations that I have been focusing upon, but the volume as a whole enacts a kind of interdisciplinary blurring that refutes the persistent tendency in Whitman criticism to isolate Whitman's sexuality from his politics, and his poetry from both. This is the primary and essential breaking of bounds in the title, for it is a central supposition of this collection not only that the issue of Whitman's sexuality cannot be separated out into a realm apart, where it will not "infect" questions of literary value or the overarching shape of this major American poet's wide-sweeping canon, influence, and reputation, but that such separations as a rule distort our readings of Whitman's corpus even when they occur in relation to aspects of his writings that would seem to be quite removed from the ones I have concentrated upon here. Thus, *Breaking Bounds* is a volume whose coherence is not so much figured as a set of shared questions about Whitman—though these are present as well—but rather as a shared set of assumptions that motivate the critical enterprise: the myriad places of Whitman's writings in his world, and the disparate places they continue to occupy in ours.

## Notes

1. The most recent manifestation of the same taxonomic imperative might be David Reynolds's inventory of Whitman's early writings:

> Previous commentators on Whitman have not placed his early poems and fiction against their popular background and have thus failed to see just how culturally representative they were. Most of his early works fit into well-established popular categories, each with its own history. Among his pre-1855 imaginative writings, fourteen (nine poems, five tales) were dark works about death or haunted minds; seven (five stories, two poems) were sensational and adventurous; four (two tales, two poems) were visionary works, picturing angelic visitations; six others (a poem, three stories, a novel, and a tale fragment) endorsed reform, especially temperance; four (two poems and two tales) were patriotic or nationalistic; four poems were political; three tales and one poem were moral; one tale was biblical. (*Walt Whitman* 85)

Among the questions this catalog begs: in what precise sense are the "patriotic or nationalistic" texts plausibly removed from the "political"? Were the "seven sensational and adventurous" texts "sensational and adventurous" with regard only to content, or were they formally daring as well? And why doesn't the sexual or the sexually explicit (not to say the homoerotic or the homosexual) make an appearance in Reynolds's order of things? If we imagine that the story Whitman first published in *The New World* as "The Child's Champion" (later "The Child and the Profligate") on November 20, 1841, is included in Reynolds's scheme under the category of the "visionary" because an angel appears at its end, or under the category of "reform" because of its focus upon alcoholic dissipation, we might still wonder where this passage from the story belongs:

> Why was it that from the first moment of seeing him, the young man's heart had moved with a strange feeling of kindness toward the boy? He felt anxious to know more of him—he felt that he should love him. O, it is passing wondrous, how in the hurried walks of life and business, we meet with young beings, strangers, who seem to touch the fountains of our love, and draw forth their swelling waters. The wish to love and to be beloved, which the forms of custom, and the engrossing anxiety for gain, so generally smother, will sometimes burst forth in spite of all obstacles; and, kindled by one, who, till the hour was unknown to us, will burn with a lovely and a pure brightness. No scrap is this of sentimental fiction; ask your own heart, reader, and your own memory, for endorsement to its truth. (322)

Such lines make clear that none of the categories Reynolds identifies can withstand interrogative pressure. It seems clear as well that this bit of taxonomic wishing-away is a remnant of a long-standing literary critical dream that Whitman in this story, as in other places in his corpus, might only be "reconciling his *private* desires with his reformist instinct toward virtuous conduct" (Reynolds 77, my emphasis), rather than, say, linking the practices and discourses of temperance reform to the public, political, adventurous, *and* moral consequences of the emotional and sexual bonds between men.

2. "But it is hard to say who will actually explore it," writes Beaver in his review of the *Columbia History.* "Students are more likely to enter it, Hebrew-fashion, from the back by making the index their point of access, thus turning this 'history' back into its constituent parts as an encyclopedia" (497).

3. Robert K. Martin offers an insightful reading of this exchange in his contribution to the Iowa centennial volume, "Whitman and the Politics of Identity." See also the final paragraphs of my " 'The Evangel-Poem of Comrades and of Love': Revising Whitman's Republicanism."

4. We might also want to notice—keeping in mind Grünzweig's concluding caveats in his contribution to this volume—how perfectly at ease Canby seems to be in 1948 with Whitman's own investments in the rhetorics and the projections called Manifest Destiny: "the lusty vigor of expansionist America. . . ."

5. Loving also misquotes the line, which, in the 1860 edition from which he says he quotes it, included the crucial qualifying word "only": "That the Soul of the man I speak for, fees, rejoices only in comrades" (*LG* 1860: 341).

6. These lines reappear in 1865 in "Over the Carnage Rose Prophetic a

Voice," one of the *Drum-Taps* poems, as predictions of the foundations upon which the nation will be restored following the Civil War (see *LG* 315–16).

7. *Newsweek* cover story, June 21, 1993: "Lesbians / Coming Out Strong / What Are the Limits of Tolerance?"

8. See Sedgwick, *Epistemology of the Closet* 7–8.

9. "Senate vote fights 'pro-gay' education," *San Francisco Examiner*, August 2, 1994, front page, afternoon edition. The amendment to the Elementary and Secondary Education Act denies Federal funding to school districts that "carry out a program or activity that has either the purpose or effect of encouraging or supporting homosexuality as a positive lifestyle alternative."

# Bibliography

Abelove, Henry. "From Thoreau to Queer Politics." *Yale Journal of Criticism* 6.2 (1993): 17–27.

Adorno, Theodor W. "On Lyric Poetry and Society" (1957). *Notes to Literature.* Vol. 1. Ed. Rolf Tiedemann. Trans. Shierry Weber Nicholsen. New York: Columbia UP, 1991. 37–54.

Alcaro, Marion Walker. *Walt Whitman's Mrs. G: A Biography of Anne Gilchrist.* Rutherford, NJ: Fairleigh Dickinson UP, 1991.

Alegría, Fernando. *Walt Whitman en Hispanoamérica.* México, D.F.: Colección Studium, 1954.

Allen, Gay Wilson. *The Solitary Singer.* 1955. New York: New York UP, 1967.

Ames, Mary Clemmer. *Ten Years in Washington.* Hartford, CT: A.D. Worthington and Co., 1875.

Anderson, Benedict. *Imagined Communities: Reflections on the Origin and Spread of Nationalism.* London: Verso, 1983.

Arac, Jonathan. *Critical Genealogies: Historical Situations for Postmodern Literary Studies.* New York: Columbia UP, 1987.

———. "Nationalism, Hypercanonization, and *Huckleberry Finn*." *boundary 2* 19.1 (1992): 14–33.

———. "Narrative Forms." *Cambridge History of American Literature.* 2 vols. Ed. Sacvan Bercovitch. Cambridge: Cambridge UP, 1995. 2: 605–777.

Aristotle. *The Nicomachean Ethics.* Trans. H. Rackham. Cambridge: Harvard UP, 1982.

Auerbach, Erich. *Mimesis: The Representation of Reality in Western Literature.* Trans. Willard R. Trask. Princeton: Princeton UP, 1953.

———. "The Aesthetic Dignity of the *Fleurs du Mal*" (1951). Trans. Ralph Manheim. *Scenes from the Drama of European Literature.* Minneapolis: U of Minnesota P, 1984.

Austin, J. L. "A Plea for Excuses." *Philosophical Papers.* 3rd ed. Oxford: Clarendon P, 1979.

Baker, Houston A. *Blues, Ideology, and Afro-American Literature.* Chicago: U of Chicago P, 1984.

———. *The Journey Back: Issues in Black Literature and Criticism.* Chicago: U of Chicago P, 1980.

Bakhtin, Mikhail. *The Dialogic Imagination.* Ed. Michael Holquist. Trans. Caryl Emerson and Michael Holquist. Austin: U of Texas P, 1981.

Barthes, Roland. *Camera Lucida: Reflections on Photography.* New York: Hill and Wang, 1981.

Barthes, *Roland Barthes by Roland Barthes.* Trans. Richard Howard. New York: Hill and Wang, 1977.

Baudelaire, Charles. *Les Fleurs du Mal.* Ed. Antoine Adam. Paris: Garnier, 1961.

Beaver, Harold. "The Endless Filament." Rev. of *The Columbia Literary History of the United States,* edited by Emory Elliott; *Scenes of Nature, Signs of Man,* by Tony Tanner; and *The Renewal of Literature: Emersonian Reflections,* by Richard Poirier. *Times Literary Supplement* (May 6–12, 1988): 497+.

Benjamin, Walter. "Central Park." Trans. Lloyd Spencer. *New German Critique* no. 34 (1985): 32–58.

———. *Charles Baudelaire: A Lyric Poet in the Age of High Capitalism.* Trans. Harry Zohn. London: NLB, 1973.

Bennett, Tony. "Putting Policy into Cultural Studies." *Cultural Studies.* Ed. Lawrence Grossberg, Cary Nelson, and Paula Treichler. New York: Routledge, 1992. 23–34.

Bercovitch, Sacvan. *The American Jeremiad.* Madison: U of Wisconsin P, 1978.

Bertz, Eduard. "Walt Whitman: Ein Charakterbild." *Jahrbuch für sexuelle Zwischenstufen* 7. Ed. Magnus Hirschfeld. Leipzig: Max Spohr, 1905. 154–287.

Bingham, Millicent Todd. *Emily Dickinson: A Revelation.* New York: Harper, 1954.

Bloom, Harold. *Poetry and Repression: Revision from Blake to Stevens.* New Haven: Yale UP, 1976.

Bohan, Ruth L. " 'The Gathering of the Forces': Walt Whitman and the Visual Arts in Brooklyn in the 1850s." Sill and Tarbell 1–27.

Boone, Bruce. "Gay Language as Political Praxis: The Poetry of Frank O'Hara." *Social Text* 1 (Winter 1979): 59–92.

Brand, Dana. *The Spectator and the City in Nineteenth-Century American Literature.* Cambridge: Cambridge UP, 1991.

Bredbeck, Gregory. "B/O—Barthes's Text/O'Hara's Trick." *PMLA* 108.2 (March 1993): 268–82.

Brown, Herbert Ross. *The Sentimental Novel in America, 1789–1860.* Durham: Duke UP, 1940.

Bucke, Richard Maurice, ed. *Calamus: A Series of Letters Written during the Years 1868–1880 by Walt Whitman to a Young Friend (Peter Doyle).* Boston: Small, Maynard, 1897.

Buckingham, Willis J. *Emily Dickinson's Reception in the 1890's: A Documentary History.* Pittsburgh: U of Pittsburgh P, 1989.

Buell, Lawrence. "American Literary Emergence as a Postcolonial Phenomenon." *American Literary History* 4.3 (1992): 411–42.

Canby, Henry Seidel. "Walt Whitman." Spiller 1: 472–98.

Carlyle, Thomas. "Shooting Niagara: And After?" *Critical and Miscellaneous Essays.* Ed. H. D. Traill. 5 vols. New York: Scribner's, 1901. 5: 1–48.

Carpenter, Edward. *Days with Walt Whitman.* London: Allen, 1906.

Cavitch, David. *My Soul and I: The Inner Life of Walt Whitman.* Boston: Beacon, 1985.

Ceniza, Sherry. Rev. of *Fanny Fern: An Independent Woman,* by Joyce W. Warren. *Walt Whitman Quarterly Review* 11.2 (1993): 89–95.

———. "Walt Whitman and Abby Price." *Walt Whitman Quarterly Review* 7.2 (1989): 49–67.

Chomsky, Noam. *Aspects of the Theory of Syntax.* Cambridge: MIT P, 1965.

————. *Cartesian Linguistics: A Chapter in the History of Rationalist Thought.* New York: Harper, 1966.

————. *Language and Mind.* Enlarged ed. New York: Harcourt, 1972.

————. "Linguistics and Politics: Interview with Noam Chomsky." *New Left Review* 57 (Sept.–Oct. 1969): 21–34.

————. *Reflections on Language.* New York: Pantheon, 1975.

————. *Syntactic Structures.* The Hague: Mouton, 1957.

Cmiel, Kenneth. *Democratic Eloquence: The Fight over Popular Speech in Nineteenth-Century America.* Cambridge: Cambridge UP, 1991.

Cogan, Frances B. *All-American Girl: The Ideal of Real Womanhood in Mid-Nineteenth-Century America.* Athens: U of Georgia P, 1989.

Corso, Gregory. "Variations on a Generation." *A Casebook on the Beat.* Ed. Thomas Parkinson. New York: Thomas Y. Crowell, 1961. 88–97.

Cowley, Malcolm. Introduction. *Walt Whitman's Leaves of Grass: The First (1855) Edition.* 1959. New York: Penguin, 1986.

————. "Walt Whitman: The Miracle." *New Republic* (Mar. 18, 1946): 385–88.

————. "Walt Whitman: The Secret." *New Republic* (Apr. 8, 1946): 481–84.

Crane, Hart. *The Complete Poems and Selected Letters and Prose.* Ed. Brom Weber. New York: Boni and Liveright, 1966.

Crane, Stephen. The Red Badge of Courage *and Other Writings.* Ed. Richard Chase. Boston: Houghton, 1960.

Crapanzano, Vincent. *Hermes' Dilemma and Hamlet's Desire: On the Epistemology of Interpretation.* Cambridge: Harvard UP, 1992.

Crompton, Louis. *Byron and Greek Love.* Berkeley: U of California P, 1985.

Dacey, Philip. "Thomas Eakins: The Secret Whitman Sitting." *Mickle Street Review* 12 (1990): 6–9.

Danly, Susan, and Cheryl Leibold, eds. *Eakins and the Photograph.* Washington: Smithsonian Institution P, 1994.

De Jean, Joan. *Fictions of Sappho 1546–1937.* Chicago: U of Chicago P, 1989.

Dellamora, Richard. *Masculine Desire: The Sexual Politics of Victorian Aestheticism.* Chapel Hill: U of North Carolina P, 1990.

Dickinson, Emily. *Letters.* Ed. Thomas H. Johnson. 3 vols. Cambridge: Harvard UP, 1958.

Diehl, Joanne Feit. "From Emerson to Whitman." *Women Poets and the American Sublime.* Bloomington: Indiana UP, 1990. 1–25.

Donaldson, Thomas. *Walt Whitman, the Man.* New York: Francis P. Harper, 1896.

Douglass, Frederick. *Narrative of the Life of Frederick Douglass* in *Autobiographies.* Ed. Henry Louis Gates, Jr. New York: Library of America, 1994.

Dummett, Michael. "Language and Communication." George 192–212.

Dunbar, Elizabeth. *Talcott Williams: Gentleman of the Fourth Estate.* Brooklyn, N.Y.: Privately printed, 1936.

Duncan, Robert. *The Opening of the Field.* New York: Grove, 1960.

Eakins, Thomas. *Photographer Thomas Eakins.* Essay by Ellwood C. Parry, III; Catalogue Notes by Robert Stubbs. Philadelphia: Olympia Galleries, 1981.

Edwards, Jonathan. *The Freedom of the Will. Basic Writings.* Ed. Ola Winslow. New York: Meridian, 1966. 196–223.

Eitner, Walter H. "Emily Dickinson's Awareness of Whitman: A Reappraisal." *Walt Whitman Quarterly Review* 22.3 (1976): 111–15.

Eliot, T. S. "Whitman and Tennyson" (1926). Murphy 205–07.

Elliott, Emory, ed. *Columbia Literary History of the United States.* New York: Columbia UP, 1988.

Ellison, Ralph. "Going to the Territory." *Going to the Territory.* New York: Random, 1986. 120–44.

———. *Shadow and Act.* 1964. New York: Vintage, 1972.

Erkkila, Betsy. *The Wicked Sisters: Women Poets, Literary History, and Discord.* New York: Oxford UP, 1992.

———. "Walt Whitman: The Politics of Language." *American Studies* 24.2 (1983): 21–34.

———. "Whitman and the Homosexual Republic." Folsom, *Walt Whitman* 153–71.

———. *Whitman the Political Poet.* New York: Oxford UP, 1989.

Ferenczi, Sandor. "Confusion of Tongues between Adults and the Child: The Language of Tenderness and the Language of Passion." *Final Contributions to the Problems and Methods of Psycho-Analysis.* Ed. Michael Balint. New York: Basic, 1955. 156–67.

Fisher, Philip. "Democratic Social Space: Whitman, Melville, and the Promise of American Transparency." *The New American Studies.* Ed. Fisher. Berkeley: U of California P, 1991. 70–111.

Fodor, Jerry A., and Jerrold J. Katz. "The Structure of a Semantic Theory." Fodor and Katz 479–518.

Fodor, Jerry A., and Jerrold J. Katz, eds. *The Structure of Language: Readings in the Philosophy of Language.* Englewood Cliffs, NJ: Prentice, 1964.

Foley, Barbara. *Radical Representations: Politics and Form in U.S. Proletarian Fiction, 1929–1941.* Durham: Duke UP, 1994.

Folsom, Ed. "Talking Back to Walt Whitman: An Introduction." Perlman, Folsom, and Campion xxi–liii.

———. *Walt Whitman's Native Representations.* New York: Cambridge UP, 1994.

———. ed. *"This Heart's Geography's Map": The Photographs of Walt Whitman.* Special issue of *Walt Whitman Quarterly Review* 4 (Fall/Winter 1986–87).

———, ed. *Walt Whitman: The Centennial Essays.* Iowa City: U of Iowa P, 1994.

Fone, Byrne. *Masculine Landscapes: Walt Whitman and the Homoerotic Text.* Carbondale: Southern Illinois UP, 1992.

Foster, George G. *New York by Gas-Light and Other Urban Sketches.* 1850. Ed. Stuart M. Blumin. Berkeley: U of California P, 1990.

Foster, Kathleen A., and Cheryl Leibold. *Writing About Eakins: The Manuscripts in Charles Bregler's Thomas Eakins Collection.* Philadelphia: U of Pennsylvania P, 1989.

Foucault, Michel. *The History of Sexuality. Volume 1: An Introduction.* New York: Vintage, 1980.

Freiligrath, Ferdinand. "Walt Whitman." *Augsburger Allgemeine Zeitung* (Wochenausgabe) 17 (Apr. 24, 1868): 257–59.

Friedman, Richard C. *Male Homosexuality: A Contemporary Psychoanalytic Perspective.* New Haven: Yale UP, 1988.

Garber, Marjorie. *Vested Interests: Cross-Dressing and Cultural Anxiety.* New York: Harper Collins, 1992.

George, Alexander, ed. *Reflections on Chomsky.* Oxford: Blackwell, 1989.

Gilbert, Sandra M. "The American Sexual Poetics of Walt Whitman and Emily Dickinson." *Reconstructing American Literary History.* Ed. Sacvan Bercovitch. Cambridge: Harvard UP, 1986. 123–54.

Gilchrist, Anne. "A Woman's Estimate of Walt Whitman." *In Re Walt Whitman.* Ed. Horace L. Traubel, Richard Maurice Bucke, and Thomas B. Harned. Philadelphia: David McKay, 1893. 41–55.

Gilroy, Paul. *The Black Atlantic: Modernity and Double Consciousness.* Cambridge: Harvard UP, 1993.

Ginsberg, Allen. *Howl and Other Poems.* San Francisco: City Lights, 1956.

———. *The Fall of America.* San Francisco: City Lights, 1972.

Goldberg, Jonathan. *Sodometries: Renaissance Texts, Modern Sexualities.* Stanford: Stanford UP, 1992.

Gooch, Brad. *City Poet: The Life and Times of Frank O'Hara.* New York: Knopf, 1993.

Goodrich, Lloyd. *Thomas Eakins.* 2 vols. Cambridge: Harvard UP, 1982.

Griswold, Charles. "The Vietnam Veterans Memorial and the Washington Mall: Philosophical Thoughts on Political Iconography." *Critical Inquiry* 12 (Summer 1986): 688–719.

Grosskurth, Phyllis. *John Addington Symonds: A Biography.* London: Longmans, 1964.

Grossman, Allen. "The Poetics of Union in Whitman and Lincoln." *The American Renaissance Reconsidered. Selected Papers from the English Institute, 1982– 83.* Ed. Walter Benn Michaels and Donald E. Pease. Baltimore: Johns Hopkins UP, 1985. 183–208.

Grossman, Jay. " 'The Evangel-Poem of Comrades and of Love': Revising Whitman's Republicanism." *American Transcendental Quarterly* 4.3 (September 1990): 201–18.

Grünzweig, Walter. *Constructing the German Walt Whitman.* Iowa City: U of Iowa P, 1995.

———. *Walt Whitman: Die deutschsprachige Rezeption als interkulturelles Phänomen.* München: Fink, 1991.

Harris, George Washington. "A Snake-Bit Irishman." Orig. pub. in *Spirit of the Times* (N.Y.) 15 (1846): 549. Rpt. *Tall Tales of the Southwest: An Anthology of Southern and Southwestern Humor 1830–1860.* 1930. Ed. Franklin J. Meine. New York: Knopf, 1937. 315–21.

———. "The Snake-Bit Irishman." Orig. pub. in *Sut Lovingood: Yarns Spun by a "Nat'ral Born Durn'd Fool."* 1867. *Sut Lovingood's Yarns.* Ed. M. Thomas Inge. New Haven: College and University P, 1966. 96–100.

Hartman, Geoffrey H. "Wordsworth, Inscriptions, Romantic Nature Poetry." *Beyond Formalism: Literary Essays, 1958–1970.* New Haven: Yale UP, 1970. 206–30.

[Hartmann,] Sadakichi. *Conversations with Walt Whitman.* New York: E. P. Coby, 1895.

Harvey, David. *Consciousness and the Urban Experience.* Baltimore: Johns Hopkins UP, 1985.

Hendricks, Gordon. *The Photographs of Thomas Eakins.* New York: Grossman, 1972.

Hesiod. *The Homeric Hymns and Homerica.* Trans. Hugh G. Evelyn-White. Cambridge: Harvard UP, 1954.

Hirsch, Arnold R., and Joseph Logsdon, eds. *Creole New Orleans: Race and Americanization.* Baton Rouge: Louisiana State UP, 1992.

Homer, William Innes. "New Light on Thomas Eakins and Walt Whitman in Camden." Sill and Tarbell 85–98.

Horace. *Complete Works.* Ed. Casper J. Kraemer, Jr. New York: Modern Library, 1936.

Hornstein, Norbert. "Meaning and the Mental: The Problem of Semantics after Chomsky." George 23–40.

Hyde, Lewis. *The Gift: Imagination and the Erotic Life of Property.* New York: Random, 1983.

Isay, Richard. *Being Homosexual: Gay Men and their Development.* New York: Farrar, 1989.

Jakobson, Roman. "Linguistics and Poetics." *Style in Language.* Ed. Thomas A. Sebeok. Cambridge: MIT P, 1960. 350–77.

James, William. *Talks to Teachers on Psychology, and to Students on Some of Life's Ideals.* 1899. Rpt., New York: Dover, 1962.

Johns, Elizabeth. *American Genre Painting: The Politics of Everyday Life.* New Haven: Yale UP, 1991.

——. "An Avowal of Artistic Community: Nudity and Fantasy in Thomas Eakins's Photographs." Danly and Leibold 65–93.

——. *Thomas Eakins: the Heroism of Modern Life.* Princeton: Princeton UP, 1983.

Johnston, John. *Diary Notes of a Visit to Walt Whitman and Some of His Friends in 1890.* Manchester: Labour P, 1898.

Kant, Immanuel. *Groundwork of the Metaphysics of Morals.* Trans. H. J. Paton. New York: Harper, 1964.

Kaplan, Amy, and Donald E. Pease, eds. *Cultures of United States Imperialism.* Durham: Duke UP, 1993.

Kaplan, Justin. *Walt Whitman: A Life.* New York: Simon, 1980.

Katz, Jonathan Ned. *Gay American History: Lesbians and Gay Men in the U.S.A.* New York: Meridien, 1992.

Keller, Elizabeth Leavitt. *Walt Whitman in Mickle Street.* New York: Mitchell Kennerley, 1921.

Keller, Karl. "The Sweet Wolf Within: Emily Dickinson and Walt Whitman." *The Only Kangaroo Among the Beauty: Emily Dickinson and America.* Baltimore: Johns Hopkins UP, 1979. 251–93.

Killingsworth, M. Jimmie. *Whitman's Poetry of the Body.* Chapel Hill: U of North Carolina P, 1989.

Kouwenhoven, John A. "Arts in America." *Atlantic Monthly* 168 (1941): 175–80.

——. *Made in America: The Arts in Modern Civilization.* 1948. Garden City: Doubleday, 1962.

Krieg, Joann P. "Letters from Warry." *Walt Whitman Quarterly Review* 11 (Spring 1994): 163–73.

Lawrence, D. H. "Whitman." *A Century of Whitman Criticism.* Ed. Edwin Haviland Miller. Bloomington: Indiana UP, 1969. 152–61.

"Leaves of Grass—Smut in Them." *Springfield Daily Republican* (June 16, 1860): 4.

Leverenz, David. *Manhood and the American Renaissance.* Ithaca: Cornell UP, 1989.

Levine, Harry Gene. "The Discovery of Addiction: Changing Conceptions of Habitual Drunkenness in America." *Journal of Studies on Alcohol* 39.1 (1978): 143–74.

Lindberg, Kathryne V. "'White Mythology' and/or Outside the Culture (Criticism) Industry." *Emergences* (Fall 1992): 170–92.

"Literary Nonsense." *Springfield Daily Republican* (Mar. 24, 1860): 4.

Lott, Eric. *Love and Theft: Blackface Minstrelsy and the American Working Class.* New York: Oxford UP, 1993.

Loving, Jerome. "Walt Whitman." Elliott 448–62.

———. *Walt Whitman's Champion: William Douglas O'Connor.* College Station: Texas A&M UP, 1978.

Lynch, Michael. "'Here is Adhesiveness': From Friendship to Homosexuality." *Victorian Studies* 29 (Autumn 1985): 67–96.

Mann, Klaus. *Der Wendepunkt.* Reinbek b. Hamburg: Rowohlt, 1984.

———. "The Present Greatness of Walt Whitman." *Decision* 1 (Apr. 1941): 14–30.

Mannheim, Karl. *Essays on the Sociology of Culture.* London: Routledge, 1956.

Martí, José. *Obras completas.* 28 vols. Havana: Editorial Nacional de Cuba, 1963–75.

———. *On Art and Literature. Critical Writings.* Ed. and introd. Philip S. Foner. Trans. Elinor Randall. New York: Monthly Review P, 1982.

Martin, Robert K. *The Homosexual Tradition in American Poetry.* Austin: U of Texas P, 1979.

———. "Whitman and the Politics of Identity." Folsom, *Walt Whitman* 172–81.

Marx, Karl. *Capital: A Critique of Political Economy.* Trans. Samuel Moore and Edward Aveling. 3 vols. New York: International, 1967.

———. *Marxism: Essential Writings.* Ed. David McLellan. Oxford: Oxford UP, 1988.

Marx, Leo. *The Pilot and the Passenger: Essays on Literature, Technology, and Culture in the United States.* New York: Oxford UP, 1988.

Mathews, Mitford M., ed. *Dictionary of Americanisms on Historical Principles.* Chicago: U of Chicago P, 1951.

Matthiessen, F. O. *American Renaissance: Art and Expression in the Age of Emerson and Whitman.* 1941. Rpt., New York: Oxford UP, 1968.

Mazzini, Giuseppe. "Europe: Its Condition." *Essays: Selected from the Writings, Literary, Political, and Religious.* London: Scott, 1887. 261–98.

———. "Organizzazione della Democrazia." 1850. *Scritti editi ed inediti.* Vol. 43. Imola: Galeati, 1926.

McArthur, Tom, ed. *The Oxford Companion to the English Language.* New York: Oxford UP, 1992.

McCauley, Anne. "'The Most Beautiful of Nature's Works': Thomas Eakins's Photographic Nudes in their French and American Contexts." Danly and Leibold 23–63.

McPherson, James. *Abraham Lincoln and the Second American Revolution.* New York: Oxford UP, 1991.

———. *The Negro's Civil War: How American Negroes Felt and Acted During the War for the Union.* New York: Pantheon, 1965.

Miles, Josephine. *Eras and Modes in English Poetry.* 2nd ed. Berkeley: U of California P, 1964.

Mirsky, D. S. "The Poet of American Democracy" (1935). Murphy 238–55.

Molloy, Sylvia. "Too Wilde for Comfort: Desire and Ideology in Fin de Siècle Spanish America." *Social Text* 31/32 [10.2–3] (1992): 187–201.

Moon, Michael. *Disseminating Whitman: Revision and Corporeality in* Leaves of Grass. Cambridge: Harvard UP, 1991.

———. "Memorial Rags." *Professions of Desire: Lesbian and Gay Studies in Literature.* Ed. George E. Haggerty and Bonnie Zimmerman. New York: MLA, 1995.

Murphy, Francis, ed. *Walt Whitman: A Critical Anthology.* Baltimore: Penguin, 1970.

Nathanson, Tenney. *Whitman's Presence: Body, Voice, and Writing in* Leaves of Grass. New York: New York UP, 1992.

Neruda, Pablo. *El hondero entusiasta (1923–1924).* 4th ed. Santiago, Chile: Ediciones Ercilla, 1940.

———. *Veinte poemas de amor y una canción desesperada.* Ed. Hugo Montes. Madrid: Castalia, 1987.

Norton, Charles Eliot. Rev. of *Leaves of Grass. Putnam's Monthly Magazine* 6 (1855): 321–23.

Nozick, Robert. *Anarchy, State, and Utopia.* New York: Basic, 1974.

Nussbaum, Martha. *The Fragility of Goodness: Luck and Ethics in Greek Tragedy and Philosophy.* New York: Cambridge UP, 1986.

O'Connor, William D. "The Good Gray Poet" (1866). *A Century of Walt Whitman Criticism.* Ed. Edwin Haviland Miller. Bloomington: Indiana UP, 1969. 19–27.

O'Hara, Frank. *The Collected Poems of Frank O'Hara.* Ed. Donald Allen. New York: Knopf, 1971.

Ostriker, Alicia. "Loving Walt Whitman and the Problem of America." *The Continuing Presence of Walt Whitman: The Life After the Life.* Ed. Robert K. Martin. Iowa City: U of Iowa P, 1992. 217–31.

Parry, Elwood C., III. "Thomas Eakins' 'Naked Series' Reconsidered: Another Look at the Standing Nude Photographs Made for the Use of Eakins' Students." *American Art Journal* 20.2 (1988): 53–77.

Paz, Octavio. *Hieroglyphs of Desire: A Critical Study.* Trans. Esther Allen. *Nostalgia for Death: Poetry by Xavier Villaurrutia and Hieroglyphs of Desire.* Ed. Eliot Weinberger. Port Townsend, WA: Copper Canyon P, 1993.

———. *Primeras letras (1931–1943).* Ed. Enrico Mario Santí. México, D.F.: Vuelta, 1988.

Pease, Donald E. *Visionary Compacts: American Renaissance Writings in Cultural Context.* Madison: U of Wisconsin P, 1987.

Perlman, Jim, Ed Folsom, and Dan Campion, eds. *Walt Whitman: The Measure of His Song.* Minneapolis: Holy Cow! P, 1981.

Perloff, Marjorie. *Frank O'Hara: Poet Among Painters.* Austin: U of Texas P, 1979.

Perry, Bliss. *Walt Whitman.* Boston: Houghton Mifflin, 1906. Rpt. New York: Chelsea House, 1981.

Peters, Robert. "Two for Walt Whitman: An Essay and a Review." *Cabirion* (Winter/Spring 1984): 10–11. Rpt. *Great American Poetry Bake-Off.* 3rd series. Metuchen, NJ: Scarecrow, 1987. 254–59.

Plato. *The Symposium of Plato.* Trans. Suzy Q. Groden. Ed. John A. Brentlinger. Boston: U of Massachusetts P, 1970.

Porter, Carolyn. "Reification and American Literature." *Ideology and Classic American Literature.* Ed. Sacvan Bercovitch and Myra Jehlen. New York: Cambridge UP, 1986. 188–217.

Pound, Ezra. *Personae.* New York: New Directions, 1926.

———. *Selected Prose 1909–1965.* Ed. William Cookson. New York: New Directions, 1973.

Quiroga, José. "Vicente Huidobro and the Poetics of Invisible Texts." *Hispania* 75 (1992): 516–26.

Rama, Angel. "La dialéctica de la modernidad en José Martí." *Estudios martianos.* Memoria *del Seminario José Martí.* Ed. Manuel Pedro González, Iván A. Schulman, et al. Río Piedras, Puerto Rico: Editorial Universitaria, 1974. 129–97.

Ramos, Julio. *Desencuentros de la modernidad en América latina: Literatura y política en el siglo XIX.* Mexico: Fondo de Cultura Económica, 1989.

Rawls, John. *A Theory of Justice.* Cambridge: Harvard UP, 1971.

Reynolds, David S. *Beneath the American Renaissance: The Subversive Imagination in the Age of Emerson and Melville.* Cambridge: Harvard UP, 1989.

———. *Walt Whitman's America: A Cultural Biography.* New York: Knopf, 1995.

Rich, Adrienne. *The Dream of a Common Language: Poems 1974–1977.* New York: Norton, 1978.

———. "The Eye of the Outsider: Elizabeth Bishop's *Complete Poems 1927–1979*" (1983). *Blood, Bread, and Poetry: Selected Prose 1979–1985.* New York: Norton, 1986. 124–35.

Roach, Joseph A. *Circum-Atlantic Performance.* New York: Columbia UP, 1996.

Roediger, David R. *The Wages of Whiteness: Race and the Making of the American Working Class.* New York: Verso, 1991.

Rose, H. J. *The Eclogues of Vergil.* Berkeley: U of California P, 1942.

Ross, David. *The Right and the Good.* Oxford: Clarendon P, 1930.

Ryan, Mary. *The Empire of the Mother: American Writing about Domesticity 1830–1860.* New York: Haworth, 1982.

Sánchez-Eppler, Karen. *Touching Liberty: Abolition, Feminism, and the Politics of the Body.* Berkeley: U of California P, 1993.

Sandel, Michael. *Liberalism and the Limits of Justice.* Cambridge: Cambridge UP, 1982.

———. "The Procedural Republic and the Unencumbered Self." *Political Theory* 12 (Feb. 1984): 81–96.

Santayana, George. "The Genteel Tradition in American Philosophy" (1911). *Winds of Doctrine.* 1913. Rpt. New York: Harper, 1957. 186–215.

Santí, Enrico Mario. "The Accidental Tourist: Walt Whitman in Latin America." *Do the Americas Have a Common Literature?* Ed. Gustavo Pérez-Firmat. Durham: Duke UP, 1990. 156–76.

Searle, John. "Chomsky's Revolution in Linguistics." *On Noam Chomsky: Critical Essays.* Ed. Gilbert Harman. Garden City: Anchor, 1974. 2–33.

Sedgwick, Eve Kosofsky. *Between Men: English Literature and Male Homosocial Desire.* New York: Columbia UP, 1985.

———. *Epistemology of the Closet.* Berkeley: U of California P, 1991.

Sedgwick, "Nationalisms and Sexualities in the Age of Wilde." *Nationalisms and Sexualities.* Ed. Andrew Parker et al. New York: Routledge, 1992. 235–45.
———. *Tendencies.* Durham: Duke UP, 1993.
Sellers, Charles. *The Market Revolution.* New York: Oxford UP, 1991.
Sher, George. *Desert.* Princeton: Princeton UP, 1987.
Shively, Charley, ed. *Calamus Lovers: Walt Whitman's Working-Class Camerados.* San Francisco: Gay Sunshine P, 1987.
Sill, Geoffrey M., and Roberta K. Tarbell, eds. *Walt Whitman and the Visual Arts.* New Brunswick: Rutgers UP, 1992.
Smith, Henry Nash. "The Widening of Horizons." Spiller, 639–51.
Sobejano, Gonzalo. *Nietzsche en España.* Madrid: Gredos, 1967.
Sommer, Doris. "Supplying Demand: Walt Whitman as the Liberal Self." *Reinventing the Americas: Comparative Studies of Literature of the United States and Spanish America.* Ed. Bell Gale Chevigny and Gari Laguardia. Cambridge: Cambridge UP, 1986. 68–91.
Spann, Edward K. *The New Metropolis: New York City, 1840–1857.* New York: Columbia UP, 1981.
Spiller, Robert E., et al., eds. *Literary History of the United States.* 2 vols. New York: Macmillan, 1948.
Stacy, Robert H. "Svyatopolk-Mirsky, Prince Dmitry Petrovich." *Handbook of Russian Literature.* Ed. Victor Terras. New Haven: Yale UP, 1985. 457.
Stott, Richard B. *Workers in the Metropolis: Class, Ethnicity, and Youth in Antebellum New York City.* Ithaca: Cornell UP, 1990.
Stovall, Floyd. *The Foreground of* Leaves of Grass. Charlottesville: UP of Virginia, 1974.
Sweet, Timothy. *Traces of War: Poetry, Photography, and the Crisis of the Union.* Baltimore: Johns Hopkins UP, 1990.
Symonds, John Addington. *The Letters of John Addington Symonds. Volume Three: 1885–1893.* Ed. Herbert M. Schueller and Robert L. Peters. Detroit: Wayne State UP, 1969.
———. *Walt Whitman: A Study.* London: John C. Nimmo, 1893.
Thomas, M. Wynn. "Whitman's Tale of Two Cities." *American Literary History* 6.4 (1994): 633–57.
Thompson, J. S. "The Reactionary Idealist Foundation of Noam Chomsky's Linguistics." *Literature and Ideology* 4 (1969): 1–20.
Thoreau, Henry David. "Resistance to Civil Government." *Reform Papers.* Ed. Wendell Glick. Princeton: Princeton UP, 1973. 63–90.
Tocqueville, Alexis de. *Democracy in America.* Ed. Phillips Bradley. 2 vols. New York: Knopf, 1945.
Trachtenberg, Alan. *Reading American Photographs: Images as History, Mathew Brady to Walker Evans.* New York: Hill and Wang, 1989.
Traubel, Horace. *With Walt Whitman in Camden.* 7 vols. Vol. 1: Boston: Small, Maynard, 1906. Vol. 2: New York: D. Appleton, 1908. Vol. 3: New York: Mitchell Kennerley, 1914. (Vols. 1–3: Rpt. New York: Rowman and Littlefield, 1961.) Vol. 4, ed. Sculley Bradley, Philadelphia: U of Pennsylvania P, 1953. Vol. 5, ed. Gertrude Traubel, Carbondale: Southern Illinois UP, 1964. Vol. 6, ed. Gertrude Traubel and William White, Carbondale: Southern Illinois UP, 1982. Vol. 7, ed. Jeanne Chapman and Robert MacIsaac, Carbondale: Southern Illinois UP, 1992.

Untitled Review. *Springfield Daily Republican* (Aug. 11, 1860): 2.

*Virgil*, with an English translation by H. Rushton Fairclough. 2 vols. Cambridge: Harvard UP, 1978.

Vlastos, Gregory. "The Individual as Object of Love in Plato's Dialogues." *Platonic Studies*. Princeton: Princeton UP, 1973. 3–42.

Waldron, Randall H., ed. *Mattie: The Letters of Martha Mitchell Whitman*. New York: New York UP, 1977.

Walker, E. C. "Should Radicals Colonize?" *Free Society* (May 15, 1904).

Ward, Geoffrey C., with Ken Burns and Ric Burns. *The Civil War: An Illustrated History*. New York: Knopf, 1990.

Warner, David. "The Good G(r)ay Poet." *Philadelphia City Paper* (Jan. 12–19, 1990): 4.

Warner, Michael. "Thoreau's Bottom." *Raritan* 11.3 (Winter 1992): 53–79.

———. "Walden's Erotic Economy." *Comparative American Identities: Race, Sex and Nationality in the Modern Text*. Ed. Hortense Spillers. New York: Routledge, 1991. 157–74.

Warren, Joyce W. *Fanny Fern: An Independent Woman*. New Brunswick: Rutgers UP, 1992.

Wegner, Armin T. "Funkspruch in die Welt." *Die Strasse mit den Tausend Zielen*. Dresden: Sibyllen Verlag, 1924.

Weisbuch, Robert. "Whitman's Personalism, Arnold's Culture." *Atlantic Double-Cross: American Literature and British Influence in the Age of Emerson*. Chicago: U of Chicago P, 1986. 83–106.

Welter, Barbara. *Dimity Convictions: The American Woman in the Nineteenth Century*. Athens: Ohio UP, 1976.

White, William. "Billy Duckett: Whitman Rogue." *American Book Collector* 21 (1971): 20–23.

Whitman, George Washington. *Civil War Letters*. Ed. Jerome Loving. Durham: Duke UP, 1975.

Whitman, Walt. "Broadway." *Life Illustrated* (Aug. 9, 1856). Rpt. in *New York Dissected*. Ed. Emory Holloway and Ralph Adimari. New York: Rufus Rockwell Wilson, 1936.

———. "The Child's Champion." *The New World* (Nov. 20, 1841): 321–22.

———. *Complete Poetry and Collected Prose*. Ed. Justin Kaplan. New York: Library of America, 1982.

———. *Correspondence*. Ed. Edwin Haviland Miller. 6 vols. New York: New York UP, 1961–77.

———. *Der Wundarzt. Briefe, Aufzeichnungen und Gedichte aus dem amerikanischen Sezessionskrieg*. Ed. René Schickele. Zürich: Rascher, 1919.

———. *Faint Clews & Indirections: Manuscripts of Walt Whitman and His Family*. Ed. Clarence Gohdes and Rollo G. Silver. Durham: Duke UP, 1949.

———. *Franklin Evans, or The Inebriate*. 1842. *The Early Poems and The Fiction*. Ed. Thomas Brasher. New York: New York UP, 1963. 124–239.

———. *Grashalme. Gedichte*. Trans. Karl Knortz and T. W. Rolleston. Zurich: Schabelitz, 1889.

———. *I Sit and Look Out: Editorials from the* Brooklyn Daily Times. Ed. Emory Holloway and Vernolian Schwarz. New York: Columbia UP, 1932.

———. *Leaves of Grass*. Ed. Sculley Bradley and Harold W. Blodgett. New York: Norton, 1965.

Whitman, Walt. *Leaves of Grass: A Textual Variorum of the Printed Poems.* Ed. Sculley Bradley, 3 vols. New York: New York UP, 1980.

———. *Leaves of Grass: Facsimile Edition of the 1860 Text.* Ed. Roy Harvey Pearce. Ithaca: Cornell UP, 1961.

———. *Leaves of Grass: The First (1855) Edition.* Ed. Malcolm Cowley. New York: Penguin, 1986.

———. *Memoranda During the War [and] Death of Abraham Lincoln.* Facsimile ed. Ed. Roy P. Basler. Bloomington: Indiana UP, 1962.

———. *Notebooks and Unpublished Prose Manuscripts.* Ed. Edward F. Grier. New York: New York UP, 1984.

———. *Poemas* (1912). Trans. and Intro. Armando Vasseur. Montevideo: García and Co., 1939.

———. *Prose Works 1892.* Ed. Floyd Stovall. 2 vols. New York: New York UP, 1964.

———. *Uncollected Poetry and Prose.* Ed. Emory Holloway. 2 vols. Garden City: Doubleday, Page & Co., 1921. Rpt. Gloucester, MA: Peter Smith, 1972.

———. *Walt Whitman of the* New York Aurora. Ed. Joseph Jay Rubin and Charles H. Brown. State College, PA: Bald Eagle P, 1950.

———. *Whitman's Manuscripts: Leaves of Grass (1860). A Parallel Text.* Ed. Fredson Bowers. Chicago: U of Chicago P, 1955.

Wilentz, Sean. *Chants Democratic: New York City and the Rise of the American Working Class, 1788–1850.* New York: Oxford UP, 1984.

Wilson, Edmund. "Comrade Prince: A Memoir of D. S. Mirsky." *Encounter* (July 1955): 10–20.

Wittgenstein, Ludwig. *Philosophical Grammar.* Ed. Rush Rhees. Trans. Anthony Kenny. Oxford: Blackwell, 1974.

———. *Philosophical Investigations.* Trans. G. E. M. Anscombe. 3rd ed. New York: Blackwell, 1958.

Wright, Henry Clarke. *The Empire of the Mother Over the Character and Destiny of the Race.* Boston: B. Marsh, 1863.

Yingling, Thomas. "AIDS in America: Postmodern Governance, Identity, and Experience." *Inside/out: Lesbian Theories, Gay Theories.* Ed. Diana Fuss. New York: Routledge, 1991. 291–310.

———. *Hart Crane and the Homosexual Text: New Thresholds, New Anatomies.* Chicago: U of Chicago P, 1990.

Ziff, Paul. *Semantic Analysis.* Ithaca: Cornell UP, 1960.

Zinn, Howard. *A People's History of the United States.* New York: Harper, 1980.

Zweig, Paul. *Walt Whitman: The Making of the Poet.* New York: Basic, 1984.

# Contributors

**Jonathan Arac** (University of Pittsburgh) is a member of the *boundary 2* editorial collective and author, most recently, of a book-length contribution on "narrative forms" to volume 2 of the *Cambridge History of American Literature*. He is currently completing Huckleberry Finn and the Functions of Criticism.

**Michael Davidson** (University of California, San Diego) is the author of numerous volumes of poetry, including, most recently, *Analogy of the Ion* (1988) and *Post Hoc* (1990). He is also the author of a study of American poetry entitled *The San Francisco Renaissance: Poetics and Community at Mid-Century* (1989).

**Wai Chee Dimock** (Brandeis University) is the author of *Empire for Liberty: Melville and the Poetics of Individualism* (1989), and co-editor of *Rethinking Class: Literary Studies and Social Formations* (1994). Her Whitman essay is an excerpt from her new book, *Residues of Justice: American Literature, Law, and Philosophy* (1995).

**Betsy Erkkila** (Northwestern University) is the author of *Walt Whitman Among the French: Poet and Myth* (1980), *Whitman the Political Poet* (1989), and *The Wicked Sisters: Women Poets, Literary History, and Discord* (1992). She is currently working on a book entitled *Border Wars: Toward a Comparative Cultural Practice*.

**Ed Folsom** (University of Iowa) is the editor of the *Walt Whitman Quarterly Review*. He is co-editor of the influential *Walt Whitman: The Measure of His Song* (1981), editor of *Walt Whitman: The Centennial Essays* (1994), co-editor of *Walt Whitman and the World* (1995), and author of *Whitman's Native Representations* (1994).

**Allen Grossman** (Johns Hopkins University) has published many works of poetry, including *Of The Great House* (1982), *The Bright Nails Scattered on the Ground* (1986), and most recently, *The Ether Dome* (1991). He is the co-editor with Mark Halliday of *Two Works on Poetry for Readers and Writers* (1991), and author of *Poetic Knowledge in the Early Yeats* (1969) and several essays on American literature.

**Jay Grossman** (Amherst College) is the author of " 'The evangel-poem of comrades and of love': Revising Whitman's Republicanism." He is currently completing a study entitled *Emerson, Whitman, and the Politics of Representation*.

**Walter Grünzweig** (University of Dortmund) is the author of *Das demokratische Kanaan: Charles Sealsfields Amerika im Kontext amerikanischer Literatur und Ideologie* (1987), *Walt Whitmann: Die deutschsprachige Rezeption als interkulturelles Phänomen* (1991), and *Constructing the German Walt Whitman* (1995).

**Elizabeth Johns** (University of Pennsylvania) is the author of *Thomas Eakins: The Heroism of Modern Life* (1983), *American Genre Painting: The Politics of Everyday Life* (1991), and many essays on nineteenth-century American painting.

**Katherine Kinney** (University of California, Riverside) is the author of "Whitman's Word of the Modern and the First Modern War" (1990). She is currently completing a study entitled *Friendly Fire: American Identity and the Literature of the Vietnam War*.

**Sylvia Molloy** (New York University) is the author of *Las letras de Borges* (1979), *Certificate of Absence* (1989), *At Face Value: Autobiographical Writing in Spanish America* (1991), and *Signs of Borges* (1994). She is currently working on a book on decadence and national health in turn-of-the-century Latin America and editing a collection entitled *Hispanisms and Homosexualities*.

**Michael Moon** (Duke University) is the author of *Disseminating Whitman: Revision and Corporeality in* Leaves of Grass (1991) and co-editor of *Displacing Homophobia: Gay-Male Perspectives on Literature and Culture* (1990).

**Vivian R. Pollak** (Washington University, St. Louis) is the author of *Dickinson: The Anxiety of Gender* and editor of *A Poet's Parents: The Courtship Letters of Emily Norcross and Edward Dickinson* (1988). She is currently completing a study entitled *The Erotic Whitman*.

**José Quiroga** (Georgetown University) is currently completing a study entitled *Cuban Homosexualities in the Tropic of Revolution*.

**Jorge Salessi** (University of Pennsylvania) is currently working on a study entitled *Medics, Crooks, and Tango Queens: Immigration, Homosexuality, and the New Argentine Subject*. He has published numerous articles on the construction of the Argentine subject.

**Eve Kosofsky Sedgwick** (Duke University) is the author of *The Coherence of Gothic Conventions* (1980), *Between Men: English Literature and Male Homosocial Desire* (1985), *Epistemology of the Closet* (1990), *Tendencies* (1993), and *Fat Art, Thin Art* (1994).

**Alan Trachtenberg** (Yale University) is the author of *Brooklyn Bridge: Fact and Symbol* (1965), *The Incorporation of America* (1982), and, most recently, *Reading American Photographs: Images as History, Mathew Brady to Walker Evans* (1989).

**Michael Warner** (Rutgers University) is the author of *The Letters of the Republic: Publication and the Public Sphere in Eighteenth-Century America* (1990) and several other essays on American literature and culture.

**Robyn Wiegman** (Indiana University) is the author of *American Anatomies: Theorizing Race and Gender* (1995) and co-editor of two anthologies: *Feminism Beside Itself* (1995), and *Who Can Speak? Authority and Critical Identity* (1995).

**Tom Yingling** (Syracuse University) is the author of *Hart Crane and the Homosexual Text: New Thresholds, New Anatomies* (1990). He was working on a study of the philosopher Wittgenstein before he died of complications associated with AIDS on July 27, 1992. An anthology of his uncollected and unpublished writings is forthcoming from Duke University Press (1996).

# Index

*Page references in italics signify illustrations.*

Printed in the United States
3320